SOCIAL MEDIA AND CAPITALISM

People, Communities and Commodities

SUDDHABRATA DEB ROY

Daraja Press

Published by
Daraja Press
https://darajapress.com
In association with
Zand Graphics Ltd
https://zandgraphics.com
2022

ISBN 9781988832890

Cover design: Alaka Anarkali
Preparation for publication: Kate McDonnell

Library and Archives Canada Cataloguing in Publication
Title: Social media and capitalism : people, communities and
    commodities / Suddhabrata Deb Roy.
Names: Deb Roy, Suddhabrata, 1993- author.
Description: Includes bibliographical references and index.
Identifiers: Canadiana (print) 20200403206 | Canadiana (ebook)
    20200403249 | ISBN 9781988832890 (softcover) | ISBN 9781988832906
    (PDF)
Subjects: LCSH: Social media—Economic aspects. | LCSH: Capitalism.
Classification: LCC HC79.I55 D42 2022 | DDC 303.48/33—dc23

This book is dedicated to the radical possibility of human emancipation – something which we need to reimagine every day and every living moment!

CONTENTS

ACKNOWLEDGEMENTS

Writing acknowledgements for a book is always an exciting process for the author, and I am no different. There are countless people who deserve a vote of thanks for enabling me to write the book. This section is a small token of gratitude to all of them from me.

Marcelle Dawson, the primary supervisor of my PhD in the University of Otago, without whose support and encouragement this would not have been possible. Marcelle has been a constant source of inspiration to me and has been instrumental in shaping my academic life.

Annabel Cooper, Simon Barber and Patrick Vakaoti – the awesome members of my supervisory and advisory panel who have been constantly encouraging me in my academic journey. An additional vote of thanks to Simon Barber, whose fantastic advice(s) about the various editions of *Capital* helped me tremendously.

Kevin B. Anderson and Peter Hudis for being constant sources of critical insights and encouraging words.

Laura and Brandon for being an awesome couple, especially to Laura for helping me work upon the initial framework which has been used throughout the book.

Christian Fuchs, who provided me with some very good editorial feedback for my first academic paper on the topic, has been instrumental in shaping the present book.

My first mentors of Marxist and critical thought in the University of Hyderabad, Professors Purendra Prasad, Pushpesh Kumar, G. Nagaraju, Satyapriya Rout and Vellikad Janardhan, without whom my journey towards writing this book would not have been possible.

Comrades and Friends across various left-wing and progressive organisations, who have been a constant feature of my life for the past decade or so.

Alaka Anarkali for the great cover.

Firoze Manji of Daraja Press who has been an absolute rockstar of a publisher! Thanks Firoze!

Debasreeta Deb for being there for me always listening to my rants and ideas. Without her spirited words, it would have been difficult to complete the book.

And finally, and most importantly, my working-class mother and trade unionist father, without whom I would not have been who I am.

Thanks to everybody! Now, let's end Capitalism!

INTRODUCTION: SOCIAL MEDIA COMMERCE AND THE MARXIST MODE OF ANALYSIS

Technology is an important part of contemporary society. Humanism, as Paul Mason (2019) notes, is facing the worst challenge since the days of Aristotle and Galileo. Contemporary society is characterised by a blatant rejection of equality and humane sentiments. Such rejection has been rendered mainstream by the way technology has been used under capitalism. Today, the threat comes from the widespread usage of technological innovations such as artificial intelligence, neuroscience, and information theory, which have reduced the social value attached to a human being (Mason 2019). The contemporary society is a society where technological apparatuses and the networks that they bring forward dominate a large part of the lives of human beings, and even non-human beings. As Aaron Bastani (2019, 'The Three Disruptions') argues, this abundance and domination of technology signal the ushering in of an era of *'extreme supply'* where machines become capable of undertaking both cognitive and manual responsibilities of the production process.

Within the overall technological milieu, which engulfs our everyday life in the contemporary world, social media has emerged as a dominant entity. It has become an integral part of the everyday lives of human beings creating newer aspects of social relationships, avenues for labour, everyday commitments, daily schedules, etc. Along with its numerous other functions, it has also evolved into becoming a digital marketplace. Social media today along with its classical functions of facilitating communication and building ties of relationships between people, also helps people engage in commercial activities – which is also the focus of this book. Commercial activities on social media are a dynamic and recent innovation within the realm of digital communication, through which, social media sites such as Facebook, Twitter and Instagram have – once again – reinvented themselves within ordinary working-class lives. Technological innovations accommodate themselves with regard to the potential weakness that human beings possess with a view to transforming the human beings themselves, in the end, into parts of the machine (Marx 1844, p. 308). No matter how much technological development capitalism brings forward, the condition of the workers remains fundamentally unchanged because capitalism always effectively means the domination of dead labour over living labour. The generation of new modes of production and newer objects of production could have positively impacted human beings and human life, but only if the regime of private property and capital did not exist (Marx 1844, p. 306). As Engels noted:

> I assert that thousands of industrious and worthy people – far worthier and more to be respected than the rich [...] do find themselves in a condition unworthy of human beings; and that every proletarian, everyone, without exception, is exposed to a similar fate without any fault of own and in spite of every possible effort (Engels 1845, p. 335)

Technological developments such as smartphones and computers have provided common users with a method of consuming different values produced through the various internet platforms (Parker, Alstyne and Choudary 2016). Gadgets that have been internalised in the everyday lives of human beings have, in turn, internalised human life within their circuits and user interfaces. In doing so, such gadgets have changed the structure of human life itself. Such innovations have rendered mainstream the surveillance of everyday lives leading to the establishment of what Zuboff (2019) calls surveillance capitalism. Surveillance capitalism is, as Zuboff (2019) says, parasitic in nature. It enables the usage of digital connections to further commercial profit: 'It revives Karl Marx's old image of capitalism as a vampire that feeds on human labour, but with an unexpected turn. Instead of labour, surveillance capitalism feeds on every aspect of every human's experience' (Zuboff 2019, 'Home or Exile in the Digital Future').

Within social media, social media commerce is a new and emerging domain of capitalist development. The peculiarity of social media commerce is that it is a physical activity – one has to actually work to fulfil it – but at the same time, it is a virtual activity as well because, as Huws (2016, 2016a) argues in the case of many platform workers, the entire structure is mediated through the internet. The internet, as Fuchs (2008) rightly says is not only a technological system but is rather a techno-social system. It is simultaneously technological as well as social and social media commerce is an important part of that overall techno-social system today. The present book is about social media commerce and its impact on the human lives entangled within it. It is not a book that emphasises social media as a virtual realm, but instead locates its influence on the concrete social reality that human beings experience on an everyday basis.

Social media commerce, in the context of the current work, refers to commercial activities on social media platforms such as Facebook, Twitter, Instagram, WhatsApp, etc. The focus of the present book, however, will be mostly on platforms such as Facebook and WhatsApp, because they are common elements of the social media landscape in both the Global North and Global South – a distinction which features throughout the work. Social media commerce, in this context, does not refer to ways in which social media sites earn their revenue directly, but rather talks about and emphasises the processes where users engage in commercial activities on social media enabling capitalism *per se* to make profits both within and outside the digital ecosystem. Such commercial activities have used the huge involvement that sites like Facebook and Twitter have in the everyday lives of individuals. The absence of any gatekeepers to manage the flow of value has enabled these websites to proliferate widely in society, and faster, giving more freedom to the consumer (Parker, Alstyne and Choudary 2016) which in the course of the book will be examined critically.

Facebook today has approximately 2.89 billion monthly active users[1], with it being the 7th highest visited website in the world[2] with almost close to 18 minutes being spent by every visitor daily each time one visits the site. Facebook thus can be said to represent an entire 'community' on its own where quite naturally, divisions between the affluent class and the working class exist. The 'blue tick' distinguishes the common users from the 'affluent users'. Bluetick users do not list things for sale on social media – neither they have to do so, nor do they want to do so. The blatant truth of social media is that one 'follows' the affluent users, while one sends a 'Friend Request' and connects to the non-affluent users. The same is the case for other social media websites such as Instagram which has close to 1 billion monthly active users and more than 500 million daily active users with an average time per user of close to 9 minutes.[3] Social media as such, never was, is not, and never will be completely free from the influence of the wider world. The analysis of social media and social media commerce from a Marxist Humanist perspective allows one to focus on the central contradictions of the capitalist system – the commodity-form and the concept of value – from a holistic perspective based on the dialectical image of the various interconnected domains of social analysis associated with capitalism.

Networking activities through social media have multiple effects on the people engaged therein some of which have wide-ranging implications on how people analyse the actual social reality around them. Commercial activities are no longer limited to large firms and online advertising but have instead become social in nature and content. Instead, these features have become commonplace (Zuboff 2019) in the overall ecosystem that human beings inhabit. The introduction of commercial activities on social media has furthered the practice of commercial trading by making it more mobile, institutionalised and popular. The overall increase in the ways in which users found themselves getting entrenched and integrated within the process occurred through the dedicated tabs on the websites and applications that the social media platforms maintain such as the designated 'Facebook Marketplace' tab in the Facebook app that allows the user to access the Marketplace option more easily in comparison with the commercial groups, for which a considerable amount of Internet data had to be used in addition to the complexities raised by the user interface itself (Deb Roy 2020). Along with the large domain of functions, that social media performs along with their primary function of aiding communication between the users, they have

---

1. See https://investor.fb.com/investor-news/press-release-details/2021/Facebook-Reports-First-Quarter-2021-Results/default.aspx (Accessed 03-10-2021)

2. See https://www.alexa.com/topsites (Accessed 03-10-2021)

3. See https://backlinko.com/instagram-users (Accessed 03-10-2021)

emerged as sites where the users, often from the working class themselves, engage with commercial and trading activities. Such activities are entrenched within the general logic of capitalist accumulation. The present book will exhibit the reasons why commercial activities within social media are not an egalitarian solution to capitalist commerce by using the Marxist Humanist idea of the importance of Hegel's Absolute Negativity (Hudis and Anderson 2021).

Social media is an integral part of the connected lifestyle that contemporary capitalism constructs and sustains in the world. It is a part of the overall productive mechanisms of capitalism, whereby capitalism posits a life of fulfilment based on continuous alienation. The popular lifestyle under contemporary capitalism is mediated by a growing culture of consumption whereby consumption has become symbolic of one's status and identity (Featherstone 1991). Lifestyles, in this context, refer to the ways in which ordinary human subjects go about in their everyday lives under capitalism. These lifestyles under contemporary capitalism have become a domain that has witnessed massive modifications in the last couple of decades. As Miller's (2011) study indicates, the highest usage of social media occurs in the form of creating content based on the everyday mundane lives of the individual users.

Social media has an indelible effect on these lifestyles. It has a wide effect on the way certain commodities and lifestyles are popularised within society. Because social media is a medium that contains the voices of actual people -people whom we meet every day – so the kind of lifestyles that these people promote immediately become relatable to a lot of other people connected to the person. One might still have reservations about a smartphone brand on seeing an advertisement on the screen, but once one's neighbour or colleague starts using and sharing the details of the usage on social media, there do not remain many reasons to doubt the brand. The branding of commodities and the way they are located in the everyday lives of human beings play a large role in the way commodities transmit meanings to their users and possessors (Wengrow 2010). These meanings constitute the dominant lifestyle in the society, which in turn, construct the everyday basis of the construction of the individual. And, it is in this everyday mundanity and banality, that capitalist monstrosity, as McNally (2011, p. 2) notes, penetrates most seamlessly through its 'elusive everydayness'. Everyday lives have become more networked in nature with individuals remaining connected with each at any given point of their everyday lives. This has been made possible by the tremendous rise of the internet over the past two decades, both in the global north and in the global south. The internet, as Terranova (2004, p. 41) says, is different than other technological innovations because of its evolution as a 'network of networks'. It has utilised existing networks to frame newer subjects that lead their lives in accordance with the norms set by it. Capitalism uses numerous tools to achieve this end. Technology is one of the most important ones, and within that, perhaps, the most important one is social media.

Commodities here occupy a central position. Social media, in fact, is itself a commodity – a fact which will be reiterated multiple times throughout the book. The analysis of social media commerce depends greatly upon the way in which one utilises the concepts of commodity as has been depicted by Marx. Marx begins the first volume of his magnum opus, *Capital* with the statement: 'The wealth of societies in which the capitalist mode of production prevails appears as an "immense collection of commodities"' (Marx 1976, p. 125). The dynamics of the capitalist social order are mediated through and dominated by commodities. All around us, we see nothing but commodities – objects which have come to dominate our lives and the way we think about our lives. The contemporary society is a society where natural needs such as hunger and sleep have become fused with the alienated social needs generated by capitalism. The difference between these two kinds of human needs only becomes visible in circumstances, where the fault lines existing in capitalist societies get exposed and thrown out in the open explicitly, mostly during social movements which protest against the very core of oppressive social systems and structures. Marx's analysis began from an analysis of commodities because a commodity is the basic unit of the capitalist production system (Dunayevskaya 1958a; Postone 1993). Commodities under capitalism, are not just an entity focused on utility but are rather focused on the creation of the class-conscious value-form – something that it draws from the very nature of labour under capitalism (Dunayevskaya 1958a, p. 85). Because the commodity inherits the inherent contradictions within the nature of labour under capitalism, the commodity, in itself, as the Marxist Humanist Raya Dunayevskaya says, 'in embryo contains all the contradictions of capitalism' (Dunayevskaya 1958a, p. 85). Commodities are located at the focal point of the ways of life of every being under capitalism. Any change in the realm of commodities, either qualitatively or quantitatively, including the ways in which they are produced, distributed and consumed, thus, has an effect on actual human lives. Capitalist production does not only produce commodities but rather produces humans as *commodiites*, the *human commodity*, the human in the role of *a commodity* such that the human being only exists in the capitalist society in a completely dehumanised form (Marx 1844, p. 284). One of the many important changes in the realm of commodities is the continuous increase in the number of commodities in society apart from the obvious proliferation of the ways in which they are finding a place within human lives. Marx (1844, p. 306) argued that the increase in the number of commodities that enter the lives of human beings under capitalism results in the increase of alien forces which oppress and subject human beings. With newer commodities, human beings tend to become poorer because, with every new commodity, the human need for money increases proportionately with the declining value of money in terms of the commodities that money can afford. Money, with the development of capitalism, becomes the basis upon which communities and individuals construct their lives. Money in many ways becomes the community itself (Harvey 2014, p. 55; Marx 1973). Within social media commerce, money occupies a fundamental position of importance as well as will be documented in this book. The importance that money possesses in the times of contemporary capitalist modernity has provided a new lease of life to these modes of commercial activities through which capitalist accumulation is taking place.

Social media commerce focuses on the way in which communities can be used for the benefit of capitalism. People are inducted into the world of social media through multiple means and for a variety of reasons (Miller 2011). Within social media, there might be different communities involving a single individual who does not intersect with each other and still be as functional as communities. Miller brings out these issues quite brilliantly in his anthropological studies (Miller 2011; Miller et al. 2016). Virtual communities in cyberspace operate through technologically mediated communication organised through globally accepted spatial and temporal regulations (Fuchs 2008). Social media has brought in a new way of living life itself. It has significantly altered the previously existing ways of life and has played a pivotal role in the creation of a lifestyle-centric way of life where the possession and flaunting of commodities have become a norm. Social media commerce uses the lifestyle-centric way of life in contemporary society to encourage people to engage in commercial activities. The desire to engage in trade is nothing new to human nature. *Homo Sapiens* have built relationships and civilisations by using trade as a tool. However, trade was never an element that could be said to be a natural element of community life (Marx 1976, p. 172). It was something that individuals and communities engaged in to survive and further the progress of their civilisation by building relationships with other civilisations. Marx theorises this from the standpoint of value production, which he refuses to identify as an 'eternal natural form of social production' (Marx 1976, p. 174) because if one does take it to be a natural element of human social behaviour, 'we necessarily overlook the specificity of the value-form, and consequently of the commodity-from together with its further developments, the money form, the capital form, etc.' (Marx 1976, p. 174). Pre-modern human societies did not produce for the creation of commodities, they do so for sustenance. Capitalism creates what Marx (1976) calls 'a society of commodity producers' (p. 172), who develop large scale commercial activities. Commodities play a crucial role in the construction of the social fabric under capitalism. They determine the 'how' and 'why' of civilisations today.

The search for a better life under capitalism has made human beings cowards. The fear of losing privileges or being outcasted from the circles of a lifestyle choice that one is privileged to make while belonging to a certain class makes one impervious to the blatant violations towards the lives of 'others' (Said 1979). The definition of a better life under capitalism is almost always mediated by the possession of commodities and private property (Marx 1844). This 'truth-like' aspect of modern life makes the *Economic and Philosophical Manuscripts of 1844* (EPM) extremely important in the context of modern capitalism because it brings forward the most fundamental contradictions between the society under capitalism dominated by private property and the actually existing individual therein. Marx's EPM outlined the theory of alienation, critique of the Hegelian dialectic and most importantly, the critique of private property, all of which went on to form the core of Marxist theory transcending narrow disciplinary boundaries creating 'a philosophy of human activity, an integrality of philosophy and economics' (Dunayevskaya 1973, p. 52).

It is of extreme importance that any book written with the purpose to investigate everyday life takes cognisance of this present state of affairs, which has been ushered because of the rapid rise of social media commerce. It is only when the working class understands the present, that it can begin to unearth the historical knowledge as a class, about its own social existence such that '...their succession, their coherence and their connections must appear as aspects of the historical process itself, as the structural components of the present' (Lukács 1971, pp. 159). Following Lukács, this can lead to the ideological construction of a world "which confronts man in theory and in practice a kind of objectivity..." (p. 159). It is also necessary, for any Marxist work, to base theories if not soundly, then at least tangentially, on the history of capitalism in general, because it is through history that one can understand the present. Summarising a few points from Lukács, which can be of extreme relevance in this context, becomes an important part of the initial setting-up of the work to follow: The social existence of the proletariat is influenced heavily by the dialectical progress of history (p. 164) characterised by '...the ending of a rigid confrontation of rigid forms, (and which) is enacted essentially between the subject and the object' (pp. 142-3), where the multiple levels of subjectivity, which constitute the true essence of man get emphasised. History, within the Hegelian way of thinking, 'is the "life-element" of the dialectical method' (p. 147) and requires a systematic and consistent methodological approach. The essence of historical progress

> ... lies precisely in the changes undergone by those structural forms which are the focal points of man's interaction with environment at any given moment and which determine the objective nature of both his inner and his outer life. But this only becomes objectively possible ... when the individuality, the uniqueness of an epoch or an historical figure, etc., is grounded in the character of these structural forms, when it is discovered and exhibited in them and through them (Lukács 1971, p. 153).

Social media is a result of this dialectical progress of history. There are certain very specific points in history from which the internet has emerged and has been subsequently ushered in into the everyday lives of individuals in the world. The development of the internet through the ages has been diverse. The development which began from conceptualising the internet as a static system of networks has now evolved into a full-fledged communicative system encompassing every aspect of human life in the contemporary world. These developments have focused on the communicative aspect of the internet. The evolution of Web 1.0 into Web 2.0 and Web 3.0, emphasising cooperation and collaboration has enabled human beings to use the techno-social domain of the internet to transmit both symbolic and economic values (Fuchs 2008). Web 3.0 has been at the forefront of enabling sharing economies and other such modes of businesses to thrive and prosper (Cohen 2016). Fuchs provides a concise thematic outline of the various levels of the development of the internet over the past few decades: 'Web 1.0 is a tool for thought; Web 2.0 is a medium for human communication;

Web 3.0 technologies are networked digital technologies that support human cooperation' (Fuchs 2008, p. 127).

The transition from Web 1.0 to Web 2.0 focused on the enhancement of the ways in which the internet changed from being a mere publishing and consumption-oriented platform to a communicative, collaborative and participative platform (O'Reily 2005; Fuchs 2008). Social media websites such as Facebook, Instagram, etc. are all parts of this transition. Platforms such as Uber, Lyft, Airbnb, Oyo Rooms, etc. have been at the forefront of this new dynamic explosion of the growth of internet-based commercial websites which have harnessed the power of Web 3.0 (Cohen 2016). Platforms are characteristic of external producers and consumers getting connected to each other through the interactive and participative structure of the platform (Parker, Alstyne and Choudary 2016). The growth of technology at an unprecedented pace has resulted in the world's largest real estate company – Airbnb – owning almost no physical property while Uber, one of the largest travel companies owns almost no physical cars (Bhanver and Bhanver 2017). All of these technological innovations have followed the phenomenal rise of the internet without the networked structure of which these technologies would have been useless and like all other common pipeline businesses (Greenfield 2017).

In the Global North, from the beginning, the Internet was embraced as an advancement of science. It gained increasing usage, made inroads into the lives of the people easily and over time became naturalised as an essential element in the lives of the common person. People used the internet because it provided them with easy access, more freedom, etc. Social movements such as 'Occupy!' have used social media extensively so as to make their demands more popular (Fuchs 2014b). In the Global South as well incidents such as the 26/11 Attacks on Mumbai in India have exposed the power which social media holds over the dissemination of critical information (Lal 2017). In the Global South, specifically in India, however, the proliferation of the internet has taken a different route. The difference, however, lies primarily in the way the internet was positioned in societies in India by the companies providing the services. The Internet was never meant to be an entity available to the common people. It was shrouded within controversies related to the indiscriminate usage of the internet for reasons often considered to be moral crimes in the country. The internet in India has been related deeply to what criminologists or the sociologists of crime referred to as 'Moral Panics' (1972). Parents tried to shield their children from its usage fearing it would push their children into morally unacceptable domains of consumption often related to pornographic content, western rationality, etc. Of course, the fear of the internet being a weapon to westernise Indian society also played a crucial role in its initial struggle to make a mark in Indian society. The internet, thus, unlike the Global North, took a much longer time to gain entry within the living spaces of the common Indian people. Of course, the impoverishment and chronic unemployment that India suffers from also played its part considering that the Internet was an expensive service to possess. There arose the business of 'Cyber Cafes' in India, which at one point in time, was one of the most lucrative businesses in urban India because everybody knew the 'Internet Boom' was just around the corner. Cybercafes were the places where a tremendous portion of the people of the current 'technocratic' generation of countries like India was introduced to the amazing 'force' of the internet. The mystification of the internet's role, or its potential role, in Indian society, along with the high exchange value that people had to pay for the service, converted the internet into an object which did not act like a way of life as it was in the Global North but rather was from the onset itself, a commodity which was located external to everyday life. Commercial activities through the internet targeted the common user thus, also took their own time to develop in India. While Amazon started its operations in the United States in 1994 with an Indian website launched in 2013, Flipkart, the first indigenously Indian e-commerce platform was established only in 2007. These platforms have benefited tremendously from the way in which the usage of the internet has proliferated in the country. At the same time, they have also been important parts of the generation of the internet ecosystem in India. The differences between how an innovation found its space within a society have an important effect on the methods in which the technology associated with it is used as history progresses.

The proliferation of the internet, however in spite of its unidentical development, has been tremendous, be it in the Global North or in the Global South. The possession of a stable internet connection has almost become a necessity of human life. In recent times, certain left-wing formations have expanded their conceptual formations around fundamental human needs to also include a stable internet connection. Covid-19, in some ways, laid tremendous credibility to this demand. One of the major critiques of these arguments can be based on the idea that no matter how much the need for the internet is described to be a fundamental need of human sustenance in contemporary society, the internet in itself will always be a commodity that will be owned by the large monopoly business in most of the major economies. It will always be a terrain where capitalist forces will use the data generated by the users themselves to exploit the users and accumulate profits. Srnicek (2017) has emphasised in his work on platforms and their relationship with capitalism that even within platform-based capitalism, there always remain certain features of capitalism that are unchanged such as capitalism's drive for economic growth and vitality – be it in the 19th Century or the 21st Century.

For example, at one point in time, India had one of the most widely functioning publicly funded internet providing services in the world in the form of the Bharat Sanchar Nigam Limited (BSNL), however, with the coming of private enterprises came in with all of their different plans surrounding the proliferation of internet-based mobile-phone possession, BSNL found itself to be at odds with the market. This is an important point with regards to the internet in India. Since 1995, the year the internet was introduced in India, it had largely been managed by the public sector. This meant that there was less competition with regard to that service in the market. When the private players came in, they brought different plans, sometimes with practically free internet such as the latest Mukesh Ambani-owned Jio Telecom. Scams in the government driving the neoliberal agenda of pushing out publicly funded players in the sector, successfully created the situation where private entities could 'roam' free in the market creating new forms of services to lure people into their connection. The Indian telecom industry is a testimony to the old Marxist idea of competition and monopoly. The Indian telecom industry is the blatant representation of how private capital systematically uproots publicly funded institutions to bring in further capitalist accumulation and valorisation.

In doing so, the internet providers created distinctions among the users of the internet. Having a BSNL connection meant you were somebody who had been stuck in the old days of pre-liberalisation India. Such documentation frequently evades the popular narratives of technological innovations and their effects on the lives of people. Capitalism, through such techniques, establishes patterns of exploitation because it realises it is the active human being who shapes and gives life to history. The patterning of the lives of individuals of which social media is an important part of contemporary society tends to erase the subjective essence of individual human beings, attempting to place everyone within a fixed spatially and temporally predictable structure. In this day and age of social media individual subjectivity, in most cases, is a myth. Technology and the networked mode of contemporary life have often resulted in the loss of human agency as Greenfield (2017) accurately informs. An understanding of how these technologies interfere with the everyday lives of people is essential to understanding the totality within which human lives sustain themselves in contemporary society. As Zuboff (2019) argues, contemporary forms of technological innovations have used the human raw data to deduce behavioural data through which they have brought in more predictability within the fold of understanding human activities. Because of the usage of human data, platforms and other such forms of commercial activities usually compete more effectively with other pipeline-based services because they rely on community reactions and feedback loops originating from the users themselves (Parker, Alstyne and Choudary 2016). Social media commerce gains momentum because it converts actual users of commodities into sellers of those commodities.

Capitalism attempts to create networked patterns of behaviour which focus on the complete obscuring of humanism within human beings. Erich Fromm identified this 'deep-set reification, with man lost in a network of things' which is characterised by a massive indifference towards the human being (Durkin 2014, p. 166). The people are the real creators of history, who do not adhere to dogmatic economic, historical, or philosophical paradigms. Marxist theory as such was never meant to be a dogma, and neither was it meant to be a sectarian discipline (Dunayevskaya 1973, p. 63). Even the French Marxist, Henri Lefebvre, at times criticised for his long association with the Stalinist French Communist Party, had said: 'Dogmatism is a great evil which comes in countless forms. If we are to exterminate it we must hunt it down in every nook and cranny and drag it from its hiding place by the tail like a rat' (Lefebvre 1991, p. 56). Going back to Marx himself, in *The Holy Family*, Marx says:

> *History* does *nothing*, it "possesses *no* immense wealth", it "wages *no* battles". It is *man*, real, living man who does all that, who possesses and fights;

"history" is not, as it were, a person apart, using man as a means to achieve *its own* aims; history is *nothing but* the activity of man pursuing his aims (Marx and Engels 1845, p. 93)

Social media commerce, as will be shown in the current book transforms the working class into objects under capitalism. It snatches the historical subjectivity of the working class and uses them as objects for the development and sustenance of capitalist accumulation. It is with the development of capitalism, that trading and other such commercial activities assume an importance that is far superior to other humane activities of the members of the social unit. Alongside this tremendous increase in commercial activities, there subsequently rises the influence of commercial capital – one of the most important elements of contemporary capitalism. But, before that, one needs to take cognisance regarding a few points related to the influence of commodities on the lifestyle centric way of life in contemporary society, the focus of which needs to be seen in conjunction with: 'Marx's ... concept of labour which revealed the labourer to be not just a force of revolution, but its Reason – meant that the proletariat was the "Subject", the *Universal* Subject that was not just a product of history, but its shaper, negating, i.e., abolishing, the exploitative reality' (Dunayevskaya 1980/2019, p. 28).

Contemporary society is a society mediated by the gains of technology, there is no way one can deny it. Technology today negotiates with the manner in which individuals form and work through their consciousness. In other words, technology today is not only a part of human beings, but rather human beings are, as Marcuse (1941) had said long ago, parts of a technological process whose roots lie in a certain capitalist technological rationality. Human life is a product of the capitalist reality that such forms of rationality create and sustain. The consciousness of individuals is in a direct relationship with their material lives which is in turn dominated by their development as productive forces under capitalism. Marx argued that the 'consciousness can never be anything else than conscious being, and the being of men is their actual life-process' (Marx and Engels 1845-46, p. 36). We are living in times when social media has transformed the objects which have extinguished their use values to their present possessors as commodities that can re-enter the market. Capitalism always has used science and technology, including the innovation and continued improvements of already existing science and technology, for furthering its own goals (Marx 1981, p. 191).

Some of the commodities which are left behind as refuse after a cycle of production-distribution-consumption has been exhausted might find a new place within the society in another form. Social media commerce accelerates these processes. Within social media commerce, commodities such as monitors, phones, cameras, etc. find a new lease of 'market-life'. At the same time, social media commerce creates the platform for numerous other commodities which would have been, under normal circumstances, labelled as pure refuse or garbage. The continued innovations in the fields of science and technology always create the potential for the production of refuse and wastes, which might result in an offshoot of the production process. Capitalism, in the process, produces a lot of commodities, which are supposed to go 'out of vogue' after a specified period of time (McKendrick 1982). Production, consumption and distribution, within this milieu, have become a unified part of a total capitalist network (Rose 1978, p. 49) that operates in the society. Social media commerce assumes an important role in this role. Technology and the digitalisation of society have made exchanges of all sorts further unequal and unjust; it makes little sense to debate whether 'fair exchange' exists or not because it does not. They have become the means through which capitalism attempts to destroy the conception of 'man [as a] "thinking human spirit"' (Marx and Engels 1845-46, p. 62), the importance of which was put forward by Marx in a marginal note in his manuscript of *The German Ideology*, the same work, in the preface of which he wrote:

> Hitherto men have always formed wrong ideas about themselves, about what they are and what they ought to be. They have arranged their relations according to their ideas of God, of normal man, etc. The products of their brains have got out of their hands. They, the creators have bowed down before their creations (Marx and Engels 1845-1846, p. 23)

Human beings are products of their needs, there is no question about that. There might be debates about the concept of 'needs', and about the causal factors behind particular needs, but what cannot be denied is that human life is an invention that had sprung up because of the way needs are structured within human modes of existence and how those needs are satisfied by the progress of history. It is the historical progress of human civilisation which has led the world into the technological epoch that one witnesses today, where smart tags have penetrated almost every technological artefact that one uses. This development has largely been due to the gains made by human society in the field of ICTs and other resource-efficient technology (Strengers 2013). Networked modes of communication and interactions have become the dominant mode of the way in which human beings experience everyday life under capitalism (Greenfield 2017). As a result of this immense proliferation of the networked modes of communication infiltrating the everyday lives of human beings, everything that human beings do get greatly affected by the technology which they use, including their needs and desires.

Every need of a human individual under capitalism is a potential site of oppression and expression, something which Marx had hinted (Marx 1844). Needs, wants and desires are interwoven within the capitalist reality of which we are a part. They are the elements that formulate the tendencies which dictate our ontology as well as our epistemological understanding of the reality around us, be it within the public space or in private spaces. In other words, they form human nature, and as such 'imperatively' need satisfaction, within certain limits of course (Fromm 1942). Apart from a few of the basic needs such as hunger, thirst, sex (and play if one takes into account the scholars who theorise leisure to be one of the foundational elements of human life such as Lefebvre (1991)), etc., human beings also have countless other needs which are essential for a fulfilling life. These needs are essential for living a fulfilling life, the indications and importance of which are found in the early Marx, especially in the EPM. Human beings come into contact with each other because of their needs, enabled by the fact that the totality of human needs in society is interwoven together in a complex web of interdependence forming the basis of human society. Needs, ideally in their unalienated form, are not created out of exchange values, but rather out of use-values. Even in their alienated form, they become the basis on which society is constructed as we know it. Even within alienated living conditions, needs still become the 'cohesive force for social life even in bourgeois society, and they ... are the real bond' (Lefebvre 1991, p. 91). Marx understood the importance of 'needs' as being the foundation of consciousness in society quite early.

> ... men must be in a position to live in order to be able to "make history". But life involves before everything else eating and drinking, housing, clothing and various other things. The first historical act is thus the production of the means to satisfy these needs, the production of material life itself. (Marx and Engels 1845-46, pp. 41-2)

The satisfaction of one need by 'the action of satisfying and the instrument of satisfaction which has been acquired, leads to new needs; and this creation of new needs is the first historical act' (Marx and Engels 1845-46, p. 42). Marx empathically put forward the argument that needs are the pivots, around which the formation of social relations and socio-historical progress in society depend (Marx and Engels 1845-46, pp. 43-4; Lefebvre 1991). Needs are the central elements of human progress and are one of the pivotal elements in the process in which human beings form ideas regarding their own selves. Capitalism tries to rob human beings of their subjective understandings of the self, reducing human beings to the point where they come to see themselves as mere machines or objects at the mercy of capitalism. Capitalism does that by generating cultural norms around certain needs and desires of the working class. It gives legitimacy to the desires which can be transformed into commodities that yield profit while neglecting others that might be more beneficial to the marginalised sections. Marx (1844, p. 308) talks about how capitalist standardisations take place in accordance with the bare necessities required by the workers to sustain themselves. By doing this, the capitalist social structure turns every 'non-essential' activity of the worker into a luxury, where it is not the worker but capital that decides what exactly is essential. This is constitutive of Marx's famous lament about the worker being 'an insensible being lacking all needs' (Marx 1844, p. 308). This conception is also related to the ways in which needs are related to the class structure in the society where particular classes are 'assigned' certain needs that 'does not coincide with their common interest', which are then 'asserted as [interests] *alien* to them' (Marx and Engels 1845-46, p. 47). Commodities manufactured for the luxury of individuals often are classified into these categories, whereby they are positioned as commodities that are out of the reach of the working class. They are not necessary to survival, as Marx writes:

> Luxury is the opposite of the naturally necessary. Necessary needs are those of the individual himself reduces to a natural subject. The development of industry suspends this natural necessity as well as this former luxury – in bourgeois society, it is true, it does so only in antithetical form, in that it itself only posits another specific social standard as necessary opposite luxury (Marx 1973, p. 528)

The current book analyses the modes of circulation of such luxury items in the chapters that follow this Introduction. But, at this particular moment, it will be sufficient to take cognisance of the idea that the changes in the mode of production within capitalism create situations whereby such luxury goods become a part of the social fabric such that life becomes unthinkable without these commodities. These commodities with time become 'naturally necessary' because of the 'historically created necessity' that Marx posits as the basic tendency of the capitalist mode of production (Marx 1973, pp. 527-28). Technological developments play a pivotal role in this regard, creating barriers between 'full production' and 'full employment' resulting in the loss of the sense of workers' skills leading to the complete subjugation of the spontaneity and subjective self of the workers (Dunayevskaya 1958a, pp. 271-73; Marcuse 1941, pp. 43-4). Consumer goods feature in at this particular juncture. They are often targeted at the prevalent culture in a society, which under the crude objectivism of capitalism along with its induced technological rationality, becomes a mode of social patterning and control along with forming an important part of the process of consumption (Mason 1981, pp. 20-1). These tendencies are often linked to social prestige as well whereby the social status of individuals gets mandated by the commodities they use or possess. These individuals remain entrapped within a bourgeois individuality, whereby, their consciousness gets framed by capitalist consumerism. Any activity that the worker partakes in which goes beyond the standards set by the capitalist as an activity for basic survival, gets labelled as a luxury. Technology is a major aspect of contemporary life that falls under this category.

There is a deep relationship between the needs of the working class and the luxuries of the capitalists, which shape the consumption market (Dunayevskaya 1958a, p. 128). What social media commerce has done is that it has worked on the latter and has transformed them into mass commodities available to everybody, albeit in a quality that will always be looked down upon by the upper class and the elites. These commodities, which the working class, has long desired to possess for itself, have now become accessible to the working class. Social media commerce has played a large role in this regard. Refurbished iPads are commonly known to be one of the highest-selling refurbished products globally. Social media commerce plays a large role in this. Some would argue that using refurbished products is a means towards the creation of sustainable economies and a sharing community that can serve as an anti-thesis to capitalist economic structure *per se* by focusing on nostalgia, care networks, etc. (Cohen 2016). However, such explanations often lack the emphasis on the manner in which even sharing networks can retain the logic of private property and capitalism. Such economies usually result from extreme conditions – either of prosperity or of poverty – which are often not accurate markers of how capitalist societies in contemporary times behave.

Marx says that during times of prosperity if the worker is poor then the causality of the impoverishment is established by citing the inability of the worker to labour to the necessary standards (Marx 1844, p. 241). While the banks and other financial institutions take all the necessary steps to safeguard themselves from any financial collapse, the small-scale trader almost always faces crises on one's own. Every user engaged in social media commerce is a potential capitalist because the individual is altering the relationship that the individual shares with aspects of property and commodities. Social media has given rise to innumerable small traders trading in commodities previously unfathomable within consumer economies. These aspects of social media commerce have been engaged with in detail in the present book. One of the important aspects of the growth of such commercial activities is that they are being done predominantly by non-capitalist classes and the commodities in which they trade are common everyday objects – objects which might not be capable of being sold at such prices. Lefebvre remains a very helpful vantage point in the discussion around anything centring on social media commerce because capitalism today attempts to penetrate everyday life at scales hitherto unknown to most forms of capitalism which make trading in such commodities possible. It becomes possible because of the changing mode of the social contract in place which gives assent to rampant commercialisation of almost everything. A society, or at least society as one knows it today, is constituted by individuals who give consent to a social contract that is accepted by the majority populace in any society.

> ... there can be no knowledge of the everyday without knowledge of society in its entirety. There can be no knowledge of everyday life, or of society, or of the situation of the former within the latter, or of their interactions, without a radical critique of the one and of the other, of the one by the other, and vice versa ... these very same causes have uniform effects, equalising social needs and bringing 'desires' in line with one another, they replace previous highly diversified 'lifestyles' by everyday ways of living which are analogous, if not identical (Lefebvre 2002, p. 11)

Capitalism wants individuals to invest in the newer products and commodities that it continues to put on the market but also does not want the workers to think of them as basic necessities. Because life under capitalism is so segmented and so infested with the inequality that even though certain commodities are 'pretty basic', they are labelled as luxury items. Culture plays a major role in the creation of social patterns around these commodities, which then go on to dominate society. Social Media has enabled the smooth transition of many such articles towards a seemingly user-mediated space – social media. On social media, the commodities which go up for sale by individual traders and users are mostly everyday items. Social media exhibits the most explicit ways in which the mundane aspects and artefacts of everyday lives are commercialised and put into everyday use by capitalist accumulation.

Capital, like light, needs to be analysed both as a process and a thing and 'a simultaneous rather than a complementary interpretation of how this duality works' (Harvey 2014, p. 70) can go miles in allowing one to understand the full impact of the power of capital within contemporary society. Capital today works as a process when it gets circulated within the society, while it acts as an entity or a thing when it takes the form of certain material objects (Harvey 2014, p. 71). The dialectical unity between both these forms produces contemporary capitalism based on, as Harvey suggests, 'a contradictory unity': 'The process-thing duality is not unique to capital. It is a universal condition of existence in nature, I would argue, and, since human beings are a part of nature, it is a universal condition of social activity and social life under all modes of production' (Harvey 2014, p. 73). Like Mandel and Engels, Harvey (2014) also focuses on the element of mobility as fundamental to the sustenance of capital. Capital without any movement loses the capacity to generate profits for its possessors: 'The Continuity of the flow is a primary condition of capital's existence. Capital must circulate continuously or die' (Harvey 2014, p. 73) – a point that has raised considerable debates and discussions. This particular book agrees with Harvey on this point, but at the same time, it also argues that the flow of capital or the necessity that capital must always remain mobile is contingent upon the production process. The point of production thus remains the primary point of the analysis – one of the core propositions of Marxist Humanist analysis of capitalism as Dunayevskaya (1965) laid out. As Marx says, 'The circulation of commodities is the starting-point of capital. The production of commodities and their circulation in its developed form, namely trade, form the historic presuppositions under which capital arises' (Marx 1976, p. 247).

Technology has become a part of our everyday life in contemporary society. Almost everybody today in the global north owns a mobile phone, or at least, has stable access to an internet connection. Gadgets and devices which make one feel safe and secured, help in connecting individuals to their friends and families, etc. In other words, technology today helps in the mediation of anxiety and fear, two of the most common elements of contemporary human life. These attributes, which have been recounted by respondents for this particular study throughout the course of the present study are important components of the overall experience of the urban space. However, anxiety and fear cannot be conflated as identical experiences. Anxiety is characterised by a range of varying emotions which include excitement, anticipation, nervous pressure, performance pressure, etc., while fear is often related strictly to behavioural tracts shown under moments of threat and danger (Kinnvall and Mitzen 2020). The feeling of safety is a critical component of the way in which anybody experiences the space around oneself, both physically and psychologically. Jabareen, Eizenberg and Zilberman (2017) argue that the feeling of being safe in an urban space is related to a combination of factors dominated by the physical environment, trusted relationships and the immediate space that individuals choose to live and thrive in. Social media provides all these to the individual user. It helps the user to negotiate with fear and lived experience, which are the basic elementary components and conditions of human lives and are important conditions that shape human existence (Arendt

1958). According to Hannah Arendt's account, the human condition has to be seen 'from the vantage point of our newest experiences and our most recent fears' (Arendt 1958, p. 5). Social media acts upon these very sentiments. It gives people an outlet for their anxieties while helping them in negotiating their fears. It is commonplace these days to witness people posting on social media regarding how bad a day they have had, or how important a particular decision is for them. Through the utilisation of groups and other such virtual communities, it has also allowed individuals to form communities on and through social media – which has been exploited by social media commerce in its drive to further capitalist accumulation. Social Media Commerce is very closely related to the influence of capital in society and the social dominance of the culture of consumption. It constitutes an important part of the circuit of capital today.

The speed of circulation of capital plays a critical part in determining the productivity of capital such that it can determine the competitive edge that the particular capitalist has over other competitors (Harvey 2014, p. 73). This also plays a critical role in the desired acceleration of the 'turnover' time in multinational corporations which often employ 'economics of scale' to produce profits at an 'alarming' rate. A political-economic analysis of the 'economics of scale' which are employed by many large-scale advanced capitalists can play an important role in our analysis. Merchants today, who come in all shapes and sizes today, have been attempting to root out the middlemen or the retailer. Social media commerce, in time, will enable all forms of capital that it entraps within itself, be it commodity capital, circulation capital or mercantile capital, to become full-fledged industrial capital. This transformation is the natural course of development because with time every form of wealth becomes industrial wealth 'the *wealth* of *labour* and *industry* is accomplished labour, just as the *factory system* is the perfected essence of *industry*, that is of labour, and just as *industrial capital* is accomplished objective form of private property' (Marx 1844, p. 293). Capital exerts power on the working class through a variety of processes – circulation is one of them. Within contemporary capitalism, this process is being increasingly mediated by technological interventions. Mainstream economics and political economists always have the habit of rendering invisible the plight of the workers under capitalism, while focusing on capitalism as a process. In the EPM, Marx (1844) said:

> Political economy conceals the estrangement inherent in the nature of labour by not considering the direct relationship between the worker (labour) and production. It is true that labour produces wonderful things for the rich – but for the worker it produces privation. It produces palaces – but for the worker, hovels. It produces beauty – but for the workers, deformity. It replaces labour by machines, but it throws one section of the workers back to the barbarous type of labour, and it turns the other section into a machine. It produces intelligence – but for the worker, stupidity, cretinism (Marx 1844, p. 273)

Social media commerce has emerged at a time and period in human history where the risk of financial collapse has increased manifold because of the globalised nature of capitalism (Castells 2010; Harvey 2014). Social media commerce helps in temporarily avoiding the acute forms of crisis because it keeps a certain amount of capital, either in the form of *hard* money or credit, constantly in circulation so that it can accumulate enough capital to further subsequent production. It is only through a crisis, that capitalism is able to ascertain the renegade elements contributing to the crisis, get rid of the same and proceed towards a new mode of profit accumulation: 'It is in the course of crises that the instabilities of capitalism are confronted, reshaped and re-engineered to create a new version of what capitalism is about. Much gets torn down and laid waste to make way for the new' (Harvey 2014, p.ix):

> Financial and monetary crises have been long-standing features of the historical geography of capitalism. But their frequency and depth have increased markedly since 1970 or so, and we have to grapple with why they are happening and what might be done about it. The compounding growth of global capital accumulation has put immense pressure upon the state-finance nexus to find new and innovative to assemble and distribute money capita in quantities, forms and location where it is best positioned to exploit profitable opportunities. Many of the recent financial innovations were designed to overcome the barriers posed by pre-existing institutional and regulatory arrangements. The pressure to deregulate seemingly became irresistible. But moves of this kind invariably create a serious probability of unrestrained financing going wild and generating a crisis (Harvey 2010, p. 54)

Social media commerce gains momentum because it is primarily an open platform. There is rarely a shroud of mystery about the processes in which the trade is executed. There are comparatively lesser things that are feudalistic about social media commerce, as opposed to the state and the other finance capitalist institutions such as banks, which have the remnants of a feudal era where their activities are secretive and cryptic with the common people denounced of much knowledge about how they function (Harvey 2014, p. 47). In spite of the mystery surrounding the way these technologies work, they do not get much attention within the public discourse because of their totalitarian nature under contemporary capitalism which has converted these institutions into everyday necessities. In other words, such financial capitalist institutions, as McNally (2011) notes, contribute to the mystification of the logic of Capital. However, in times of distress, such as the Covid19 Pandemic, the activities of banks and other financial institutions came into the fold of public scrutiny.

The most important aspect of Marx's theory is the element of the value-form, and the means by which society can transcend the logic and rule of the value-form (Hudis 2012). Marx talked about numerous factors involved in the entire production and circulation process. These factors include the aspects of circulation time, the role of continuous buying and selling, raw materials, transportation, etc. The worker who receives the money in exchange of the labour-power from the capitalist spends the money on a variety of commodities that satisfy the needs of sustenance of the worker. In other words, the worker spends the money on 'articles of consumption' (Marx 1992, p. 113). Marx's brilliance lies in the fact Marx does not talk about consumption as consumption per se, but rather about consumption being a part of production while still holding on to the primacy of capitalist production being the focal point of his critique (Marx 1992, 1973). Social media commerce has created avenues for personal properties of the working-class users to enter the cycle of capitalist circulation under circumstances that capitalism creates especially for the working classes subsumed by it. These are then used by capitalism for the fulfilment of reciprocal needs and requirements, especially through trade and commercial activities (Engels 1843). It has done so by bringing forward digital modes that encourage such commercial practices and subsume the working class within these modes of circulation.

Marx characterises 'capital' not as a thing or an object of analysis but rather as a relation existing and dominating the social reality: 'capital is not a thing, but a social relation between persons which is mediated through things' (Marx 1976, p. 932). Social media commerce aids the transformation of the personal properties of workers into commodities suited for commercial trade. In doing so, social media commerce leaves an indelible footprint on the social relationships existing between the workers, who also constitute the highest proportion of its users. The present book argues that the rapid growth of social media commerce, which is emerging as a tool of profit accumulation through indirect means, aided by the crisis of neoliberal capitalism, is converting the society into a society of working customers where people are working towards becoming an effective customer by providing free labour to the growth of commercial capitalism. Like all other platforms, social media commerce uses and affects the spare capacities and communities built around commodities (Parker, Alstyne and Choudary 2016). It supports capitalist accumulation, both digitally and physically, either directly or indirectly by exploiting the perennial social crisis and rampant consumerism already existing within society (Deb Roy 2020).

The constant technological developments continuously reduce the socially necessary labour time to produce commodities. The reduction in the socially necessary labour time is, as Dunayevskaya (1958a, p. 105) stated, the result of the process in which the machine interferes with the concrete labour of human beings transforming 'all concrete labours into one abstract mass'. The technological developments of capitalism have an indelible effect on the way social relations are structured: '*The relations of production in their totality constitute what are called the social relations, society,* and, specifically, a society at a *definite stage of historical development,* a society with a peculiar, distinctive character' (Marx 1849, p. 212). Capital is the all-encompassing reality of contemporary everyday life just like it was during Marx's time. The temporary affluence that social media commerce provides to the worker is nothing but a marker of the increased affluence of capital itself as Marx (1849, p. 220) had noted, because to capital the maintenance of the 'social gulf that separates the worker from the capitalist' is central to the maintenance of the power of capital. The analysis of capitalism thus has to start from the commodity itself – the genesis of capitalism as a social force – from which it has to extend towards constructing the social foundations of various facets of contemporary capitalist reality such as social needs, exchange relations, consumerism, and the like. This is also the trajectory that this book follows.

The history of human civilisation is the history of human labour, and nothing – absolutely nothing – can substitute the effects of human labour on the dialectical progress of history, and this is the central point about which capital clashes with labour. This is the most important Marxist Humanist concept which has reverberated throughout the book. Concrete events, epochal ones included, such as the introduction of social media commerce cannot be analysed with a one-sided view but have to be situated within the broader processes of value creation and commodity production (Dunayevskaya 1958a, p. 102). The current book locates the 'event' of social media commerce within the broader literature on capitalism and is driven mainly by the idea that it is only a negative – and pessimistic – analysis of a situation that can lead to positive and optimistic results just as how Marx had theorised it to be following Hegel.

Note on the Text

For the current study, a total of 25 Facebook groups and over 100 Instagram and Twitter accounts were examined. The location of these accounts and groups were based in New Zealand, the United States, India, Bangladesh, the United Kingdom, Nepal, etc. Virtual social media groups dedicated to 'Buy and Sell' purposes were critically engaged including 'Hyderabad Buy and Sell', 'Delhi Exchange Zone', 'Otago Flatting Goods', 'Dhaka BuY & SeLL', 'New York Offers – Buy. Sell. Trade', etc. The users in these groups mostly focus on the trading of used products, with only occasional new products being listed. Some of the most commonly listed or sold items on the groups are apartment rentals, clothes, electronics, books, household amenities, etc. In addition, there are also occasional listings of flats and other accommodation-related products. Interviewees included students, professionals, manual workers, housewives, etc.

Some of the words in the text are used interchangeably. Interviews for the qualitative data presented in the book were conducted mostly virtually. The countries included here are New Zealand, the United States, India, the United Kingdom, Bangladesh, Nepal, etc. The terms 'Global North' and 'Global South' have been used mostly interchangeably with 'West' and 'East' respectively. The author remains aware of the larger debates about the terminology, but for the purposes of simplicity, this approach has been taken. For the purposes of maintaining a certain universality, the author has largely abstained from mentioning the names of individuals and their countries. However, in cases, where a specific characteristic has been noted, that has been very specifically mentioned.

Care has been taken to use gender-neutral pronouns throughout the text. However, many of the quotations used in the book come from texts that were written at a time when the convention was to use male pronouns when referring to people. These have been left unchanged.

1. CAPITALISM'S COMMODITY

The Russian revolutionary, Vladimir Ilyich Lenin (1899/1977), was one of the first Marxists who could theorise the centrality of the economy surrounding the commodity-form under capitalism. It is the growth of the commodity-economy, as Lenin himself put it, which gives rise to other kinds of institutions for capitalism to exploit and extract profits from. Commodities under capitalism, along with their objective domination over the human subject have become the subjective foundations upon which human beings concretely construct and think about their everyday lives. Commodities have helped capitalism in maintaining the control it possesses over the everyday lives of workers through a modification of the structure of needs of the working class. For the current generation, the differentiation between natural needs and social needs is extremely thin. For some, it might not even exist. Capitalism, through its many techniques, influences human beings to become machines working relentlessly in the service of capitalist accumulation (Dunayevskaya 1958a, 1965).

In her classic work on the Marxist conception of 'Needs', Agnes Heller (2018, p. 21) had argued that the quality of labour-power that the worker sells is directly proportional to the needs of the worker, which determines the amount of productivity of the worker at any particular time. This productivity, as is popularly known, determines the amount of labour-power which a commodity is embedded and thus also determines the value of the commodity – the actual value – which then goes on to determine the price of the commodity when the capitalist tries to extract the profit from the commodity to further the domination of capital in the society through accumulation. Entrenched within this process is the circulation of commodities in the society through the market, which is governed by the corresponding values of the commodities influencing the way in which the workers satisfy their individual and collective needs. These in turn, as Balibar (2007) notes, affect the manner in which social relations – including relations within the community and the family – get shaped within the capitalist reality. Commodities, thus, as one can see, lie at the root of this entire process. Before proceeding further, it will be useful to put forward a definition of the *commodity*. In the first volume of his magnum opus *Capital*, Karl Marx defines a commodity in the following way:

> *An external object, a thing which through its qualities satisfies human needs of whatever kind. The nature of these needs, whether they arise, for example, from the stomach, or the imagination, makes no difference. Nor does it matter here how the thing satisfies man's needs, whether directly as a means of subsistence, i.e. an object of consumption, or indirectly as a means of production* (Marx 1976, p. 125)

The value of a commodity can only be realised if it is embedded within some use-value, even though the commodity in itself might be completely indifferent to the useful form in which it is used (Dunayevskaya 1958a, p. 128). In the context of the current work, numerous examples can be cited – Computer Monitors, Television sets, Flowers, etc. The commercial exchange which goes on surrounding these commodities often takes place not in their original intended purposes but rather along what usefulness they can fulfil apart from their usually designated functions. During the Covid19 Pandemic, an increasing number of old TV sets suddenly started to be traded as 'Second Monitors'. Similarly, old mobile phones, which have perhaps lived out their utility as phones began to be traded as 'webcams' because their cameras were still functioning effectively. In whatever form the commodity is traded, the fundamental idea that the more human labour that is embedded within a commodity, the more profit that the commodity can produce for the capitalist, remains unchanged. Marx explains this process through his exposition on the dual-process in which capital makes a profit: 'first, by the division of labour; and secondly, in general, by the advance which human labour makes on the natural product' (Marx 1844, p. 249).

Money then acts as an agent which completely externalises the human labour embedded within these commodities to produce spiralling capitalist valorisation processes and methods of profit accumulation (Murray 1993, p. 43). Marx (1976) describes commodities, as has already been stated, to be objects which is located external to the human being and is characteristic of something which satisfies some form of human need. Marx argues: 'Objects of utility become commodities, only because they are products of the labour of private individuals or groups of individuals who carry on their work independently on each other. The sum total of the labour of these private individuals forms the aggregate labour of society' (Marx 1976, p. 165).

Following Marx's own expositions on the concept of 'commodity' under capitalism, many scholars over the years have brought forward their own interpretations of the relationship between labour, commodity, time, culture and capitalism. These include scholars such as Adorno (1991), Lukács (1971), Soth-Rethel (1972, 1978), Cleaver (1979/2018), Mosco (1989), Postone (1993), Huws (2003), and Balibar (2007) among others. Capitalism understands that in order to extract the surplus value from the labour of the working class, it must extend the rule of commodities in society (Huws 2003, p. 61). The commodification of society by capitalism affects the fundamental existence of the workers in society, both at an objective and at a subjective level. This commodification is firmly established in society by erasing the exploitation which goes into producing the commodity. Almost every commodity that finds wide usage in society – from a tiny hairpin to a small spoon to a very large aeroplane – is extracted from the earth and human labour, and as such is exploitative in its very nature of existence (Morrison 2008). This is the history of any commodity that capitalism attempts to hide. At the same time, it also tries to establish 'this' commodity as the central point of everyday life (Lefebvre 1971; Goldman 1983/1984).

For capitalism, the establishment of the rule of the commodity form in the society is quintessential to its existence as a dominating mode of production. In doing so, it performs some very specific functions, one of the most important among which is the expansion of the 'Market' overcoming some of the traditional modes of exchange and processes of formation of social bonds among people in the society (Harvey 2009, pp. 55-64). The market has been propagated by capitalism as a force that forms the basis of the society, regulates the various subjective human positions in the society, etc, while remaining outside the control of the majority of the societal populace (Barbalet 1983, pp. 89-92; Harvey 2010, p. 42). Social media today is a part of this capitalist market. There is a growing literature – both academic and non-academic – about how social media has created a democratic space or a space that has allowed ordinary individuals to freely voice their opinion, which is all quite legitimate (Fuchs 2014c). But, at the same time, social media is also a part of the capitalist system and its associated market regime – *this is the fundamental reason why this particular book exists.* Social media is the final culmination of a capitalist developmental project, which was set in motion a long time ago when the industrial age progressed towards the post-industrial age. The post-industrial age or the 'Post-Industrial Society' as Daniel Bell (1973/1999) would term it, is a major conceptualisation of the contemporary day and age. Brought forward by massive changes in the social structure which resulted in changes in the management of the industries, the post-industrial society results in an immense proliferation of employment in the professional and technical sectors (Bell 1973, pp. 13-7). Along with the immense improvement of the technological systems and innovations which continuously intervene in the lives of human beings, this kind of society is also characterised by the change from a goods-based economic structure to a service and information-based one (Bell 1973).

While theorising social media commerce, this argument has to be extended and modified, because through the proliferation of platforms like 'Facebook Marketplace' and 'Instagram Shops', what one witnesses is a physical mode of commodity circulation within the working class being promoted by a digital platform. The primacy of the information-based economy still holds but it is characterised, in certain cases like the present one, by a complicated web of social capital circulation based upon the exchange of physical commodities. Without the physical circulation of capital through the exchange of commodities, the digital platforms cannot sustain themselves as the latter can only remain free and counter its own lower marginal costs by economies of scale if the former keeps on accumulating profits and diverting those in the form of investments to the latter. So, while the "new men" like the mathematician and the scientist (Neilson 2018, p. 885) still hold a dominant position in society, they cannot, on their own, be the controllers of the society since the reproductive value of the commodity produced by them is extremely low (Marx 1976). There, thus, arises the requirement of a physical circulation model, which can concurrently exploit, the material needs of the people as well the digital labour of the people entwined within the alienated production process in the society.

Social media commerce facilitates the process of creation of capital of a new kind in the information society, where the relation between the price of the commodity and its value is different than what it had been under pure industrial capitalism. The value of a commodity, according to Marx (1976) is determined by the addition of three factors – constant capital, variable capital and surplus-value while the price is fixed, as Rigi (2014) summarises, through a process that takes note of the supply and demand existing in the market. The price often exceeds the value, thereby paving the way forward for the creation of profits. The realisation of this surplus-value and profit occurs in different forms such as interest, rent or through profits drawn from the market, or by reducing the variable capital involved in the production process (Marx 1894). Along with these forms of contemporary capitalist accumulation, there is an additional accumulation of digital rent on information and advertising (Rigi 2014) as well, which has become a vital aspect of the sustenance of digital monopolies like Google and Facebook. Through the ushering in of countless gadgets, many of which have allowed human beings to remain connected to each other on an everyday basis, capitalism has invented newer methods of exploiting and controlling the workers. In other words, as Boltanski and Chiapello argue, capitalism has successfully managed to provide a new lease of life to capitalist domination in the society through 'internalisation of a certain spirit of capitalism' (Boltanski and Chiapello 2005, p. 25). This internalisation entails within itself the constitution of a sense of justification of the capitalist ideology, not only at a superstructural level but also at a subconscious level. It furnishes the possibilities of self-criticism and eradication of practices unsuitable for profit accumulation, while at the same time, also creating avenues where individuals can voice their differing opinions so as to 'establish various reality tests, and thereby to provide tangible evidence in response to condemnations' but within the ideological boundaries constructed by capitalism (Boltanski and Chiapello 2005, p. 26).

In doing so, capitalism ensures that individuals remain compliant with the norms set by capitalism. This nature of capitalism has turned capitalism into something which is more than a mere disciplining or controlling force. Capitalism, today, ruptures the basic idea of being human. It turns human beings into commodities and commodities into 'spiritual beings'. In such circumstances, struggling against merely the economic aspect of capital is not sufficient, and it is necessary to struggle against the core of capitalism – the dehumanisation of human life and the commodity form. Dunayevskaya (1980) suggests in her *Preface to the Iranian Edition of Marx's Humanist Essays* the necessity of combining the Marxist philosophy of revolution with actual revolutionary praxis, one of the primary elements of which was the articulation of the domination of dead labour over actually existing living labour, which converts human beings to parts of a capitalistic social machine. To counter such tendencies under capitalism, it is necessary that Marxism comes out of the narrow confines of disciplinary sectarianism (Dunayevskaya 1965).

While speaking about contemporary capitalism, it is not sufficient to talk only about the economic aspects of capitalism, but rather one always has to speak about capitalism as a whole social system. Understanding capitalism and its impact through social media commerce on the lives of people requires an understanding of the commodity and its significance within capitalist societies and state forms. Capitalism increases the global demand for commodities and transforms the very definition of the necessities of life that the working class actually needs to live in society (Marx 1976; Morrison 2008). This is done through massive reorganisation of the structure of society, where everybody can aspire to become a part of the improving standards of living in the society. This aspiration, *which should have been normal and there is nothing wrong it had capitalism not existed as a systematic mode of exploitation*, makes the working class completely subsume itself within the relations of capitalist production. Under a society dictated by the modes of social media, this aspiration becomes commonplace and creates new modes of capitalist accumulation. Social media creates apparent images of a good life attesting to the idea that it is only under capitalism that an individual can obtain a good life. This encapsulates the constructed necessity of a commodity economy and a capitalistic way of life divorced from natural human relationships. Commodities are offered as a way of enrichment – often as the only way of enrichment. This is not something that is alien to Marxist thought since Marx (1844) had very eloquently referred to the process in his EPM. Capitalist ideas surrounding enrichment use the existing social value systems and position particular social aspects as enriching experiences to further the goals of accumulation. Possessing a new commodity is seen to be the solution to all problems. This gives birth to new forms of cultural economic activities, which lay the groundwork for the advancement towards, what Boltanski and Esquerre (2020, p. 301) term, a new *society of enrichment*. The unique aspect of enrichment capitalism is that it does so through processes that portray that the oppressor actually works for the greater good (Boltanski and Chiapello 2005a, p. 173; Mies 2014). Alterations within the relationship between the people and the objects around them (Boltanski and Esquerre 2020, p. 301-302), create a new ruling class along with the existing one which then creates a new 'value (a "greatness") that will convey their hold on the world' (Boltanski and Chiapello 2005a, p. 173).

In this age, when capitalism is increasingly being mediated by digital means, this stratification is being performed through digital means. People having access to faster internet connections are parts of the fortunate few who have the privilege to access the massive collection of data and resources which are out there on the internet. Social media commerce does not have an effect on the overall class structure of the society – it just maintains the status quo already existing in the society. It might be successful in elevating a few individuals momentarily out of their personal crises, but it cannot resolve the larger contradictions found within the capitalist mode of production. Capitalism, as Dunayevskaya (1980) pointed out works through the conversion of human beings into parts of a *well-oiled* machine. This machine works for the furthering of profits of capitalism, while at the same time, keeping the working class under control. Under capitalism, individuals engage with each other as representations of their particular class interests and class locations (Marx 1976). Under the digital mode of capitalist sustenance of the market society based on exchange-values, these relations are expressed through the internet. The internet, and its proliferation both in the global north and in the global south, has enacted newer ways for individuals to establish and propagate their class positions in society. The proliferation of internet accessibility in the Global South thus cannot be analysed as a mere developmental project of capitalism. It is not that capitalism cares about the people and wants to improve the lives of the people living under its domination. History has proved that capitalism cares the least about that.

Capitalism, on entering the post-industrial age, understood, that the central problem with the kind of society that it itself had built upon was, as Bell (1999, p. 29), the management of the extremely complex and large-scale systems of commodity production, circulation and consumption. To do that, it required a system that integrates or has the potential to integrate over time, the immense mass of populace which contributes to its growth. In other words, the labour of the individual needed to be socialised to an extent, where the very individualised nature of its existence itself becomes shrouded under layers of mystification. An individual's labour becomes social under capitalism because it acts as a means of determining the value of a commodity, and further enables the determination of the price of that commodity. The exchange relations existing in the society put the different actors essential to the circuit's existence into contact with one another. According to Marx (1976), it is the form of exchange relation which exposes the social character of their labour as: 'the labour of the individual asserts itself as part of the labour of the society, only by means of the relations which act as exchange establishes directly between the products, and indirectly, through them, between the producers' (Marx 1976, p. 165).

There are various dynamic tendencies existing within these networks of exploitation, many of which cannot be explained in simple terms, and neither there should be any attempts to do that. There seldom exists any overtly simple 'law-like' explanation in the social sciences. Likewise, the tendency of people to engage in trading also does not have one simple explanation. There are multiple reasons for the same, which sometimes work in isolation with one process overdetermining the others, while at times, work in combination with each other with multiple processes exerting themselves in similar proportions. Bell (1999, p. 9) argued, and quite correctly, that the social dynamics existing in a society cannot be understood by ways of simple observation, because to accurately take cognizance of the progress of history, one needs to take into account the various fluxes and contingencies that social progress presents to social theorists and social scientists. At the centre of historical progress, lies the dialectical relationship between the subject and the object, i.e., living labour and dead labour, or 'to put it differently, the conception of reality as a totality, the unity of inner and the outer; the relationship between the whole and the parts which constitutes the passage from existence to reality' (Dunayevskaya 1958b/2002, p. 95). If post-industrial society is not analysed dialectically, then, one will again be prone to making crude analysis of the social structure under capitalism (of any kind). Thus, a dialectically critical look at the relationship between philosophy, organization and the social reality that we inhabit, not only allows one to look at the overall totality of existent reality but also enables one to delve into the multiplicity of issues that co-exist within any society, most precisely within any moment with revolutionary possibilities. Dunayevskaya's (1987/2002) philosophical vantage point on dialectics as a philosophy of revolution remains a highly relevant tool in any contemporary revolutionary analysis. Her focus on the Hegelian concepts of 'Abstract Negativity' and 'Concrete Universality' helps in understanding the nuances of the Marxist mode of Dialectical thinking which can provide pathways toward a more detailed comprehension of the revolutions taking place in underdeveloped or developing nations (Dunayevskaya 1979; Anderson 2020, p. 189). Dunayevskaya's approach becomes relevant because she did not succumb to either crude materialism or to romantic idealism. Instead, she focused on the co-existence of both co-existing in a dialectical relationship. Her's, and Anderson's ideas about dialectics and its centrality are based on the elements of both idealism and materialism being co-existent in Marx's EPM.

This is an attitude that Dunayevskaya utilised in analysing the role of Lenin, someone who is often known to be the person who rescued Marxism from the *Das Kapital* (Gramsci 1917/1977). The revolutionary legacy of Lenin, as Dunayevskaya argues, has to be found in the dialectical arguments made by him and taking his theories in light of the existing praxis of the times in which he was writing as a holistic model to be referred to, not imitated, in the contemporary struggles as Anderson (2020, pp. 53-4) further argues following Dunayevskaya's arguments. In this light, Dunayevskaya's argument on the dialectical Lenin, with regard to national liberation struggles, can be taken up as a case-in-point: 'as opposed to Bukharin's (and many others') concept of capitalist growth in a straight line, or via a quantitative ratio, Lenin's own work holds on tightly to the dialectical principle, "transformation into opposite"' (Dunayevskaya 1967, quoted from Anderson 2020, pp. 69-70). Societies do not progress in straight lines (Dunayevskaya 1979, 1983). The influence of the internet and social media thus, cannot be streamlined to fit into particular models, but rather have to be analysed subjectively. They have to be analysed as parts of the overall mode of production in the society, which need to be analysed as actual revolutionary revolutions which would enable Marxist theory to come to terms with the fact that some societies can 'choose a different path' (Dunayevskaya 2002, p. 259).

There are considerable differences between how people engage with social media commerce in the Global North and in the Global South. While in the Global North, the engagement is largely determined by needs, crisis and a certain notion of affluence towards articulating possibilities of 'upgradation', in the Global South, the engagement is mostly along lines of getting rid of commodities. It is true that even in the Global South, some amount of engagement – a good proportion of it as has been revealed by the author's numerous conversations – is because of needs, but those needs are also generated by a certain affluence. It is mostly people who are relocating or are having to sell their commodities because they are looking forward to something new in their lives. These people categorically state the dire state of affairs of transportation services in India as being a primary driving force in having to sell. In the Global North, however, and especially in New Zealand, transportation and delivery services are mostly performing well above the average expectations, hence the dire need to necessarily sell is absent in most cases. In other words, the use-value of a commodity, once it is within the everyday life of people, has more chance of getting realised to its full extent in the latter case than in the former.

One can understand this point, perhaps more clearly, if the concept of use-value is taken into consideration. Commodities one buys within any capitalist system, always have two values- use-values and exchange-values. Harvey (2014, p. 15) argues that the primary contradiction leading up to a crisis within capitalism is the very contradiction between these two forms of value. The major difference, in quantitative and qualitative terms, between the use-value and the exchange-value of a commodity is that while a commodity can have many use-values depending on where and by whom it is being used, the exchange-value is usually a homogenised and quantified value assigned to the commodity. Marx (1976) argued that for a commodity, the use-value was its natural form, a form in which its social character was not to be realised under capitalism. But it is only within the contours of the exchange-value that the object obtains for itself a social form- a form in which it finds itself entrenched within capitalist social relations. Dunayevskaya (1952/2019, p. 62) proposes the value-form within capitalism's organisational structure, to be the primary driving force of the perversion of the relationship between 'man' and 'machine' – in the current case, between human beings and machinic philosophy of social media.

Not all use-values can be quantified as commodities on the market as some use-values of certain objects can be extremely cultural in nature. The relationship between use-value and exchange-value also determines the availability of the product or the commodity in the market, which reinforces the importance of this relationship for the capitalist mode of production. Use-values can exist without exchange-value, but exchange-value cannot exist without use-value (Heller 2018, p. 22). The underlying meaning of the statement is that exchange-values, which are often expressed quantitatively as 'price' – an immaterial part of the value of the commodity (Balibar 2007) – cannot exist if there is no use for the object in question. For capitalists, the relationship between value and price is one laden with contradictions and always creates a problem, often for the workers. Capital tends to fetishise the price and neglect the value of a commodity. Values remain an abstract notion under capitalism because there is no easy quantifiable way in which one can identify the actual value of the commodity in the market. One reason is that prices can be fixed by the capitalist under capitalism, whereas value is something that is almost always relegated to a certain temporality. Values, as Harvey (2014, p. 31) opines, cannot be easily identified, which discourages their usage in the market under capitalism where money acts as a medium to put a label on the commodities. In other words, the process of putting an 'asking price' on the commodities becomes a norm, while objects begin to be labelled in terms of money becoming commodities for capitalism. The price asked for a particular commodity is 'the price [which is] actually [supposed to be] realised in an individual sale ... [depending] on particular conditions of supply and demand in a particular place and time' (Harvey 2014, p. 31). With the expansion of the market, or rather the forces associated with the market, the price of a commodity becomes personified in the commodities themselves.

It is the use-value of an object which plays a pivotal role in its transformation towards becoming a commodity under capitalism. The use-value of any commodity is influenced by the 'need' of the worker actually using the commodity, such that the 'worker sells his labour-power to the capitalist: [the worker] gives up the use-value and, in return, receives exchange-value' (Heller 2018, p. 21). If someone does not have a use-value for a cell phone, the exchange-value of the same is useless for the person. For capitalism, this is critical. The bare purpose of capitalism – accumulation – cannot take place through a commodity if the commodity does not have a use-value. The state of needs and crisis in the society plays a pivotal role in the determination of the exchange-value of the commodity as Marx (1976, pp. 132-34) argues. The analysis of these needs, however, needs to be focused on the state of the relationship between living and dead labour in society. It is in the moment of production itself under capitalism that forms the core of capitalist exploitation (Dunayevskaya 1965). All capitalist innovation in the field of production is done in order to reiterate this violent core of capitalism. It is the invention of the phone call itself which has to be problematised. It is futile to talk about how use-values are not realised or how the unused use-values are ending up in the realm of exchange-values without talking about the causes of the commodity itself.

Crisis in the society under capitalism has an important effect on the individual as it unfolds through the numerous tragedies – both physical and psychological – in the individual's modes of being and thought (Dunayevskaya 1968). Needs and crises are important elements of the process in which a commodity finds its use-value in any society. The exchange-value of the commodity is also contingent upon the time and place in which the commodity finds itself (Marx 1976). The price of a phone call from a quiet little town in Canada will be significantly different if that same phone call is made from a war-ravaged Middle Eastern town, even if other factors remain consistent for both towns. Social media commerce acts as the balancing force in these situations. It can manipulate not only the exchange-value but also the use-values of commodities in accordance with the situations in which it finds itself. A diaspora Indian, who had a tremendous collection of electronic items reveals how the prices varied when the person travelled to his home country following Covid19. He could sell his electronic goods which included a laptop and a tablet for a greater amount of money in the west than he could in India. The need for a laptop, a costly one, at a used price is more in the west than in the east. Brand culture in the west is significantly more developed than that in the east.

Another example in this regard can be taken with regard to the garments and apparel business. In the Global North, there is a growing tendency to sell used garments. A plethora of such items can be seen in the social media market. Individuals engage in selling their used suits to their wrongly sized undergarments, all with an intention of either getting rid of the objects or gaining some extra money. The intentional drive is more often towards the latter in the case of individuals with low socio-economic credentials. Even with the former option, most of the respondents confirmed that once they got rid of their old objects, newer commodities took their place. An interesting point in this regard was referred by a South Asian person, who hinted at the way in which such items exhibited the way social media commerce intersects with ideas of race and class in the west. Most of the people listing used clothes in the west, at least in New

Zealand, remain to be from the dominant race – there is nothing surprising in it. The minority of sellers from other races who sell clothes on social media narrate their experience to have gone smoothly when the buyers do not request to meet personally, especially if they are not from the same community to which they belong. Similar is the case with Muslim sellers in Hyderabad in India. Most of the commercial relations around used goods are actually associated with bodily attributes and are associated with a previous utility that requires actual body-to-body contact. Such trading mostly occurs within the particular community, creed, caste or race to which the original user belonged to.

These commercial relations have not been formed out of a vacuum, but rather are manifestations of the systemic global crisis in different societies. With every crisis, there occur certain alterations within the societies which become characteristic of societies as history moves forward. The present crisis, which has slowly but definitely becomes a permanent feature of lives under contemporary capitalism has forced the working classes to transform their personal properties into commodities. Personal properties are different from private property as they do not naturally, without a market to appropriate it, have the ability to generate profits. Social media commerce provides this market to encompass all the use-value of commodities within the capitalist accumulation circuit thus promoting contemporary capitalism from being an agency of formal subsumption to an agency of real subsumption (Negri 2003). This process where the productivity of labour becomes redundant because the production process itself becomes a commodity through a complete reorganisation of work through the application of communication technology constitutes what Negri (1989), based on Marx's (1867) theory, calls real subsumption, the unequivocal and complete realisation of the law of value (Negri 2003, 1989). Under capitalism, it is the value-form of the commodity, and value production, which becomes the basis of the organisation of the society and produces other conditions for the sustenance of capitalism, so 'every single thing that issues from the process of production has the *value-form*. The commodity itself is not a product of the market. *It arises at the point of production itself and reflects the dual character of labour*' (Dunayevskaya 1952/ 2019, p. 62). Dunayevskaya (1965) analyses the Marxist idea of value form to be one that Marx drew quite heavily from the practical struggle of the Communards during the Paris Commune, whereby value is not only understood economically but also socially and psychologically in relation to the dominant ideology in the society.

When users use Facebook to *sell on the go*, they are not only being exploited on the basis of unpaid digital labour (Fuchs 2014a) but also on the basis of the exploitation of their productive forces which no longer determine the value of their labour-power (Negri 2003). It is the dominant bourgeois ideology in the society which renders this oppression invisible in advanced capitalist societies (Marcuse 2002). As Dunayevskaya (1965, p. 67) notes, under advanced forms of capitalist societies, all kinds of philosophy are reduced to false consciousness among the workers and the intellectuals, so as to create a society where any dialectical progress of the working-class movement becomes difficult. Theories, as Adorno (1973, p. 4) notes, in advanced capitalist societies, are only offered as alternatives and competing opinions to other theories in the marketplace – *nothing however escapes the market*. Theories about capitalism need to focus on the commodity and the value represented by the commodities which is the final and the most explicit manifestation of capitalism (Dunayevskaya 1965, p. 69). The fetish of the market has been critiqued by many citing that it often makes theories negligent of the core contradictions of capitalism. The relationship between the value of the commodity and labour-power becomes further complicated when the same kind of product is continuously used for profit accumulation. The act of resale through social media does not generate profit for the capitalist directly but rather, it creates the conditions that make capital accumulation possible. So, while for the seller, it is true, that there is no profit because the resale usually gathers a lower price than the original one, the point that has to be studied is the direction of investment or expenditure of the generated price in the case of a resale. Harvey (2006) correctly argues that under a system that depends on commodity production, it is the process of exchange that determines the relationship between (or separates the aspects of) production and consumption. Drawing from Marx (1867), Harvey argues that the concept of use-value is the determining factor in establishing the relationship between commodities and human needs. However, use-value is almost always related to the qualitative aspect of economic relationships while exchange-value is related to the quantitative dimension. Under real subsumption, it is this relationship between the use-value and exchange-value that gets blurred because all use-values, already utilised or hitherto unutilised, become potential avenues for the generation of exchange-values. Social media commerce aids the working class to make use of the unutilised use-value of the commodity. Hence, even though the resale of the used goods on social media does not make any profits for the working class, it does allow the working class to invest that money back into the market. If the resale had not taken place, and social media would not have accelerated or facilitated the process, this investment would not have taken place. Additionally, the person buying the commodity also pays for a certain amount of use-value that the commodity can still offer, as a part of the same has already been used, and inevitably finds himself/herself again in need of the very same commodity in the future.

Mandel (1975, pp. 525-26) characterised the primary sustaining factor of the socio-economic fabric of the capitalist mode of production as the generalisation of commodity production. Social media commerce aids the sustenance of generalised commodity production in society by temporarily enabling the working class to satisfy its needs for consumer goods by consuming the commodities which have already been produced so that new commodities of the same kind can be produced for more consumption at a rapid pace. This new cycle of production requires investment from the working class at regular intervals. Many interviewees affirmed that they do in fact, buy or have to buy, the same kind of consumer goods, with the money they earn by selling their personal property. This temporary monetary capital or financial stability generated by the sale, thus, again gets accumulated as new profit for the capitalist producing consumer goods which in turn generates profits for the capitalist producing producer goods. In doing so, capitalism re-uses the labour-power contained in the means of production in the form of machinery as well as exploits new labour-power. It is this quantified form of the workers' labour that the commodity embodies within itself (Marx 1976), where 'Value is simply expended labour' (Sayer 1979, p. 16). In other words, 'in bourgeois society, the commodity form of the product of labour — or the value-form of the commodity — is the economic cell form' (Marx 1867c/1996, p. 8) and it is this 'value-form of the commodity [which is] ...the social form of the commodity' (Marx 1867d/1978, p. 134).

It is this transcendence of the value-form, and then subsequently the total apparatus of surplus-value creation, itself which has to characterise the revolutionary movement against capitalism (Hudis 2012, p. 6). Everything that arises out of the capitalist production system has a value-form, such that 'the commodity itself is not a product of the market' but it 'arises at the point of production itself and reflects the dual character of labour' (Dunayevskaya 1952/2019, p. 62). It is the point of production itself that creates the distinction between the use-value and exchange-value of objects under capitalism. Once a commodity passes through the capitalist production system, it cannot possess any other value than the exchange-value. However, to the common worker, it is the use-value that matters (Perlman 1972/2016). Capitalism attempts to obscure the relationship between the worker and the use-value of the commodities possessed by the worker in its drive for value-creation. If one is to think about dismantling the power of capital on a global scale, it is imperative on their part to take the use-values of commodities under capitalism into consideration. In the first volume of Capital, Marx (1976) continuously provides the readers with an analysis of the importance of use-value. Commodities under capitalism, however, do not have any 'businesses' to conduct with use-values. For them, the primary element – the base of their existence – is the exchange-value and the price of the commodity. Appadurai (1986) perhaps is the most important contemporary figure in this regard who has written exclusively and extensively on the cultural value of commodities under capitalism. Although writing from a perspective, whose basic aim is to critique the concept of the commodity within Marxism, Appadurai's (1986) excursions into Simmel (1978) and Marx (1976) do prove helpful to understand the cultural side of commodities, even if one does not agree with him completely. Simmel's (1978) arguments surrounding the way in which demands influence the value of a commodity roughly translate into proposing that 'the economic object does not have an absolute value as a result of the demand for it, but the demand, as the basis of a real or imagined exchange, endows the object with value' (Appadurai 1986, p. 4). Appadurai's concept of the commodity revolves around three factors, 'commodity phase' referring to the idea that things can move in and out of the commodity state, 'commodity candidacy' based on the 'symbolic, classificatory, and moral' standards through which the exchangeability of an object or thing is determined within a particular socio-historical context, and 'commodity context' referring to 'the variety of social arenas, within or between cultural units, that help link the commodity candidacy of a thing to the commodity phase of its career' (pp. 13-15). In order for something to be classified as a commodity, it has to be found in the commodity phase, Through these argumentative positions, Appadurai (1986), writing from an anthropological perspective, proposes that it will be overly simplistic to analyse commodities merely as a manifestation of western capitalism and instead argues that '*the commodity situation in the social life of any "thing" be defined as the situation in which its exchangeability (past, present, or future) for some other thing is its socially relevant feature*' (Appadurai 1986, p. 13). He clarifies it further by saying that *commodisation* (not *commodification*) of a society is, simultaneously, a 'temporal, cultural, and social' affair (15). His theories point one to believe that commodities can become 'not commodities' under specific cultural points, even within capitalism.

Under social media commerce, this statement can be placed, but in a reverse manner, because what one is witnessing in social media commerce, is the commodification of objects which were 'not commodities' previously. Exchange-value is the basis of the commodity-form, but use-value is the way in which commodities get utilised by individuals. Consumption of commodities thus 'needs to be considered as a complex, multivalent phenomenon, a manifestation of economic, social, cultural, historical, and psychological processes and effects' (Dunn 2008, p. 4). The act of consumption as Dunn (2008) states, is placed at the conjunction between 'commercially based commodification and subjectively based satisfactions and meanings' (4). Used garments in the west, have been commodities for decades now. However, they have not been so in the east, where they are traditionally articulated as gifts or donations based on one's class, gender and caste position in society. Alternatively, customised t-shirts focused on a fixed audience are increasingly becoming a commodity in certain fixed and spatially restricted markets in India. More often than not, such garments find a market where an already existing fetish is operating in society – in the form of an institution or a *monument*. Conversations with student sellers located in Hyderabad and Delhi, as well as a few of them located in the far-flung states in India expose this point. These sellers have confirmed the process in which social media has helped them garner customers and a market for their products.

Brick and mortar markets never provide the extensive social penetration that social media does. Social media helps them in targeting their potential customers. They use the networks they already possess on social media platforms to sell their products. The fact that social media has become an almost institutionalised means for semi-closed communities such as universities and colleges to inform the stakeholders has aided social media to become a successful platform for student sellers. Such sellers have been engaging in commercial trading of numerous commodities, which are at times very unconventional – cakes, arts and crafts, hand-crafted beer, etc. Within such platforms, commodities, normally not profit-making objects for individuals producing on a small scale, have suddenly been offered a completely professional commercial set-up. These commodities, as a crafts seller informed the author, were always a part of the community, but were never produced for profit: 'We used to make these long before Facebook came along. Then, we used to sell these in community fairs and stuff like that, but now it's like 365 days, 24×7 marketplace'. Similarly, an amateur baker from India tells the author: 'I used to bake cakes since I was 15 or something. I used to hold treats then for family or friends at times. When Facebook and Instagram became a thing, I considered why not turn into a full-time baker selling cakes instead of giving them away for free'.

Raya Dunayevskaya (1973) informed her readers that when considering social relationships under capitalism, one should always see them as relationships between things. Under the regime of value production, nothing – absolutely nothing – can escape from the idea associated with the dominant logic of value production within capitalism (Dunayevskaya 1952). Appadurai's partial agreement with Marx that it is under capitalist societies, that an increasing number of previously cultural material objects might end up becoming commodities, thus is nothing but the reassertion of Dunayevskaya's theory of the centrality of value production under capitalism. His conception of commodities however remains more cultural than economic. Commodities for him, have to share a meaning within the community they are exchanged, a point which was also later raised by Bauman (2001) albeit in a different manner. Bauman (2001) argues that society itself is composed of shared meanings. Similarly, Appadurai (1986) also argued that the commodities are not the markers of *only capitalism* but rather 'refer to things that, at a certain phase in their careers [through production to distribution or circulation and then finally onto consumption] and in a particular *context*, meet the requirements of commodity candidacy' (Appadurai 1986, p. 16). The use-value of objects becomes particularly interesting in this kind of analysis. However, even if the use-value occupies the central and pivotal position within cultural accounts, it is the very purpose of the exchange-value, or more precisely, the price in contemporary capitalism, to dissolve these qualitative differences between the different use-values of an object in such a way so that there comes alive a form of commodity exchange in the society which is not only generalised but also normalised. In other words, the exchange of commodities becomes the soul and substance of the society, just as how Marx (1976) had predicted it would be under capitalism.

2. THE FETISH OF THE COMMODITY

Commodity fetishism is an intrinsic character of capitalism. Social media commerce under capitalism also does not evade this generalisation. Commodity fetishism dominates the social relationships which arise under capitalism, at the core of which lies the commodity-form – regarding which Karl Marx had said:

> ... the commodity form, and the value-relation of the products of labour within which it appears, have absolutely no connection with the physical nature of the commodity and the material relations arising out of this ... (the commodity) is nothing but the definite social relation between men themselves which assumes here, for them, the fantastic form of a relation between things (Marx 1976, p. 165)

This statement from Marx also serves as the basis for a theoretical excursion into the world of the idea of *Commodity Fetishism*. Commodity Fetishism, as an idea, is intimately related to the processes of needs generation, capital circulation, and capitalist sustenance. Balibar (2007, p. 59) proclaims fetishism to be the means through which capital achieves the complete realisation and expansion of value fundamentally important to the capitalist idea of continuously feeding on the living labour of the workers, while continuously valorising the value of dead labour. This was one of the most important points raised by Raya Dunayevskaya (1965, 1980) as well. Even though Marxists differ among themselves regarding a whole plethora of different issues, there does exist a broad consensus about commodities within Marxists of all hues. Almost every Marxist *worth one's salt* will believe in the process in which commodities exploit human beings under capitalism and create the conditions for capitalist domination in society. Raya Dunayevskaya (1958a, 1965) and later Peter Hudis' (2012) analysis of the role of the fetish within capitalism, however, remain the most strikingly important ones to the current author, because of their dialectical analysis of the role of the commodity within the society. The basic cause of the emergence of fetish under capitalism, according to Dunayevskaya (1965) remains the 'perverse relationship of subject to object – living labour to dead capital' (Dunayevskaya 1965a/2019, p. 42). Commodity fetishism is the stage of capitalist development where the relationships between human beings are no longer mediated by human sentiments or spontaneity, but rather by capitalist alienation and commodities. In other words, commodity fetishism becomes the living soul of capitalism itself. Commodity fetishism is not an abstract notion under capitalism, rather it is a living force that plays a crucial role in alienating human beings. The social state of fetishism is the naked reality of capitalism: 'Under capitalism, relations between men appear as relations between things because that is what "they really are."' (Dunayevskaya 1958a, p. III).

Dunayevskaya (1965, p. 63) sees commodity fetishism as a central element within capitalism, along with the accumulation of capital. Fetishism creates a barrier between the complete realisation of the mental and manual potential of human beings in a way that represents the ' "Positive Humanism" [which] begins "from itself" when mental and manual labour is reunited in what Marx calls the "all-rounded" individual' (Dunayevskaya 1965, p. 72). Dunayevskaya posited two basic arguments from Marx as being fundamental to the Marxist analysis of capitalism – commodity fetishism and the Marxist analysis of value along with the accumulation of capital (Dunayevskaya 1965, 1981) – which she qualified to be, and rightly so, the basis of the theories of alienation and historical materialism within Marxism if they are dialectically understood. Dunayevskaya's analysis of the commodity and value form results from her understanding of history being a struggle between the oppressor and the oppressed. Her ideas rest upon a 'non-truncated' Marxism which analyses the continual logic in Marxism rather than focusing on narrow segments (Dunayevskaya 1976a, 1987).

Commodity fetishism has been the subject of numerous theoretical and practical studies over the course of history. Some have theorised about commodity fetishism from a vantage point influenced by the distinction between money and money capital (Lotz 2016), while there are others who have focused on how the concept of fetishism is a process through forgetting or the state of 'historical amnesia' is institutionalised socially (Jameson 2007, p. 15). There are others as well, who have approached the topic more philosophically, such as Slavoj Žižek, who refers to commodity fetishism as 'the unconscious of the commodity form' (Žižek 2009, p. 9). The contemporary English usage of the word 'fetish' draws from the Latin word *factitius* which means 'made by art' and the Portuguese word *feitico* meaning a charm or some form of sorcery referring to some objects deemed illegal or taboo in the Middle Ages (Pietz 1985, p. 6). However, the usage of the word, with its present connotations as Pietz (1993, p. 134) argues, seems to have been drawn from the work of Charles de Brosses in the 1760s who had used the word to describe aspects of religious practices associated with object worshipping (Simpson 1982). So, it cannot be deemed unnatural for somebody like Karl Marx to refer to concrete examples situated within the realm of religion to clarify his positions regarding the relationship between commodities and fetishism. Of course, the actually existing material conditions of the times in which Marx was writing about commodities and fetishism, also played a major role in the process of the selection of examples by Marx to make his theories relatable to the everyday reader.

An object cannot possess or come to possess any special social value unless its intrinsic meaning has been completely displaced by the logic of capitalism and the consumer culture that capitalism establishes in society. For example, one can always refer to products from Apple, an example, which will be used in abundance throughout the work. Brands such as these are near-perfect examples of how certain brands and their commodities possess certain special social values. The social values of these commodities might be economic or cultural. They might also possess some cultural value because they already harbour some kind of special economic value within themselves or vice versa: 'Affording a new iPhone is difficult for me with the wages I draw, getting it on Facebook is easier. It always is a bit old, but if I can test it and it works fine, I guess that is okay for me. In this case, Facebook Marketplace has been an awesome thing for me'. The desperate need to obtain an iPhone by young people is the idea that creates the value for these commodities. Social media commerce does not dissolve the crisis itself, but rather it acts as an agent to further subsume the worker within capitalist relations of production, something that the worker was not a part of till the purchase was not done.

Marx (1976) argues that the 'real' value of a commodity only gets exposed through the relationship within which it finds itself. These relationships, more often than not, are actually existing social relationships between human beings, which are formed through the exercise of labour-power producing the commodities under capitalism. One aspect of the increasing dominance of commodity fetishism is to render obsolete the intrinsic essence of these relationships formed out of the labour-power of human beings, be it within any socio-political system or within the realms of production and consumption. The complete control of the commodity form over the society creates the ground for human beings to analyse other human beings as possessors of commodities only, or worse, as commodities themselves. These are some of the intrinsic ideas which can be fathomed from the ideas presented by Karl Marx and by the many others who have written about the topic after him. Commodity fetishism is a result of the production relations existing under capitalism. As Dunayevskaya (1958a, p. 89) argues, the shift in Marx's theoretical excursions 'from the history of *theory* to the history of *production relations*' allowed Marx to develop a 'theoretical expression of the instinctive strivings of the proletariat for liberation'. This theoretical expression of the process of abolishing inequality in society remains true even in the day and age of social media commerce, which attempts to propagate the archetypal production relations solely based on exchange-values under capitalism, throughout the society at a level that is far more individualised and universal in nature than previous forms and methods.

Use-value in classical Marxism, as has already been stated, refers to the use that the commodities have for human beings and are realised in the sphere of direct consumption. Exchange-values, on the other hand, dwell within the value that these commodities come to represent within the society and are often quantifiable in nature (Marx 1976, pp. 126-28). A sketchy theorisation would reveal that use-values can be attributed to a certain individuality because of the possibility of the existence of diverse nature of usages. But exchange-values can only exist socially – they are objective in nature. Use-values can be only realised in consumption, while exchange-values are realised in society (Marx 1976, p. 126). Commodities under capitalism are all social commodities in nature because they do not exist because of their use-values, but purely because of their exchange-value, which is the basis of all capitalism (Marx 1976). Everything today is part of the social network of production and contributes in some way or the other to the growth of the capitalist production-consumption network. Scholars such as Heller (2018) have used the concept of 'need' to explain the relationship between production and consumption. To understand the relationship between production and consumption, it is necessary to understand the antagonistic relationship between use-value and exchange-value under capitalism. Marx says that if the use-value is abstracted from the commodity, all that remains within the commodity is the labour of the worker (Marx 1976, p. 128). This particular book is not about providing a discussion about use-values and exchange-values, but these two are concepts that are intrinsic to the topic which this book attempts to treat and analyse. For these purposes, and to provide a clearer explanation of use-value and exchange-values, one can always go back to Marx from the first volume of *Capital*:

> The usefulness of a thing makes it a use-value... This property of a commodity is independent of the amount of labour required to appropriate its useful qualities. ... Use-values are only realised in use, or in consumption ... Exchange-value appears ... as the quantitative relation, the proportion in which use-values of one kind exchange for use-values of another kind (Marx 1976, p. 126)

Commodity fetishism is a domain of Marx's *Capital* where philosophy and economics effectively fuse with capitalist politics and human history (Dunayevskaya 1965, p. 67). It complements the Marxist idea of 'value-producing' labour and alienation (Dunayevskaya 1965, p. 68). For the purposes of the present work, the two definitions reproduced above will prove extremely valuable to the readers. The current work is not supposed to be extensive work on the concept of 'value'. This book bases itself on the differences between use-values and exchange-values, which are intrinsically related to the dialectical relation between production and consumption, something which becomes one of the major focal points of this work. Karl Marx in his three volumes of *Capital* as well as in his *Grundrisse* understood consumption as a part of the overall production process. For Marx (1976, 1993), production and consumption were definitely related to each other. Even though production and consumption are processes that move along with each other, it is production that determines consumption. It is the relative abundance of certain commodities which instigates the process of consumption at a pace that favours capitalist accumulation. Social media commerce is no exception to this general rule. It is production that determines the various processes associated with consumption – supply chain mechanisms, price determinations, etc. – while consumption in itself is only a part of the capitalist production process. Consumption cannot go on without production and vice versa, but even in this kind of relationship, the realm of production possesses a certain autonomy because of the direct control that capitalists possess over innovations and the scale of production. Price is an important point to consider in this regard. The 'proper' pricing of any commodity can go a long way in making the commodity more suitable for both production and consumption. The word 'proper' is used here to refer to two processes: (a) so that the price offers a sufficient amount of profit to the capitalist; (b) so that the price also offers a 'well enough value' to the consumer so as to encourage the purchase. In other words, a proper price can enable the continued sustenance of the production-circulation-consumption under contemporary capitalism.

Users of social media commerce spend an immense amount of time determining the price of the commodity they intend to sell. On Facebook Marketplace, the potential customer can also check and verify if the product they want to buy has had a price amendment or not. Such advancements have made people think more about the relationship between price and time (for which the commodity has been listed). At the same time, it also reflects how desperate a seller might be under specific circumstances. Individuals from both sides of the globe have emphasised this point. The commodities for which the prices fluctuate 'more than the usual' on a downward spiral are more likely to be picked up. There is a strange, yet obvious, intersection between the way in which human users on social media perceive the social situations of others, based on the way in which they alter the prices of the commodities on their 'Commerce Profile'. It points them towards determining, speculatively, the social condition of other users. They act just like how capital would have wanted them to behave. Interviews with people who have extensively used social media, across the east and the west, have said that they paid particular attention to checking if the price of the commodity was reduced. Some of them also pointed out the descriptions of the commodities which are listed which often described the situations under which the seller is in. Stimulations caused by words such as 'need money', 'sell out' and 'move out' play a major role in this regard. Social media commerce increases, and to a certain extent, socialises the propensity of the working class to exploit the working class, something which Fleetwood (2008) had theorised in the context of the actual interactions which take place in different shops and businesses. Human beings under capitalism are alienated from the experience of freedom, which makes them submissive to various kinds of authority (Fromm 1942/2001). These are all the processes that the false consciousness under capitalism promotes. The constant judgementalism about others' social position, the desire to oppress and the competitive attitude towards possession at the cost of inflicting harm or benefiting from the problems of oppression of fellow workers.

This oppression within social media commerce takes place mainly through the price set for a commodity. The price becomes the quantified value attached to a person's needs and social situation. The price of a commodity, according to Marx is 'The exchange-value of a commodity, reckoned in *money* is what is called its *price*' (Marx 1849/1977, p. 201). Marx (1859) subsequently also talked about the subtle differences between value and price, when he says: 'The commodity as such *is* an exchange value, the commodity *has* a price' (p. 308). The price is the final alienation of the product from the labour of the producer i.e. the worker, such that it is the price expressed in money that quantifies the individual labour 'contained in the commodity can only through alienation be represented as its opposite, impersonal, abstract, general – and only in this form social-labour, i.e., money' (p. 308). Going by this definition, he qualifies 'wages' to be nothing more than a specialised name for the 'price' the capitalist pays for human living labour 'which has no other repository than human flesh and blood' (Marx 1976, p. 201). The relationship between wages and prices was seen to be an intimate relationship by Marx (1849, p. 204-205). The prices that one sets for commodities on social media are not arbitrary ones. They are fixed by the individual through complex analysis. This is also a point where Dunayevskaya's (1976a) critique of Mandel becomes very important. She critiques Mandel for his overemphasis on the idea of the market under capitalism. Dunayevskaya's (1965a, pp. 72-78) critique runs along with the idea that in the process of emphasising the influence of the market, some theories often render invisible or do not give adequate attention to the core contradictions of capitalism, the contradictions surrounding capital, wage and labour. Dunayevskaya (1958a, p. 106) argues that the domain of circulation is an insufficient tool to analyse capitalism. She critiques them because such theories fail to acknowledge the impact of the factory on the market but rather take the market to be an all-encompassing manifestation of capitalism. The articulation of the contradictions of capitalism needs a unifying theory that takes the entire society into perspective. Dunayevskaya (1958a, p. 126) emphasised the relationship between production and consumption and related that relationship to the core problems of capitalism, i.e., the problem of the realisation of surplus-value and reproduction of capital itself.

Some of the sellers in the west fix the prices following standard norms of the market rates. However, this practice is relatively absent in the Global South. This was also expected, as most countries in the Global South are not acquainted with the system in which used commodities can be priced within a set standard. In the course of the research, it was found that, and quite unsurprisingly, a mobile phone in almost the same condition, was priced differently with a very high price-gap, at two ends of a city in India. One of the most common techniques of fixing prices of used goods was, according to sellers themselves, to fix the price at half the marked price for the brand-new commodity. However, this technique only works in cases where there is a standard mechanism for determining the condition in which a particular commodity is at the time of being sold. Pricing, a trivial matter, to the common observer, is deeply laden with the contradictions of the capitalist system in itself, which come out in all its complexity in Marx's *Grundrisse*:

> In present bourgeois society as a whole, this positing of prices and their circulation etc appears as the surface process, beneath which, however, in the depths, entirely different processes go on, in which this apparent individual equality and liberty disappear. It is forgotten, on one side, that the presupposition of exchange-value, as the objective basis of the whole of the system of production, already in itself implies compulsion over the individual, since his immediate product is not a product for him, but only becomes such in the social process, and since it must take on this general but nevertheless external form; and that the individual has an existence only as a producer of exchange-value, hence that the whole negation of his natural existence is already implied; that he is therefore entirely determined by society; that this further presupposes a division of labour, etc.,

in which the individual is already posited in relations other than that of mere exchanger, etc. (Marx 1993, pp. 247-48)

Prices are fixed by the struggle between the consumers and the producers. The power to negotiate, possessed to a certain extent, by both the producer and the consumer within social media commerce, provides an empowering agency to the consumer therein. At the same time, it also creates the grounds for the exploitation of the worker by another worker (Fleetwood 2008). Many sellers within social media commerce engage with the same kind of commodity. This is nothing new to Marxist analysis, as Marx himself had noted: 'It is essential that the immovable monopoly turns into the mobile and restless monopoly, into competition; and the idle enjoyment of the products of other people's blood and sweat turn into a bustling commerce in the same commodity' (Marx 1844, p. 267). This competition is important to capitalism in many ways, aspects of which will be engaged in detail in the subsequent chapters. To the consumer, it looks as if the opposing individual is dictating the prices, whereas, in reality, it is the capitalist system itself, which employs various factors including social needs, crisis, massively heightened commodity production, etc. to dictate how sellers – mostly workers within social media commerce – behave and influence the prices:

> The same commodity is offered by various sellers. With goods of the same quality, the one who sells most cheaply is certain of driving the others out of the field and securing the greatest sale for himself. Thus, the sellers mutually contend among themselves for sales, for the market. Each of them desires to sell, to sell as much as possible and, if possible, to sell alone, to the exclusion of the other sellers. Hence, one sells cheaper than another. Consequently, *competition* takes place *among the sellers*, which *depress* the price of the commodities offered by them (Marx 1849/1977, p. 205)

The prices of commodities, the process of fixing which falls at the behest of the workers' labour-power which goes into producing the commodity for the capitalist manufacturing process, puts the worker directly within the capitalist relations of production and exchange. Prices fluctuate under capitalism because capitalism wants to keep the wages of the working class intact *where they are* while still being able to generate more surplus value and profit from the commodities in the market (Marx 1865/1985, pp. 105-106). There are many factors that determine the process of fixing prices, a topic that is beyond the scope of this book. Capitalism uses pricing to exploit human labour, even under the aegis of social media commerce. Price is basically, the means through which capital quantifies human labour (Marx 1849, p. 208). For the worker, who doubles up as a consumer, price is the first quality of the commodity that the worker gets affected by. For the development of mass consumerism as an ideology, it is of utmost importance that different sectors of the populace find themselves within the ideological gambit of consumerism (Milanesio 2013). Social media commerce has been performing this function for capitalism in contemporary society. The relation between capital and the consumer, who is often a worker, is mediated through price at a superficial level. The modern consumer, according to Dunn (2008), also produces surplus value for the capitalist like the worker, as does the factory worker. In other words, if one can extrapolate from Tronti's (1962) workerist ideas, the consumer is the *social proletariat* for the capitalist. However, this idea only achieves its complete fruition when seen in conjunction with Dunayevskaya's (1965) dialectical analysis revealing the causes of the capitalist labour process itself. In other words, while Tronti (1962) highlights an extremely important social manifestation, Dunayevskaya (1965) grabs its genesis.

The success of capitalism today depends upon the ways in which it can propagate capitalist values to the very core of everyday working-class lives. This includes manipulating the workers to oppress themselves and their fellow workers when they act as consumers of customers (Fleetwood 2008). This is performed so as to camouflage the bourgeois economists' failure to comprehend the reason behind 'why a certain amount of money is given for a certain amount of labour' and as such fail to understand the causal roots of the supply-demand problem (Marx 1985, p. 117). Marx argued that the supply and demands relating to a particular commodity in the market are directly related to the amount of money that is supposed to be paid for the labour-power which produces that commodity: 'Supply and Demand regulate nothing but the temporary fluctuation of market prices. They will explain to you why the market price of a commodity rises above or sinks below its *value*, but they can never account for the *value* itself' (Marx 1985, p. 118). The market price of any commodity can be at its real value only when the law of supply and demand ceases to act:

> At the moment when supply and demand equilibrate each other, and therefore cease to act, the *market price of a commodity* coincides with its *real value*, with the standard price round which its market prices oscillate. In inquiring into the nature of that *value*, we, therefore, nothing at all to do with the temporary effects on market prices of supply and demand. The same holds true of wages and of the prices of all other commodities (Marx 1865/1985, p. 118)

Capitalism manipulates the waves of supplies and demands as and how it deems fit. Social media commerce 'almost' humanises this process. It makes human beings propagate capitalist values and norms. Social media commerce and its success reflect the ideological power of capital. It acts similar to the Ideological State Apparatuses of Althusser (1970). Within contemporary capitalism, speaking in the language of Althusser (1970, 2014), the Ideological State Apparatuses (ISAs) through the usage of media and education, attempt to portray consumption as a marker of social status which not only represents commodities in accordance with heretical notions (Soper 2020) but also takes an active role in the creation of new needs – one of the intrinsic elements of capitalism according to Marx (1845-46/1973). Targeted advertisements on social media are today a part of these ideological arsenals of capitalism by making workers believe that the solution to their problems lies in the acquiring of all forms of commodities (Mulcahy

2017). Commodity fetishism involves the social negotiation and sharing of the overall cultural meanings of the object in question. Commodity fetishism, often through the usage of advertisements and aggressive public display methods, is that it transforms the objects from mere materials of everyday life to objects of fantasy and desires which increase the overall capacity embedded in the object (Dant 1996, pp. 511-12). Consumer activists often try to identify and expose the hidden history of the generation of these capacities, which underline the 'fantasy-slick surface of the commodity', such as to rupture: '... the dual fantasy of the commodity is that the commodities are created without human agency (the fantasy of omission) and that the purchase and use of the commodity will result in a magical transformation for the consumer, again, without human agency (the fantasy of addition)' (Duncombe 2012, pp. 372-73).

The essential characteristic of a commodity is its ability to get transferred from one person to another shifting its use-value in the form of a relationship that is mediated by an exchange-value (Marx 1976). One can buy a mobile phone, new or used, and might use it for a variety of purposes. Some might use the phone for talking with friends, while some might specifically use it for accessing the internet. Some might use it for both. But the exchange-value of the commodity remains the same. The price of the commodity determined by the labour-power embodied within the commodity and the profit it seeks for the capitalist through its sale, who manufactures the product, remains unchanged. The prices of commodities such as these, and all others, serve the purpose of establishing the commensurability of the object when it finds its way as a commodity in the market. It is the method in which the differences in use-value of any commodity are mitigated and the commodity is standardized with respect to other commodities available in the market (Sayer 1979, p. 16). The state of workers' needs and the perpetual crisis that capitalism produces within the society make it imperative for the working class to trade their daily necessities while engaging in fierce competition surrounding the price of any commodity with other individuals of their own class. Such negotiations often, in the real world, produce conditions of antagonism between the groups and individuals with differing immediate interests, but similar overall interests. This 'hostile antagonism of interests, the struggle, the war is recognised throughout political economy as the basis of social organisation' (Marx 1844, p. 260). As long as the marginalised classes and groups continue to compete within themselves and continue to view each other as nothing but 'competitors', capitalism is in safe hands (Marcuse 1941).

Marx (1976) talked about the price of a commodity as a general form of the relative value of a commodity which provided it with a certain social validity and consistency, along with creating a form of commensuration in society (Harvey 2014, 2017). Money under capitalism becomes the medium in which the value and prices of all commodities are expressed (Marx 1976, 1993). Money completely renders invisible the actual conditions under which the commodity is produced by converting the commodity into a 'number'. It does not take into account that the productivity of the workers, which is the source of all commodities, is contingent upon numerous factors. It depends upon the technology that is employed in the workplace, along with the form of the organisation for or within which they work. One of the major traits of any successful capitalist enterprise is to pay for the labour-power of the workers after the production process has been completed and to buy the means of production prior to production (Harvey 2014). The final result of the entire production process is a new commodity that then finds its place in the market at a price that provides the capitalist not only a *return on investment* (popularly known as ROI) but also a surplus to carry forward further production. The depersonalisation of commodities, i.e., the process in which these commodities become autonomous objects (Marx 1976) within the exchange relations, something which becomes its apparent form to its users and possessors. This apparent form, i.e., semblance, is an authentic one from the point of view of the general worker, who also doubles up as a customer for the capitalist. However, this semblance of the object merely being a commodity with no apparent history of its own also creates an inauthentic semblance as well which is that the commodities only have a value, but no separate use-value (Skotnicki 2020, p. 371). The commodities seem to be completely depersonalised forms of social labour, thus becoming 'imperceptible' giving rise to their status as 'anonymous' commodities.

The commodity is the very foundation of all forms of capitalist exploitation. A Commodity carries a fetish within itself. Commodities make 'the despotic *conditions* of capitalist production as if they were self-evident truths of social production' (Dunayevskaya 1958a, p. 99). This is also the basis of the reified state of social consciousness. Commodities, under capitalism, are from the onset, manifestation of a certain duality – created out of the combination of use-value and exchange-value – 'which, in embryo, contains *all* the contradictions of capitalism' (Dunayevskaya 1958a, p. 99). Commodity fetishism takes root not only from the dual character of the commodity but also from the dual character of labour itself, the fundamental basis of capitalist production (Dunayevskaya 1982, p. 188). It is the commodity and the relationship between the commodity and the individual, which occupies a central position in any Marxist theorisation of capital and capitalism, including that of Lenin as had been also stated at the very beginning of this chapter: 'Lenin's profound grasp of the universal, and the individual in Hegel made him realise, however, that all the contradictions of capitalism are included in the simple exchange of commodities' (Dunayevskaya 1969/2002, p. 155). This constitutes the basic foundation of all fetishist relations. The task of a Marxist theory of contemporary fetishism is to dissect the depersonalised nature of commodities and argue for complete destruction of capitalism itself – which will take down the idea of the 'commodity' with it.

There have been numerous accounts highlighting the significance of the word 'fetish' (Pietz 1993, Chin 2007, Sutherland 2008). Among them, there are some such as Pietz (1993, p. 140) and Chin (2007; 2016, pp. 26-7) whose analysis somehow paints the fetishists as being people who were outside the dominant hegemonical discourse of western civilisations. Making reference to some if these thinkers, Skotnicki (2020, p. 365) argues that there are three major interpretations of commodity fetishism, as an error of cognition, as an illusion or what Marx called 'false consciousness', and as a subjective element of human life defined by capitalist domination. All these three interpretations, to him, act in consonance with each other to produce the combined effectual nature of commodity fetishism in capitalist societies. While explaining the idea of commodity fetishism, Marx used religion as an analogy and saw it as the process in which '... the products of the human brain appear as autonomous figures endowed with a life of their own, which enter into relations both with each other and with the human race' (Marx 1976, p. 165). The 'socio-natural' aspect of production that Marx (1976, pp. 164-65) was talking about gets completely erased from the investigative realm of public analysis when an object finds its way into the market as a commodity with a price. This initiates a process, which after a cycle of time, results in the complete domination of human beings by commodities through a process of capitalist reification. According to Berger and Luckmann:

> ... reification is the apprehension of the products of human activity as if they were something else than human products – such as facts of nature, results of cosmic laws, or manifestations of divine will. Reification implies that man is capable of forgetting his own authorship of the human world, and further, that the dialectic between man, his products is lost to consciousness (Berger and Luckmann 1966, p. 89)

Reification, for all practical reasons, refers to a system of social structuring where subjective individuals are coerced into thinking about other objects and human beings in a manner that sees them only as 'things' from which they can profit upon. In other words, human beings begin to analyse and witness other human beings and their own capacities as human beings, like commodities, as mere profit-bearing objects. This is the most common understanding of reification (Lukács 1971; Honneth 2008). Horkheimer and Adorno (2002) in their celebrated text *Dialectic of Enlightenment* referred to reification as an act of forgetting, similar to how Jameson (2007) labels forgetting as one of the prime elements of capitalist control in contemporary society. But as Honneth (2008) rightly analyses in his book, under contemporary capitalism, it becomes crucial to examine 'Who is doing the forgetting? What is being forgotten? And will remembering suffice to produce a change in actual social practices and institutions?' (Jay 2008, p. 5). For Lenin (1901/1961) and Lukács (1971), the working class armed with the vanguard party's socialist consciousness would be at the centre of the revolution against capitalism. This notion can be and has been debated widely within the left-wing circles (Gorter 1921; Shipway 2013) and is not our primary concern at this point. What matters, at this point, is the centrality of the working class at the centre of the oppression that capitalism inflicts. Chari (2015) recently describes Lukács position on reification as such:

> Reification, he argued, is above all, an unengaged, spectatorial stance that individuals take toward the social world and toward their own practices – it is the subjective stance individuals take toward a society in which the economy exists as a separate, self-grounding, and autonomous realm of social life, operating in a way that is seemingly independent of human will (Chari 2015, p. 5)

The human consciousness under a reified existence is a subjective power that renders capitalist oppression of the worker invisible to the worker (Chari 2015). The capitalist domination of the worker is not only objective but also subjective. It not only attempts to colonise everyday life through objective forces but also does so through manipulation of the many subjective realities (Lefebvre 1971; Lukács 1971; Vaneigem 2012). Reification is a very important part of this critique of capitalism because of the way it emphasises the constant subjection of working-class subjectivity to capitalist objectivity in the form of commodity relations in society. According to Lukács, the theory of reification argues that '...men... erect around themselves in the reality they have created and 'made', a kind of second nature which evolves with exactly the same inexorable necessity as was the case earlier on with irrational forces of nature' (Lukács 1971, p. 128) such that '...even the complete knowledge of the phenomena could never overcome the structural limits of this knowledge, i.e. in our terms, the antinomies of totality and of content' (pp. 132). The domination of reification processes over the human individual, to a large extent, depends upon the mystification of the commodity form in society.

As Marx (1976, pp. 164-65) argues, the process of mystification does not depend upon the use-value of the commodity but rather it depends upon the way commodities hide the social labour which goes into their production. The complete obscuration of the labour itself is the basic form of commodified social relationships under capitalism. Social media commerce thrives within this aspect of contemporary capitalism whereby it allows the continued circulation of consumer goods in the society, making the individuals privy to the possession of such goods, albeit in a roundabout way, increasing the possibility of the establishment of capitalist reification as social psychology. This particular book is not about reification as a concept, and neither does it proclaim itself to be taking sides in the various debates over the subject. However, to understand the domination of commodities in society in the age of social media, reification does indeed play a critical role. In this regard, Lukács raises two points: the first being that

> 'the powers that are beyond man's control... (transform into a) blind power of a-fundamentally-irrational fate, the point where the possibility of human knowledge ceased and where absolute transcendence and the realm of faith began' (Lukács 1971, p. 129); and the second about the philosophy of the contemporary human '...who proceeds immediately from ready-made ideological forms and from their effects ...consisted simply in applying to society an intellectual framework derived from the natural sciences' (p. 130).

Society gives rise to 'social institutions (reification) strip man of his human essence and that the more culture and civilisation (i.e., capitalism and reification) take possession of him, the less able he is to be a human being' (p. 135). Commodities appear to the human self as objects where the labour-power and the social relationships formed by the various modes of labouring activity have been rendered invisible. As soon as an object becomes a commodity:

... it changes into a thing which transcends sensuousness. It not only stands with its feet on the ground, but, in relation to all other commodities, it stands on its head, and evolves out of its wooden brain grotesque ideas, far more wonderful than if it were to begin dancing on its free will (Marx 1976, pp. 163-64)

Buck-Morss (1977, p. 96) argues that while Marx's theory about commodity fetishism was emphasising the forces of capitalist production, the materialistic hermeneutic ideas of Adorno (1973) were aimed at unearthing the nuances of the capitalist social totality manifested by the object, of which social relationships and interactions are an integral part. The social interactions, as has been argued by theorists such as Kellner (1989) and Collins (1989), are not only managed by commodity relationships but rather are negotiated through varying layers of meanings associated with commodities that characterise social relations – in other words, the worst form of reified capitalist social relationships. When different commodities, with the same or different quantities of labour embedded within themselves, are priced, unequally or equally, within the market, the socially productive relations between the labour invested in the creation of the commodity become invisible and the price of the commodity appears as something naturally attributed to the commodity. This is reminiscent of the way in which the analytical Marxist, Gerry Cohen, argued about the process in which capitalism expresses 'the social character of production [which] is expressed only in exchange, [but] not in production itself' (Cohen 1978, p. 119). The manufacturing process of established noodles brands such as Maggi and Top Ramen, might be exactly similar to how a community-based production unit located in the outskirts of Auckland, Islamabad or New York, manufactures its noodles, but, when it comes down to the cost price of these commodities and their ability to accumulate capital, it can be said with reasonable certainty that the established brands would win the battle 'hands down'. Commodities, thus, are not mere economic categories. There are cultural dimensions to every commodity, which finds its place in the market.

Social media commerce often emphasises the cultural dimension of commodities. The immense number of posts that come up on social media create a semblance of the commodity in question being something more than mere commodities. Corporations such as Nike, Adidas, Apple, Google, etc., repeatedly engage in such activities to market their goods. In the process, Apple becomes more than an electronic good producing brand but rather becomes a symbol of status in society, while Starbucks offers taglines, which are immediately accepted by the working classes, such as 'we are so much more than what we brew' (Starbucks 2011, quoted from Duncombe 2012, p. 360). In other words, they help capitalism to create systems through which individuals can be classified in accordance with the consumer goods they purchase (Baudrillard 1970). Commodities thus are directly made to have an impact on the subjective existence of the working classes. The non-possession of a particular commodity drives the working class to work harder to possess the commodities guaranteed to offer them pleasure and satisfaction – to further the accumulation of capital while being ignorant of the same. In other words, they work towards the complete reification of the society that the bourgeoisie desire 'in the forms of the generalised "commodification" of social activities' (Balibar 2007, p. 59). This process is intimately connected to how individuals experience the commodities in the market. Every commodity embodies within itself certain cultural ideas and sensibilities which make them appeal to different individuals belonging to different classes in different ways (Hetherington 2007). However, the common element binding all those different interpretations remains their objectification of the entity they witness and experience as a commodity divorced from human labour.

As Lukács (1971) notes 'this transformation of labour into a commodity removes every 'human' element from the immediate existence of the proletariat, on the other hand, the same development progressively eliminates everything 'organic'...so that socialised man can stand revealed in an objectivity remote from or even opposed to humanity' (p. 176). To become conscious of oneself, the working class needs to be aware of the existing commodity relationships in society. It is here that one can realise the reified structure of the social totality and begin to understand one's own social position and ontology (p. 180). Certain (kinds of) commodities within the market, might assume a certain status quo, among others of their kind. These may be simple products, but they might be performing certain very important functions for capitalism – such as stratifying the population. Certain commodities act as systems of signs, which then go on to stratify the consuming subjects through differentiation of consumer objects (Baudrillard 1972). Duncombe (2012) uses the example of Starbucks to make his point. His argument stated that with the coming of Starbucks, coffee was transformed into something which was more than any regular drink containing caffeine. The coffee of Starbucks assumes a special character of its own – a haunting one if one speaks in the language of Derrida (1994) – when the coffee from Ethiopia is served along with a service composed mainly of affluent looking and mostly middle-class hospitality workers. The combined experience of the product with the service produces 'a fantasy [which] cloaks the "true" history of the commodity and offers up a created ideal in its place' (Duncombe 2012, p. 360).

The importance accredited to emotions and the interpretation of a certain commodity bring forward a certain subjective dimension within the idea of commodity fetishism. Scholars such as Lotz (2014, p. 365) have attempted to speak about commodity fetishism from a perspective informed by both subjectivism and objectivism, arguing that fetishism within capitalism is a subjective relation that exists objectively. The basic core of the proposition is the one that Marx (1976, p. 165) proposed, which was that fetishism was a quality that was inherently attached to the 'object' as soon as it became a commodity under capitalism and that is what objectively gave wind to their production under capitalism, which is in itself a result of the social character of subjective individual labour. Many years prior to Lotz (2014, 2016), Lukács, had also suggested a similar point while furthering his arguments about the process of reification:

> Corresponding to the objective concealment of the commodity form, there is the subjective element. This is the fact that while the process by

which the worker is reified and becomes a commodity dehumanises him and cripples and atrophies his 'soul' -as long as he does not consciously rebel against it—it remains true that precisely his humanity and his soul are not changed into commodities (Lukács 1971, p. 172).

Under advanced capitalism, it can be said beyond reasonable doubt that some, or most, of the famous brands effectively become cultural objects, which supersedes their use-value. For example, taking an example from the Global South, 'Cadbury' in India and in most other developing nations, does not simply mean 'a chocolate bar or a toffee manufactured by Cadbury' but rather it means 'the chocolate'. Arguments such as these have been used by theorists such as Guillory (1993), and Sherlock (1997) to hold the labour theory of value to account, which to them is often an insufficient tool to analyse the contemporary capitalist market. His argument puts forward the point that certain products or commodities have a far superior market value because of their charismatic and aesthetic dimensions. He critiques the 'orthodoxy' in certain accounts, following Guillory (1993), to separate the use and exchange-values of objects with the former becoming a mere appendage to the latter within the level of consumption that people engage in under capitalism. The aesthetic value of a commodity, in the accounts of such 'orthodox' thinkers such as Adam Smith (1776/1999) and Karl Marx (1976), to Sherlock (1997, pp. 62-3) gets lost within its drive to analyse the exchange-value and the labour embedded within the commodity. Following Guillory, Sherlock argues for the necessity of a pluralistic discourse-based analysis of value under contemporary capitalism by deconstructing the use-exchange segregation of Marx. This to him, had the potential to open up the path towards the analysis of the labour of consumption itself which could further problematise the relevance of the experience of consumption. Kate Soper (2020) argues:

> Postmodernity just allows for a plurality of lifestyles, tastes and opinions to find an outlet among consumers with enough money. Theorists who celebrate this individuation and diversification of choice do so without acknowledging the implications of consumption for projects of solidarity, in which indeed they show no interest. Consumers are here theorised as if the behaviorist enactment of an 'aesthetics' or 'ethics' of the self were their only desideratum, and they had no concern for any more stable and collectively effective form of empowerment (Soper 2020, Ch. 'Neither heroes nor dupes')

With a plurality of lifestyles, it is obvious that not all commodities will hold the same cultural value even if they are composed of the same materials and are produced through the same process. Some brands are often labelled as being luxury brands and come with a certain status attached to them for their users. This status is reflected not only in the way in which their outlets and brand ambassadors conduct themselves but also in the way these brands advertise themselves to the population. These brands often utilise the emotions of the individuals, in creating a situation where that particular commodity becomes something radically different from others of the same kind. The emotional satisfaction caused by such commodities, one of the most important of which among the affluent classes, is the fear of losing one's status within the society. Similar to what Benjamin (1968) described, these commodities do not have any inherent properties but were only significant because of the position attached to it in the larger corpus of networks within the total social system (Benjamin 1968). Commodities have no exchange-values independently, but rather they possess that only when seen in relation to other objects already existing in the market. This exchange-value, or more precisely the price of the commodity, renders invisible the concrete labour invested in the commodity and transforms all the labour embedded within the object into abstract labour. If commodities are separated from the dehumanising impact of the production process aimed at modifying nature characterised by, in the words of Wolin (1994, p. 236), 'technical exploitation', the commodity can be analysed as an object 'ensouled'. This would allow the object to regain its actual essence by a reinterpretation of the commodity's nature – the one held by its form in pre-capitalist social formations to its integration into the capitalist production process. The mere shift of the theoretical vantage point from the side of production to that of consumption runs the risk of reproducing the duality – this can be said with reasonable certainty.

The abstract nature of fetishism under capitalism renders it as an intrinsic force of capitalist exploitation. Social media commerce makes commodity fetishism socialised within society. It makes it 'everyday' through its proliferation into the behavioural cognition of the working class, as such transforming it into an ideological force. As Dunayevskaya (1982, p. 189) notes, the 'absolute' – the universality – of fetishism can only be countered through the 'freely associated labour'. Commodity fetishism can only be stripped off by the 'freely associated' human beings, who could expose the labour embedded within the commodity (Dunayevskaya 1982, pp. 143-44). In the process, they would completely destroy the mystified nature of the commodity under capitalism, which exercises subjective domination over human beings under capitalism, the influence of which reaches far beyond the objective domination that political economists credit. Commodity fetishism is the force that transforms the living worker – the historical subject – into an object, a thing, nothing more than a cog in the giant wheel of capitalism.

3. THE COMMODITY SOCIETY

Commodities are central to the generation of false consciousness among individuals (who are both consumers and workers) under capitalism who define themselves in accordance with their possession of commodities – both qualitatively and quantitatively. This is the point that Marx (1844) and later Marcuse (1941, 2002) and Lukács (1971) tried to establish through their writings. It is the society of commodities that social media commerce bases its operation within. Social media commerce enables the wider circulation of commodities across the society, so as to posit the commodity and its associated fetish as the central element in the society. It tends to establish commodity production – the root of all circulation – as a natural law in the society that 'cannot be abolished at all. The only thing that can change, under historically differing conditions, is the form in which those laws assert themselves' (Marx 1868, p. 68).

The analysis of commodities and their influence on human society has not evaded the attention of even poststructuralists and postmodern Marxists. Theorists such as Baudrillard (1970, 1988) and Derrida (1994), both of whom are often admitted into Marxist and anti-capitalist discussions with a pinch of salt, have also talked at length about commodities and their domination in modern society. For example, Baudrillard (1988) argues that the modern world is characterised by fetishised social relations:

> Use-value is an abstraction ... It is just like the abstraction of social labour, which is the basis for the logic of equivalence (exchange-value), hiding beneath the "innate" value of commodities. In effect, our hypothesis is that needs (i.e. the system of needs) are the equivalent of abstract social labour: on them is erected the system of use-value, just as abstract social labour is the basis for the system of exchange-value. This hypothesis also implies that, for there to be a system at all, use-value and exchange-value must be regulated by an identical abstract logic of equivalence, an identical code (Baudrillard 1988, p. 65)

Baudrillard however possessed a very discouraging, and a rather plastic, notion of humanity in itself, whereby capitalist oppression has become the 'permanent refraction of our least movements, we are no longer confronted with our own will. We are no longer even alienated, because for that it is necessary for the subject to be divided in itself, confronted with the other, contradictory' (1985, p. 580). For him, human beings do not anymore possess the capacity and revolutionary vigour to generate a successful resistance to break the circuit of capitalist manipulation and oppression in the contemporary age of media and information-oriented social structure and are destined to remain trapped within a 'permanent autointoxication' (Baudrillard 1985, p. 580). Scholars such as Kellner (1989) and Jhally (1987) have critiqued Baudrillard's reading of the Marxist idea of use-value and have argued that his reading has not considered Marx's theory about human needs being contingent upon historical development and socially produced under capitalist modernity. Among the two, especially Kellner (1989) has critiqued Baudrillard for refusing the acknowledge the dialectical thinker in Marx and for completely overlooking the dialectical development of the commodity under capitalism. Any philosophical vantage point which does not consider the development and dynamics of the commodity form runs the risk of reiterating the bourgeoisie mode of consciousness because it is fundamentally segregated from the roots of the capitalist structure and its mode of production. It is worthwhile, at the point to refer to Lukács (1971), who begins his critique of bourgeoisie philosophy by stating, 'Modern critical philosophy springs from the reified structure of consciousness. The specific problems of this philosophy are distinguishable from the problematics of previous philosophies by the fact that they are rooted in this structure" (pp. 110-11). For Lukács, the classical philosophers such Kant and others of his time analysed the world, as it existed – as a (divine) pre-existing creationist disposition – while modern rationalist philosophy mostly conceives of the world to be a material creation of human beings themselves (p. 112) and claims to have '...discovered the principle which connects up all phenomena which in nature and society are found to confront mankind' (p. 113). However, even though 'classical philosophy mercilessly tore to shreds all the metaphysical illusions of the preceding era but was forced to be as uncritical and as dogmatically metaphysical with regard to some of its own premises...the grandiose conception that thought can only grasp what it has itself created strove to master the world as a whole by seeing it as self-created' (pp. 121-22). As Lukács argues, 'Their underlying material base is permitted to dwell inviolate and undisturbed in its irrationality (...) so that it becomes possible to operate with unproblematic, rational categories in the resulting methodically purified world' (p. 120). This results partially because of 'the failure to make man dialectical (which) is complemented by an equal failure to make reality dialectical' (p. 187).

The final effect of fetishism, according to Sayer (1979, p. 33) is to separate, both in form and content, the products of human labour from their producers and 'deny their constructed character'. Taking a cue from Sayer, the commodity in a fetishised state can be compared with religion which Marx described to be the 'opium of the masses' (1843). Just like religion, a commodity in its alienated and fetishised form, completely disjointed from the historical and social situations from which it has emerged, is always beneficial to capitalism. One of the major characteristics of classical philosophy was its acceptance of the struggle between form and content, which gave rise to the 'nascent' dialectical system, but the strong belief that they harboured for their own bodies of ideas often gave rise to irrationality and a form of dogmatism (Lukács 1971, p. 118). The adherence to a mathematical/natural scientific idealised experimental model devoid of the differences between '"creation" and the possibility of comprehension' (p. 119) led '...to the (dogmatic) rejection of every "metaphysics" [...] and also to positing as the aim of philosophy the understanding of the phenomena of iso-lated, highly specialised areas by means of abstract rational special systems, per-fectly adapted to them and without making the attempt to achieve a unified mastery of the whole realm of the knowable' (pp. 119-20). In spite of 'the turn taken by critical philosophy towards the practical, [it] does not succeed in resolv-ing the antinomies... (but rather) fixes them for eternity' (p. 133). Dant's (1996) four-point critique of Baudrillard emphasises this very idea of divine creation-ism found in Baudrillard's theories, which finally leads to his argument that Baudrillard becomes progressively disinterested in the process in which objects become objects of human fetish while being entrenched within the everyday mundanity:

> First, objects seem to have only two social dimensions; function and ostentation. ... [But] there are a number of forms of social relations with objects that could lead to fetishization. Secondly, ... (there is a need to understand and analyse) the relation between sign value and practical use-value. Thirdly, ... it is not clear ... to what extent all commodities are fetishes and, if they are, whether they have the same fetish qual-ity. ... Fourthly, ... the source of the sign is progressively disconnected from social practices until it becomes 'hyper determined' (Dant 1996, pp. 508-9)

Everyday life under contemporary capitalism revolves around the usage of objects for varied purposes and their ability to be of use to human beings entrenched within the exploitative paradigm of capitalism. Social media, now a feature of most people's habits, create the pathway for individuals to become entrenched within these relations of production. Habits can be described as activities, done through memories formed by the influence of external events (de Certeau, Jameson and Lovitt 1980, p. 40), which focus on the actor who is con-sciously aware of one's action, its context and future implications (Cohen 2016). Under capitalism, however, the consciousness itself is a reified one. It is this rei-fied consciousness that determines the manner in which individuals form their habits, which are often engulfed within capitalistic relations of production and socialisation. Zerubavel (1981, p. 138) quite correctly argued that one of the most important aspects of contemporary societies was the multiple levels of partici-pation that individuals have to assure in order to feel welcome into the society. Participation on social media is a means for them to become 'one with the soci-ety' which they inhabit. There are countless individuals who start using social media because of peer pressure. For them, social media is not just a means of connecting with the people they want to connect or remain connected with, but rather it often becomes a necessity for them. For example, there are countless educational institutions in the Global South, that use social media to keep their students abreast of the latest developments in the institutions. The maintenance of the institution also creates grounds for further reduction of the costs associ-ated with website maintenance, domain hosting, etc. When students get used to social media at a formative age, the probability of social media becoming a part of their everyday life increases manifold. These very students of the yesteryears are the contemporary sellers on social media, who have been using their expertise on social media to generate profits for capitalism.

In the Global North, people use social media differently than those of the global South. One of the easiest contradictions to notice is the way people add 'Friends' and 'Followers'. In the west, social media has mostly remained a way of connecting with people whom users already know. In the east, however, the usage has mostly been towards garnering more networks of acquaintances in the hope that some of those acquaintances will turn out to be friends. This also has effects on how these people engage with social media commerce. This is also a reason of the proliferation of small-scale businesses on social media in the Global South because most users on social media in the Global South make active efforts in creating a community. These two aspects of social media and social media commerce are related. Individuals 'have to' participate in social media to secure themselves of the opportunities which emerge on and through social media. These opportunities may be materialistic or psychological. These multiple levels of participation, under capitalism, produce a split between the 'person' and the 'role' (Zerubavel 1981, p. 141), with the former relegated to the insignificant and mundane habits of the private sphere while the latter is promoted significantly within the society as the public self of the individual. The dialectical movement between the private spheres and public lives of individuals forms a community and society as one knows it. As the French Marxist Henri Lefebvre had said:

> Everyday life ... defined by "what is left over" after all distinct superior, specialised, structured activities have been singled out for analysis, must be defined as a totality. Considered in their specialisation and their technicality, superior activities leave a "technical vacuum" between one another which is filled by everyday life. Everyday life is profoundly related to all activities, and encompasses them with all their differences and their conflicts; it is their meeting place, their bond, their common ground (Lefebvre 1991b, p. 97)

The driving idea behind Lefebvre's conceptualisation of everyday life was that once the superficial or the 'spectacle' is removed from everyday life, the remnant of the social existence – the mundane, the trivial – is the underlying philosophy of the raw human nature of individuals and communities which these individuals form. Ontological security, in the words of Giddens (1991) is a direct consequence of the ways in which these individuals fragment their time and space, which again can be related to the mundane nature of everyday life and the processes in which identities are stabilised. For a south Asian, thus, taking a bath early in the morning following the schedule usually followed in one's native place is a means through which the individual feels at home in the spaces he/she/they inhabits. Under capitalism, these activities translate into avenues for profit. So, one is not only focused on the act of bathing but is rather also emphasising the commodities which facilitate the process of bathing – soaps, shampoo, etc. Community-oriented shops use social media to popularise their products.

These shops do not market their commodities as commodities but rather as community traits. A South-Asian restaurant has built up an entire economy of *desi* food relying entirely on social media connections. People consume the food for the cultural and aesthetic value that it represents for them, regardless of its status within the economy. Little does it matter that the particular chain was running without the necessary food and health certificates for a long duration time and was a manifestation of extreme marginality considering that the people who had started the venture did so out of extreme necessity and not for fulfilment or a feeling of service to the community. Such commodities are examples of situations where people fail to realise that there 'is a mirror, and the commodity form is also this mirror, but since ... it no longer plays its role, since it does not reflect back the expected image, those who are looking for themselves can no longer find themselves in it. [Human beings] no longer recognise in it the social character of their own labour' (Derrida 1994/2006, p. 155). This complete abstraction of the labour embedded within a commodity compels the hauntological significance of Marx to again come into relevance under contemporary forms of consumer capitalism. These forms of domination of the commodities and their forms over and above the actual living souls render these living human beings to the status of 'ghosts'. Derrida argues that any commodity:

> ... must ... have at least promised it to iterability, to substitution, to exchange, to value; it must have made a start, however minimal it may have been, on an idealisation, that permits one to identify it as the same throughout possible repetitions, and so forth. Just as there is no pure use, there is no use-value which the possibility of exchange and commerce .. has not in advance inscribed in an out-of-use – an excessive signification that cannot be reduced to the useless (Derrida 1994/2006, p. 160)

Derrida argues that an alternative approach toward the rule and domination of commodities in modern lives can be brought forward through an approach centred on reading the objects similar to what is done in the case of texts. This approach could potentially enable us to understand the hidden meanings of the very idea of consumption whether it means the mere usage of the object or whether it refers to the symbolic and economic meanings which an object garners as it moves through the production-distribution-consumption network. Anderson (2020) argues that Derrida's contribution to Marxist theory needs to be analysed in an appreciative manner because of Derrida's 'hauntological' insistence on the much-needed academic emphasis on the original writings of Marx himself. However, that being said, it is also necessary to pursue a dialectical opposition to Derrida's work where applicable because of his notion of the permanence of fetishism and his idea of Marxism being 'an attempted (undialectical) exorcism of the fetish' (Anderson 2020, p. 174-175). Though more radical than others of his genre and line of thought, Derrida's analysis of the commodity too has its own issues.

Derrida assumes fetishism to be a permanent feature of almost all social conditions (Anderson 2020). Dunayevskaya (1973) wrote that within a fetishised society, reification does indeed become the dominant thought of the period. Dunayevskaya (1981) in her subsequent writings, constructed fetishism as a subjective category, which is almost always taken to be an objective factor under capitalism (Hudis 2012; Anderson 2020). Commodity fetishism, analysed dialectically, leads one to analyse it as both a subjective and objective force of capitalism, which is intrinsically related to the dual character of the commodity under capitalism (Dunayevskaya 1952). It is true that a theory that accounts only for productive labour, as is 'orthodox economistic Marxism' often critiqued to be (Vogel 1996, 2013; Deb Roy 2020a), cannot provide a contemporary critique of commodity fetishism within contemporary consumer capitalism, where the aesthetic and cultural values of objects plan an important role. Under consumer capitalism, people do not buy mere objects constituted by human labour but '... are buying the image created by [factors such as] advertising, and [which transform the cost associated with these factors] not just a cost-related [to the] distributing information about a product, [but, rather a cost which] is essential to the worth of the objects' (Hall and Neitz 1993, p. 148). Fetish usually stems from such objects which find extraordinary meaning within a whole gambit of other similar but not identical objects. Say, for example, the case of *Kentucky Fried Chicken* (KFC). In many cities across the Global South, taking inspiration from the model propagated by KFC, there have arisen many such outlets which focus their attention on selling fried chicken, which looks similar to the chicken that KFC sells. Some might even taste the same, but the market share of KFC, at least according to mainstream public opinion, remains unchallenged. Similarly, another example can be taken from the numerous technology companies such as Apple and the innumerable Asian companies, which actively attempt to reproduce the user interface of Apple devices. This attempt can be explained by focusing on the fetish created around the object of the iPhone. It is not so that the software and hardware components of devices and gadgets from Apple are something which is 'other worldly', but rather because they exercise certain domination over the subject so as to coerce the user, or the potential user, to dominate others.

The individuals possessing such commodities do not realise that they are also, in turn, objectified and utilised by capitalist production mechanisms to further their profits and surplus generation. They instead remain embedded within a notion of individual sovereignty and free will, both of which are impossible to attain within capitalism of any kind. As the Slovenian Philosopher Slavoj Žižek argues:

> On an everyday level, the individuals know, the individuals know very well that there are relations between people behind the relations between things. The problem is that in their social activity itself, in what they are *doing*, they are *acting*, as if money, in its immediate material reality, is the immediate embodiment of wealth as such. They are fetishists in practice, not in theory (Žižek 2009, p. 28)

Žižek's argument revolves around the idea that people misrecognise themselves and their activities encompassing their social understanding within the capitalist reality, which is guided by a 'fetishistic illusion' (2009, p. 28). Fetishism allows for a critical analysis of the field of consumption, but one in which the entire sphere tends to be treated as merely a 'false' representation, consequent of other spheres (Miller 1987, p. 44). With the onslaught of capitalist modernity within our lives, the social lives of individuals have been entrapped within a network of money and value-forms, which makes any attempt to uncover the fetish embedded within these commodities, as Zukin (2004, p. 268) notes, attempts to shake the foundations of our social relationships themselves. The objective experiences of capitalist reality frame the subjective mental aspects of the human conditions which include as Arendt (1978, pp. 70-1) describes, thinking, willing and judging. Arendt's arguments in the book stem from her theory surrounding the dominance of a world order which is obsessed with high levels of semblance. The disruption of the dominance of the semblance does not merely mean removing the falsity of the consciousness, but rather it means one has to begin with reinterpreting the meaning of which the semblance is constituted as well as the ones that it itself creates.

Fetishism, however, has not always been conceptualised as an illusory subject within human sustenance. Ollman's (1976, p. 199) conceptualisation of commodity fetishism revolves around the idea that people acquire their consciousness from their objectively lived reality and this concept of their own reality on their own terms determines their ideas about their own experiences. Today, people's own actions come back to them in a hauntological fashion, almost like an image of 'an alienated object of subjective activity' (Hetherington 2007, p. 70). Elster (1985, pp. 96-9) in his account on 'Fetishism' refers to it as something which performs the activity of making human beings impervious of certain ideas about society through the usage of psychological manoeuvring. Fetishism, in the words of Marx, is a stage of society where economic categories have been elevated to the level such as that they look like '... qualities inherent in the material incarnations of these formal determinations or categories' (Marx 1976, p. 1046). Under a system that actively promotes and sustains commodity fetishism, the value of a commodity becomes intrinsically tied together with the use-value of the object. The power of capital to impose exchange values and prices on commodities, which under normal conditions would be considered to be arbitrary rights held by capital, becomes a natural right held sacredly by capital. This becomes further accentuated under capitalist alienation – the dominant mode of social consciousness in society.

Workers live their lives under the alienated conditions of sustenance that capitalism creates and sustains in society. Alienation is one of the central concepts of Marxist theory. Under capitalism, social life is constructed in a manner that keeps on reproducing and expanding the capitalist ideas of society (Perlman 1972/2016; Lefebvre 1991b). Dunayevskaya (1965b) argued that the concept of alienation was one of the central elements of the theories which Marx drew from Hegel, 'from which he concluded that the alienation of man does not end with the abolition of private property – *unless* what is most alien in all of bourgeois society, the alienation of man's labour from the activity of self-development into an appendage to a machine, is abrogated' (Dunayevskaya 1965b, p. 32). The freedom from capitalism, thus, remains the complete unshackling of the chains of capitalism.

Plamenatz (1975) argued that in Marx's works, one can find two kinds of alienation – the social and spiritual (Sayers 2011). However, the dominant trend is to separate Marx's theories of alienation into four different kinds: Alienation of the worker from the products of the workers' labour; Alienation from other workers and in the process from the society itself; Alienation from the process of production and objectification itself including the tools through which the worker engages in production; Alienation from one's species life (Marx 1844; Ludz 1973). Alienation is the process in which the existence of the human being is separated from the essence of being human (Fromm 1961). The growth of the individual human is structured and constrained by the social conditions – social conditions which have become increasingly solitary and infused with a sense of aloofness from society (Fromm 1942). Marx's criticism of Hegel, as Dunayevskaya notes, stems from the Hegelian ideas about appropriating 'objects as thought and movements of thought' which often led to a certain uncriticality (Dunayevskaya 1973, p. 57). However, like Hegel in *The Philosophy of History* (Hegel 1837/2004), Marx also believed that the history of human evolution under capitalism is the history of the progressing alienation of human beings (Fromm 1961). It is the socio-historical dimension of human progress which produce contradictions and social theories based on them. Be it Hegel, Darwin or Marx, all of them have taken inspiration from actually existing conditions around them and as such have inspired thoughts from both the political left and the right (Beiser 2005). In Hegel's writings, elements like contradiction are usually presented within the realm of human consciousness which though 'rooted in the experience of human labour, is privileged over the fulness of human praxis, both mental and manual' (Hudis and Anderson 2020). But, with Marx, this notion of 'contradiction' finds a materially tangible basis within the realm of political economy, that was the significance of the Marxian critique of Hegel which focused on the conservative aspect of Hegelian socio-political theory and emphasised the ideas of Hegel which bring forward the centrality of the dialectical mode of thinking.

Marx develops alienation from his theories about bourgeois society and capitalism in general by evoking terms such as 'estrangement', 'objectification', etc. Some thinkers have argued that there is a qualitative difference between the way Marx (1844) uses the terms 'estrangement' and 'objectification' (Wendling 2009, p. 110). However, that is not something that the present work focuses on. It is simply not possible to write any book on Marxist theory or politics without making a reference to the concept of alienation, which is one of the most important aspects of Marxist theory. Alienation, under capitalism, is not only a result of the labouring process but rather embedded within the labouring process itself (Marx 1844). Because of the complexity associated with the concept, it has received both subjective and objective analyses, which have often been pitted against one another (Geyer and Schweitzer 1976). Alienation, as Dunayevskaya (1969a) argues following Hegelian methods, is a process that dampens the process of the workers' formation of selfhood further enabling Hegel's positing of dialectics not only as a method but rather as a critical perspective on the social reality itself. Capitalist alienation of the worker makes the worker perform labour in accordance with the wishes of capitalism, thus the consciousness formed by the worker under capitalism is characteristic of the very capitalist objectivity that oppresses the worker (Dunayevskaya 1976/2002). Under capitalism, more so under consumer capitalism, there thus cannot be any such thing as a purely unalienated social relation. Henri Lefebvre, in this regard, had famously remarked:

> ... with the forms of exchange and the division of labour which govern it, there is no social relation – relation with the other – without a certain alienation. And each individual exists socially only by and within his alienation, just as he can only be for himself within and by his deprivation (his *private* consciousness) (Lefebvre 1991, pp. 15-16)

Alienation under capitalism hinders one from understanding the true causes behind one's actions and thoughts, either in the public sphere or within the private sphere, creating an essentialist ambiguity within the understanding of life under capitalism (Lefebvre 1991, p. 18). Capitalist alienation results in the complete disjunction between the labour of the human being and the actual individual (Marx 1844; Dunayevskaya 1958a). The results of these actions, as Lefebvre goes on lie within the uncertain human actions 'which go on around us; they escape us just as our own selves escape us' (Lefebvre 1991, p. 19). Social media commerce is an important element of this milieu. It has become such an integral part of human lives that it has penetrated the very unconscious of human life. It is because of this high level of proliferation of social media in the everyday lives of the workers, that social media commerce has become such a successful aspect of social media itself. This success not only is a testimony to the pre-existing success of social media, but also a manifestation of the domination of exchange relations in society.

Scholars such as Skotnicki (2020, p. 372) argue that there are two major interpretations of commodity fetishism: one engaging with the authentic semblance of the depersonalised commodities and the other engaging with the inauthentic interpretations of these exchange relationships to be natural. They argue that these two interpretations, while remaining related, are also distinct from one another and that the exchange relation itself does not have a direct bearing on how one interprets the commodities involved in the exchange. However, this is precisely the point in which his reading of Marx also runs into a few problems. For Marx, both of these interpretations were interrelated to each other dialectically – there cannot be a fetishist reality without depersonalised commodities, and vice versa. Individuals engaged in exchange relations are 'misled by the fetishism attached to the world of commodities, or by the objective appearance of the social characteristics of labour' (Marx 1976, p. 176). The commodity-form is not a natural entity in society, it is rather, an invention of capitalism, which designs such forms to instigate domination in society. The commodity becomes the social form of the labour which exists in the society (Marx 1976, p. 164), which exploits the social labour under capitalism (Dunayevskaya 1958a). In this regard, Marx draws upon the 'double form' of the commodity (Marx 1976, p. 138). Marx argued that every commodity becomes a commodity because of its ability to assume two forms – one based on its nature, and one based on its value. All commodities, at the same time, are objects with specific use and also possess a value, as has already been stated right at the beginning of the book. This is the dialectical relationship between use-value and exchange-value. Analysing one, disregarding another would yield results that are massively short-sighted in their outlook and analytical prowess. In other words, what Marx was saying was that while analysing the effects of commodity production on the individual and the society, the analysis has to encompass the totality of the society, in a way that takes multiple variables into account (Marx 1976, Footnote No. 35, p. 175) as Marx notes:

> The economists ... who lay a special claim to critical acumen, nevertheless, find that use-value of material objects belongs to them independently of their material properties, while their value, on the other hand, forms a part of them as objects. What confirms them is ... the peculiar circumstance that the use-value of a thing is realised without exchange, i.e. in the direct relation between the thing and man, while inversely, its value is realised only in exchange, i.e., in a social process (Marx 1976, p. 177)

Using Dant's (1996, pp. 510-11) classification, it can be said that material objects perform six functions as a commodity: It extends or enhances human capacities, creates a sense of belonging ('social group membership'), has desire-arousing capabilities, is a manifestation of accumulated knowledge, aesthetically sound, and enhances communicative powers, among other capabilities which a material object might possess. These attributes all conform, more or less, to the way in which Marx defined commodities in *Capital Volume 1* which was focused on the 'socio-natural' history of any commodity and the manner in which these very commodities, stem from actually existing material conditions, begin dominating and altering the material conditions themselves: 'Humans bow down before the commodities that they themselves have created, and we become mere consumers of a world already produced for us. This, of course, quite accurately describes the contemporary world of consumer capitalism' (Duncombe 2012, p. 372).

Within a system that promotes commodity production, 'the product assumes the commodity form (possesses exchange-value in addition to use-value) and labour, in addition to being useful in private and, through its equalization in exchange, abstract' (Sayer 1979, p. 31). The forces of commodification work within the domain of social media as well. There might be countless debates over whether social media is itself a commodity as well. In the view of the present author, social media is a commodity. It establishes itself firmly within the domain of what Marx (1992) was talking about in terms of commodities themselves creating the avenues for the further valorisation of other commodities. Social media does it through targeted advertisements and by creating commercial platforms such as 'Marketplace' and 'Shops', where they engage in activities that regulate and initiate the flow of certain values back into society. One of the major aspects of Adorno's theoretical excursions into the idea of commodification is based on the problems associated with the extent to which this drive of commodification controls the various institutions which dominate our lives (Rose 1978, p. 48). Even today, Adorno remains a very important source of critique of the dominant culture, one which can be related to the critique of commodity fetishism as well (Habermas 1975). Adorno however, almost never presupposed the complete domination of the user of the commodity over the commodity or vice versa. As Buck-Morss notes, following Adorno: 'If in thinking about reality the (reified) object was able to dominate the subject, the result was the reification of consciousness and the passive acceptance of the status quo; if the subject dominates the object, the result was the domination of nature and the ideological justification of the status quo' (Buck-Morss 1977, p. 186).

The continuous increase in the quantity and quality of commodities under contemporary alienation is nothing surprising, given that Marx had talked about this as early as 1844. More commodities mean more means of alienation and further means of oppression through the naturalisation of private property. To achieve this, capitalism uses numerous methods, such as the utilisation of enjoyment as a saleable factor, the generation of new needs, the fetishization of money as a commodity, etc. It is worthwhile here, to quote Marx in full:

> We have seen what significance, given socialism, the wealth of human needs acquires, and what significance, therefore, both a new mode of production and a new object of production obtain: a new manifestation of the forces of human nature and a new enrichment of human nature. Under private property their significance is reversed: every person speculates on creating a new need in another, so as to drive him to fresh sacrifice, to place him in a new dependence and to seduce him into a new mode of enjoyment and therefore economic ruin. Each tries to establish over the other an alien power, so as thereby to find satisfaction of his own selfish need. The increase in the quantity of objects is therefore accompanied by an extension of the realm of the alien powers to which man is subjected, and every new product represents a new potentiality of mutual swindling and mutual plundering. Man becomes ever poorer as man, his need for money becomes ever greater if he wants to master the hostile power. The power of his money declines in inverse proportion to the increase in the volume of production: that is, his neediness grows as the power of money increases (Marx 1844, p. 306)

Capitalist development occurs hand in hand with the alienation of the proletariat, in a manner "When confronted by the rigidity of these 'facts' every movement seems like a movement impinging on them, while every tendency to change them appears to be a merely subjective principle" (Lukács 1971, pp. 184). The task of a dialectical struggle is to destroy the primacy of these facts, and thus open up 'a complete penetration of the forms of reification' (p. 185). Reification, to

Lukács is the 'immediate reality' of a capitalist society which can only be negated through the development of consciousness regarding the totality and its relationship with the contradictions therein (p. 197). The proletariat identity is an identity based on a 'real historical and dialectical process', whereby it generates the foundations of praxis necessary to overcome reification (pp. 204-05).

The relationship of dependency between capitalism and the working class is one of the most important relationships within the total gambit of social relationships under capitalism. However, relationships formed out of technological mediations, are often at odds with the actually existing human being. Relationships formed within technological circles can, at times, empower the worker. Some of the functionalities in digital spaces and online platforms which allow the individual to hide or alter one's identity can in fact be highly efficient in temporarily dislodging the dominant dynamics of power existing in society. Commercial activities on social media have created 'sellers' out of introverts, 'buyers' out of misers. In these transformations, commodities are the effective agents in the formation, sustenance and dissolution of human relationships. They are 'brought into relationship with one another as values or made to appear as exchange-values' (Marx 1976, p. 158), with commodity fetishism becoming one of the major aspects of the various facets of the social fabric which define our everyday reality in the contemporary times. The relationship between the value of a commodity and the exchange of the commodities is not determined by the act of exchange but rather by the production of the commodity itself: 'it is not the exchange of commodities which regulates the magnitude of their value; but, on the contrary, that it is the magnitude of their value which controls their exchange-proportions' (Marx 1976, p. 156). The struggle thus needs to begin at the point of production, a theme that will continue to reverberate in the entire book.

4. THE SOCIAL MARKET

Ideology is no good if it does not help one to understand everyday reality as Marx says in *The German Ideology*. Like all other forms of capitalist oppression and exploitation, commodity fetishism also takes root in the everyday reality of human existence on the earth. The purpose of an ideological offensive against commodity fetishism thus needs to base itself on the actually existing everyday lives of the people who actively regenerate commodity fetishism every day. Social media is one of the main staying elements of the struggle, either as a force to be resisted or as a force to be used in the resistance. The number of people who remain connected to each other through social media is tremendous. Continuous developments of technology and machinery result in the continuous altering of the nature of social labour which is embedded in the commodity form. Commodity fetishism plays a large role in the creation, sustenance and popularisation of the platforms and production processes that occupy the central position within capitalism today. The influence which commodities play within capitalist modes of production, along with its associated fetish, makes the oppression of capitalism look natural to the working class. The dual character of the commodity – as a use-value and as an exchange-value – and the dialectical relationship formed between these two characters is a direct manifestation of the dual character of labour such that 'It is, from the start, a unity of opposites – use-value and value – which, in embryo, contains *all* the contradictions of capitalism' (Dunayevskaya 1958a, p. 99).

The possessor of a commodity becomes one with the commodity, ensuring that the possessor cannot be anything that the commodity is not. The Asian seller the author encountered in Dunedin cannot be anything more than the commodity that the seller has put out in the market. A Muslim young person, who sold off his mobile phone on social media, is identified directly with the commodities they sell. The value which these commodities represent becomes the values of actually existing living human beings. Social media commerce makes these values attached to human beings commonplace in society. Interviews with people who sell or buy regularly on social media reveal the pre-existing biases which they hold when they interact with fellow users. A Caucasian person never buys clothes from a person who comes from a different race, because that is something that the person does not hold to be a practice informed by good hygiene. Similarly, even within social media commerce, Muslims find themselves severely disadvantaged because the commodities they sell are not easily consumed by the dominant section of the populace, especially if they demand bodily interactions of any kind such as food, clothing, etc. A couple of sellers interviewed revealed how they change names on social media so as to completely do away with these issues. The influence that such practices hold on individuals is of paramount importance, which includes the loss of self-identity, and reassertion of their stigmatised minority status, among others.

The Marxist analysis of capitalism argues that 'value is the cornerstone of the system of economic contradictions' (Marx 1847, p. 120). The constitution of value is intimately related to the way in which capital moves through society. The movement of capital takes place through a complex social mechanism, whereby it takes many momentary forms only to be surpassed by another: 'It begins as money-capital before taking on commodity form passing through production systems and emerging as new commodities to be sold (monetised) in the market and distributed in different forms to different factions of claimants (in the form of wages, interest, rent, taxes, profits) before returning to the role of money cap-ital once more' (Harvey 2018, p. 3). The most important characteristic of 'Cap-ital' as Harvey (2018, p. 4) describes it, following *Capital Volume 1*, is that it is value that has been set in motion. Once value is set in motion, it becomes fur-ther abstract in nature, in the sense that the useful and concrete labour-power which forms the basis of ascertaining the value of a commodity, gets expressed in terms of the abstract labour contained in another commodity (Sayer 1976, p. 26). In the words of Marx (1976, p. 209) 'concrete kind of labour [gets counted] as merely abstract universal labour, between the conversion of things into persons and persons into things'. This also forms the basis of the relationship between the private labour embodied in one commodity and the social labour embodied in another:

> The value of every commodity is now ... not only differentiated from its own use-value, but from all other use-values generally, and is, by that very fact, expressed as that which is common to all commodities. By this form commodities are ... effectively brought into relation with one another as values, or made to appear as exchange-values (1976, p. 66)

Once the capitalist market is firmly established in the society and begins to act as the functional and structural logic of the society (Sayers 1979), it begins to classify and label commodities in terms of one single homogenous equivalent – Money, which becomes the 'universal equivalent': 'The specific kind of com-modity with whose natural form the equivalent form is socially interwoven now becomes the money commodity or serves as money. It becomes its special social function, and consequently its social monopoly, to play the part of the univer-sal equivalent' (Marx 1976, p. 162). A capitalist market is established in the soci-ety with the assumption that commodities have both an economic, as well as a cultural aspect (often propagated through luxury brands), which money seeks to express in the form of numbers. The processes through which capitalism dom-inates the working class today are increasingly reliant on, in addition to the economic forces, the paradigms of 'beliefs, desires, perceptions, affects and atti-tudes' (Chari 2015, p. 6). Capitalism today produces newer subjectivities on an everyday day basis (Hardt and Negri 2012) through the manipulation of the senses. Chari (2015) poses the theory of reification as an approach that could become helpful in this regard. In her opinion, capitalist reification today works through the construction of a veil between the economic and political structures of capitalist exploitation and uses both Adorno's (1973) and Lukács' (1971) points to present her ideas (Chari 2015, p. 165). She appreciates Adorno (1973) because of his emphasis on the role of experience and critiques him for his separation of the political realm from the economic. Every economic act, it must be remembered, is a political act in itself. The two circuits of capital usually found in society, Commodities-Money-Commodities (C-M-C) and Money-Commodities-Money (M-C-M), with the latter being the pivotal form of circulation of capital under capitalism, cannot function if politics and economy do not go hand in hand. Brands cannot sustain themselves if they do not toe the lines of the dominant political ideologies in any society.

Innovations in the digital field have exploited the domination that commodities exercise over the material selves of human beings. Technology does not operate within a vacuum. Since Facebook draws a huge share of its revenue from advertisements (Fuchs 2008, 2014c), it has an implicit interest in keeping its advertisers afloat and thus also has a stake in avoiding the economic crash be it through an accumulation crisis (O'Connor 1984) or through an overproduction crisis (Mandel 1978) or through any other forms of crisis. This again calls for an understanding of communication that can analyse social media use as a material practice itself (Fuchs 2020; Mosco 2009) and social media's utilisation as a facilitator of capital accumulation. The integration of the digital ecosystem with the physical "brick and mortar" framework of profit-accumulation is essential because, as Fuchs (2019a) rightly mentions, digital capitalism today, co-exists with 'finance capitalism, hyper-industrial capitalism, crisis capitalism, authoritarian capitalism, neoliberal capitalism, mobility capitalism, global capitalism, etc.' (Fuchs 2019a, p. 3). Markets have become, in the contemporary digital age, omnipresent in human lives. They have become deregulated and globalised (Castells 1996; Sassen 1999), often at the expense of public services in advanced industrial nations as Harvey explained in his theory of 'Accumulation by Dispossession' (Harvey 2014, p. 84). Most of the left-wing arguments against neoliberalism tendencies in both the Global North and the Global South advocate a certain form of deepening of the control that the state possesses on the essential services which get taken over by capitalism thus often meaning more conflict within the execution of these services (Harvey 2005). Raya Dunayevskaya, CLR James and Grace Lee Boggs, the primary proponents of State Capitalism Theory have theorised about this tendency of the state perhaps in the greatest of details. Freedom does not mean the transfer of power, nor does it mean replacing the 'Capitalist' with the 'Communist' rather it means the complete dissolution of power itself. The basic contradictions within both these kinds of societies – societies where central power is posited – is that they both follow a structure of domination based on the central contradictions which Marx posited in *Capital*, i.e., the law of value and the law of motion of capital (Hudis 2021). Such economies still rely, as Hudis argues further, on the benefits of commodity production which make them at par with any normalised capitalist economy. As Žižek argues, the major challenge for the left today remains the reintroduction of:

... the Leninist opposition of 'formal' and 'actual' freedom: in an act of actual freedom, one dares precisely to *break* this seductive power of symbolic efficacy. ... the truly free choice is a choice in which I do not merely choose between two or more options *within* a pre-given set of coordinates rather I choose to change this set of coordinates itself (Zizek, 2017, 'Introduction')

The economic categories that Marx puts forward are themselves class conscious in nature, which applies to capital and capitalism only (Dunayevskaya 1965, p. 69). The distinctions between use-value and exchange-value only make sense if they are posited within a capitalist society. The capitalist market is a product of the production relations within capitalism. It does not exist independently of the production relations and the division of labour in society. The Marxist law of value, which Dunayevskaya (1965) proclaimed to be the fundamental idea of Marxism, applies only within a capitalist framework, and not beyond it – the past or the future (Hudis 2012; Anderson 2020). In this context, the market is important to capitalism. It serves numerous purposes for capitalism as a whole, such as integration of exchange systems, facilitating the satisfaction of private interests, generating competition, quantification of the society, and establishing the domination of *the price* (Slater and Tonkiss 2001).

However, to posit the market as the only intrinsic logic of capitalism means doing away with the other contradictions of capitalism, which exercise much greater power over the methods through which capitalism sustains itself within contemporary society. It means the complete rendering absent of the important factors such as the division of labour and the commodity form which are fundamental to capitalism. The emphasis on the market as a fundamental part does not take into account the division of labour in the society which gives rise to the entire structure of capitalism – the commodity economy (Lenin 1899; Marx 1976). The fundamental part of capitalism is the commodity. As Lenin articulates: 'The market is a category of commodity economy, which in the course of its development is transformed into the capitalist economy and only under the latter gains complete sway and universal prevalence' (Lenin 1899, p. 31). Under capitalism, the anarchy of the market characteristic of the class relations in the society becomes the general law under capitalism, as capitalism's 'law of motion is impelled by reproduction according to socially necessary labour time set by the world market, and thus even if all conditions are met as to planning in the factory, external planning as to market, and labour paid at value, the incessant revolutions in production of necessity mean the "development of productive forces of labour at the expense of the already created productive forces"' (Dunayevskaya 1949, p. 9217, quoted from Hudis 2021, p. 69).

Money plays a crucial role in this expansion of the influence of the market in society – both physically and psychologically. Marx (1976) argues that the domination of money as a social medium of exchange coexists with the complete dissolution of all the intermediate steps which determine the value of a particular commodity. The evolution and domination of money actually render invisible the innumerable quantity of human labour which goes within a commodity. Taking an example from the words of David Harvey (2014), the food at the breakfast table becomes merely some things one picked up from the market and does not represent the labour that has been invested in the products by the countless workers to transform the raw materials and transport the finished product as a meal on to the breakfast table. Money quantifies and dehumanizes the entirety of the productive labour entrenched with a certain commodity and expresses it in the form of a number such that 'the movement through which this process has been mediated vanishes in its own result, leaving no trace behind' (Marx 1976, p. 187). Value only represents the labour embodied within a commodity till the point when the commodity and 'value' remain attached to each other. The moment one puts a 'price' on the commodity, any intrinsic value that the commodity had possessed gets destroyed and fully consumes the commodity, i.e., the value of the commodity becomes extinct.

Use-values, like exchange-values are also signs of riches for their possessors, but they are so because of their inherent qualities, for the purpose they fulfil for the possessors. In other words, quoting Marx: 'Riches which are identical with use-values are properties of things that are made use by men, and which express a relation to their wants' (Marx 1863c/1971, p. 129). But, when the market reigns supreme, use-values get superseded and completely obliterated by heightened exchange-values expressed in the form of prices. This stage of capitalist development and its insurgency into the social relationships formed by men under capitalism results from capital's disgrace over the fact that value, in its purest form, can be variable because of the presence of value in the pre-exchange commodity (Sayer 1976, p. 38). It is here that Marx states:

> Historically ... the search for value is at first based on money, the visible expression of commodities as value and that consequently the search for the definition of value is represented as a search for a commodity of 'invariable value' or, for a commodity which is an 'invariable measure of value' (Marx 1863c, p. 145)

With the exchange of commodities in society becoming the norm, money becomes an important point of analysis. It mediates the relationship between value and price (Marx 1865, 1976; Brunhoff 1976), establishing a general commensurability for every commodity that capitalist production system produces (Marx 1859). The ushering in of money as a universal form of value (Marx 1976, p. 162) greatly affects the social relationships existing in the society, which are themselves formed along the lines dominated and dictated upon by commodities. Since '... as values, commodities are social magnitudes, that is to say, something absolutely different from their 'properties' as 'things'. As values, they constitute only relations of men in their productive activity' (Marx 1863c, p. 129). The value of a commodity, as Marx (1976), is manifested in the manner in which the use-values of other commodities can be potentially exchanged for them. The digitalisation of the mode of exchange has facilitated a wide variety of commodities, which previously had limited exchange-values to become significant aspects of further accumulation of profit. Capital has become financial money capital, a form where it becomes absolute and does not distinguish between producer and consumer goods during accumulation (Luxemburg 1915). Overproduction and its associated economic crisis (Mandel 1978) have also contributed to this popularisation of social media commerce. The existence of a huge inflow of consumer goods within the market with the majority of the population unable to buy those creates exactly the kind of problem that Bauer had rejected as Kowalik (2014) elaborates. In spite of the fact that platforms such as Facebook Marketplace allow the users to fix prices of their own, these prices are mediated by a complex web of social crisis and the resulting natural or social needs. The prices of these existing range of commodities determine the value that the working classes put on their personal properties for sale on social media.

The freedom and accessibility provided by Facebook in listing the commodities can be seen in the light of the argument made by Fuchs (2016, pp. 37-42; 2016a) that within capitalist structures, there is always a provision of relative freedom, which the system provides to the working class to express themselves but within certain limits – as long as the freedom provided to the workers does not curtail the power of accumulation possessed by capitalism. Social media commerce enables the sellers to generate exchange-value out of items that were only of use-value previously and it does so by hinging on the continuous state of crisis and ever-increasing need within capitalism, both of which are dialectically related to each other. There are countless examples regarding the causality behind certain commodities ending up on the social media market. The research conducted for the book revealed some of the inhuman situations, including homelessness, under which individuals engaged in social media commerce. The crisis in their lives forces the users to keep the prices low so as to facilitate a quick sale, thus bringing in a new dimension to the procedure in which capitalism utilises the element of "time" for domination (Shippen 2014). In the case of social media commerce, this domination is performed through a continued easing of the process of subsumption of the working class within the capitalist circulation process by exploiting the state of crisis and immediate needs of the working class. This is also reminiscent of Engels's (1872) arguments about the housing properties owned by the working classes whose prices vary significantly due to other associated processes which are outside their own control:

> The growth of the big modern cities gives the land in certain areas, particularly in those which are centrally situated, an artificial and often colossally increasing value; the buildings erected on these areas depress this value, instead of increasing it, because they no longer correspond to the changed circumstances. They are pulled down and replaced by others. This takes place above all with workers' houses which are situated centrally and whose rents, even with the greatest overcrowding, can never, or only very slowly, increase above a certain maximum. They are pulled down and in their stead shops, warehouses and public buildings are erected (Engels 1872, p. 319)

The autonomy of the working class, in a manner that reminds of Engels's (1872, p. 319) description of housing, is at the mercy of capitalism in spite of the ownership of property, a theme that will be dealt with in considerable detail in later chapters. The sustenance of social media commerce depends on the sustenance of the crisis within the society, both materialistically and psychologically. In the Global North, this crisis is seen in its starkest form. The research for the book exhibited a plethora of reasons surrounding the causes behind why individuals engaged with social media commerce, a major portion of which were because of the dire situations in which they found themselves at various points in time. In the Global South, the causality was largely related to inter-city and inter-regional shifts. Some of the users engaged because they wanted to build careers in the electronic goods' repairing sector in the cities they belonged to. Some engaged to get rid of their old furniture, while some others exploited social media as a community of users to sell merchandised goods that they had got manufactured. Taking note of some of the responses which were revealed during the many interviews which were conducted by the author in the Global North, the relation between needs, crisis and the act of selling become explicitly established. Responses ranged from people having to sell because of losing their jobs, to being rendered homeless by the landlord on an immediate basis. Many of the people who participated in the study confessed to living in almost dire conditions – some with moving costs associated with shifting houses, while some losing their jobs while still having increasing amounts of bills due.

The analysis of the multifarious engagement with social media commerce reveals the high subjectivity and variability of the situations in which the individual interviewees found themselves, which prompted them to enter the social media market. Social media commerce shares a dialectical relationship with the existing human knowledge on housing, its financial aspects, rentier capitalism, etc. Within developed capitalist societies, houses are speculatively custom built to be sold on the market in the future, the value of which depends upon the total constellation of the factors which the property represents or possesses or both such as its location, proximity to other services, gentrification, etc. Another example in this regard might be cited as tobacco, whose status in the market depends upon other commodities such as filters, papers, lighters, etc. That is to say, without a lighter, a cigarette or tobacco holds no use-value for the possessor. Such commodities can be analysed by employing the theory of the 'Commodity text' (Sherlock 1997) derived from the ideas of the Marxist critic Walter Benjamin. For Benjamin (1968), objects were of no use in isolation only by virtue of their natural or historical properties, but only made sense to the individual when they are related to each other within a system (Sherlock 1997, p. 72) – an idea which is also found in the works of Baudrillard (1972). Under the social conditions of commodity fetishism, commodities become something more than mere material objects. Social media and some of the commodities on sale therein only make sense within a totality of other commodities. For example, the merchandised t-shirts often sold on social media in India only make sense to a niche range of customers, who are already associated with certain other commodities – and under contemporary capitalism, everything, from education to oxygen, is a commodity. Similar is the case for merchandised coffee mugs in the west. The effect of social media commerce on such sales has been that they have become more frequent and more widely practised, as a frequent small-scale student seller informed the author. The power of connectivity has been used by communitarian commodity dealers to create commercial practices. This interconnected nature of certain commodities brings to attention Benjamin's (1968) theories surrounding the *'Task of the Translator'*, using which Sherlock brings forward an advanced definition of the commodity. He defines the commodity under capitalism in these words:

> If production for the capitalist marketplace, for exchange, involves a certain violence to the "natural properties" of the thing through packaging, marketing and enclosing the thing, the moment of reception on the part of the consumer also involves a rearrangement, or translation, of the "elements" of the commodity into a constellation (Sherlock 1977, p. 72)

This definition can be used effectively in the case of numerous brands which end up on the social media market. In India, most people cannot afford to own an expensive piece of technology such as the iPhone or the iPad but have a very strong desire to possess those. However, it is also commonly known that once anybody purchases an Apple product, the individual will, more or less, be likely to purchase, or rather have to purchase, other Apple products as well. There are numerous ways in which Apple entices individuals to buy into its ecosystem of products. An iPad makes sense to a consumer only if it is paired up with an iPhone or a MacBook. In New Zealand, and in the United States as well, individuals frequently engage in social media commerce to make an inroad into the Apple ecosystem. Social media commerce has provided an output to these desires of the individuals. Desires, which under normal circumstances, would have taken them years to fulfil probably. However, the way such commodities are interpreted by individuals varies widely.

However, whether the idea of reading the commodity as a text can lead one to a reinterpretation of the very idea of consumption remains to be seen. Sherlock (1997, p. 76) makes a crucial point in this regard when he emphasises the above strategy to be one where the commodity formed out of human labour and capitalist subjectivity of the market becomes interpreted with reference to how the user interprets it. Sherlock informs that 'The commodity text, written in the language of production, is not simply "consumed", but rather is potentially translated into something "beyond" mere consumption. ...the "properties" of the commodity can be "consumed" by a new "property-owner" -an autonomous subject with needs to be fulfilled by the object' (Sherlock 1997, p. 71). Consumers give new meaning to the commodities they inhabit through their usage of the commodities in their everyday lives (Collins 1989). Social media enables the fast propagation of these meanings. Under normal circumstances, the meaning of consumption associated with any particular commodity might have taken months to become properly grounded within the society, but with the continuous resales of used commodities, the speed with which the meaning is translated is heightened.

Most of the commodities that people use in their everyday lives are not defined by any rigid meaning but are rather characterised by a certain fluidity in the way they are interpreted by the consumers which then went on to characterise the social relationships formed by these consumers as individuals (Collins 1989; Kellner 1989) – a criticism which was primarily aimed at Baudrillard (1972, 1973) who emphasised the rigidity of the functionality of the commodity 'code' or sign in advanced industrial societies. The social media market cannot exist without the proliferation of the cultural meanings of commodity consumption. It is imperative for capitalism if it has to sustain itself, to continuously innovate within the domain of existing commodities. Commodities such as phones, laptops, etc. are also built so as to retain a part of their total value even when their initial usefulness (i.e., the use-value) runs its course. Although multinationals are attempting to do away with the element of repairable spare parts, they are meeting with strong resistance from their users and consumers. Contemporary capitalism actively uses human relations to further its cause of accumulation. In the preceding decades, this relationship was restricted to advertising. In other words, capitalism manipulates the state of crisis in society in such a way as to lead the workers into acting as living advertisements for their products and commodities. In the modern era, this management has surpassed the interpersonal domain of advertising, where there is only one desired commodity and countless consumers. It has converted every thinking human being into an advertiser for its commodities. Commodities of everyday use, which constitute the bulk of the total commodities within social media commerce, regulate the processes of cohesion and conflict in the everyday lives of individuals in society. Most social media commerce occurs at the local level, and it is this level of the social whole that becomes critically important in the envision of a social revolution aimed at complete de-alienation of the everyday reality of capitalism (Vaneigem 2012, p. 11; Lefebvre 2008, pp. 15-16). Everyday lives are immensely powerful locations of analysis if one is to envisage social change in a radical manner (Goonewardena 2008, pp. 117-21). But everyday lives are also highly indeterminate in form and content because under capitalist social alienation, 'Many men, and even people in general, do not know their own lives very well, or know them inadequately' (Lefebvre 1991b, p. 94).

Capitalism, as Lefebvre (1991b, p. 157) argued, produces individuals who do not have any right over the various objects which constitute the space, both physical and digital, and the society in which these individuals live and survive. Social media commerce, like capitalism, poses commodities as a process of knowing the world they inhabit. Used goods play a pivotal role in this regard. They serve the purpose of creating adequate low-priced commodities for the working class to spend their wages upon, following which they appropriate – or are made to appropriate – the meanings associated with these commodities. Sections of the population, who discourage themselves, for varying reasons, to get expensive goods often attempt to use a cheaper or ex-lease version to ascertain the suitability of the product for their purposes. Previously, the space for this test of suitability was performed by brick-and-mortar shops. In the age of social media, it is social media that is performing this task. The only difference is that while in physical stores, one need not spend money for testing a commodity, within social media commerce, one spends money to possess the commodity and then test its suitability. The cheap availability, ease of transaction and the structural notion of a 'false' community, make social media commerce seem like a nice, friendly space where individuals get to 'exchange' their physical goods, while in reality, it is a manifestation of a new regime of capitalist accumulation where social networks – pre-existing or newly formed – enable the total commercialisation of everyday life. This is one of the many ways in which the influence of online social media commerce has altered the socio-economic practices existent in the society, at the centre of which lies the commodity.

5. THE CONSUMER SOCIETY

Consumers form an important part of the capitalist production process. The spread and rise of consumerism in society is both an economic process and a cultural phenomenon. There are many diverse aspects of everyday reality which contribute to the formation of a specific type of consumer society. Don Slater (1997) in his acclaimed book *Consumer Culture and Modernity* argues that consumer culture *is* the dominant mode of cultural reproduction in the global north. This particular book, however, theorised and extends the spread of consumer culture from the west to the east. In other words, the book argues that consumer culture is not a characteristic feature of the global north, but in the 21st century, is also an intriguing factor of the global south as well. Consumerism, as Miles (1998, p. 5) suggests 'can be defined as a psycho-social expression of the intersection between the structural and the individual within the realm of consumption. The consuming experience is psycho-social in the sense that it provides a bridge that links the individual and society' (Miles 1998, p. 5). It encompasses both the experience of consumption and the ideological power of consumption. Consumption studied socio-historically, exposes issues of 'modernity, capitalism, democracy, the marketplace, and collective identities' (Milanasio 2013, p. 9). At the same time, modes of consumption also indicate the extent to which capitalism has penetrated as a living ideological force into the lives of human beings, especially the working class and other marginalised sections of the population of any society.

The Marxist roots of the theorisation of the consumer society lie in Marx's EPM, where Marx talks about money being the sole need generated by the capitalist economic system, with '*Excess* and *intemperance* [coming] to be its true norm' (Marx 1844, p. 307). The continuous creation of fetishes, fantasies and whims legitimises them through the positing of money as a means through which everything is quantified as a value including the natural elements (Murray 1993). Money is the basis upon which the consumer society is constructed. Construction of the consumer society cannot take place until value itself is rendered abstract. Money again plays a crucial role in this process in being the primary agent through which some of the prime processes associated with the consumer society take place – continuous exchange of commodities, hoarding of money for further consumption, etc. Social media commerce depends upon these tendencies being pre-existing in society to make inroads within the society.

When the individual acts as a consumer, the individual does not think critically but rather mediates his/her existence by a tendency of 'giving in' to the ideals preached by capitalist forces such as advertising, media campaigns, etc. This process is a uniform one, be it in the global north or in the global south. Most of the people who have participated in this study affirm that once they had engaged in commercial activity through Facebook or any other platform, they have rarely saved up the money, or invested the money in any long-term banking structure. Rather, the money that they earned has almost always ended up again in the market. They confirm that the moment they came into possession of the money (through the sale), their first response, almost like a reflex action, is to reinvest the money into some form of commodity. So, a person who sold off his Samsung Phone in New Zealand used the money that he got and added in a few hundred dollars of his own, to buy a more expensive phone, again from Samsung. Similarly, in India, a person sells his washing machine on Facebook, and then buys a new washing machine – an upgraded one. Both of them, however, retain a similarity, which is that they analysed social media as a platform where they could fulfil their desires of getting an improved commodity – an upgrade from their state of existence. Both these individuals saw the possession of commodities as an articulation of their being, a point made by Marx (1844) quite forcefully.

Dunayevskaya (1958a, p. 126) divided political economy into two broad theories between which the discipline oscillates: '(1) that production creates its own market; and (2) that it is impossible for the worker to "buy back" the products he himself produced'. The contribution of Marx was that he could dialectically relate the two theories. While the dominant idea did remain that it was production that created the market for newer goods as Marx had formulated in *The German Ideology*, it was also true that within capitalism there was a definitive problem associated with conceptualising the limits of human consumption (Dunayevskaya 1958a). The coming of the consumer society has been theorised in many ways over the past years (McKendrick et al. 1982; Benson 1994). Miller (1998, p. 85) asserts the centrality of consumption to capitalism in a way in which individuals are turned into consumers whose 'purpose is to annihilate, destroying but also incorporating the objects of desire' (Miller 1998, p. 86). The act of consumption, in Bowlby's (2001) opinion, 'involves much more than the situations in which actual buying takes place' (p. 6). It is intimately connected to the way in which individuals perceive society around them. The consumer society has evolved from being centred around the neighbourhood departmental store and the supermarket. Today, it has reached the living spaces and bedrooms of individuals through social media. Horkheimer and Adorno (2002) argued that it is the development of urban social spaces which resulted in the creation of a mass society that further led to a wide array of consumer goods appearing in the market. In this day and age of digital capitalism, it can be said that it is not only the urban social spaces that lead to the introduction of such goods but also the virtual spaces which do so, perhaps in a more trans-spatial way than material urban spaces ever could. Consumerism conceptualises a consumer society, which is highly deterministic in nature and is mandated by the ideals of mass consumption and increasing manufacture of consumer goods at rates higher than usual (Lefebvre 2002, p. 10). The underlying aim of this increased production lies in the desire of capitalism to manufacture, not commodities, but also consumers who are actual human beings made of flesh and blood. The basis for a consumer society comes into being when capitalism garners enough resources to sufficiently replenish the labour-power and means of production. All the conceivable aspects of a capitalist system play a role in this process including consumption (productive and unproductive). Capitalism uses many techniques to do that – innovations within the production mechanism, increasing the range of commodities by bringing forward sub-brands within an established brand, and other such means. Similar to the many paths that capitalism adopts to increase the propensity to consume, the theorisation about consumer society has taken place through many routes, some focusing on industrialisation (McKendrick 1982; Miles 1998), while there are others who have placed 'consumers' as a social category even in pre-industrial societies (Appadurai 1986; Braudel 1974). Some like Benson (1994) have focused on the increased capacity of consumption in the society to be the foundation of the consumer society. McKendrick however, provides one with the accurate characterisation of the kind of consumer society that this particular book is focused upon:

> What men and women had once hoped to inherit from their parents, they now expected to buy for themselves. What were once bought at the dictate of need, were now bought at the dictate of fashion. What were once bought for life, might now be bought several times over. What were once available only on high days and holidays through the agency of markets, fairs and itinerant pedlars were increasingly made available everyday but Sunday through the additional agency of an ever-advancing network of shops and shopkeepers. (McKendrick 1982, p. 1)

The birth of a consumer society as McKendrick (1982) informs, is related to the increasing standards of living, the desire to assert status and wealth, and most importantly, to complete commercialisation of the society itself. Consumer society is not an economistic society. The perils of an economistic analysis of consumer society would be the complete obscuration of important facets which are absolutely essential to the sustenance of the consumer society under capitalism which includes factors related to culture, geopolitics, biological and social attributes. Marx in *Wage, Labour and Capital* had proposed what would turn out to be the basis of the consumer society under capitalism. Marx (1849/1977) spoke of competition – inherently part of the capitalist social system – between the buyers of any particular commodity 'each of whom desires to get one [of the commodities in question], and if possible all' for themselves (Marx 1849, p. 206). This is the main driving force behind consumer societies of all varieties. Competition between the buyers is the soul of consumer societies and of consumerism in general.

This competition among buyers cannot come about without sufficient production taking place at a pace, which is perhaps far greater than what is required or necessary. Fromm (1956) quite correctly noted, a long time ago, that the western world has produced an immense mass of commodities and is the wealthiest society recorded in human history, yet there is no other stage of human evolution where more people have lost their lives, belongings, and above all, selfhood. Amidst all of this, the market is posed as a solution to the problems while it continues to give rise to new problems. Important post-Marx theorisations of the consumer society include works by the likes of Zygmunt Bauman and Jean Baudrillard, two theorists with a Marxist past but who in their later years largely went on to be recognised as scholars who abandoned Marxism as a paradigm in their later years (Kellner 1989; Blackshaw 2005; Best 2013). Bauman (2000) argued that contemporary society has progressed from a stage of solid modernity i.e., from a society of producers to being a society of consumers with liquid modernity. Consumption, to him, is a concept, which is inherently related to the ideas of desire and possession. Bauman (2003a, p. 9) writes that desire is the very root of consumption. It is the desire to completely consume a commodity or a metaphysical entity such as a relationship. Bauman's major contribution to this debate remains his theorisation of 'Liquid Modernity', whereby the society is conceptualised as a society of consumers – a society that likes a certain non-orderliness in the society and its institutions where no event is more likely to happen than another (Bauman 2000). Such a society places consumption at the centre of its existence establishing, as Dunn (2008) says, the relationship between economy and culture:

> The essence of consumerism is the principle that consumption is an end-in-itself, its own justification. Deeply rooted in the profit motive, consumerism is now a widely shared ideology and worldview capable of creating strong attachments to consumption as a way of life, based on a belief in the enduring power of material possessions and commercial distractions to bring happiness and personal self-fulfilment. (Dunn 2008, p. 8)

A consumer society is a society where consumer culture reigns supreme within the social structure. Consumerism is a result of the combined effects of commodity fetishism and capitalist alienation. A consumer society needs innumerable objects as a precondition to its formations – objects which can be destroyed and replenished at the will of capital. This proliferation of objects for consumption is propagated as a marker of democracy and growth (Baudrillard 1970, p. 51). Growth, however, does not come without its own refuse. The environment is living proof of that. Centuries of human growth, combined with massively declining climatic conditions for the sustainability of the human race, have resulted in the creation of an uncertain future for the human race – environmentally as well as socially (Mann and Wainwright 2018). Consumerism has the ability to channel these fears towards practices of effective accumulation for capitalism. There are responses to the crisis from all ends of the political spectrum (Aronoff, Battistoni, Cohen, and Riofrancos 2019; Pettifor 2019; Malm 2020), but to the point to which they all agree, in some way or the other, is that it is the drive towards the relation of a society based on limitless consumption that is causing the climate crisis that the world finds itself engulfed in. Shrestha (1997) defined this in one of the best possible ways: 'The poor are forced into a situation in which they either have to spend what little money or resources they have on senseless consumer objects rather than basic necessities in order to deflect total social humiliation or face the prospect of being teased and laughed at' (Shrestha 1997, p. 26).

Social media revolutionises this process because this provides the avenues for the transformation of commodities that would have normally ended up in the garbage bins into the market. From a sustainability point of view, this would have been a welcome step, provided capitalism was not involved. Interviews with sellers engaged in the sale and purchase of commodities manufactured out of refuse (both recyclable and non-recyclable) such as eggshells, paper, etc. reveal the manner in which social media influence the market for such products. Individuals who are environmentally conscious and whose posts on social media are engaging with issues of environmentalism, get targeted by advertisements focused on 'Green Products' which eventually lead them to more 'Marketplace' recommendations, further on towards these sellers. These sellers, it must be said, are environmentally conscious people, they have their hearts in the right place. However, whether the market can be used for the purpose is something that can be debated. This is true for both the Global North and the Global South. In India, 'green' commodities are usually marketed through platforms such as WhatsApp and now, *Signal*. Sellers attempt to target a specific corpus of customers generated through personal networks. In the hinterlands of India, companies like Amway and Avon have for decades, employed these techniques to generate profit. However, because of the restrictions imposed upon networking and communication by traditional modes of communication, their reach mostly was generated through in-person human connections. With social media and messaging platforms such as WhatsApp, and its associated groups, such commodities become easily transmittable within the community. Interviews with many small-scale sellers in the Global South confirmed this aspect of social media commerce. They confirmed the process in which they creatively used the various WhatsApp groups that they have been added to over the course of years. These sellers use their family networks, circles of friends, and official links to perpetuate through the complex web of individualities in the community. The primary benefit that social media provides them with is that it significantly reduces the efforts that these sellers and businesspeople have to do to build customer bases. Dunayevskaya (1958a, p. 270) spoke about the importance of time within the capitalist mode of production, and how capitalism uses technology to substitute human efforts by incorporating them into a machine reducing the requirement of individual efforts and further workers and increasing the productivity of those already working. As Marx had noted: '... the size and value of the machines employed grow as the productivity of labour develops, but not in the same proportion as this productivity itself, i.e. the proportion to which these machines supply an increased product' (Marx 1981, pp. 203-04).

Social media commerce is important because it represents the methods in which such commodities, which are definitely environmentally conscious, can be made to end up within the fold of the capitalist market through the utilisation of social media. Within social media commerce, the factors of trust and reliability, which might have otherwise been important factors in the commercial trading of these commodities are negotiated through personal communication directly between the manufacturer and the customer. These individuals, bound by a mechanism of trade, try to establish a relationship with each based on the commodities they possess. Consumerism today has spread globally (Dunn 2008; Bauman 2000, 2007). Social media commerce uses social media and its associated power over the users to generate a more penetrative consumer culture that voraciously 'lends itself to images of unconscious imprisonment' (Bowlby 2001, p. 3). Social media commerce makes capitalism more intrusive and more acceptable to the workers. It makes capitalism look sane and supportive of the workers because it allows them to be happy with the tiny respites which they can gather under capitalism because selling is a much happier and less painful activity in itself than working under capitalism (Perlman 1972/2016).

One of the major aspects of these commodities is that they are temporarily outside the capitalist pricing system, and as such, they do not have any fixed 'Retail Price' and are open to negotiations. Social media focuses on the element of community prevalent among social media users within a particular social space and its associated factors such as security, trust and goodwill (Bauman 2001), to further the spread of commercial activities in society. The usage of these factors by capitalism, or capitalistic tendencies in society, is nothing new. Capitalism has been using these for decades now to further its own growth and accumulation. From the departmental store in the neighbourhood to the mall, communities have always been used by capitalism as means of reaching the individual consumer. Capitalism's approach uses the cultural modes of consumption and production prevalent within a community or a cultural system to increase the penetration of its commodities into an individual's life. Both in the Global South and Global North, individuals confirm to have ventured into social media for some commodity but have ended up getting into exchange relations with other people for some other commodity. With improved search optimisation, social media sites now allow users to search for commodities in the same way as any normal e-commerce website. These characteristics are typical of modern-day shopping processes whereby people feel completely susceptible to the innumerable attractions of the shopping site (Bowlby 2001).

Miller (1987, pp. 190-91) theorisation of consumption as being a social practice that does not only include the mere practice of buying commodities but also includes within itself the way in which human beings use, enjoy, dispose and 'abuse' the objects becomes a particularly interesting way of analysing such practices in the current context. Material objects are different from other cultural objects such as extended familial ties, religious beliefs, etc. The primary focus of our analysis is material objects. Even though cultural objects can easily end up in the commercial sphere (Adorno 1991), they are not the primary concern as far as the present volume is concerned. Material objects have a certain physical attribute that corresponds to their material attribute such as shape, colour, etc (Dant 1996, p. 510). Some of these attributes are natural attributes of any commodity which are provided by nature itself upon which human labour is exercised (Marx 1976, p. 133). Most of the commodities are naturally found in this state, as Marx says:

> Commodities come into the world as use values and material goods, such as iron, linen, corn, etc. This is their plain, homely, natural form. How-

ever, they are only commodities because they have a dual nature, because they are at the same time, objects of utility and bearers of value. Therefore they only appear as commodities, or have the form of commodities, in so far as they possess a double form, i.e., natural form and value form. (Marx 1976, p. 138)

Secondly and Thirdly, Dant (1996) further argues that material objects have a certain cultural meaning embedded within them – taking a cue from arguments which he borrows from Baudrillard (1970, 1975, 1981) – which are located spatially and temporally by the signs which signify the object. The fourth aspect of such objects revolves around the 'surface for linguistic or quasi-linguistic texts to play across' such as advertisements, promotional banners, etc (Dant 1996, p. 510). Consumption, as the sociologist Robert Dunn argues 'is shaped and conditioned by a multitude of material and nonmaterial factors' (Dunn 2008, p. 3). Under contemporary capitalism, the act of consumption is as important as the act of production. A society of consumers as Zygmunt Bauman informs is a society that has transcended the desire for stability and moved towards a certain fluidity in their lives aimed more toward self-development as consumers (Bauman 2007) rather than human beings. Smart (2010) talks about some of the aspects of modern consumption, which are integral to contemporary social subjects. These aspects include the ability of consumption to provide happiness and satisfaction (Tonkiss 2006). This constitutes the foundation of the consumerist economy under contemporary capitalism. However, as Baudrillard (1970) rightly notes, the happiness one derives within a consumerist economy is not intrinsic happiness but is rather a happiness that is drawn from acts of consumption and possession of consumer goods. In other words, in a consumer society, factors of happiness have to be tangible commodities; happiness and well-being consequently are searched in concrete commodities through the quantification of happiness by focusing on the commodities one possesses (Baudrillard 1970, p. 50). Commodities within the consumer society are produced to live out their utility within a short period of time, so as to enable the generation of newer desires frequently. These new desires, as Slater (1997, p. 100) puts it, seemingly remain fulfillable only by the possession of commodities.

Commodities which are the results of the growth of the consumerist attitudes in society are often endowed with a 'false appearance', drawing the term from Adorno, in the sense that they portray themselves to be something different while in reality, they are merely extensions of the previous commodity from which they are derived. While such commodities can be said to be a result of consumerist production mechanisms, in reality, these two processes are largely complementary to each other. The growth of such consumerism and its associated commodity fetishism has received considerable attention from the Frankfurt School theoretician, Theodor Adorno, who remains a more radical figure in comparison to other postmodern thinkers. His analysis of the 'false appearances' of the commodity point toward a theoretical paradigm that can point one towards an analysis of a 'near-total reification' (Sherlock 1997, p. 66) and the possibility of envisaging a world external to the force of the commodity. For

Adorno (1991), everything within the society was at the risk of getting commercialised or commodified by the forces of capitalism. In advanced capitalist societies, the relationship between use-value and exchange-value, quite in line with Marx (1976, 1981, 1992), dissolves in such a manner that all use-values become a kind of false appearances to the user (Rose 1978, p. 49). What matters to capitalism is nothing but pure exchange value – a conceptualisation of a kind of value that yields profit.

Social media today, has to be analysed as an apparatus at the hand of capitalism. Big capital has invested a huge sum of money into developing the social media platforms which are used by millions of users online. Individuals are products of the social apparatuses of capitalism within capitalist society (Horkheimer and Adorno 1972/2002, p. 125), whereby educational qualifications for the working class merely means '*submission to the dominant ideology* and, for the agents of exploitation and repression, reproduction of *its capacity to handle the dominant ideology*' (Althusser 2014, p. 145). Social media also, to some extent, operates along these lines. It creates compliant subjects – subjects who are so firmly entrenched within the dominant social idea that anything that comes up on social media becomes the instant truth for them. One can witness such power of social media in the recent election campaigns by the far-right forces globally (Chaturvedi 2016). These campaigns have used the power of social media to garner support for their views regarding society. Social media, today, is an important agent of social change. It has been repeatedly used by activists and political personalities for effecting social alterations, reiterating that social media is an important element in the social fabric today. It can be said, in very plain words, that whatever happens on social media iterates and gets iterated by the actually existing society, including the market that social media contains *in its belly*.

The random chance of whether a commodity will yield a profit or not is the truth that marketing professionals have to live through day in and day out. Naturally, because of the huge amount of randomness and domination of probability involved here, there inevitably results in a massive quantity of commodities in the consumer market. Some of these commodities become massive profit generators for the capitalists, while some of these result in failures. While it is a common conception to think that the capitalist loses money, in reality, the market is structured in such a way that the capitalist is the most unlikely to lose the capital invested in it. Multiple techniques including the reduction of wages, credit payments, etc are used to ensure this. This is the 'naked' truth of neoliberalism – the market dominates the state, the state protects the market and the marginalised sections of the society face the highest risk of impoverishment. Capital may lose or concede to workers' demands at the point of production but regain what has been conceded or lost (and then some) by excessive extractions in the living space. High rents and housing costs, excessive charges by credit card companies, banks and telephone companies, the privatisation of healthcare and education, the imposition of user fees and fines, all inflict financial burdens on vulnerable populations even when these costs are not inflated by a host of predatory practices, arbitrary and regressive taxes, excessive legal fees and the like (Harvey 2014, p. 84).

The consumer society is one of the recent manifestations of such tendencies on a global scale. In the global north, society as a consumer society has been there for a very long time. In an affluent society, individuals are surrounded by objects (Baudrillard 1970, p. 25) – Marx's (1976) commodities. Baudrillard (1970, p. 32) defines 'affluence' as 'merely the accumulation of the *signs* of happiness'. For Baudrillard (1972, 1975), the act of consumption is not only about consuming the commodities but rather is also about the signs and meanings that those commodities represent. Consumer goods, according to him, possess a certain power that gives vent to the demand and desire for growth in the economies. Growth here refers not only to the growth of the potential of individual expenditure but also encompasses the increasing expenditure from other concerned parties to encourage the individuals to do that (Baudrillard 1970, p. 37). This might include the reduction of taxes, doing away with the middlemen, etc., anything which would promote general happiness in the society – an essential aspect of consumer society (Baudrillard 1970, p. 49). The consumer society stems from the domination of the commodity in the modern society under capitalism in a way that any product created out of labour always ends up becoming a commodity.

Most of the powerful merchants today control the entire process from production to final retailing. They reduce the cost by employing economics of scale through which they ensure that their production or acquisition prices remain abysmally low such that they can sell the product at a price that is lower than even its production cost. It is customarily understood that this entire process is characterised by the intense exploitation of labour and produces alienation that far surpasses any form of alienation in the preceding era. Harvey (2014, p. 75) analyses these strategies taken up by capital as parts of its overall plan to increase and hasten up the process of circulation and turnover time. These strategies, as Harvey continues, are also not free from demerits. Because of their pivotal role in smoothing out the process of circulation of capital, these strategies often result in the creation of powerful and dominating groups within the merchants. In the advanced capitalist countries, capitalism tended to pay more attention to a scheme that emphasized the effective management of the conditions required for the proper realisation of value. As Harvey (2014, p. 81) recounts, this tendency ran into problems wherever there arose strong organised labour movements, which forced capital to transfer its emphasis onto more direct surplus-value production which included strategies aimed toward reduction of all real wages at a social level and further heightening social control (Hardt and Negri 2000). Social control is applied through the exercise of the domination of commodities, which rapidly proliferate in consumer societies 'as part of the rise in the standard of living' (Baudrillard 1970, p. 40). Consumer expenditures also result from the rising expenditures which a person has to undertake to access the commodities – to buy a book from a bookstore, one has to travel to the bookstore or to work at the university, one has to travel to the university. Under neoliberal capitalism, where everything comes at a price, these activities cost money. But digital commerce does not have such costs. It does not matter if it is raining, or there is a tornado at the shores, the market is always open.

6. TECHNOLOGY, COMMUNICATION AND CULTURE

Technologies are not alien elements that are just introduced into society but are rather socially shaped as Mackenzie and Wajcman (1999) argue. The kind of impact these technological innovations have over the overall shaping of an individual or a community can be immense. For example, they can reduce the time one has to spend outdoors, and further regulate the time one spends in various activities while indoors. In other words, a simplistic understanding of technology can point one toward concluding that they help individuals in gaining better control of their lives. Some technological innovations help in the manufacturing of routinisation and regularisation of the lives of individuals by interfering with the, as Reckwitz (2002, p. 255) mentions, routines of how individuals move and interact with each other. They can produce routes towards individualisation and the creation of 'atomised individuals' who are divided between their private lives often portrayed as being self-sufficient, and social life based on needs that can be fulfilled in relationships with other individuals (Lefebvre 1991b, p. 91). The influence of technological innovations facilitates the integration of everyday life into a 'technological milieu', where objects are previously seen as only appendages to social existence become essential artefacts influencing the rhythm or style of human existence (Lefebvre 2002, pp. 74-5). Such technological equipment often restricts the need for movement of the individuals and allows them to utilise their private spaces by making them completely segregated from the overall social space. Such technologies often act like individuals who provide not only physical comfort to their users but also provide mental security. Bruno Latour (1987) argued that such objects and artifacts play similar roles to human beings in the overall social network. These technologies have become important actors in the fulfilment of everyday lives under capitalism (Greenfield 2017).

Such objects, including social media, are in effect means of communication used by capitalism for furthering its drives or accumulation. Communication has often been labelled as the foundation upon which the socio-economic fabric of society is constructed, and social media is an important component of the same within the information society of the twenty-first century where it is not only a technology but rather a techno-social system (Fuchs 2014c). Burston, Dyer-Witheford and Hearn (2010) also associated this digitalisation of the society with the actually existing socio-political realities, and opined, *'the term "digital" does not simply refer to digital machines and processes but to the entire political, social and economic context and infrastructure within which they have emerged. This is how we now live in the "digital age"'* (Burston, Dyer-Witheford and Hearn 2010, p. 215). While the previous centuries were dominated by industrial and finance capitalism, contemporary society has witnessed a gradual evolution towards the primacy of information (Castells 2009), where information has become a major aspect of the capitalist production and circulation process. This alteration of the capitalist production and circulation process was done through an emphasis on the utilisation of information and communication technologies (ICTs) such as computers and televisions, which function digitally and not mechanically. Castells (1996/2010) rightly extends this by saying that though "information" has been central to human societies for a long time, the peculiarity of the contemporary usage of ICTs is that communication and information have evolved into being a raw material for the production of surplus-value (Deb Roy 2020). Raymond Williams was one of the first Marxists of repute to analyse the means of communication as a means of production (Williams 1980). The means-of-communication debate within Marxist debates is often focused on the positions taken by Williams (1980) and Althusser (2005). While *Althusserian* theory focused on overdetermination and *determination in the last instance* (Althusser, Balibar, and Ranciere 2009), Williams (1977) saw the concept as a mere reproduction of the economistic side of Marxist theory, which proclaimed everything to be a superstructure to economic foundations of the society. This is the vantage point from which Williams approached the issue. The means of communication within Marx's (1992) own writings were more or less analysed as the factors of transportation, and more specifically as a relation of production, which has its own share of impact on the value of a commodity. For Williams, 'Marx ... had correctly stressed the connection between culture and economy but had badly mistaken the nature of that connection' (Higgins 1999, p. 110).

There is something common about the structural Marxism of Althusser and the cultural Marxism of Williams, which is that they both worked through a concept that distinguished between the base and the superstructure. As such, this allowed for the development of a gulf between culture and economy. It is necessary to understand here that dissolving the distinction between base and superstructure in the society completely in any analysis is a tendency that encapsulates within itself the risk of the analysis becoming too negligent of the material conditions of human existence producing accounts that are 'counter ... to the revolutionary materialism of Marx' (Dunayevskaya 1973, p. 163). Following Dunayevskaya's (1973) critique of Mao's retrogression, Anderson (2021) argued that such complete dissolution of the differences between the base and superstructure, as it occurred under Mao's leadership in China, tends to create alienated subjectivity which fails to take into account actual objective material conditions thus failing to evolve into a 'revolutionary humanist subjectivity' (Anderson 2021, p. 331).

An analysis of the seemingly explicit dichotomy between economy and culture becomes the point where Marxist Humanist analysis becomes a useful force for analysis of contemporary capitalism. Marxist Humanist theory attempts to liberate the human being from the *totality* of all oppressions instead of an undialectical emphasis on the individual as a 'subject of domination' which leaves little scope for understanding and analysing the 'varying forms of collective self-consciousness and resultant collective action for self-liberation' (Anderson 2017, p. 74). Dialectics as Dunayevskaya notes is to be recreated continuously in light of the 'spontaneously [emerging and developing] Subject', the Subject being the working class (Dunayevskaya 1973, p. 73). A dialectical view of society encapsulates the unity of the opposites. Economy and culture or economy and philosophy need not be seen as separate distinct categories but can exist together as one holistic system in a way where *The positive is negative, but what is most negative is also what is most positive* (Lefebvre 1991b, p. 72). In other words, as Dunayevskaya (1973, p. 13) argues, following Hegel's *Logic*: 'The positive is contained in the negative, which is the path to a *new beginning*. This is not only the *Logic* but life; or, more correctly, it is a movement ... in dialectics in general, because it is a fact of history as of life. It is a ceaseless movement, a veritable continuous revolution. It is the lifeblood of the dialectic'.

Social media commerce is one of the most recent developments in the field of technology. Its rapid usage has come at a time when working-class individuals have perhaps been going through one of the worst periods in the history of capitalism in general. Social media commerce is not an automated technology *per se*, such that it requires actual human beings to perform functions and work through the interface. Huws (2016) describes this process in great detail in her account of labour performed within the *logged-in* paradigms of different platforms, where ICTs occupy a central position in managing and coordinating the labour of a vast section of the workers engaged therein – which has as Huws (2016, 2017) describes has effects on both ends of the spectrum. The involvement of ICTs in such acts of coordination brings in a certain notion of automation within the process, and this is where the Marxist Humanist critique of technology becomes extremely relevant. Marxist Humanism allows one to look at technology dialectically without resorting to either indiscriminate demonisation or positivistic appreciation.

Dunayevskaya's (1958a) analysis of technology, which was primarily through the vantage point of automation but is highly relevant in this case. She analyses automation from the vantage point of the working class who felt threatened by the increased production capacities of the machinery. Small scale businesses globally have been very vocal about the kind of problems that large e-commerce platforms such as Amazon have been causing for them. For many of them, there was no option left but to integrate their businesses with the digital ecosystem. Many small businesses have begun to get integrated into the Amazon ecosystem in India through multiple means – registering as sellers, opening storefronts, etc. Similar is the case with a website known as 'The Market' in New Zealand, which has become a major platform for small-scale businesses to integrate themselves and build customer bases in a networked world. The impact however has been different. In the west, businesses have developed and thrived. Small businesses usually are mostly impacted positively by this step because they usually have either a flagship brand value associated with niche commodities or have used such platforms for becoming more sophisticated in nature to the customer by using their automated and digital systems in place. One example can be cited of stores such as 'Actiontech' or 'Rubber Monkey' which engage very specifically with certain commodities such as drones, e-ink devices, etc., which do not have a huge distribution network in the country. Social media commerce for such businesses has been indeed beneficial, because it has enabled them to make wider inroads into the market through their social media pages, groups, etc. Social media has helped them in overcoming the restrictions that their spatial location imposed on them. Similar is the case with some of the entrepreneurs located in the far-flung corners of India. Social media has enabled them to reach a wider audience. There are countless examples of how small-scale set-ups in India's Northeast have got national viewership now because of social media. At the same time, it cannot be denied that such businesses always face a threat of being taken over by other large corporations or being forced to integrate themselves with other established brands, considering that

Technology, as Dunayevskaya (1958a) notes, was analysed and perceived differently by different workers depending on the hierarchical structure to which they belonged (Dunayevskaya 1958a, p. 268). She brings out the worst aspect of the work that capitalism has put machines to – putting workers out of work, increasing their insecurities, etc. Dunayevskaya (1958a, p. 269) predicted the way in which technology and automation could divide the working class based on their knowledge of the machines, which were finding space in the capitalist production systems. Similar to the way in which television sets and mobile phones have begun to be used and perceived as computer monitors and webcams by a specific section of the working class and the middle class possessing the requisite technological knowledge to do that, social media commerce as well has been perceived differently by different people. In the east, conversations reveal that social media commerce has been a great advancement for potential small-scale entrepreneurs. Social media has enabled these individuals to come directly under capitalist production and distribution relations.

Marcuse (1941) argued that technology under capitalism was no better than capitalism itself. Like capitalism, technology too 'as a mode of production, as the totality of instruments, devices and contrivances which characterize the machine age is thus at the same time a mode of organising and perpetuating (or changing) social relationships, a manifestation of prevalent thoughts and behaviour patterns, an instrument of control and domination' (Marcuse 1941/1998, p. 41). Technology is an integral part of capitalism which has contributed to the production of what Marcuse called 'technological rationality' (Marcuse 1941, p. 44) which destroys individual rationality and makes human beings unable to critique the way machines dominate the everyday lives of human beings. Gadgets such as smartphones, smart displays, etc. have become a part of the everyday lives of the working class in such a way that many of them have become an extension of the personality of their respective users. These gadgets often work as signs and symbols of one's status and social occupation. In other words, commodities become coded cultural symbols and as such are less about satisfying needs than about the creation of meanings (Dunn 2008, p. 6). Social media has become increasingly important in this domain. Through the usage of pictures, videos and a mechanism through which people can constantly keep others updated about their lives. The influence of the technologies which facilitate the spread of social media in the everyday lives of human beings has modified the very fabric of the society that human beings inhabit, both in the global north and the global south. Communication is fundamentally important to human society because it is the process through which individuals construct their sociality and become parts of social groups, relations and other collective social institutions (Fuchs 2020), either voluntarily or involuntarily. Capitalism uses this sociality of human beings as a weapon for domination. Rosa Luxemburg (1913/2003) in her seminal work *The Accumulation of Capital* stated, 'the process of production is based on the continuation of two different, though closely connected factors, the technical and social conditions – on the precise relationship between men and nature and that between men and men' (Luxemburg 2003, p. 4).

The relation between actually existing human beings is in no way inferior as an analytical tool in theorising the contemporary modes of capitalist exploitation. This relationship between human beings is mediated by various means of communication. Thus, the overcoming of the marginalisation of communication within Marxist theory (Fuchs and Mosco 2016) is critical if one is to analyse contemporary social relationships, which are products of the enclosures enforced upon society by digital capitalism (Hall and Stahl 2012). Such an analytical perspective is especially important when certain forms of technology have become so normalised that they have become an integral part of human sustenance itself. It should be noted here that most of the technological innovations that have been normalised in the daily lives of people are communicative in nature. Greenfield (2017) brings forward the dominance of communicative technology in the everyday lives of individuals. Social media is a dominant part of this networked communicative framework. Social media has the ability to shape perceptions and ideas about society. People today, carry smartphones all throughout the day – the contemporary urban person is woken up by the alarm in the smartphone after getting his sleep analysis done by the smartphone. As Greenfield (2017) informs, this rapid surge in the usage of smartphones and their associated services is a global phenomenon not restricted spatially to any part of the globe. These devices are being maintained by and through the internet, which again comes with all its various networks embedded within itself, created with the purpose of extracting profit from every click and every move that one does while being connected to the internet.

The idea that communication has always been an important factor in the generation and sustenance of class inequalities (Fuchs and Mosco 2016), is further validated when these normalised communicative technological advancements are used for the accumulation of profits, as is the case of social media commerce in the context of the working-class property. The digital means of value creation use the relationship between labour and digital technologies along with the existing modes of social organisation within capitalism to continue alienating the workers from the means and products of their own production (Fuchs and Sevignani 2013, p. 204). Keeping up with this evolution, social science has also brought in new techniques and conceptual paradigms to analyse the new form of society such as 'free labour' (Terranova 2000), 'immaterial labour' (Hardt and Negri 2000), 'digital labour' (Fuchs and Sevignani 2013), and the like. One of the primary aspects of almost all these various understandings of labour within contemporary society is the emphasis on how labour as a conceptual element intersects with the political economy of ICTs (Briziarelli 2014) within digital capitalism.

Social media within social media commerce is used as a means of production. To qualify this, one has to go back to how Marx talked about the means of production in society. Marx (1859) argued that 'In the social production of their existence, men inevitably enter into definite relations, which are independent of their will, namely relations of production appropriate to a given stage in the development of their material forces of production' (Marx 1859, p. 263). The forces of production in any society constitute the foundation of that society, which Marx characterised as the base of the society upon which the entire social superstructure was built. Some have critiqued Marx for his overtly and seemingly economistic analysis, including Williams (1960, 1980) who argued that Marx uses the terms merely as an analogy. However, Williams (1977, p. 11) himself was not averse to placing something as the central element of a society, which to him was 'culture' rather than 'economy'. Theorists such as Eagleton (1989) and Milner (1994) have critiqued Williams for his culturalist opinions at this point, and rightly so, by saying that 'there is a strong implication through ... Williams' work ... to label a phenomenon "superstructural" is somehow to assign it a lesser degree of effective reality than an element of material reality' (168). Marx included in his definition of the means of production, everything that allows and facilitates the production process which is again inevitably linked with capitalist accumulation. Without the desire to accumulate, capitalist production (which today includes innovation as well) would have no purpose to exist as well.

It is true that Marx (1859) talked about raw materials and labour mainly. His analysis of technology is integrated with the critiques of political economy. Williams (1960) sees the notion of industry as a historical project, where human qualities such as perseverance and skills, became institutionalised with time to mean a specific entity in human civilisations. Cohen (2000) has also argued that the notion of raw materials includes factors such as emotions, intelligence, etc., and rightly so because, without such factors, production cannot go on. Technological innovations, including social media and Computers, are creations of human intelligence, done in specific contexts created by either crisis or prosperity or at times, a combination of both. Social media also arrived at a very specific point in human history. It harped on the desires of multinationals, states, and individuals, to create a multi-modal networked platform, whereby ideas, and most importantly money, could flow. It is true that technology has been the cause of many problems in the social lives of human beings, but without the important intervention of modern technology, some of the very basic characteristics of contemporary human existence would not have been possible, as Hardt and Negri (2017) in their work *Assembly* quite correctly state. But, that in no way, means that one has to disregard the dehumanising role of technology and question the very humanism that technology wants to create, something to which scholars such as Dunayevskaya (1958a) and to which Marcuse (1941) devoted considerable attention.

The vulnerabilities, of both the overall techno-social system and the working class therein, have long-term effects. The influence of gadgets has been such that almost every modern human being has been converted from being a biological being per se, into a cyborg, whereby the rigid distinctions between human beings and machines have disappeared (Haraway 2016). Hands (2019) designates this kind of life as a 'gadget life', where gadgets occupy such a central position in contemporary lives that it becomes imperative to look at how they are functioning and most importantly, how they influence human behaviour and affect collective alterations at a social level. In general, gadgets, according to Hands (2019) have some common features – 'ingenuity, intelligence, multifunctionality and [the ability to expand] human capacity' (p. 3). These are some of the primordial qualities of gadgets that make them such an attractive entity to the common individual. Their fetishistic existence within the human social reality makes them exercise a certain kind of domination over human life in such a way that they obtain the power to influence the lives of the people associated with them, and also at times, transform them (Callon 1991). One can practically conceptualise this with regard to the power of brands and their associated products today. The individual can replicate the power of the fetish if the individual can identify oneself with the object, which forms the basis of the fetish. In today's world, the individual likewise identifies with the smartphone, and through the smartphone with social media. The users rarely care about the human labour, which is involved in the creation of the platforms, but rather they see it merely as a commodity – to be used, and often abused.

A fetish is created by hiding away the human labour which has gone into the production of the commodity possessing or generating the fetish. Innovations under the capitalist mode of production attempt to further the regime of value in the society – the main staying element of capitalist domination in the society. The development of technology and machinery under capitalism creates further alienation of the working class because the general labour of the society then does not present itself within the working class and their struggles but in capital increasing its productivity and ability to accumulate (Marx 1973, pp. 694-95). Social media, one of the most recent advancements in technology, bases itself on communication and uses communication to extract further profits and surplus value from the working class. Primarily, it does so through targeted advertisements and encouraging the users to spend time on the platform (Fuchs 2019a 2015, 2014c). This encouragement occurs through masking its capital accumulation model (Fuchs 2017) by making platforms free to use. It also attains a high level of participation because it provides the users with a brief respite from capitalism's mass scale alienation (Fuchs 2017). Social media commerce, especially within the working classes, capitalises on this very element of respite by using digital communities and spaces created by the users for promoting commercial activities between them and thus again pushing the working class into an alienated existence dominated by capital.

Contemporary capitalism creates situations where human beings become extensions of technological developments and automated machinery used in the service of capitalist commodity production (Dunayevskaya 1980). Technology, as Marcuse (1941) rightly analysed, cannot be merely analysed as a disjointed arte-fact, but rather is a process that is directed by the individuals and groups asso-ciated with the technological form as creators, users, etc. In other words, the users themselves are part of the technological form in existence and cannot be detached from the same. However, users are not free individuals but are rather part of a process of social control, whereby almost every aspect of human life, previously spontaneous, becomes part of technological rationality in both form and content, lacking all spontaneity and humane aspects (Marcuse 1941). Marx's analysis of machines and technology was influenced by the manner in which he analysed political economy. Marx (1973, p. 679) analyses machines and techno-logical development as a part of the capitalist production and circulation sys-tem. Machines and money become the exemplars of fixed and circulating capital in Marx's account of machinery which aim to increase the profits and surplus value amassed by the capitalist (Marx 1973, pp. 686, 692, 694). Machines become the representations of capital as value which are put into action by capital to accumulate further value (Marx 1973, p. 694). According to some scholars such as Wendling (2009) and Negri (1992) to a certain extent, for the Marx of *Grun-drisse*, machines and money, both, become destructive forces under capitalism. It is only under the alienated mode of living that capitalism promotes that these objects turn towards becoming oppressive agents (Wendling 2009). In *Grundrisse*, Marx takes a different route towards analysing technology and machinery. As Wendling (2009) argues, the Marx of *Capital* was speaking from a perspective, which had taken the alienated mode of existence as a pre-existing condition of the object under analysis. But the Marx of *Grundrisse* however agrees upon the possibility of deploying technology for the betterment of the working-class con-dition, whereby the 'workers [after the revolution] need not to smash but to own machines, for in doing so they reclaim the accumulated wealth of their class' (Wendling 2009, p. 100). Machines, to Marx (1973, p. 694) always represent the collective capitalist accumulation and absorption of skills, knowledge and the 'general productive forces of the social brain'.

There was no 'break' between Marx's ideas on machinery and technology. He continued to analyse machinery as an alienating force under capitalism, right from his *Grundrisse* to *Capital Volume 1*. Marx (1973) argues that the objectifi-cation of labour becomes a distinct tangible reality with the proliferation of machinery within the production mechanisms under capitalism (pp. 703-04). For Marx, machines were always a part of the capitalist structuring process in soci-ety. Machines bring into effect newer divisions of labour in society. Functions, erstwhile of actual living human labour, become a part of the overall network maintained by machines. Machines become a part of the process of automation which is increasingly finding a place in capitalist production. In this situation, it is a kind of automation itself that moves other parts which are also in automa-tion. Marx argues that with the development of capitalist production systems, the process of production itself becomes the process of labour with no particular importance being accredited to the actual worker. Machines, under the highly developed form of capitalist production, become the production process itself with workers – the actual living labour – becoming mere linkages or parts of a total system. At such a stage, it is the machine itself that possesses productivity and other qualities traditionally attributed to the worker and is often 'itself the virtuoso, with a soul of its own in the mechanical laws acting through it; and it consumes coal, oil, etc., just as the worker consumes food to keep up its perpetual motion' (Marx 1973, pp. 692-93). In other words, as the Marx of *Capital* would interpret this subsumption: 'The worker has been appropriated by the process, but the process had previously to be adapted to the worker. This subjective principle of the division of labour no longer exists in production by machinery' (Marx 1976, p. 501).

There is a critical relationship between machinery, living or dead labour, and capitalist accumulation. Machines can perform the task of replacing a certain portion of living labour with machinery (Marx 1976, 1973). As Marx further states, 'In machinery, objectified labour materially confronts living labour as a ruling power and as an active subsumption of the latter under itself, not only appropriating it but in the real production process itself' (Marx 1973, pp. 693-94). This creates the basis for the conceptualisation of machinery as fixed capital whereby it gets related to the individual value created by the worker in the production process. The complete proliferation of machinery in the system of production creates an appearance of individual units of labour scattered across the productive spectrum (Marx 1973, p. 693). Machines have always been an important part and parcel of human development. The innovation in the realm of energy and its impact on the existing forms of energy development had a tremendous impact on the general organisation of society (Wrigley 2010). However, as Wrigley (2010, p. 4) argues, even though the impact of the Industrial Revolution cannot be denied, there also cannot be any completely objectively 'correct' way of defining the industrial revolution or any other technological watershed moment because 'a description and explanation which are satisfactory in the context implied by one definition are unlikely to carry conviction when the [moment] is differently defined'. If one goes back to Marx at this point, one can notice how Marx was analysing the dialectical relationship between machines and human beings as workers:

> The machine, which is the starting-point of the industrial revolution, replaces the worker, who handles a single tool, by a mechanism operating with a number of similar tools and set in motion by a single motive power, whatever the form of that power. Here we have the machine, but in its first role as a simple element in production by machinery (Marx 1976, p. 497)

> In machinery, objectified labour itself appears not only in the form of product or of the product employed as a means of labour, but in the form of the force of production itself. The development of the means of labour into machinery is not an accidental moment of capital, but is rather the

historical reshaping of the traditional, inherited means of labour into a form adequate to capital (Marx 1973, p. 694)

Technology has always featured in Marx's works in a dialectical fashion. Marx never takes one-sided opinions in the case of machinery, but rather he always views machinery as a force whose effects, in the end, depend on how it is used and by whom. In *Capital*, it received largely a negative connotation, such as his polemics on the conceptualisation of tools and machines as being independent of human interventions which seek to replace 'man' with a 'mechanism' and the distinction between the 'motive power' of the machine and (Marx 1976, pp. 493-94). The machines that Marx was talking about were, of course, not the modern machinery and technology that one is accustomed to today while speaking about machines. However, what was implicit in Marx's depiction of machines was that machines had an immense influence on the human life of the time in which a particularly 'revolutionary' machine or technology was introduced. Social media is the 'revolutionary' technology of the 21st Century. Social Media, Computers and other technology have their own sets of impacts on the lives of human beings. Accordingly, some scholars raise objections to the usage of the work 'impact' over the word 'effect' (anonymous reviews and personal communication). The current author, however, uses the word in the exact same way that the word 'impact' is supposed to mean. The literary notions associated with the usages of these words might seem trivial in the context of the current work, but it is highly relevant in this context. The usage of 'impact' emphasises the potential dehumanising notions of technological artefacts in the everyday lives of human beings. Social media tends to convert people to mere objects. In a recent book, Richard Seymour states, and he makes a very convincing argument as well, that within social media and its constant encouragement to individuals to let the world know about their lives, the person is often converted into a 'user' akin to those who are addicted to drugs (Seymour 2019). The technologies, in themselves, also have a human aspect to themselves as has been highlighted by scholars such as Latour (1987), most notably known for his theories surrounding actor-network theory (Latour 2005). Just like human beings, they have the power to coerce human beings or to make them cooperative. Under contemporary capitalism, the usage of technological innovations in regulating everyday lives and social patterning has been one of the mainstays of the dynamicity of social reality. Material objects often have the ability to shape the everyday life of human beings and influence the social forms in place (Latour 2005; Mylan and Southerton 2017). Technology and the appliances associated with them today are more than mere material objects, but rather are instruments that enable structural changes in the everyday lives of individuals. The rise of technological intervention into the everyday lives of the people have not been able to do away with the trivial aspects of everyday reality (Lefebvre 2002) which have extraordinary qualities and implications for society as a whole (Lefebvre 1991b), shaping and structuring contemporary human lives.

Technological artefacts, with widespread usage, are also associated with their own sets of 'meanings, relations and effects' (Michael 2006, p. 4). In any urban centre with a widespread culture of walking or travelling by trains, buses, etc within the limits of the city every day, it is common to see people wearing headphones. Some say that they do so to reduce the effects of the distance by diverting their minds off the road, while some others use it to look the part of a student in the twenty-first century. The use of headphones within domestic and public spaces thus has to be seen as something which is only tangentially related to the traditional effects of music in everyday human life (De Nora 2000) but is more often than not related to the efforts that individuals put in to create boundaries around themselves. Thus, the functions which an actually existing living human being performs in a network of actors are different from the way in which technologies function in those networks. The influence of technologies creates a new kind of social structure where networks become the main factors of newer networks which then go on to create the total social structure itself (Castells 2010, p.xviii). Factors like cooperation between different actors (Negri 1989a 1989b) play a major role in this kind of social structure. One of the most prominent distinctions between networks of human beings and networks formed by the intervention of technology can be theorised by focusing on the manner in which individuals continued to engage with the community during the global Covid19 pandemic. Social media and other platforms which encouraged virtual interaction between individuals were the primary means through which individuals kept in contact with each other in situations where physical in-person interaction was not possible. While these could be a means of extending the social relationships between two individuals, and a means to extend their professional or personal network, there are considerable differences between the acts of conversing with people in person and on the internet virtually:

> There is a different between chatting with people whom I know and chatting with people whom I don't know. Within the workplace, if I have to take a meeting online, which is very common nowadays, it is very easy to do so, if I already know the person. I just have to transfer the dynamics which we share offline to the online mode. While, if I do not know the person, I will often have to conduct the meeting in a very professional manner without much regard for human emotions.

Technologies are not autonomous entities in themselves. They do not exist in a vacuum, as has been emphasised many times in the current work. Hence, any discussion about technologies or machinery needs to talk about many associated processes, all of which are a part and parcel of the overall social space within which the technology exists. Social media, also, has its own space – a space by which it gets modified, and which in turn, modifies social media itself. Social media commerce helps capitalism in the development and scattering of networks, which as Banaji (2020) describes, is one of the most important properties of capitalist accumulation strategies. Marxist terminology terms this very quality, as Banaji (2020) mentions the moment of circulation within the capitalist cycle of accumulation. The development of these networks also emphasises the shift from industrial capitalism to newer forms of capitalism. In the contemporary society dominated by digital capitalism, social media takes up the task of generating these networks of circulation, which were previously dominated by merchants and traders (Banaji 2020). This functionality also makes social media a typical case of the techno-social model (Fuchs 2013) that emphasises the social character of technological innovations under capitalism. Facebook brought forward 'Facebook Marketplace' in the year 2016 as an extension of its already well-established technological framework. The official declaration from Facebook regarding the ushering in of Marketplace on the social media platform stated,

> Facebook is where people connect, and in recent years more people have been using Facebook to connect in another way: buying and selling with each other. This activity started in Facebook Groups and has grown substantially. More than 450 million people visit buy and sell groups each month – from families in a local neighborhood to collectors around the world. To help people make more of these connections, today we're introducing Marketplace, a convenient destination to discover, buy and sell items with people in your community. Marketplace makes it easy to find new things you'll love and find a new home for the things you're ready to part with. We'll continue to build new options and features to make this the best experience for people[1] (Facebook 2016)

As is evident from the statement itself, Marketplace or FM, was designed so as to exploit the relations of communication that users had built up on the social media platform. "Marketplace makes it easy to find new and used items such as clothes, furniture, cars and even your next home to rent".[2] FM encourages the usage of social media as a means of intra-working class or intra-user commerce. FM, in some ways, capitalised upon the practices of "Buy and Sell" groups on Facebook. These "Buy and Sell" groups, however, operated more as normal groups, where the user had to describe manually the details of the product listed. FM did away with all of these lengthy procedures and made it easy to list commodities for sale with a full-fledged user interface integrated within Facebook to aid in listing the commodities and accurately describing the state of usage they are in, which points toward, in Marxian terms, the unused use-value of the commodity on sale. Technology has created a situation whereby it has revolutionised the ideas surrounding the actually existing class dynamics in society. The existing condition of a 'Digital Divide' which has engulfed society has created a scenario whereby the basic categories of being 'rich' and 'poor' have been de-economised in the public discourse, of course, with its own limitations. 'Rich'

---

1. See https://about.fb.com/news/2016/10/introducing-marketplace-buy-and-sell-with-your-local-community/

2. See https://www.facebook.com/marketplace/learn-more/buying

in the discourse of 'Digital Divide' means somebody who has access to social media, has the potential (social, cultural and spatial) to use social media for personal benefits and has the capacity to spread the culture of social media and digital capitalism today. It is a technocratic society, especially in the kind of world that Covid19 has created. Technology can bring in many different kinds of alterations, both at a social and an individual level. Some of the people in the global south, who are engaged in social media commerce affirmed that for them, it was the easy access to social media which made them think about engaging in commercial activities in the first place.

Individuals affirmed the process in which they were integrated into the digital world. Some had been integrated because of their necessity, while others became integrated going with the flow of the society. There are no fixed routes through which people get introduced to social media, but once they do and possess high-speed internet access, they get absorbed by the technology. The subjective-objective relationship was explored by Dunayevskaya (1958a) quite in detail where she argued that the interpretation of technological development varied immensely among human beings. Likewise, it is near impossible to predict how an individual might get absorbed into social media. It is also very difficult to predict how the individual will use social media, but it can be said with absolute certainty that the person will get absorbed into it, and once it happens, will be used for profit accumulation by capitalism. However, it is absolutely essential here to realise that the development of capitalism does not occur like a natural law. It can take different routes in different societies, and as such, anti-capitalist theories also need to do the same.

The understanding of Marxism as science has often relegated Marxism to a positivist science. Raya Dunayevskaya following Marx's EPM critiqued the crude materialist ideas behind the creation of veils between the ideas of social and individual life and science (Dunayevskaya 1973, p. 53). The explicitly naturalist and radical humanist Marx (1844, p. 304) of the EPM expounded upon how 'the *social* reality of nature, and *human* natural science, or the *natural science of man*, are identical terms'. It was this Marx which informed the entirety or the whole of Marx in the years to come when he produced the *Manifesto of the Communist Party* (Marx and Engels 1848) and *Capital* (Marx 1867). Dunayevskaya (1973) draws her inspiration from Marx himself:

> We see here thoroughgoing Naturalism or Humanism distinguishes itself both from Idealism and Materialism, and is, at the same time, the truth uniting both. We see, at the same time, how only Naturalism is capable of grasping the act of world history (Marx 1844, quoted from Dunayevskaya 1973, p. 53)

Harvey (2014, p. 70) is right in analysing those contemporary natural sciences often carry within themselves a certain non-dialectical (and at times, anti-dialectical) notion which infests the ideas about other areas of social knowledge as well. Dunayevskaya (1965, p. 73) mentions: 'The challenge of our times is not to science or machines, but to men. The totality of the world crisis demands a new unity of theory and practice, a new relationship between workers and intellectuals'. It has to take cognisance of the fact that modern ideologies commentating on social forms and content inevitably get impacted by the rise of modern technology and science. It is almost inevitable that technological progress will lead technology to become a dominant discourse (Gouldner 1976). However, in the analysis of science and technology, and its influence on human life, it is essential to remain free from the deterministic biases of natural sciences. It is thus of utmost essentiality to remember the ideological nature of science and technology. The task of any ideology, in its purest sense, is to inculcate among people the potential, or the idea that they have the potential, to alter society as they deem fit. As Gouldner (1976, p. 68) argues, it is the task of ideology to empower or provide a feeling of empowerment, to individuals regarding their ability to act without the approval or consent of anybody else. Gouldner (1976) also says that one of the major tasks of ideology is to enable the individual with a 'self' to overcome the anxieties of isolation from traditional networks as well as from the position one is ascribed to. Political regimes, including left-wing ones, often resort to this blatant determinism (Dunayevskaya 1958a). Both academic sociologists and 'scientific' Marxists often fall into the trap of positivism by wishing 'to extend the method of the exact sciences into a new area that [to them] requires it, the study of human relations' (Gouldner 1976, p. 5). However, as much as Marx was enthralled by the laws of thermodynamics and its laws (Wendling 2009), Marx was well aware of the fact that history was not dictated by doctrinaire laws, and neither could human beings who made that history as he himself often said.

Under conditions of contemporary capitalism, when it is often accorded that 'the individual no longer has a fixed and given position in society [and that the] very notion of a social 'place' or 'station' has all but ceased to have any application' enabling individuals to 'choose their social place and the role and, in doing so, create their own identities' (Sayers 2011, p. 10), it is of utmost necessity to understand the revolutionary dialectics of Marxism. Lukacs' (1975) case can also be taken at this point referring to his often-neglected work '*The Young Hegel*', where he attempted to recover the revolutionary dialectics of Hegelian-Marxism from crude materialist writings which had dominated much of the revolutionary praxis of the twentieth century. Lukács was one of the first Marxists of his time, who argued about the centrality of the 'standpoint of the proletariat' (Lukacs 1971) and the criticality of the idea with reference to how he views the totality being in a dialectical relationship with the actually existing capitalist reality (Anderson 2020, p. 132). According to Anderson (2020, p. 139) Lukács arguments get weakened by the outright rejection of any romanticism in the Young Hegel. Lukács' Hegel is more concerned with economics and labour in a relatively crude materialistic manner, which can be analysed as a practical necessity because of the pressure exerted by the USSR under Stalin (Anderson 2020, pp. 133, 140, 150). These points raised by Anderson become critical if one is the analyze the fetishist desire among most of twentieth-century Marxists to explain and counter philosophical questions at the level of human praxis (Anderson 2020, p. 53) through crude materialist praxiological understanding. This becomes further clear if one considers the point that historically crude forms of Marxism have always '... returned most of Marxism to such crude materialist and positivist views for many years. Even Trotsky, despite his political opposition to Stalin, certainly never freed himself from positivist and Kantian categories at a philosophical level' (Anderson 2020, p. 133). The crude materialist fetishism of human praxis often makes theorists blind to the importance of theory within the revolutionary struggles. It is a theory that makes it possible to challenge common-sensical beliefs about human freedom under capitalism. Individuals under capitalism (or even under despotic 'communism') are never free (Dunayevskaya 1958a). Evidence in this regard can be cited from the condition of Dalits in India in the Global South or African Americans in the broader Western world, who cannot be categorised as being the affluent section of the society. The affluent citizens can make their own decisions, they have access to multiple resources, which can aid them in mobilising their will and their material forces towards the fulfilment of their desires. However, for the worker, there is no freedom to choose an identity or a role, the worker, under the *spirit of capitalism*, is destined to work for the furthering of capitalist accumulation, either in the factory or on social media.

7. NEEDS, CAPITAL AND SOCIAL MEDIA COMMERCE

Human needs under capitalism are not only focused on sustenance but are culturally ordained in accordance with the socio-cultural values that certain commodities represent. An iPhone in the Global South is not just a phone, but rather it represents a constellation of meanings. It is not only an object with an exchange value (of course, it has that), but rather, if one refers to Smart (2007, p. 14), such an object has the ability to empower its possessor with certain happiness or satisfaction from the mere act of having the commodity within one's possession. Under capitalism, consumption is only to further production, and subsequently more consumption such that 'future work and future productivity become the justification of all forms of consumption' (Wendling 2009, p. 110). Automation of the modes of production and digitalisation of the means of consumption is resulting in a situation where capitalism has been able to further streamline its mode of accumulation and circulation of capital – with the 'conscious' support of the working class. Human needs, as Hudis (2012) correctly notes following Marx, are a result of the capitalist value-production processes and their associated social relations which operate independently of human needs and capacities (p. 7).

Social media commerce within this socio-political and cultural milieu is a site where there is a direct overlap between the existing economic system and the manner in which people use a certain technology, i.e., social media. The expansion of the term 'digital' can also be used to put into perspective in relation to the capitalist strategy to allow people to sell physical 'items' to other people directly, in the process turning them into commodities, without any intermediary except the digitalised medium facilitating the exchange. This exchange can be looked at either through a simplistically optimistic or through a critically informed paradigm. There are significant voices that have argued, from the former perspective, that with a mass-scale social level digitalisation of everything, capitalism will eventually come to an end because it will lose its ability to draw surplus value from most of the commodities (Mason 2016). However, this view does not take into account the power of capitalism to restructure itself with the changing dynamics of society. In the consumer society, consumption assumes a central position in society whereby it is placed as an instrument through which human beings negotiate with their individuality which is very closely related to the beliefs these individuals hold regarding the satisfaction of their needs and desires (Dunn 2008). Quoting Henri Lefebvre at this point seems worthwhile:

> Without the experience of need and want, without actual or potential pri-
> vation and destitution, there can be no being – consciousness, and free-
> dom will never spring forth. In the land of its birth – 'nature' and the
> unconscious – being remains a prisoner. It is in and through need that
> freedom is born and finds ways of acting, and if it is to modify the real,
> there is a fissure in its hard surface which it must discover and penetrate.
> Finally, need defined as want is the starting point from which man begins
> to explore a world of possibilities, creating them, choosing between them
> and making them real (Lefebvre 2002, pp. 5-6)

In pre-capitalist societies, it was the use-value of the commodity – the material
usefulness of the commodity – which facilitated the exchange of the commodity
(Hudis 2012). This relationship under capitalism gets perpetrated by abstract
exchange value (Hudis 2012, p. 7), which becomes the foundation of capitalist
society itself creating as Marx notes in *The German Ideology* new needs and
desires. In the EPM, Marx says, 'Man produces even when he is free from physical
need and only truly produces in freedom therefrom' (Marx 1844, p. 276). The
physical needs that Marx was talking about are the needs of individual human
sustenance – food, shelter, clothing, etc. These needs are often labelled as natural needs or needs of sustenance as they are critical to human life as we know
it. Most of the needs today are reduced to their bio-psychological nature, which
is appropriated, and are more often than not, created by capitalism (Heller 2018,
p. 26). The forces of capitalism render invisible the social content of these needs
and instead transform them into basic survival needs. Heller argues that the category of natural and social needs appears differently in various writings of Marx.
The Marx of *Capital* defined 'natural needs' in accordance with the views on
'labour power' which as he described were to be determined by the overall value
of the life-sustaining resources of life that an average worker needs:

> (Man's) natural needs, such as food, clothing, fuel, and housing, vary
> according to the climatic and other physical conditions of his country. On
> the other hand, the number and extent of his so-called necessary needs, as
> also the modes of satisfying them, are themselves the products of history,
> and depend therefore to a great extent on the level of civilisation attained
> by a country; in particular they depend on the conditions in which, and
> consequently on the habits and expectations with which, the class of free
> workers has been formed. In contrast, therefore, with the case of other
> commodities, the determination of the value of labour -power contains a
> historical and moral element (Marx 1976, p. 275)

Marx in the *Grundrisse* talked further about social needs, which are needs created
and sustained through the historical progress of the mode of production. Marx,
here, does not posit commodities arising from needs but rather needs from commodities. The centrality of commodities and their associated fetishism has been
engaged in detail in the previous chapter. This chapter will progress further from
then. One of the pivotal notions of Dunayevskaya (1965) was that Marx posited

his theories based on the centrality of commodities right at the core of capitalism – the point of production. Social needs are the ones that capitalism focuses on in its course of development which is critical to the way it poses money capital and commodity capital's importance in society. There are two quotes from Marx which are worth reproducing at this point:

> When the aim of labour is not a particular product standing in a particular relation to the particular needs of the individual, but money, wealth in its general form, then, firstly, the individual's industriousness knows no bounds; it is indifferent to its particularity, and takes on every form which serves the purpose; it is ingenious in the creation of new objects for a social need, etc. (Marx 1973, p. 224)

> ...needs are produced just as are products and the different kinds of work skills. Increases and decreases do take place within the limits set by these needs and necessary labours. The greater the extent to which historic needs – needs created by production itself, social needs -needs which are themselves the offspring of social production and intercourse, are posited as necessary, the higher the level to which real [capitalist social] wealth has become developed (Marx 1973, p. 527)

Heller (2018) later argues that along with 'Natural' and 'Social' Needs, one can also find within Marx other categories of needs such as 'Necessary' Needs, 'Physical' Needs, etc. An elaborate discussion on all of these categories is beyond the scope of the current work. With the development of capitalism, as Heller (2018) rightly argues, every need gets reduced to mere physical needs which can be fulfilled only under the alienation that capitalism perpetuates throughout society. This causes the basis for the domination of private property in the society where possession becomes the sole desirable outcome of any need-fulfilment process. The category of 'Natural Needs' also undergoes considerable changes from the *Grundrisse* to *Capital*. In *Grundrisse*, as Heller (2018, p. 29), there is a similarity between natural and necessary needs. In *Capital*, however, she notes that Marx emphasised this difference so as to put forward that life cannot be led only by the fulfilment of natural needs such as hunger, sleep, sex, etc. Heller (2018, pp. 29-30) argues that the necessary needs in *Capital* are:

> not dictated by mere survival; the cultural element in such needs, the moral element and custom, are decisive, and their satisfaction is an organic part of the "normal" life of people belonging to a particular class in a given society. The quantum which we refer to as the "necessary articles or means of survival" at a given time or for a given class serves to satisfy vital needs and "necessary needs" (Heller 2018, p. 29)

Heller (2018, p. 21) critically appreciates Marx because of the concept of need playing the role of a hidden prime mover in his writings, but also critiques him for never formulating that as a prominent concept *per se*: 'Marx's categories of need ... are *not* as a whole economic category. He tends to treat concepts of need as non-economic categories, as historical-philosophical, that is as anthropological value categories, and therefore as not subject to the definition within the economic system' (Heller 2018, p. 24). Heller's general argument can be summed up in the following way:

> It is bourgeois society that subordinates the human senses to "crude, practical needs" and makes them "abstract" by reducing them to mere needs of survival. For this reason, needs aimed merely at survival cannot form a general historical-philosophical group of needs which is independent. Later, as a consequence of the economic point of view, a classification [between natural and socially produced needs] becomes necessary. ... the economic point of view is an explanation of the origin of surplus labour and surplus value and of the possibility of their existence. But it is also motivated by the *status quo* in capitalist society as the point of departure of Marxist analysis, and by the discovery of exploitation as a leading motive in the critique of capitalism (Heller 2018, pp. 25-6)

Social needs stem from the actually existing material conditions that capitalism creates in society (Heller 2018). The need to engage in social media commerce among the working class also is a manifestation of this concrete reality created by capitalism, which leaves the working class vulnerable to the byproducts of capitalist development in the fields of production, digital media and means of communication. Engaging in commercial activities through social media is significantly different from other digital e-commerce platforms like Amazon or eBay because social media commerce is a site of the direct exploitation of communicative and social media labour where the combined labour of users is exploited in creating the symbolism associated with the technology (Fuchs 2015; Hardt and Negri 2000). While for Amazon or eBay-operated marketplaces, the communication follows the actual exchange, for FM, it is communication itself that facilitates the exchange. Communication here, as Fuchs (2015) has highlighted, becomes a material force of exploitation within society. The desire to use communication as a material tool of accumulation has contributed to social media commerce emerging as a popular tool for digital commerce among common people. Though there is a dependency on the kind of commodity offered for sale, there is a general consensus about social media being the first place to look for the desired commodity among the people in the Global North (Deb Roy 2020). This popularity becomes exceptionally high in the case of used commodities, for two reasons: the lower price of the commodity, and the ease of trading.

The major difference between established e-commerce websites and social media commerce is that while in the case of e-commerce sites like Amazon, it is the economic structure in its entirety that more often than not determines the price of the product or the commodity on sale, but in the case of social media commerce, price is determined by a coalition of various factors such as the state of social crisis and the personal need of the seller. Needs, as Marx (1973) pointed out, can be both natural and socially produced. Capitalism depends on the latter more than the former to produce surplus value. It is within the paradigm of the latter where it can produce consumerism which hinges upon an everlasting state of continuously evolving needs, which is a significant driving force behind the proliferation of commercial activities through social media in the hope of generating some individual monetary capital, even if temporarily. These needs are crucial for capitalism because as O'Connor (1984) argues, the needs of the working class determine the demand for consumer goods, and if the demand for consumer goods increases, also the value composition of capital itself increases (O'Connor 1984, p. 157). Social media commerce caters to the process of satisfying this growing demand for consumer goods by temporarily allowing the working class to control some amount of the exchange value of the commodity. The challenge for social science today is thus to come out with a holistic understanding of the term accumulation itself and the process in which it is being performed in the information society. It is something, which cannot be done unless one takes into account communication within the larger gambit of social processes, especially communication through digital means and the relationship that this form of communication shares with its non-digital predecessors.

Social media has been particularly useful to middle-class women. In India, there have erupted a host of different 'Pages' and 'Accounts', which cater to a certain section of the populace – the women. In the case of men, however, this tendency is still quite limited. The proliferation of entrepreneurs in the garment and jewellery sector has been a very interesting process. There are today an increasing number of women who are engaging their time in doing commercial activities on social media. Some of the commodities which are mostly sold by them include sarees (a traditional Indian garment) and other associated clothing, jewellery, etc. Many of these women, at least among those with whom the author had conversations, were married women. An increasing number of these women confirmed that without the presence of social media they would not have turned into businesswomen. For these women, being a businesswoman, even if that is in a virtual medium, provides them with a certain agency and autonomy. These women, many of whom come from the middle classes and the upper-middle classes in India, see social media as a site where they can exercise and assert their identities as citizens and active producers. Social media commerce attempts to solve the problem of women's agency in contemporary society by using the marketplace. In doing so it tends to forget that it is the market and capitalism itself which was the basis of the problem something that early predecessors of the socialist tradition understood (Deb Roy 2020). However, the solutions posed in this regard through social media commerce, as one can easily understand, remain highly bourgeoisie in form and content as Tiersten (2001) shows us in her book about French consumer culture and the role of women in it. Consumer culture possesses an ability to lure women into it because it makes them empowered in comparison to the situation they find themselves in every day under contemporary conditions of capitalism and patriarchy. It allows them to move away from the confines of home and its moral structures and work with other aspects of their personality (Tiersten 2001).

Capitalism always allows the working class to enjoy a brief moment of affluence before it begins its drive to 'squeeze them dry'. Capitalism which allows women, especially the bourgeoisie women, to articulate their freedom within a paradigm informed by its desires for further profit accumulation, uses social media commerce to further worsen the condition of women in society. It operates on a basis that takes the economic aspect as the only attribute of women's autonomy and independent existence in society (Lysack 2008). In other words, the economic agency is posed as a solution to problems, which are much larger than any constricted domain of study can provide solutions for. Capitalism uses social media commerce by posing it as a viable alternative to the requirement of jobs and work for women. So, while there is a continuous reduction in jobs and employment, there is at the same time, a further popularisation of social media commerce. Amidst all this, the basic question of employment, jobs and the creation of new avenues for providing women with the opportunity for struggling toward true human emancipation is lost. As Marcuse (1941) would say, every other thing gets subsumed under the rationality that capitalism wants the oppressed masses to adhere to, and willingly. Most of the women engaged in social media commerce running their own personal brands, take help from the members of their family, including their husbands and fathers. There are instances where it is the husband who actually owns the business, but it is the wife who merely manages it. There are broader issues of unpaid labour which take place in these circumstances, which are beyond the scope of the current work. These sellers can control the exchange value and prices of the commodities they sell, to a certain extent provided they could satisfactorily negotiate their terms with the merchants who sold them the commodity in the first place. It is worthwhile to mention in this regard that a lot of such businesses are not petty production units but are rather distribution units. Simply speaking, most of these sellers buy commodities from one place and then distribute them through their networks. Running their businesses allows these women to negotiate with their patriarchal social settings, gain financial autonomy to a certain extent, and also fulfil their own desires as active consumers.

It cannot be denied that the women engaging in social media commerce thinking that it is their 'own little business', are at risk of becoming commodities themselves every day (Lysack 2008), provided that social media is a space that is in itself a part and parcel of the social patriarchy that exists unilaterally in both the Global North and the Global South. That capitalism can manipulate these women into disregarding such risks and accepting social media as an emancipatory force proves the ideological nature of contemporary capitalism, working through the creation of universal consumerism and an all-encompassing commodification, which in turn, keeps on replenishing the old needs while at the same time, creating new needs within the society, which can only be satisfied by monetary capital. This entire process of the creation of new needs within society leads to the analysis of the production of new modes of consumption (Harvey 2006, p. 8) and takes one back to Marx's statement about money being the alien essence that dominates and subsumes human existence (Marx 1844, p. 172). As Marx (1973, p. 408) mentions, the production of new consumption can only be produced through three distinct methods, 'firstly quantitative expansion of existing consumption; secondly: the creation of new needs by propagating the existing ones in a wide circle; thirdly: production of new needs and discovery and creation of new use values' (Marx 1973, p. 408). Social media commerce allows capitalism to give vent to the above-mentioned processes. It gives the working class access to a certain amount of capital, the usage of which depends upon external factors beyond their own control. The constant creation of new needs, either out of crisis or out of the consumerist nature of capitalist society, enables social media commerce to be a vital aspect of capitalist accumulation because it temporarily counters low wages in the economy, which cannot be mediated through normal e-commerce websites like Amazon where the relations between the value and the price of a commodity are more rigidly established.

Marx (1976, p. 505) argues in the section on machinery and large-scale production that a change in one mode of production necessitates the subsequent change in other modes of production. These are modes of production that are segregated by the division of labour existing in the society where they are meant to be producing different independent commodities for capitalism. But, even if the commodities they produced were distinct, they were all 'separate phases of a process' – the process of capitalist commodity production and accumulation through the generation of consumption. The changes in one segment set the process in motion for a complete reorganisation of the 'social processes of production' (Marx 1976, p. 506). Marx evaluated the means of communication and the means of transportation as the social processes of production. These means are connected to other factors such as circulation, the time associated with it, consumption, etc., all of which feature prominently in the second and third volumes of *Capital*. The critical part of understanding Marx and his critique of the overall system of capitalism needs to be based upon the dialectical understanding of all these components in relation to the capitalist whole.

In the second volume of *Capital*, Marx argues that the 'product of the production process is not a new objective product' in the cases of the communication and information industry (Marx 1992, p. 134). Marx's reasoning for the same was related to the manner in which commodities were transported and the way in which the 'place of production' plays a role in altering the exchange value of certain commodities, and the role that transportation industries played in the process (Marx 1992, pp. 134-36). In these cases, the exchange value and price of the commodity are based on the production process itself, the value of which is at times, consumed directly resulting in the increase or decrease of its price. In other words, in the cases of the means of communication, interpreted most explicitly as the means of transportation in Marx, the final product's increased exchange value is not a result of modifications in its material properties 'for it is the production process itself, and not a product separable from it, that is paid for and consumed' (Marx 1992, p. 135). Needs under capitalism, also entrench within themselves the possibility of creating surplus-value, especially in situations like those in consumer societies where society produces much more than the requisite amount sufficient to satisfy the 'vital needs' of the society (Heller 2018, pp. 21-2).

Social media commerce uses human beings as actually existing means of communication in the production process. Human beings play the role of increasing the value of a commodity through their impact on the circulation of these commodities. This process is most easily observed in the way in which comics are sold on social media. The rarer it is, the more costly it is. Rarity is determined, on the other hand, by how rarely individuals had bought that commodity when it first appeared, or was abundantly available, in the market. In other words, a subjective human decision taken in a certain context becomes the basis of capitalist value creation – *only maybe 10 or 20 years later*. With social media, an increasing number of sellers have erupted on various social media platforms. While from a left-wing point of view, this might seem like an improvement from the conditions of monopoly. But, in reality, this is one of the worst aspects of capitalist markets. The huge influx of sellers who are engaging with selling their old comics or other forms of art on social media have no idea regarding the pricing mechanism of old and rare comics. Of course, the pricing mechanism, usually followed in the west, is an exploitative one, but there still is a logic – though capitalist – behind it. In the Global North, sellers on social media follow the pricing guidelines to some extent, but in the global South, there is no such resource to fall back on. Social media has created a market, where pieces of art such as comic books are listed with indiscriminate prices on Facebook and Twitter. An increasing number of small businesses engaging with comic books also use WhatsApp to further their business, by creating dedicated groups focused on a particular publisher, a particular city, etc. As part of the research for the current project, the author became a part of some groups created on WhatsApp by various sellers. A lot of discussion on these groups revolved around what Walter Benjamin (1936/1968, p. 221) would have referred to as the aura of the piece of art, which gets destroyed once it undergoes mechanical reproduction under capitalism. Customers' requests for old reprints are valorised and an entire production mechanism is built up based on these requests.

The sellers use these groups to not only build their customer base but also to actively engage in dialogues with their existing customers. With improving payment techniques such as the *Vyapar App*, which have made it extremely easy for people to set up small e-commerce platforms, these groups, have become active hubs of commercial trading in such niche commodities. Commodities such as comics, which enjoy relatively lesser reproduction materially become privy to manipulations of value based on their 'aura' more often than not. It is here that it becomes imperative for capitalism to use, not only the industrial means of production but also the social processes of production to further the domination of value in society. Baudrillard (1970) provides a useful explanation in that regard when he argues that objects today are not produced and presented to the consumers alone but rather are done so within an overall system of objects, whereby the total system assumes a use-value that is peculiar and far greater in utility than the individual object. This is performed through the proliferation of brand culture and advertising methods as Baudrillard (1970) argues. This all becomes possible in a situation when there are too many commodities, or objects in the language of Baudrillard, around. Quoting Baudrillard:

There is all around us today, a kind of fantastic conspicuousness of consumption and abundance, constituted by the multiplication of objects, services and material goods, and this represents something of a fundamental mutation in the ecology of the human species. Strictly speaking, the humans of the age of affluence are surrounded by not so much by other human beings, as they were in all previous ages, but by *objects*. (Baudrillard 1970, p. 25)

Social media makes these objects much more visible than they were a decade ago. Capital's usage of the social and digital means of productive communication to further its own agenda of accumulation results in the creation of the process in which innovations become an active part of the process of capitalist accumulation. They are not only instruments that are the results of capitalist production, but also instruments that result in further capitalist production, and accumulation. In doing so, capitalism affects the existing condition of needs in society. According to Marx:

Capital's ceaseless striving towards the general form of wealth drives labour beyond the limits of its natural paltriness, and thus creates the material elements for the development of the rich individuality which is all-sided in its production as in consumption and whose labour also therefore appears no longer as labour but as the full development of activity itself in which natural necessity in its direct form has disappeared; because a historically created need has taken the place of the natural one (Marx 1973, p. 325)

Agnes Heller (2018) argues that the most critical element of Marx's classification of needs is their division on the basis of their objectification referring to how and through which objects they come to be satisfied under contemporary modernity. This also encompasses the feelings of joy, despair, and other such emotions of satisfaction, which might be evoked within the individuals. There are two major kinds of needs, natural and socially produced. Natural needs correspond to the biological requirements of the individual's sustenance and self-preservation, while social needs correspond to the needs which are generated by society (Heller 2018). They are related to the existent status quo within the society, as well as to the idea of enrichment of the individual. Human life as we know it today does not only sustain because of its purely physical biological needs but needs attributed to human life by society play an important role as well. Certain spiritual and immaterial needs act in addition to material needs and create conditions of enrichment for human beings. The basic foundation of capitalism is that it creates a situation where the activity of even enriching oneself becomes a part of the capitalist accumulation process (Boltanski and Esquerre 2020).

Under consumer capitalism, the emphasis is not so much on needs as they are on desires. It is infested with the idea of a multiplicity of desires, which are susceptible to being satisfied with commodities, providing happiness and gratification (Bauman 2007). Lefebvre was one of the first Marxists to work towards distinguishing 'desire' from 'needs' in a way that focuses upon their role within the overall social consciousness, i.e., in the construction of the *total man* and 'Man appropriates his integral essence in an integral way, as a total man' (Marx 1844a/1975, p. 351). He does so by working along the lines in which Marx (1973) defines the distinction between natural and socially produced needs. One of the first distinctions that Lefebvre makes while talking and discussing needs in society is between 'needs in general' and 'need for this or for that'. Specific Needs are those needs that are touted to be potentially resolved by some commodity available in the market controlled by forces of capital. The human consciousness creates and sustains 'needs'. These needs are generic in nature, as Lefebvre (2002, p. 7) puts forward, simplistically determined quantitatively. 'Desires' on the other hand, bridge the gap between individual and the social and are mainly determined socially through a commodity of one kind or another. Dunn (2008, p. 12) argues that needs should be understood as those which are required for survival, while desires are something that is related to the broader social and individual processes such as appetite, passion, longing, etc. This kind of theorisation often resorts to classifying needs as something quantitative while desires being of a qualitative nature.

Lefebvre, however, labelled this kind of classification overtly simplistic in nature. He argued that needs and desires cannot be classified in the sense that one is psycho-social and the other as biological or physiological (Lefebvre 2002, p. 8). Lefebvre argues that there are 'needs' that can be 'desire-like' and 'desires' that can be 'need-like'. Lefebvre proposes a dialectical distinction: 'A single human reality appears with two faces, one brutally objective – social need (for this or for that), the other subtly subjective – desire (for this or for that or for something else by means of this or that, or even for nothing or for the infinite or for a pure surprise), with motivations which give meaning to the desired object and to desire itself' (Lefebvre 2002, p. 8). The process of the formation of a desire has to be mediated in a manner that is accepted within the broader contours of the social contract, which is in place in the society, in addition to the commodities with the potential to satisfy those desires already existent in the society (Lefebvre 2002). The existing culture, value systems, shared and collective history, social aspirations, etc contribute to the mediations between the conceptual categories of 'needs' and 'desires'. The dialectical tension between needs and desires is summed up by Lefebvre in the following manner:

> a) Desire is profoundly different from need. It can even go so far as to struggle against it, until it frees itself; b) Initially, however, there is no desire without a need as its nucleus, its point of departure, its base of 'foundation'. A desire without need can only be purely artificial, an extreme case which even the most subtly refined moral or aesthetic values or artificial modes of behaviour find difficult to create, c) Sooner or later desire turns back towards need in order to regain it and to regain itself. By reinvesting itself within it, it rediscovers spontaneity and vitality. It is a return journey which crosses through the objectivity, impersonality

and indifference of social needs, as it is conveniently understood (Lefebvre 2002, p. 10)

For Henri Lefebvre, it is this struggle between needs and desires that gives the dialectical sense to everyday life. 'Desires' desire to alienate the human existence from its intrinsic essence, by rendering the uncertainty of fulfilment of any and all potential desires as the ultimate truth of life. However, this uncertainty is in itself a part of the pattern under capitalism's technological rationality (Marcuse 1941), whereby individuals come to like or even admire, this uncertainty. This remains one of the fundamental propositions that Bauman (2000) makes. Contemporary capitalism creates a rupture between 'needs' and authentic 'desires' through the domination and fetishism of commodities in the society that Marx (1976) and Dunayevskaya (1965) considered to be the absolutely fundamental aspect of capitalist society. Commodities work to alienate and *motivate* human beings as 'concrete motivations' so that 'Desires no longer correspond to genuine needs; they are artificial. Needs no longer get modified into desires automatically and "The process becomes complicated, or disintegrates"' (Lefebvre 2002, p. 11). However, in spite of that, the process does not disappear and continues to manifest itself in various forms between the domains of essentiality and sociality as Lefebvre informs us so eloquently. Lefebvre argues that the 'system of needs', which had assumed a significance of utmost value within Hegelian theories no longer holds the prominence it once did within the everyday lived reality of human sustenance. The colonisation of our everyday life and the all-encompassing nature of capitalist alienation by the sustained promotion of consumerism, rapid technological innovation and mass consumption (Debord 1968; Lefebvre 2002) has created a scenario where the first task remains to rescue 'needs' from 'desires' and then the rescued 'needs' again from 'needs' again.

Needs and desires are a component of the overall value system under any social structure. Baudrillard argues that objects are signs entrenched within a code of 'significatory value that can be manipulated between the two registers of functionality and ostentation' which places Baudrillard into a relationship with Veblen's conspicuous consumption (Dant 1996, p. 504). Under capitalism, these signs that the object represents become the symbols of status within the society. Veblen (1899/2007) theorised this process through the theory of 'conspicuous consumption' based on how the affluent classes emphasise the aspect of flaunting the commodities they possess. He argued that since commodities cost money, their possession becomes a symbol of one's honour and status in society. Veblen's leisure class, which is infested with the desire for conspicuous spending, creates a structure of emulation in the society, whereby the ideals and morality possessed by the classes at the highest echelons of the society trickle down to the lowest levels. Capitalism progresses in a manner in which newer commodities become commonplace every day. Individuals take to consumerism and buying as means to get integrated into society by showing off their possessions. In other words, as Bauman (2007) argues, and as the current book has narrated in the context of the women entrepreneurs on social media, being a consumer becomes an effective way of asserting social belongingness. In situations such as these, the accumulation of private wealth becomes a social goal scattered uniformly across the society through the commodification of conspicuous leisure (Mason 1981). Commodities in this situation are valued both because of their functionality and their ostentatiousness because both these qualities play a role in making the old object, now rendered useless or 'temporarily out of use', replaceable by a newer or an advanced version, merge 'pure gratuitousness under a cover of functionality, pure waste under a cover of practicality' (Baudrillard 1981, p. 32). It is futile to expect that technological innovation would not produce any kind of refuse, although this statement can be scrutinised and critiqued by the many proponents of 'green science'. The waste or refuse of innovation can, however, be both physical and ideological. The complete exhaustion of the 'repair' generation, in both the west and the east, by the 'replace' generation is a testimony to the way in which technological innovation and new inventions can fundamentally alter the basic way in which individuals interpret the commodities they possess. The cheap price of smartphones is a case in point in this regard. Fuelled by the repressive labour management structures in China, manufacturing companies and Industrial capitalists have found it extremely easy to manufacture new products on a large scale, which are then marketed as upgraded products and status symbols. However, at the same time, this continuous expansion of production mechanisms, which is a natural desire of all capitalist production structures, also creates certain problems: 'We know how much the affluence of rich societies is linked to waste, given all the talk of a 'throwaway society' and the fact that some have even envisaged a 'garbage-can sociology': 'Tell me what you throw away and I'll tell you who are you' (Baudrillard 1970, p. 42).

Social Media commerce operates within these contours. It provides the users with avenues to dispose of their 'material wealth' in exchange for the remaining 'use value' of the object in question. Social media commerce exploits, in most cases, the system in which various objects and consumer goods are created within capitalism. Baudrillard (1981, p. 55) takes the example of television to make further explorations into the topic. According to him, the commodity of the television, located within the socio-economic reality of capitalism, is a scarce one for many people struggling to make ends meet which transforms the commodity into a 'pure fetish' (Baudrillard 1981, p. 55) while for some others it is merely just another object. The television, in other words, makes sense, as a commodity or a fetish, only when it is analysed in relation to other objects. For Baudrillard (1968, 1981), everything that one finds within a system (our homes can be categorised as one for instance) '... finds meaning with other objects, in difference according to a hierarchical code of significations' (Baudrillard 1981, p. 64). Baudrillard (1981, p. 85) argues that consumer needs for such objects under contemporary capitalism are generated through a 'strategy of desire' which creates an ideological impact on the social system thriving on an exchange of signs. He proposes the concept of 'consummativity' as a juxtapositioned idea to the orthodox Marxist concept of productivity (Baudrillard 1981, p. 83). Consummativity is a theory that proposes that the system of needs, including the need to have a choice, is imposed upon the individual consumers. As Dant (1996, p. 505) writes, 'Needs cannot be derived from a humanistic notion of the free, unalienated, a social individual driven by craving or pleasure or even by some essential needs'.

Needs, according to Marx change over time (Marx 1847). Social media today under capitalism has become a generator of new needs in society which it accomplishes through creating networks of users who interact with each other creating new needs among others by working upon human feelings. The system of needs in society is dependent on the way in which the social division of labour is structured in the society, which also finally affects the accumulation of capital (Perelman 1981) – the final goal of all forms of capitalist social structures. Marx's (1847) conception surrounding needs is very similar to that of Hegel's (1820), who also insisted on the continuous multiplication of needs being a fundamental part of the expression of human universality and the human transcendence of the natural restrictions on other animals (Lebowitz 2003). Lebowitz (2003) asserts the centrality of the production system in his discussion of needs as well, following Marx (1847), but to him, it is not only capitalist production but also capitalist circulation, which becomes critical in establishing the system of needs in the society. Lebowitz's arguments are valued ones precisely because he establishes the importance of circulation and consumption without resorting to completely obscuring the role of production in the process like Boltanski and Chiapello (2005, p. 369) who argue that 'Firms have sought to achieve a level of mobility tailored to the supposed volatility of consumer desires. ... They produce exactly what consumers want when *they* want it'. Lebowitz (2003) argues that it is capitalism's desire to accumulate endlessly on an expanded scale that makes it imperative for capitalism to innovate in the realm of circulation by finding newer avenues for the creation of markets to destroy the barriers to further production, in the process creating new needs and new use-values. Under advanced and more exploitative forms of capitalism, most of these new needs remain unfulfilled for a large section of the populace. The inability of the society to render its members capable of fulfilling their needs is contingent upon the social system within which the individual with the need is structured into. The system of needs is contingent upon the way in which the productive capacities and processes of the society are constituted (Marx 1847, p. 119). Needs are manufactured through a complex network of technological innovation, capital's rising desire to accumulate profits and the socio-political reality. Under market and consumer capitalism: 'Wealth is concentrated in huge multinational enterprises. Resources are badly allocated and income unequally distributed. Within the market's sway, larger or lesser groups of people lack the resources to translate some of their basic needs into "effective demand"' (Heller 2018, p. 12). Social media commerce allows them to fulfil some of their basic social needs, but at the cost of constantly reproducing newer social needs.

Whether a commodity will satisfy a social need depends upon the social properties that the commodity possesses, and rarely on its intrinsic needs as Marx had described being the basic character of any commodity under capitalism (Lebowitz 2003; Marx 1976). Social needs are often mediated and expressed through desires (Lefebvre 2002). New desires proliferate in direct proportion to the fulfilment of previous desires within social media commerce. Technologies play a major role in this regard. The constant innovation and the constant generation of new needs play a role in the creation of the basis upon which capitalist society is built (Marx 1844). For Baudrillard (1981), the exchange of the symbolic value for the sign that a commodity possesses is one of the major characteristics of contemporary capitalist modernity. As has been noted in the previous chapter, Appadurai (1986), in a roundabout way, also agrees tangentially at this point. Sometimes, commodities are priced in accordance with their spatiality as Marx (1992, p. 135) had predicted. When it happens, the means of transportation and communication itself become the production process, through which they produce new values. Even though Baudrillard's account does not take into account the historical analysis of commodities under capitalism, his accounts do provide certain interesting arguments, such as his emphasis on objects making 'sense' within a system of objects (Baudrillard 1968). As Kellner (1989) argues, Baudrillard's theory is basically based upon 'the framework of a subject-object dialectic in which the subject faces a world of objects which attract, fascinate and sometimes control his or her perception, thought and behaviour' (p. 8). Following on from other theorists such as Lefebvre (1991a, 1991b), Baudrillard (1968) provides a theoretical excursion into the ways in which commodities penetrate into the everyday lives of individuals. Attributes such as colour, form, and style create newer modes of living for human individuals (Kellner 1989, p. 10). Commodity fetishism targets the human desire for worshipping this system of differences that are entrenched within various commodities. It dwells in the ideological sensuality that the object comes to represent to the individual consumer alienated by the capitalist social system.

The capitalist bourgeois society 'has its own way of manipulating the needs arising out of a specific stage of civilisation' (Lefebvre 1991, p. 33). Like consciousness, needs are also a definite part of the process in which social reality shapes human beings who experience the social reality on an everyday basis. Needs within capitalism are primarily based around the idea of a good life – not a satisfying life, but a good life. It is about what can make one happy, rather than what 'will' actually a person happy (Segal 2017). If one goes back to how Lefebvre (1991, p. 51) looks at this, one gets the idea that people today want to move beyond insecurities and poverty in their lives. In other words, as he argues, they want to bring some 'solidity' into their lives through achieving some form of material security. Under contemporary capitalism, money exists as a 'fetish' that has its own identity independent of the actual subject possessing it. It has achieved an autonomous existence, something which has been critiqued by Marx heavily all throughout his works, especially in his three volumes of *Capital*. However, reductionist political economy has the tendency to focus on only this particular aspect of contemporary capitalism (Lefebvre 1991, p. 58), in other words, in spite of their Marxist claims, they fail to realise that: The whole point, however, is that Marx ... did not confine himself to 'economic theory' in the ordinary sense of the term, that, while explaining the structure and the development of the given formation of the society exclusively through production relations ... (he) clothed the skeleton in flesh and blood' (Lefebvre 1991, p. 3).

Contemporary capitalism engages fundamentally with 'concrete' needs of human beings. Capitalism uses everything in its repertoire to generate these 'precise' and 'concrete' needs, which can be satisfied by the purchase of certain commodities. Often, these needs are satisfied by-products already in existence, but sometimes, these needs pave the path for new needs as Marx notes in his *Grundrisse* and *The German Ideology*. The specificity of these needs and the precise nature of the goods which satisfy them is dictated by capitalism as a life that is located within a certain mould of bourgeoisie tangibility dominated by a consciousness that reinforces the ideological justification of a society created by private property but '... the apparently clear concept of satisfaction and of the fulfilment of a need – the need for *this* or *that* – is in reality very obscure' (Lefebvre 2002, p. 6). Classical Economists, conventional empirical sociologists and uncritical Marketing professionals often, and unsurprisingly, talk of needs in reference to certain commodities. They reduce an expression of human sustenance to a certain commodity that finds its place in the market because of the demand that is there for it. For Marxists, as Lefebvre (2002) argues, the primary issue is to analyse the transformation of the *need in general* which is a manifestation of human existence to the specific needs' category. For this he says:

> We will have to bring together an analytic presentation of needs and a dialectical determination of desires. If we are to arrive at a theory of the situations (concrete, of course) of social man, we must not lose track of the generic or general concept of man as 'being of need' when confronting the mass of contemporary facts (Lefebvre 2002, p. 7)

Human consumption and its associated processes are a complex network of social and individual relationships that shape and get shaped by the existing reality. It has numerous symbolic dimensions which makes it abnormally difficult to reduce these processes to some form of the absolute basis of determination that stands true for all (Soper 2020). However, this diversity is something that capitalism does not like which it tries to dismantle through the generation of needs in the society that are directly related to the immense number of commodities that it produces. Baudrillard (1970, 1972) argues that 'the entire system of production produces a system of needs that are rationalised, homogenised, systematised and hierarchised' (Kellner 1989, p. 15). The consumer does not buy a single commodity, but rather the consumer buys into a (commodity through which one is inducted into the) total system of commodities – this becomes the basis upon which the consumer constructs individuality and integration into the (consumer) society (Kellner 1989). The distinction between the roles of consumers and citizens has been the subject of numerous debates historically which has also at times, resulted in the creation of hybrid identities such as citizen-consumers or consumer-citizens (Warde 2017, p. 17). Social media commerce enables the further integration of the individual within the consumer society. Consumer culture places consumerism as a path towards the realisation of one's individual self within a capitalist democracy's framework of pleasure and self-fulfilment (Dunn 2008).

In conventional media, a term is often invoked – 'entry point'. For people who are highly integrated into the Apple ecosystem of products or the Amazon ecosystem of services, it should be very easy to comprehend this point in real-life terms. In some ways, this is perhaps, the easiest and the messiest, the example of Adorno's (1973) theory of reification based on one's lived experience. There is always a distinction between buying these commodities – often status symbols – brand new and buying used ones. In the Global South, such commodities have a negligible chance of ending up on social media commerce because these commodities are accredited with inhuman importance within the individuals' lives, something that they possess and interpret as a symbol that marks their success in their lives. The used market for such commodities on social media proliferates in the Global North, where they are largely everyday items, where the fetishism associated with them has become an everyday feature of life under capitalism in the west. People have confirmed buying such commodities on social media, but at the same time, what they have also confirmed is their desire to somehow hide the fact that they have bought them on social media from their peers. An Asian person, with whom the author had had a very detailed conversation admitted to buying half the electronic items that he owns on social media, but he continues to hide the markers of the act because he believes that if people get to know about the place from where he got those, he will be labelled as 'another of those wanting to use the stuff without having the resources to get it'. The possession of commodities thus becomes the basis of the determination of one's status and prestige in society. Mason (1981, pp. 29-31) would argue that such behaviour – the act of buying a used high-end commodity and then camouflaging it as a brand new one – are the moves that an individual makes towards achieving a certain social consensus, acceptability in the society in addition to demonstrating the individual's impressive choice of consumption, which translates into social status and social acceptability.

The question of needs, desires, and their relationship has to be analysed today in relation to diverse philosophical and sociological viewpoints, some of which might be very economistic in nature, while some may be extremely culturalist in nature (Appadurai 1986; Althusser 2005). Based on their ideological ideas, these explanations might be very different, and even though the shared philosophical resources of multiple movements and their ideologies might pose no guaranteed 'black and white' political conclusions, the political and social responsibility and the revolutionary prospects of building alliances between different ideas and movements is a very important matter under contemporary capitalism and cannot be simply made to pass on (Benton 1993). Everyday lives, under capitalism, are 'doubly determined... at one and the same time as *unformed*, and as *what forms contain*' (Lefebvre 2002, p. 64) through an interconnected network of alienation, fetishism and reification which facilitate the transformation of needs into desires (Lefebvre 2002, p. 66). Under capitalism, commodities are no longer merely objects to satisfy human needs, but are artefacts that are precisely introduced into the society to negate any efforts towards generalising autonomous production -production meant only for the generation of use-values negating the capitalist domination of production for exchange values. As Gorz (1987) shows, the rule of capital is prolonged through the establishment of the complete use-lessness of autonomous production to the working class, either through cooperation or coercion.

Like being on social media is not an act born out of human sensations, consumption and buying things on social media are also not acts performed under a state of needing those, but rather are means through which individuals get integrated into society. Trading has today emerged as a new means of socialisation. In the Global South, individuals on social media resort to multiple techniques to garner new circles of influence which include sharing news, working as unpaid public relations 'managers' of their favourite celebrity, etc. In the Global North, such tendencies are much less prevalent. The consciousness of users differs based on the way they were integrated into the capitalist society, as well as the kind of capitalism they have experienced. But under all forms of contemporary capitalism, the 'spiritual' dimension of human activities, reminiscent of the pre-capitalist formations, become extinct (Benton 1993, p. 49). In its place, the world gets exposed to the dominating logic of the commodity market and the power of money, both as a medium of exchange and as capital. Money attempts to become the sole need of every individual such that:

> The need for money is therefore the true need produced by the economic system, and it is the only need which the latter produces. The *quantity* of money becomes to an ever greater degree its sole *effective* quality. Just as it reduces everything to its abstract form, so it reduces itself in the course of. its own movement to *quantitative* being. *Excess* and *intemperance* come to be its true norm. (Marx 1844, p. 307)

Needs always possess some sort of 'social' content imbided within themselves. This social nature of needs stems from their relationship with the division of labour in society which is responsible for the generation of the relationship between the individual's family interests from the individual's social interests. In other words, there is a mutual interdependence always at work in the society which has a bearing on the 'general interest' of the society (Marx and Engels 1845-46, p. 46), which makes the means which individuals adopt to satisfy those needs themselves social in nature (Marx 1973) – because the hunger satisfied with the help of a knife and fork is very different than what can be satisfied with raw meat:

> ... the object is not an object in general, but a specific object which must be consumed in a specific manner, to be mediated in its turn by production itself. Hunger is hunger, but the hunger gratified by cooked meat eaten with a knife and fork is a different hunger from that which bolt down raw meat with the aid of hand, nail and tooth. Production thus produces not only the object but also the manner of consumption, not only objectively but also subjectively (Marx 1973, p. 92)

Heller (2018, p. 27) argues that if one is to analyse needs as being structured within the society in relation to the social relations existing in the society, in totality, which would then imbibe even the natural needs with a certain social character. Even the satisfaction of natural needs cannot take place in a vacuum. The satisfaction of such needs such as hunger also has some culturally ordained modes. Similar is the case for other consumer needs, whereby the individual or the group 'in addition to a general culture' also reacts to other sub-cultures to which they belong or can somehow relate themselves (Mason 1981, pp. 20-1). Benton explains this by taking the example of the human need for the satisfaction of hunger through the consumption of food:

> The distorted, or pathological relation to food induced by starvation in humans is ... a specific distortion or pathology of *human* feeding activity ... the object of hunger exists merely as food, its sole significance is that its consumption will satisfy the hunger. ... This feeding activity is means/ends activity, not activity with its own intrinsic satisfaction (Benton 1973, p. 49)

Acts of consumption are cultural processes, as much as they are economic processes. Human beings consume certain products and reject certain products depending upon these two processes and the relationship between them. Something might be culturally very appropriate to consume but it might be economically unsustainable for certain sections of the population. The logic of consumption under capitalism is significantly towards obliterating the previously existing modes of social values, with a new system of social structuring. Baudrillard (1970) refers to this process as a process that generates a certain 'code' among the individuals in the society, which is different from other historically existing modal structures of values and morals. Old moral and ethical values also get abandoned at this point (Thompson 1963/2013, ch.4, 7). Social media plays a crucial role in the nexus of commodities becoming part of the everyday lives of people. Some commodities can be economically much more viable, but they are not culturally ingrained or accepted within society. Take the example of Beef in India – it is widely known that communities that are often at the bottom of the economic hierarchy have to consume beef to sustain themselves and fulfil their requirement for protein. However, the far-right in its recent political activities has actively turned towards violently repressing the right to consume beef in the country. So, even though India remains one of the highest exporters of beef in the world, there are few people within the country who can say that they can consume beef in peace. The paradox in this matter is that the 'public', which completely detests beef consumption, has no problem with the nation earning through its export – which effectively also means slaughtering. The dislike for beef, however, cannot be understood completely if one restricts oneself merely to beef as a commodity. As one can see, the general populace does not have a problem with it acting as a commodity from India in the global market, but rather it has a problem with it acting as one in India.

Similar conclusions can be drawn from the case of clothing as well. In New Zealand, the sale of clothing on social media is a decentralised affair. There are very few concentrated sellers on social media selling garments. Most of the people, who actually do so, engage in the trade of homespun clothing or knitted woollens. The cultural mode of consumption in the West plays a role in the way in which this market is structured. With longstanding segregations between common supermarket clothes and branded or boutique clothing, it would have been difficult to carve a market for commonly manufactured or distributed clothes – as has been the case in the East where social media sellers have taken over the task of the small-scale garment dealer. So, the trade in the West usually occurs within the used clothes section, albeit with its own racial connotations. Used clothes carry with them no markers of social status, but they do construct a mode of consumption in the society which points towards the human desire to consume, but within a framework acceptable to the society, just as Lefebvre (2002) argued. There are certain socially normative regulations that govern the existing mode of consumption of any commodity (Benton 1993, p. 50). These regulations also play a part in not only determining the individual modes and processes of consumption but also the distribution of these commodities of consumption within and beyond the community. This makes certain commodities culturally ingrained within certain communities, and then onto the 'imagined communities' that these communities form (Anderson 1997). Even if needs are simply biological or economical in nature, there is always embedded within them a social character that is often mediated by culture. This cultural mediation is indicative of the model or 'ideal' life one wants to lead under capitalism which is, as Soper (2020) argues, not only damaging to society and nature but is also lined with negative effects on the practising subject itself. Buying commodities for use, not because one wants them but because one wants to 'want them' is the new norm under capitalism. This characteristic of contemporary society produces numerous emotional factors which go on to play pivotal roles in how human beings witness and analyse society, as well as how they see other human beings. Human beings today, almost 'unquestionably accept the notion that ownership of particular luxury goods like diamond earrings [or the new iPad] is not the exclusive right of the upper classes' (Matt 2003, p. 3). Matt (2003) in the book 'Keeping up with the Joneses' provides a descriptive analysis of how and in what circumstances, both social and cultural, emotions such as envy and emulations become a part and parcel of everyday middle-class lives. The contribution of factors such as advertising, and forms of mass culture such as magazines and catalogues, also play a role in this regard. Modern human society does not detest envy or jealousy, instead, it thrives on the same. Consumer capitalism cannot survive if such emotional outbursts from people do not take place. The desire to upgrade, the desire to carry an Apple device, and other desires, create the fundamental conditions because which companies survive. Social media has made it easier for people to exhibit the various commodities they possess and use. In other words, flaunting possession has become an everyday use, which has, prefiguratively, made desires to possess luxury consumer goods more rampant in society.

Soper (2020) provides the framework of 'alternative hedonism' which takes into account the regrets that human beings share regarding the pleasures they can no longer enjoy in reality as well as the negative effects of the contemporary capitalistic way of affluent and 'good' living. Her fundamental thesis rests on the assumption that people today tend to show little tendency of reducing the commodities they shop for in spite of their way of life producing innumerable difficulties in their own lives, including those associated with over-work, degraded health conditions and deteriorating mental health of the society (Soper 2020). Commodity relations under contemporary capitalism are transformed into naturalised processes where they have replaced the natural relations that human beings share with other human beings and the environment around them (Soper 2020). This becomes particularly important in an economy mediated by digital means. Digital spaces are not natural spaces, but rather they are spaces that are dominated by a certain artificiality that obscures the real problem of cyberspace – the actual situation of the user in the actual social reality (Nunes 2006) – considering the fact that under contemporary capitalism the screen (even the computer monitor) becomes for the individual the real reflection of social reality which one seeks to reproduce in real life (Adorno 1991), including the exchange relations therein.

The consumer society, which breeds itself under contemporary capitalism, is dependent upon the human acceptability of the fact that spending is only natural as Shrestha (1997) notes. The integration of the 'Marketplace' tab on Facebook is thus a natural extension of the Facebook ecosystem itself. Digital spaces do not exist in a vacuum, rather they are part of the overall social structure in place – reflecting and reiterating the dominant values of the society. 'Needs' of the individuals, which get expressed through social media commerce in the digital space, thus should not be seen just as another character of the individual but should be analysed as parts of the capitalist reality itself (Baudrillard 1970). Marx separated himself from the economistic understanding of needs in 1844 itself as is evident from his ideas on alienation, naturalism and humanism. Individual needs cannot be seen as distinct from social needs if one is to go by how Marx articulated the concept of Individual and the social in the EPM. The end result of any kind of production, thus, must be the satisfaction of social needs which would necessarily also fulfil the individual needs. This constitutes one of the primary sites of struggle within social media commerce.

8. THE 'FULFILING' LIFE

The notion of freedom is a central element of Marxist analyses which is concretised through the progress of the history of capitalist development (Dunayevskaya 1965, p. 65). Freedom means a life without alienation. It refers to a life where life becomes, as Dunayevskaya (1958a, p. 10) says, 'the play of human faculties'. This freedom can be attained only if human beings understand and realise, consciously, the dialectical progress of history, whereby they realise their own potential as actually living actors capable of effecting change (Dunayevskaya 1973, p. 74). As she said: 'Man's true history does not begin until he is free, can develop all his innate talents, which class society, especially value-producing capitalism, throttles' (Dunayevskaya 1973, p. 74).

In a free society, the individual does not live for extrinsic social needs, but rather internalises the society within oneself and realises the true notion of individuality. Under contemporary capitalism, Individuals live their lives under a social system that by itself determines the needs, desires and aspirations of the individuals, promoting competition within the individuals of the society converting them into beings who are entrapped within a duality of 'permanent defence and aggression' (Marcuse 1966, p. 65). They live under a system that decides, without taking the concrete individual into account, their production processes, distributional mechanisms, consumption preferences, needs and desires (Marcuse 1966, pp. 65-6). Fully developed or advanced industrial production not only allows one the opportunity to satisfy the 'natural needs' of human beings but also aids in dissolving the distinction between natural and social needs (Heller 2018, p. 28-30). This dissolution creates the fertile ground for *Big Capital* to advertise and propagate non-essential technology and luxury goods in society. The struggle for a happy and fulfilling leads to the complete self-development of human beings, which capitalism provides to human beings only as an illusion in the form of possession of property and participation in exchange relations (Fromm 1942, 1961; Dunayevskaya 1958a, 1973; Lefebvre 1991b 2002). Capitalism poses 'money' as the solution to every problem faced by individuals in society. Capitalism not only stops at the production of new needs (Marx and Engels 1845-1846), but at the same time, it also turns money into a collective representation of social wealth such that money itself becomes the society (Marx 1973). The success of capitalism in propagating this view depends upon the extent to which it has successfully brought the workers under its control so as to make them receptive to its ideals, or as Marx explained:

> The ideas of the ruling class are in every epoch the ruling ideas: i.e., the class which is the ruling material force of society is at the same time its ruling *intellectual* force. The class which has the means of material pro-

duction at its disposal, consequently, also controls the means of mental production (Marx and Engels 1845-46, p. 59)

Capitalism continuously impoverishes the working class, a view that Marx had continued to hold dear to his thoughts (Marx 1844), while 'coercing' the worker to feel oblivious to the impoverishment and refuting the role of capitalism as a systemic structure in the continuing deterioration of living conditions for the working class. Social Media commerce utilises the labour of the working class to increase the total wealth at the disposal of capitalism. The cultural approval for the process is gained through the process of equating the benefit of the working class with that of capitalism in general. As Bauman (1988, pp. 61-2) illustrates, the market provides the individual with a certain social legitimacy by destroying hesitancies and insecurities in the process. The proliferation of trade and commerce in the 21st century, even at a personal level for individuals, stands testimony to the fact. Even though people have engaged in trade and commerce, even at a personal level, in the hope of earning money with a desire to create for themselves a 'fulfilling life', that desire is articulated within an alienated social reality. Dunayevskaya (1973, p. 5) argues that both the abolition of private property and the emancipation of 'creative human relationships' under capitalism have to go on together if the struggle is to reach a successful humanist and fulfilling life for everybody in contemporary society. These struggles have to pose an antithesis not only to the material accumulation of wealth by capitalism but also to the theoretical and ideological justifications of capitalist accumulation in society. Human relations under capitalism are perverted relationships formed out of false consciousness and because of false needs, where the human starts getting dominated and controlled by the production process.

The generation of consumerism in society is intimately related to capital's drive for accumulation. Capital's very purpose of existence is not to be spent, or be redistributed but rather, in its essence, is to be used for further accumulation of capital for a particular social class, the bourgeoisie. Marx (1976) had argued that capitalism allows commodities to be expressed as the magnitude of values of other things for this very purpose. Accumulation is an intrinsic part of the reproduction of capitalism. Accumulation enables capitalism to continuously reproduce itself through means which can be either external or internal to it or even be a combination of both. Social media commerce is a testimony to this. The idea surrounding the affluent society (Galbraith 1969) and the consumer society (Baudrillard 1970) are related ones. Without affluence, there cannot be consumerism and vice versa. However, the theorisation of societies in the global south in terms of affluence will surely raise some eyebrows with regards to how societies perpetually haunted by the horrors of colonisation, poverty, and other such evils can be categorised as being affluent. But what these ideas do not take into account is that, within a society such as India, there are multiple societies existing simultaneously. While one section of India suffers from poverty and hunger, there is also an urban India populated by a rising middle class and professional-managerial class, which enjoys considerable consuming prowess and mobility. Most social media users, both in the global north and in the global south are part of the affluent society, or at least they try to maintain a lifestyle that is akin to those in consumer societies. In the context of social media commerce, this is the section of the populace, which forms the base of the users and consumer base of these platforms. Goldthorpe and Lockwood (1968-69, quoted from Slater 1997, p. 12) perhaps put forward the relationship in the best way possible: 'The Consumer is the "Affluent Worker"'. The rise of consumerism is associated with some of the most important labels attributed to modernism in the west – freedom, individuality, the power to choose, etc. (Slater 1997). The expansion of the neoliberal market globally has provided a certain legitimacy to the belief that within capitalist markets, consumer choices are sovereign and autonomous, while in reality, they are, as Marx (1847) said, determined and dominated by the ways in which production is oriented in the society.

The sovereign consumer under capitalism is not a real individual but is rather part of a rigid patterning of individual subjectivities which conform to a fixed conceptual argument that justifies neoliberal ideologies such as consumerism and consumer sovereignty (Olsen 2019). The market functions as the agency providing the social legitimacy to the individual choices (Bauman 1988, p. 64) that the market itself creates for-profit accumulation by capital. The construction of the seemingly autonomous market and the free consumer therein requires, as Bauman (1988, p. 67) further says, a certain 'affluence' in terms of the number of commodities within the market. The machine in this case which often becomes the prime mover of heightened production systems, cannot be seen as something distinct from the capitalist mode of production designed specifically to increase productivity and exploit the labour-power of workers (Dunayevskaya 1958a, p. 94). Social media commerce operates within the society whereby the real inequalities in the society have no space in the symbolic construction of the virtual reality or 'spectral illusion' that it creates for its users as Žižek (2002) would have argued. The individuals are enticed into the market relations because of the seemingly autonomous ontology which they see within the space created by the market in such a way that eventually 'they depend on it for enjoying their freedom without paying the price of insecurity' (Bauman 1988, p. 62). The loss of decision making, the complete subjugation of the right of the individual to make choices for oneself is undermined in favour of planning towards getting engaged in preparatory, or coaching, courses for clearing the examinations for admissions into empowering institutions – professional or educational. In other words, typical to Horkheimer and Adorno's (2002, p. 117) arguments, 'chance and planning' become two identical parts of the same social process which emphasises the similarity between the competitors: 'Chance itself is planned; not in the sense that it will affect this or that particular individual but in that people believe in its control' (Horkheimer and Adorno 2002, p. 117). The denial of free will to human beings reduces them to mere commodities under capitalism represented only by their labour power (Adorno 1973). Adorno further argues '... the doctrine of free will which in the middle of the commodity society would abstract from the society. The individual himself forms a moment of commodity society: the pure spontaneity that is attributed to him is the spontaneity which society expropriates' (Adorno 1973, p. 264).

Free will under capitalism becomes a myth that exists in reality only for the elites. As Dunayevskaya (1973, p. 10) notes, dialectics should be analysed 'as a continuous process of self-development, a process of development through contradiction, through alienation, through double negation. It does not stop at the negation of mere bondage, but rather continues onwards to the complete realisation of freedom. If a fulfilling and unalienated life is to be established under capitalism, its articulation has to be along the lines of the development of the human species as being alive 'history from bondage to freedom' (Dunayevskaya 1973, p. 10), rooted in the historical development of capitalism and the workers therein. It is this historical development of capitalism that has created social media commerce, where individuals' lives are opened up to endless possibilities – all of which can only be satisfied by some or other commodity – in such a way that they get entwined further within the alienated society so that even the 'consciousness of alienation is largely repressed' (Marcuse 1966, p. 65). The seemingly prosperous nature of social media commerce in the sense that it allows the workers to get easy access to consumer goods, is merely an illusion of freedom. While the widespread dominant ideology might posit social media commerce to be an empowering factor in the lives of many who otherwise, would not have been having the commodities they can now possess, the reality remains that social media commerce is nothing but another manifestation of the problems created by capitalist production through its continuous desire for widespread accumulation. Social media commerce can result in a life of momentary alienated happiness, but it can never be the route towards a fulfilling life – the conceptualisation of which remains beyond the scope of bourgeois economics. The idea of a fulfilling life is something that classical economists fail to account for. It is very unlikely for classical economists to:

> According to the political economists, the interest of the worker is never opposed to that of society: (1) because the rising wages are more than compensated by the reduction in the amount of labour time along with other factors such as the division of labour, the increase in social productivity, etc. (2) because in relation to the society the whole gross product is the net product, and only in relation to the private individual has the net product any significance (Marx 1844, p. 240)

Marxist theory attains a differing dimension because it not only foregrounds the problem associated with equating the benefits of the worker with the capitalist social structure in general but because it evaluates all the categories involved in the generalisation critically from a viewpoint informed by the state of the working class. As Lukacs (1971, pp. 163-64), the knowledge and ideologies that the working class constructs 'stands on a higher scientific plane objectively'; it does, after all, apply a method that...provides the adequate historical analysis of capitalism" (pp. 163-64) through an application of Marxist dialectics, where the objective existence of an object itself becomes a dynamic revolutionary 'process' within the system of overall capitalist reproduction (p. 180). The working-class vantage point is ideologically superior to the capitalist vantage point, not only because it forms its ideas out of the struggle it engages with against capitalism, but also because it suffers from the effectual conditions created by capitalism in society. The capitalist abstract theory, in other words, becomes the concrete reality for the working class. Marx, rightfully, not only questions the classical bourgeoisie theories but questions the material conditions that the bourgeoisie constructs in the form of the capitalist society: 'While the interest of the worker, according to the political economists, never stands opposed to the interest of the society, society always and necessarily stands opposed to the interest of the worker' (Marx 1844, p. 240). Marx continues: 'Society in a state of maximum wealth – an ideal, but one which is approximately attained, and which at least is the aim of political economy as of civil society – means for the workers static misery' (Marx 1844, p. 241). Marx substantiates this point by arguing that during the period when the society is suffering from a decline in wealth or productivity, it is the working class who suffers the most because of being doubly oppressed both by virtue of the worker's position in the society and the society's position in general. Classical political economy works by dehumanising the worker. It considers the worker to be merely a unit of labour. In other words, capitalism does not take the workers as human beings but rather as commodities – which can be sold and bought at the market: 'Political economy knows the worker only as a working animal – as a beast reduced to bodily needs' (Marx 1844, p. 242).

History and Marxist dialectics develop in a continuum where '...the objective reality of social existence is in its immediacy 'the same' for both proletariat and bourgeoisie. But this does not prevent the specific categories of mediation by means of which both classes raise this immediacy to the level of consciousness, by means of which the merely immediate reality becomes for both the authentically objective reality...' (Lukacs 1971, p. 150). Human beings, in their interaction with this objective reality, modify and get modified by '...the objective structure, the actual content of the individual phenomenon-as individual phenomenon' (p. 152). It is this 'same reality' which restricts the bourgeoisie to an 'immediacy while forcing the proletariat to go beyond it' and the changes within this reality enable the proletariat to derive meanings as a class (pp. 164-71), which counter the problems caused by the methodology of treating individual historical phenomena in isolation from the totality (p. 152). This would allow the worker – the proletariat – to achieve 'the transformation of the objective nature of the objects of action' (p. 175). The moment class consciousness arises within the proletariat, the laws operating within capitalism 'fail and become dialectical and are thus compelled to yield up the decisions regarding the fate of history to the conscious action of men' (p. 178). It is only the class that can 'relate to the whole of reality in a practical revolutionary way' (p. 193).

In a world dominated by capitalism, the working-class consciousness is dominated and completely subsumed by capitalism. The struggle for altering the consciousness of the working class cannot take place without a struggle against the rampant material inequality existing under capitalism. This was one of the important points made by Marx and Engels (1845-46, p. 30). It stemmed from the understanding that the limitations that people face in their lives are not products of imagination, but that they are actually existing hurdles to the realisation of human potential. Social media commerce sustains the alienating illusion that a successful trade or a successful commercial practice is the final aim of human life. It does not provide the workers with any substantial base for the construction of a fulfilling life. It merely provides the workers with a temporary luxury, without resolving any fundamental contradictions within the capitalist society. It further enables the construction of the individual human being as a manifestation of possession, of either money or commodities or both. In the EPM, Marx had already distanced himself from the economistic understanding of society. Referring to the understanding shared by some of the classical political economists, Marx had argued, 'everything that goes beyond the more abstract need – be it in the realm of passive enjoyment or a manifestation of activity -seems to him (the economists and the classical political economists) a luxury' (Marx 1844, pp. 308-09). Social media commerce expresses the fundamental problem with individual needs within a society, i.e., it restricts the fulfilment of needs in an individual's life within narrow economic paradigms. In the process, it encapsulates the complete obscuration of any harm that it causes on an everyday level to the possibility of human development.

For Marx, an *ideal* human life was not about possession, but rather it was about fulfilment. Marx was of the opinion that mere possession of a commodity cannot make anybody attain a 'fulfilment' in their lives. This is something that political economists fail to articulate in Marx's view, because to them, every individual is a mere collection of needs to another individual, who exist to become a mutual means to each other to satisfy their needs (Heller 2018, p. 23). Consumerism as an ideology becomes the basis on which individuals have begun to frame their individuality (Dunn 2008). An individuality formed in this way does not have an ounce of universalism in it, but is rather a highly determinist one, which restricts the human development of the individual within the rationality put forward by the consumerist market – the creation of the point of production under capitalism. Understood in this manner, capitalism usually conflates needs with demands, and does so intentionally, because doing that provides capitalism with the necessary impetus towards further monetisation of the society. Needs are distinct from 'demand'. There is a tendency to conflate these two conceptual ideas within market-based theories whereby the presence of a 'need' justifies or foretells a 'demand'. Demands are often purely economic in nature, while needs are more about the actual living conditions of human beings. Capitalism creates demands, and the law of supply and demand posing it as a law that guides the global order (Marx and Engels 1975, p. 48). It is only within a society based on capitalist alienation that demands can overcome human existence as the primordial element of social sustenance. The supernatural attributes accredited to 'trading' which as Marx rightly says is nothing more than a mutual exchange in his *The German Ideology*, are largely due to the theories stemming from bourgeoisie economists. However, as Heller (2018, p. 12) informs, some of the orthodox economists, such as Alfred Marshall (1890/1964) did talk about the differences between 'necessities' and other commodities, but even then, the market was seen to be a remedy to all the problems 'and "need" was condemned to be seen as a phantom idea outside the writings of utopians and socialists'.

Heller (2018, p. 23) argues that the reduction of the concept of 'need' to its mere economic essence is further alienation of human needs under capitalism – a system that priorities profit valorisation over and above human development and human satisfaction. It also inevitably leads to a situation where 'needs' only get manifested as markers of 'effective demand' within the market. This tendency within capitalism also puts a limit on how much time and money can the working class spend to satisfy their needs. The constant drive of capital to increase the labour time coupled with the continuously increasing prices of the commodities, which far exceed their value, completely jeopardize the efforts of any social arrangement aimed at inculcating the freedom or sovereignty necessary to achieve a 'true' satisfaction of one's needs or desires. The sovereignty of an individual within capitalist societies is constructed on the terms dictated by capitalism itself. Since, the individual, who is also a consumer belongs to a society characterised by rampant consumerism, it is only natural for the consciousness of that individual to be entrapped within the dominant mode of thought production in the society – controlled by bourgeoisie consumerism and capitalism. The complete subjugation of the individual to these modes of thought converts the existent system into an independent being in itself, which becomes independent of human intervention, at least to the individual.

Conditions like this lead the individual to conceptualise all others around his own self as being entities that are external to himself and most likely, 'in opposition to himself' (1991, p. 93). As Lefebvre continues, the perfect bourgeoisie would be the near-perfect personification of the desires of capitalist accumulation, which remains the primary goal of the very existence of capitalism itself (Lotz 2017). Capitalism when coupled with full-fledged bourgeois democracy creates a situation that manifests itself through a complex web of multiple contradictions within a social totality (Lefebvre 1991b, p. 91). This society entails within itself a maximum level of alienation – the most that capitalism can bring into effect – encompassing individual, political, economic and social alienation in totality and completely:

> It perfects the opposition between public and the private, between community and slavery. It mystifies every individual by granting him a place both in slavery and in community, in fiction and in reality. It allows him an apparent independent, because he] takes 'the *unbridled* movement of the spiritual and material elements which form the content of his life' for total freedom. (Lefebvre 1991b, p. 91)

This sets the individual up for complete subsumption within the capitalist modernity. It transforms the individual into a subject who is not only alienated from his/her own human living subjectivity but also becomes at one with the subservient social order akin to a machine. Consciousness becomes an important element in this milieu. It 'joins forces with the need for other people which is determined by the situation the individual is in; together they transform needs into desires, decisions into actions; or conversely, the one inhibits the other' (Lefebvre 1991, p. 93). Lefebvre spent a considerable amount of time on the concept of consciousness in his work on everyday life – which he believed to be the critique of 'capitalist' everyday life as we know it itself (1991, p. 92). Lefebvre analyses the web of needs, desires and consciousness of the human self from a materialistic perspective. It is the context and the objective conditions, he says, which determine consciousness like Marx (1973). However, the consciousness of the workers under capitalism is not a product of their activity but rather it is the reflection of the capitalist domination over the society: 'The production of ideas, of conceptions, of consciousness, is at first directly interwoven with the material activity and the material intercourse of men – the language of real life. Conceiving, thinking, the mental intercourse of men at this stage ... appear as the direct efflux of their material behaviour' (Marx and Engels 1975, p. 36).

The human consciousness is a reflection of the social life around the individual. However, as Lefebvre (1991, p. 92) argues the reflections of social life can be wholly different from the actual objects which source the reflection. In other words, 'A Reflection in a consciousness, or a reflection which constitutes a consciousness, can be incomplete, mutilated, inverted, distorted, mystified; it is a reflection and yet in the generally accepted sense, it is not a reflection' (ibid.). The individual is a reflection of the existing mode of production in society, but 'the mode of production must not be considered simply as being the reproduction of the physical existence of the individuals. Rather it is a definite form of activity of these individuals, a definite form of expressing their life, a definite *mode of life* on their part' (Marx and Engels 1975, p. 31). The individuals express their life as they are under capitalism 'both with what they produce and with how they produce. Hence what individuals depend on the material conditions of their production' (Marx and Engels 1975, pp. 31-2). The individual, sadly, even though occupies the central position in society as Marx (1844) himself had posited, has always received very little attention within most Marxist accounts (Dunayevskaya 1973, p. 53; Lefebvre 2016). The individuality, which leads to a fulfilling life, is to be based on the dialectical relationship between the *Abstract Universal* and the *Concrete Individual*, the movement between which is through a *specified particular*. Lefebvre (1991, p. 81) argued that the conflict between individualism and the individual carries within itself the tension between the ontology of the bourgeois individual, who is isolated from the lived reality of the innumerable others in the society, and the *real individual*, drawing the terminology from Lefebvre, who is the active and labouring element in the society:

> The individual realises that in bourgeois society the way he represents himself, for others and for himself, is contradictory, in that it splits him in two. On the one hand it isolates him as 'private', atomising him, dividing him; and that is a false image: atoms have no needs, they are self-sufficient, without needs, contented, perfect. Then on the other hand, the individual realises that each of his activities, his 'properties', his impulses, involves a *need*. This need brings him into relationship with other people (Lefebvre 1991b, p. 91)

These are the conditions under which an individual constructs one's conscious-ness under capitalism, which is so burdened by capitalist alienation. In the EPM, Marx was resolute on the point that 'the individual is the social being' (Marx 1844, p. 299). For Marx, there was a continuum existing between the individ-ual and the society. In previous chapters, the book has suggested that the dom-inance of exchange values in the public sphere is related to the obliteration of use-value, which is realised in direct consumption (Marx 1976), from the pub-lic sphere. Lefebvre (2002, p. 6) argued that the consciousness of human beings within the society is shaped by the overall social consciousness, but the individ-ual consciousness also shapes the social consciousness in return. This dialectical relationship between the society and the individual forms the basic elements of the structure of the society (Lefebvre 1991b). It is through this dialectical rela-tionship that a philosophical understanding of the needs and wants of the indi-viduals within society needs to be constructed and analysed. The individual's needs are also social needs because the individual is related to society dialecti-cally (Lefebvre 1991, 2002; Marx 1844):

> Above all we must avoid postulating 'society' again as an abstraction vis-a-vis the individual. The individual is *the social being*. His manifestations of life – even if they may not appear in the direct form of *communal* man-ifestations of life carried out in association with others – are therefore an expression and confirmation of social life (Marx 1844, p. 299)

Socialism does not mean the dissolution of consciousness, but rather means the complete realisation of one's individual potential – in its unalienated form. For the *total man* to emerge, one of the requisites is the dialectical integration of the individual and the social (Lefebvre 1991b, p. 73). Marx was never in favour of cre-ating a rift between the individual and society. It is also highly uncharacteristic of Marx, a dialectical thinker of repute, to do that. The individual and the society are dialectically related. They are not completely antagonistic to each other, but neither they are completely subsumed by one another. According to Lefebvre the man and the human (as a species) always construct a dialectical whole through negotiations of contradictions and alienating mechanisms operating within the society: 'As for the total man – *universal, concrete* and alive – ... can only be con-ceived of as a limit to the infinity of social development. ... The *total man* is but a figure on a distant horizon beyond our present vision. He is a limit, an idea, and not a historical fact' (Lefebvre 1991b, p. 66).

Society itself is a development of the relations between human beings, just as much as human relations are a product of social development. This is the point Marx makes in his EPM (Marx 1844, p. 298). Both private property and the indi-vidualisation of human beings occur throughout history (Dunayevskaya 1973, p. 68). Social activities, forms of enjoyment and forms of anxiety are all products of the development of society in terms of the 'mode of existence' (Marx 1844, p. 298). These practices and forms are as much social as they are individual as the being which performs them or feels them is actually a human being: 'Not only is the material of [the] activity given to him as a social product: his own existence is a social activity, and therefore that which he of himself' (Marx 1844, p. 298). The individual constructs selfhood under the conditions and preconceived unconscious of being a social being, and it is only in a society that the constructed selfhood can make sense. The completely developed 'social individual' is a form that has completely freed oneself from everything which interferes with the full development of the idea of *universal* freedom within the individual's existentiality (Dunayevskaya 1973, p. 43). In the movement towards achieving this freedom, human beings have no other option but to struggle for that freedom, i.e., progressing towards the realisation of absolute freedom from the logic of capital itself and not merely the capitalist economic form. Theory for the realisation of such freedom comes from the people themselves who negate the alienated philosopher's influence before negating the capitalistic form which that influence sustains. As Dunayevskaya rightly said, '...in our age theory can develop fully only when grounded in what the masses themselves are doing and thinking' (Dunayevskaya 1973, p.xviii).

Unless the consciousness of the people is freed from capitalist domination, there cannot be any free individual in society. The ideas possessed by the dominant section of the society become the dominant ideas in any period of history (Marx and Engels 1845-46). These are the ideas that produce the needs and desires in the society through their relationship with the production process existing in the society:

> It is not consciousness that determines life, but life that determines consciousness. For the first manner of approach the starting-point is consciousness taken as the living individual; for the second manner of approach, which conforms to real life, it is the real living individuals themselves, and consciousness considered solely as *their* consciousness (Marx and Engels 1845-46, p. 37)

The free society that Marxism endeavours to create is a society where the individual needs of every individual become the responsibility of the social division of labour as a whole (Marcuse 1966, p. 74). It is the conceptualisation of leisure time itself through which the ideas surrounding administering, organising or controlling the leisure time of the individuals come up (Marcuse 1966).

Social media users do respond to the suppression and repression in society, but they do so while being under the influence of complete social alienation (Marcuse 1972). Alienation, which has become *'constant and everyday'* (Lefebvre 1991b, p. 167) and engulfed the human self under contemporary capitalism, aids in establishing the methods in which technical small equipment shape the ways in which the individuals interact with the community and how those modes of interaction impact their interpretations of the space around them. They influence the potential activities of the individuals towards *localisation*, which in the current context, does not only mean 'mastering everyday mobility ... [but] it is about excavating urban space and disclosing the activities places permit and the experiences they elicit' (Buhr 2017, p. 11). Being *local* thus means the complete realisation of the social totality – the *full and complete space, physical and digi-*

tal. It is within this *total* social reality composed of the private lives in the bed-rooms, domestic lives at dinner tables, and the public lives in the offices, parties, etc, that the community of which the individuals are a part of constituting the premise of a potential ground for constructing an idea of human life in the every-day spaces, of which the digital spaces are an integral part. The trivial yet extra-ordinary aspects of the individual's life constitute the overall social life where '*each individual exists socially only by and within his alienation*' (Lefebvre 1991b, p. 15). This becomes true in a capitalist society because of the social space's manip-ulation in such a way that true individuality is able to develop only when one is not formally within the productive process (Lefebvre 1991b, p. 30). In other words, the productive relations of the society form the basis of individuality under capitalism. According to Lefebvre (1991, p. 30), the quest for *real individu-ality* has always involved a contradictory relationship between the two basic ele-ments of human sustenance- work and leisure, which makes the imagination of a 'work-leisure' unity absolutely essential to rupture any and all forms of alien-ation in the society.

In today's world, social media has become a primary element of leisure. Talk-ing about social media cannot evade discussions about leisure. A large section of the population, globally, analyses and engages with social media as an activity deemed fit for lazy afternoons or relaxed evenings. However, for young people, social media has almost become a part of life. The proliferation of the internet has made social media a part of the leisurely hours of almost everybody on the planet, be it from the Global North or the Global South. On the other hand, the leisurely activities of the workers also are very much within the fold of cap-italist accumulation. Social media is a stark example of this. Targeted advertise-ments, corporatisation of everyday life, etc. play a pivotal role in this regard. Human needs today are increasingly getting mediated by technological and cul-tural innovations. Social media, in this regard, can also be analysed through the 'Serious Leisure Perspective' (Elkington and Stebbins 2014; Stebbins 2020) whereby leisure becomes a conscious and devoted aspect of life. Individuals have used social media for knowledge and news for years now. Conceptualised in that way, the usage of social media often is not an act of leisure in its pure form, i.e., '*un-coerced, contextually framed activity engaged during free time, which people want to do and, using their abilities and resources, actually do in either a satisfying or a fulfilling way (or both)*' (Elkington and Stebbins 2014, p. 5). Technology has made it very easy to engage with serious leisure, and social media is at the centre of it. Most of the sellers who sell professionally on social media have learnt the nuances of social media during their 'leisure' time, or the time that they understood to be leisure. One of the sellers on social media in India said that it was his expertise on social media which led him to trade on the platform. Social media is not a necessary requirement for commercial activities, but because its easy access and because people are more familiar with the platform made it one of the most accessible and popular ways of doing business.

Perspectives such as 'Serious Leisure' would have been seriously critiqued by Marcuse (1966). For him, the Marxist conception of 'free time' cannot be 'leisure time' of any kind – serious or not – because the complete development of the individual human potential is not something that anybody attains in leisure (p. 74). Marcuse goes on to say: 'Free time [only] pertains to a free society, leisure time to a repressive society' (p. 74). In the Global South, 'Doing Mobile' or 'Doing Computer' had become an activity in itself in the last decade and a half, which individuals engaged in during their leisurely hours. Years after, those leisurely hours have finally become the source of active value production for capitalism through social media commerce. The generation which grew up 'doing computers and mobiles' remains the largest proportion of users of social media commerce and as such constitutes more than 50% of the interviewees for this particular work. Cybercafes, as noted in the *Introduction*, were the genesis of this activity and are accepted as a normative mode of life, which got further domesticated when smartphones and laptops became commonplace. With the pandemic, these gadgets have become essential aspects of daily life. E-commerce platforms have 'essential' labels on commodities that under normal circumstances would have been classified as luxury or optional. Many such commodities today have become a part of our everyday lives just as Marx (1973) had predicted regarding the evolution of luxury goods, through history, to becoming necessary goods and the relationship of this evolution to capitalism and its associated alienation. These so-called luxury goods, are the necessary arsenal for the enjoyment of leisure today, pushing human life towards more luxury goods. These tendencies restrict the human journey towards radical individuality by not allowing human beings to negate the various forces of alienation that capitalism puts into work in society. Consciousness for a free society requires the negation of the established societal ideologies, both psychologically and physically as Dunayevskaya (1958a, p. 11) would say. Dunayevskaya (1958a) understands freedom to be fundamentally dependent on the amount of time that a person possesses for unalienated existence – an existence where, in the words of Lefebvre (1991b), there occurs a unity of work and leisure. In other words, a free society is a society where 'the individual's "occupation" is the shaping of his free time as his own time, while the process of material production, organised and controlled by free individuals, creates the conditions and means for the exercise of their freedom or "enjoyment"' (Dunayevskaya 1958a, p. 10).

Work under capitalism monopolizes life, *even the best kinds of work* (Weeks 2011). Social media in the case of many people who use it to inform, and influence has become 'work' and the workplace simultaneously. The problem with social media both as work and as a workplace is that it often does not feel like a workplace, nor does it look like a workplace. Camouflaged by the rhetoric of a community, social media makes work feel like 'not work'. Weeks (2011) correctly argues that it is within the workplace that people form the basic relationships that inform their life as a whole. Alienating workplaces, and their tremendous influence on the workers who work in them make the argument from Lefebvre (1991b) that it is only outside the capitalist productive cycle that effective and fulfilling social relationships can be created. In the process, it makes the liberation from work, as advocated by Gorz (1987), more difficult and possibly impossible to imagine as Fisher (2009) would say. Social media commerce helps commercial capital by extending the working hours of the working class, without the working class actually recognising it. As Erich Fromm noted: 'We today have more free time available than our forefathers dared to dream of. But what has happened? We do not know how to use the newly gained free time; we try to kill the time we have saved and are glad when another day is over' (Fromm 1956, p. 5). Time has always been an important factor in capitalism, Lefebvre (1991b, p. 139) talks about the way in which leisure has been colonised under capitalism such that the modern human being '...possesses everything it is possible to possess: money, property, leisure, talent, thought. And yet he possesses nothing, and knows it, and says it: "I believe I am brave enough to doubt everything, to fight against everything; but I am not brave enough to recognize nothing, to possess nothing"' (Lefebvre 1991b, p. 139). The perennial desire of capital is to reduce the amount of time it employs the actual living labour of the workers to the 'necessary minimum and constantly shorten the labour needed for the creation of a product by exploiting the social productivity of labour, i.e. economising as much as possible on directly applied living labour, so it also has the tendency to apply this labour, which has already been reduced to its necessary amount, under the most economical circumstances, i.e. to reduce the value of constant capital applied to the absolute minimum' (Marx 1981, p. 180). A life centered on gadgets becomes a very effective tool in obtaining this target. In this situation, it becomes essential to talk about the centrality of gadgets and technology in contemporary life because 'their centrality in modern society, economy and culture, what we do with them – as active agents, citizens and workers – will have a profound impact on the future. This means [we have to be] looking at their social and economic place, [how] they function in relation to politics and power, and above all in relation to collective thought, will and action' (Hands 2019, p. 5).

Most people today live a life that is highly routinised in nature, where certain equipment and technology are endowed with the capacity to provide them happiness. Fromm (1942) and Perlman (1972) have both shown that the nature of that happiness under capitalism is determined by exchange relations and capitalist alienation. Happiness is a marker of freedom in unalienated conditions. It is intrinsically related to free will and the exertion of one's free will. Contemporary capitalism rests on the positing of new oppression in place of the old forms, reason as indifference, human will without any impulse, and unfreedom as a conscious and *good* state of existence (Adorno 1973). The consumer society gains social legitimacy by providing certain freedom to its inhabitants who do not enjoy much freedom elsewhere. It is this supposed freedom towards realising individual choices that make consumer markets attractive to individuals even though it is the market itself that exists as a force of social control reproducing capitalism not through the suppression of individual freedom but through its realisation in a form mediated by the market, within the market (Bauman 1988, p. 61). Consumer markets, in other words, act in ways similar to other emotional regulatory frameworks under capitalism employed to control the emotional display of workers (Gross 2013). It interferes most fundamentally with what Dunayevskaya (1973, p. 26) refers to be the subjective determination of selfhood and 'the need to master' oneself. The consumer is always entrapped within a paradigm invented by capitalism itself, whereby the consumer is supposed to be always happy. Being a consumer under capitalism means performing emotional labour where the private individual interacts with the public sphere through emotions (Hochschild 1983). Emotions, as Illouz (2007) mentions are more than mere psychological entities, they are integral to the cultural articulations of selfhood within the relationships that human beings find themselves in affecting and getting affected by the unconscious. According to Baudrillard:

> There is no question for the consumer ... of evading this enforced happiness and enjoyment, which is the equivalent in the new ethics of the traditional imperative to labour and produce. Modern man spends less and less of his life in production within work and more and more of it in the production and continual innovation of his own needs and well-being. He must constantly see to it that all his potentialities [and] ... consumer capacities are mobilised. If he forgets to do so, he will be gently and insistently reminded that he has no right not to be happy (Baudrillard 1970, p. 80)

This momentary happiness, however, is the very means capitalism uses to keep them under control. Sometimes, technological instruments enable the formation of a cocoon around individuals, protecting them from potentially unpleasant events and experiences. In reality, social practices help in demarcating the lives of individuals in accordance with their convenience and schedules, which is also a means of demarcating the space around individuals along with the meanings these spaces hold. The partitioning of space also reflects the desires of the ways in which one wants to partition their social life (Zerubavel 1991, p. 6). Social media sites like Facebook offers numerous ways in which individual users can limit the audience of their posts. Within its Marketplace framework, Facebook allows users to hide the commodity they listed from their friends. In doing so, it allows the sellers to shield themselves from potential emotional troubles which might arise out of the activity usually in the form of inferiority complexes, self-pity, etc. More than half of the people interviewed for the current project said that they have used the function to hide the commodity they put up for sale fearing that their peers might start 'judging' them. Such acts are usually mediated by cultural norms associated with emotions which often develop in tandem with the development of capitalism itself (Illouz 2007), and are related to other issues of class, gender, race, etc.

Capitalism tries to control the different social practices which define how human beings live because habits define the processes in which human beings affect and get affected by the space around them. Thus, if there is a mechanism to control the habits of human beings, it opens up a distinct route toward controlling the way in which human beings interpret the space and time around them. Reckwitz (2002, p. 249) defines 'practices' as being 'a routinised type of behaviour which consists of several elements, interconnected to one other: forms of bodily activities, forms of mental activities, "things" and their use of background knowledge in the form of understanding, know-how, states of emotion and motivational knowledge'. The construction of reality by individuals actually living it is not based on perception but is rather contingent upon these practices that Reckwitz (2002) talks about which result in the construction of differences between the various facets of the everyday practices of individuals (Giddens 1991, p. 43). The differences between the ways in which various individuals experience everyday life give rise to certain codes, forms of knowledge and means of interpretive action (Suttles 1973, p. 36), which then give shape to the codes of commodities that Baudrillard (1970, 1972) talks about. These codes are sustained within the community through layers of horizontal and vertical relationships, which as Fennema (2004, p. 435) suggests, are present in a combined fashion across society – from the streets to the bedroom, from the real space to the virtual space.

The routine that an individual constructs, and the social practices enmeshed within it, are important for the continued sustenance of the individual's 'protective cocoon' (Giddens 1991, p. 56), and is also as much physical activity of boundary construction as much as it is a mental activity of interpreting and creating an interactive framework with social reality (Reckwitz 2002, p. 251). Domestic and private spaces are traditionally understood as places of refuge (De Certeau, Giard and Mayol 1998) which are supposed to accelerate the processes of social belongingness under normal circumstances. They are spaces where individuals feel secure and safe. In a society where commodities are markers of individualities, engaging in social media commerce can also be compared to how Mason (1981, p. 29) theorises conspicuous consumption is a means to gain legitimacy within the society for non-affluent individuals and groups. People indulge in social media commerce because they get happiness out of it, there is no way one can deny that. However, the idea that one can get happiness out of selling and purchasing commodities is a capitalist construct. Capitalism constructs certain social practices and social identities through its forces which dominate the working class. Kate Soper (2020) quite rightly argues although she does so from an ecological standpoint, that the emphasis today has to be on understanding the complete apparatuses at play that promote these characteristics or traits at a social level to make them everyday identity-oriented practices. Analysis has to be constructed in a way in which the analysis of consumerism goes beyond its conceptualisation as a mere unconscious way in which a person lives or theorising the act of consumption as a distinguishing and status-altering activity (Soper, 2020). It has to be all-encompassing – taking the entire social form into its fold. Any constructive notion of any form of social justice under contemporary capitalism has to engage with everyday life, that was Lefebvre's golden notion as reflected in his *Critique of Everyday Life* (1991: 46). No amount of development of the productive sources will be sufficient enough to usher in socialism because: 'Men do not fight and die for tons of steel, or for tanks or atomic bombs. They aspire to be happy, not to produce' (Lefebvre, 1991b: 48).

The establishment of a free society, which leads to fulfilling lives, requires the complete abolition of all forms of repression. Social media commerce is a part of this overall system of repression within capitalism. It produces through the system of needs a voluntary servitude to itself, the destruction of which is necessary to the constitution of freedom in the society. Any movement for liberation which attempts to achieve freedom from such institutions of repression needs to demolish, at first, the need for 'liberation from servitude, prevalence of the need for liberation' (Marcuse 1967, p. 78). True freedom can only be achieved through a qualitative change in the society which as Marcuse (1967) says, requires changes at a social level – 'to the very system as a whole' (p. 79). True freedom results in the complete destruction of alienation of all forms – one of the final goals of all revolutions seeking their origin in Marx. Lefebvre perhaps wrote this is in the most beautiful way possible: 'For Marx, the revolution was to continue a historic moment, a leap into freedom, the end of alienation' (Lefebvre 2016, p. 20).

The autonomist argument that workers produce new forms of subjectivity every day through their own activities and that these new subjectivities can pave the way for a restructuration of the labour-power itself (Hardt and Negri 2000), proves helpful in exhibiting the Marxist importance of the spontaneity of social relations which human beings produce unconsciously while being engaged in their productive activities, which was taken to be one of the most important achievements of Marx (Dalla Costa and James 1975). True autonomy can, potentially, be achieved when the working class reclaims the element of 'Humanity', the basis of all autonomous human activity, first within itself, and then within its immediate community, before being converted into a full-fledged political tendency. Such freedom cannot be achieved through objective measures only, but neither can it be achieved through only subjective articulations. True freedom, rather, is a quality, where 'The objective may outweigh the subjective but unless we see the unity of the two and grapple with the truth of both, we will never be free. And freedom is what all the striving is about' (Dunayevskaya 1981, p. 144).

Social media commerce is a part of the overall system of capitalist exploitation and accumulation, whereby capitalism reconstructs the world in its own image similar to Marx and Engels' description of the bourgeoisie reconstruction of the world (Marx and Engels 1848, p. 488). Within such reconstructions, the easiest and most highlighted solution remains the appeal to individuals 'to become bourgeois themselves' (Marx and Engels 1848, p. 488). Social media commerce does exactly the same within contemporary society. It posits happiness and aesthetic fulfilment in terms of commodities emphasising the contemporary society being a society of commodity producers (Marx 1976, p. 133). Social media commerce makes it impossible to attain any fulfilment in life for the individual because it continues to entrap human beings within the commodity economy and the process of capitalist value production. It keeps on generating newer social needs by working upon common human emotions, which under conditions of capitalist alienation, by reducing human existence to 'archaic' forms of possession of commodities as Fromm (1976, p. 22) would say – within a life which is never fulfilled, never complete.

9. COMMODITY CIRCULATION AND CONSUMPTION

The circulation of commodities in society is quintessential to capitalist suste-nance. Production is only one aspect of the process of capitalist control. It is circulation that actually keeps the economy going on, by increasing consump-tion and profit accumulation. The general form of circulation of commodities is the transformation of commodities into money followed by the re-conversion of money into more commodities (Marx 1976, pp. 247-48). This forms the basis of the primary element of all capitalist economies i.e., buying in order to sell, production merely for the sake of more production so as to initiate more accu-mulation. This process can be represented as Commodity (C) – Money (M). But, as Marx (1976, p. 248) also says, it is also necessary to explore the roots of the creation of 'C' which is through 'M'. Thus Marx says that within the circuit of C-M-C, there is also embedded within it, another circuit which is: M-C-M (p. 248). The theorisation of money and money capital stems from this point because money is always entrenched within the system and begins functioning as capital when capital *per se* might not even be existing. The circuit through which cap-ital appears and then goes on to dominate the society by working through the various institutions, social processes and individuals in the society is a socio-eco-nomic and cultural process that involves both production and circulation (Marx 1992, p. 139). The importance which Marx himself gave to the circulation and dis-tribution of commodities can be summed up thus:

> In society, however, the producer's relation to the product, once the latter is finished, is an external one, and its return to the subject depends on his relations to other individuals. He does not come into possession of it directly. Nor is its immediate appropriation his purpose when he produces in society. *Distribution* steps between the producers and the products, hence between production and consumption, to determine in accordance with social laws what the producer's share will be in the world of producers (Marx 1973, p. 94)

The liberal understanding of the consumer under contemporary capitalism is that the consumer is always an independent and sovereign person free to make choices, at least in formal terms. These views ascribe certain self-determination to the individual which is considered to be the basic cornerstone of all existing democratic set-ups. However, the choices that these individuals make 'need to', within capitalism, be in line with the basic tenets of capitalist modernity which privileges the individualization of all needs and desires (Soper 2020). Soper mostly uses the word 'private', but the current author uses the word 'individual' to refer to the points Soper is making because the notion of individuality emphasizes the self-reflexive subjectivity of the human being more than 'private'. The market takes up the responsibility of furnishing before the individual consumer innumerable products, each catering to some need that the consumer may or may not have experienced till the point the actual commodity is noticed. For example, to get to the point in simpler terms, one can take the example of the latest technology in digital reading devices. Many technological multi-national companies today are experimenting with the idea of digital paper which encourages the further usage of digital means in aspects of human lives engaged with concerns such as taking notes, reading PDFs on-screen which are like paper, etc. These innovations, largely portrayed to be for ecological concerns, are rarely driven by eco-sensitive desires on the part of the manufacturing companies. Instead, they produce a whole new area of need for the people. Before Digital paper technology (DPT) came up as a commodity, people did not even conceive of that as a possibility. But now that it exists, there is a new need (mainstream management professionals would term it as a 'demand') growing for it. Holding a DPT device, in certain spaces, has become a status symbol because of the way they are priced. At the same time, they are seen to be more efficient, potentially 'cool' and an essential and much-desired part of being a serious 'note taker'. A generic response to the query posed regarding the possession of such a device usually runs like this:

> I used normal paper notebooks previously. But one day, I saw this advertisement on social media where they said they have a device which could take notes like paper, but it is run on battery. You know, like a Kindle or a Kobo. I was instantly attracted to the product, although it did cost me some money initially, but it would be offset by the price I pay for paper plus its eco-friendlier.

On being asked whether it did reduce their cost, most people say something along these lines:

> You know, I never really calculated. But I surely do not need to count the pages or keep on thinking about buying a notebook or a journal for these purposes. Does it save time? I think so. Does it save money? I am not sure.

In other words, this line of thinking lands one back to the age-old debate within the political economy- the relationship between production and consumption. It is production that creates the necessary ground for consumption. In reality, the consumption market, which many on the left tend to fetishise, is a limited one – extending only up to the luxuries of the capitalist or the needs of the workers (Dunayevskaya 1958a). It never focuses on the production relations existing in society. Lenin perhaps explained the relationship between production and consumption in the best way possible and argued that it is petty bourgeoisie economics that would have people believe that production follows consumption, whereas 'Marx shows that the connection is an indirect one, that it is connected only in the final instance because in capitalist society consumption follows production' (Lenin 1899; Dunayevskaya 1958a, p. 131). Petty bourgeoisie economists desire to establish the rule of the market, not only in society but also within the anti-capitalist thought processes operating within capitalism. The relationship between production and consumption is a part of this ideological suppression of the basic contradictions of capitalism. As Dunayevskaya notes:

> The preponderance of production over consumption was considered to mean the "automatic" collapse of capitalist society. Where the classicists saw only the tendency toward equilibrium, the petty-bourgeois critics saw only the tendency away from equilibrium. Marx demonstrated that both tendencies were there, inextricably connected (Dunayevskaya 1958a, pp. 131-32)

The market cannot be posited as an alternative to commodity production in the social analysis of capitalism. Commodities find their way into the market through the establishment of exchange values and then prices. When a commodity attains a price, it becomes ready to enter the sphere of circulation (Marx 1859, p. 323). The exchangeable value that these commodities possess are only the 'social functions of these things and have nothing at all to do with their natural qualities' (Marx 1865, p. 121). The social functions of the commodities are created through the labour which is spent on producing the commodity 'not only *Labour*, but *social Labour*' (Marx 1865, p. 121). Labour is the source of all value the market seeks to make this labour invisible. The market seeks to establish the law of supply and demand as the basic law of capitalism, while in reality, it is the dialectic relationship between the use-value and the exchange-value of the commodities along with the law of value, which is of great importance to Marxist analysis. As Marx (1847, p. 137) argues, the supply and demand of commodities do not dominate the production of commodities under expanded conditions of production, because 'forced by the very instruments at its disposal to produce an ever-increasing scale, [capitalism] can no longer wait for demand. Production precedes consumption, supply compels demand' (Marx 1847, p. 137).

Consumers are themselves determined by the class position at which they locate themselves: 'The use of products is determined by the social conditions in which the consumers find themselves placed, and these conditions themselves are based on class antagonism' (Marx 1847, p. 133)

The circulation of commodities is essential to this continuing relationship which is fundamental to capitalism. A high magnitude of circulation of commodities increases the overall exchange and monetary value of the commodities, which allows capitalism to fulfil the basic underlying aspect of any circuit which enables the sustenance of capitalism to remain the valorisation of value (Marx 1992, p. 159). The circuit of Capital, in the words of Marx (1992) consists of three specific stages:

> *First Stage*: The Capitalist appears on the commodity and labour markets as a buyer; his money is transformed into commodities; it goes through the act of circulation *M-C*; *Second Stage*: Productive consumption by the capitalist of the commodities purchased. He functions as a capitalist producer of commodities ... his capital passes through the production process. The result: commodities of greater value than their elements of production.; *Third Stage*: The capitalist returns to the market as a seller; [the] commodities are [now] transformed into money, they pass through the act of circulation *C-M*. Thus the formula for the circuit of money capital is M-C...P...C'-M'. (Marx 1992, p. 109)

The first component of the circuit (*M-C*) represents the process of the conversion of a sum of money into a group of commodities. This is the first, and probably the most important, part of the process. These commodities generate the revenue for the capitalist to further invest in extending the production of newer commodities by splitting up the revenue to either invest in further labour-power (L) and means of production (MP) or rejuvenate the already existing capacities of the same. In simpler words, the commodities aid the capitalist to buy further means of production and labour-power. In other words, as Marx said, highlighting the intrinsic relationship between money capital and commodities: 'The money M divides into two portions. The two sets of purchases pertain to completely different markets, p.one to the commodity market proper and the other to the labour market' (Marx 1992, p. 110). It is here that some of the most important arguments surrounding the Marxist theory of consumption can be based. The division of M, into the two portions – L and MP – is a social affair, as Marx (1992; 1981) repeatedly highlights. Both labour-power and the means of production are not economistic commodities, they are 'social commodities' affected greatly by other aspects of capitalism such as commodities and its associated fetishism the centrality of which was emphasised by Dunayevskaya (1965). The concept of commodity fetishism is directly interwoven into the method which Marx adopts in analysing capitalism. Without commodity fetishism, which is itself almost always an ambiguous concept to the human being who actually experiences it in the sense that the individual, because of alienation, cannot really understand, 'whether it is really an object or whether it is part of the self. A fetish [conceptualised this way] can be thought of as existing in a free space between the subject and the object' (Levin 1984, p. 42). Social media is an intrinsic part of that fetish in contemporary society. Marx rightly says that once the circuit of M-C [and further into L and MP] is complete, the capitalist does not only increase the means of production and labour-power at the disposal of the capitalist but also possesses a greater ability to put these entities into motion. Under more automated and mechanised means of production, the workers are always at the receiving end of capitalist exploitation, and in a heightened fashion (Marx 1849, p. 226). Enabled by digitalisation, the modes of commodification of capital in society have undergone massive changes over the past few years. Capital does not commodify itself in the same way as it used to do a decade ago. Betancourt's (2016) arguments surrounding the causes why digital capitalism, or more precisely, the commodification of digital products under capitalism is potentially more harmful than other such processes because it seemingly creates a notion that producing something digitally has no expenditure. The magnitude of fetishism associated with a commodity can be significantly higher in the digital space than in the real space because of the innumerable forces of mystification which work within the digital space.

Theories about social media have emphasised the element of communication and its usage for digital profit generation by using communication as a production process in itself (Fuchs 2020; Williams 1980). While for the workers, it is the exploitation of variable capital by the capitalist in the form of wages that increase the profits of the capitalist, for the capitalist however it is the entirety of the social capital which produces the surplus-value and in turn, helps in increasing the rate of profit (Rigi 2014). By using the power of communication, the entire structure attempts to remain at equilibrium by providing the capitalist with enough social capital to invest in producer goods by increasing the circulation of consumer goods through social media. The consumer goods produced from the producer goods would again be out in the market with exchange values and the cycle of profit-accumulation, thus, continues. The major advantage that social media possesses, is its inherent culture of participation, where 'consumers are invited to actively participate in the creation and circulation of new content' (Jenkins 2008, p. 331). Because of the culture of participation, social media has the capacity to be the foundation of an alternate media that can destroy the monopolistic control over media by a few capitalists. However, as Fuchs (2014b, 2014c) shows, social media is not a completely democratised space but rather is an extension of the authoritarian social system. This relation between technology and society has tremendous influence over the everyday lives of people as technological advancements, in every era, have come to define what Gardiner (2000) calls the *style of life*. The digital space on social media is an extension of the actual space. The tranquil nature of life in every epoch is disturbed by a technological innovation that suddenly appears and ruptures the social fabric as one knows it. This has been the mode in which history has been functioning. From the steam engine to the computer, technological developments have ushered in revolutionary changes in the everyday lives of individuals.

Developments such as the iPhone have become watershed moments in the history of techno-cultural advancements in human history, because of their course-altering effects on human life and organizational systems (Qui, Gregg and Crawford 2014). Going by Crawford's description: the iPhone is 'a key moment of metastasis when an already intimate, popularized technology expanded to encompass a host of media forms' (Crawford 2012, 219). Social media commerce, similar to the iPhone, is one such archetypal moment because it has fundamentally transformed the ways in which the non-capitalist classes engage in the circulation and distribution process (Deb Roy 2020). It has significantly altered the dynamics of ownership by ensuring a constant circulation of both commodities and money within the capitalist society which allows it to further accumulate profits. The uniqueness of any social media commerce platform is that these platforms work as a model that is based mostly on communication and accumulation through indirect sales. However, with more and more multinationals and large-scale manufacturers adding the 'Shop' button on their social media pages, the world should now prepare itself for a complete reorganisation of the digital space.

Traditionally, social media commerce platforms are different from other platform models such as the one used by Airbnb and Uber because the former's use for commercial activities is provided free of any cost. This free-ness of social media has been an instrumental factor in attracting users to engage in commercial activities on these sites. A significant number of users in the Global North have attested to this idea. Fieldwork in India revealed that the free nature of social media has enabled the middle class and the working-class users to put more and more commodities online. Sites like OLX and Quickr have been struggling for years now in India. These were revolutionary websites when they were initially launched allowing individuals to sell their old commodities for money. With the coming of social media commerce, these sites have become almost ousted from the competition. Reasons for this are multiple. From poor user interfaces to the interventions by social media, these websites have not been able to retain their popularity among the users.

Social media commerce platforms are potentially more exploitative than other platforms because even though they do not charge a fee, it encompasses within their platform a diverse range of accumulation strategies, especially the kind of advertising that feeds on the user's cognitive instincts and commerce, which involves direct physical exchange. While other e-commerce websites work on a model based on the primacy of accumulation through direct sales, Facebook works by encouraging users to GET involved in resales so as to increase the direct sales of others, which are the platform's potential advertisement and financial sources. Fuchs (2017, 27, 293) argues that platforms such as Airbnb builds their capital accumulation model on individuals' alienation from the community in order to promise community experiences via Airbnb and commodify the community. Community as ideology helps to mask platforms like Airbnb from their "for-profit capitalist businesses aiming at making monetary profits" (Fuchs 2017, 27, 293), but also helps them in gaining a high level of social acceptability. Thus, although the exchange of commodities for money within the working class is not entirely new with websites like TradeMe and eBay doing it for years, the new medium through which this exchange is being propagated within the society certainly demands academic attention because of its uniqueness in comparison to other established modes of this form of exchange. Coupled with cybernetic domination (Norbert 1961), it creates a scenario where every click and every message become a part and parcel of the profit-making mechanism of capitalism. Under this current mode, it does not matter if one is merely browsing or scrolling through social media. The entire digital ecosystem works in a manner that encourages and enables every activity into becoming a potential source of capital accumulation. A political-economic analysis of social media commerce that proliferates through Facebook and the groups therein reveals the integration of social media commerce into the broader contours of the general structure of the capitalist economy that revolves around profit generation.

Facebook groups created for the purpose of commercial activities do not earn any revenue for the users or their facilitators. In an indirect fashion, they help keep Facebook and other social media platforms free by diverting profits to its financiers by exploiting the constantly changing working-class composition that results in a constantly varying pool of needs and requirements within society (Hardt and Negri 2004) as well as the existing culture of consumerism at a mass scale (Fuchs 2019a). This culture of consumerism works through the conversion of human beings into nothing but profit-making machines (Engels 1845). The conversion of individuals into appendages of the broader system of profit-accumulation is one of the most important effects of the rampant consumerisation of the society where each individual witnesses another individual as a consumer and not a fellow human being. In other words, individuals become, as Engels (1845) says, a source of capital for further accumulation.

The free access to social media platforms like Facebook and Twitter as opposed to platforms like Airbnb where for the final product one has to pay a fee (Fuchs 2017) can be explained through two interrelated theoretical arguments. At first, one needs to acknowledge the relevance of Marx's (1867) insight that products of science, which are primarily products of mental labour, are almost always priced lower than their value because the labour-power required to reproduce the same is often significantly lower than the original labour-power invested. Taking a cue from that, one can then refer to Staab and Nachtwey (2016) who take this further by saying that digital capitalism attempts to tackle this particular problem by reducing the market price of the products of science so that lower profits can be nullified by an economy of scale (Staab and Nachtwey 2016). So, in spite of the fact that a huge amount of investment goes into, both in terms of constant and variable capital, creating an algorithmic platform like Facebook Marketplace, which can facilitate commercial activities on social media, charging rent or a fee for access would simply encourage other platforms to invade the niche space that platforms like Facebook have carved out for themselves. This becomes especially relevant in the case of Third World economies like India where sites like Airbnb and Uber have been facing tough competition from local platforms like Oyo Rooms and OLA. Free access to Facebook has not generated such competition (Deb Roy 2020). Additionally, the press releases made by Facebook regarding its free access to users establish a public consciousness that helps retain its tremendous user base.[1] Facebook's economy of scale makes it easy for the platform to popularise any new development that it introduces. Facebook's task, in popularising parts of its framework like Marketplace, becomes easier because it is already a part of the digital eco-system in the

---

1. Facebook has made many such statements over the years. In 2018, it said, https://www.daily-mail.co.uk/sciencetech/article-5600803/Facebook-WONT-charge-users-subscription-fee-opt-targeted-ads-completely.html. Again, in 2019, https://www.businessinsider.com/facebook-changes-free-and-always-will-be-slogan-on-homepage-2019-8?r=AU&IR=T

domain of communication and advertising, with the latter constituting the bulk of its revenue model (Fuchs 2014c, 2015). The only thing which Facebook had to do to make Marketplace a dominant mode of distribution and circulation was to encourage its 2.45 billion[2] users to start using it to sell their personal property. For achieving this aim, Facebook made FM more accessible and did away with any trading fees, which most other domains charge. These combined and interrelated processes contributed to Facebook's monopolisation of social media commerce.

Mobile applications have aided the rise of these monopolies in the digital world by emphasising the communicative nature and participatory culture. These monopolies use the already existing 'feel of a community' within their systems to promote commercial activities. Engaging in commercial activities through Facebook nullifies some important factors which previously acted as hindrances within sites like eBay, TradeMe, OLX, Quickr, etc. such as initial investment, time and ease of access. With them, one needs to go through a certain process while listing the commodity, which is both time-consuming, at times expensive and a bit complicated. Sites like Facebook, on the other hand, allow one to sell, "*on the go*" for free and with no success fees, i.e., the fee payable to the website if the product gets sold. In other words, while on eBay or OLX, the listing process is more mechanical in nature, the listing process on Facebook is in a way organic in nature, which enables the user to make use of their spontaneous will and freedom. Reproducing some of the responses which were invoked by participants in a 2020 study conducted by the current author, can substantiate this point: "Facebook as a medium, as opposed to something like TradeMe, has the advantage of not requiring an investment to sell an item. So, I can get more out of the sale, as opposed to when I have to sell on TradeMe"; "It's an excellent platform, free and easy to use. I stopped using TradeMe completely because the fees got too high"; "I reckon it's an easy platform to sell things and better than TradeMe because TradeMe has the extra cost that goes to them whenever you sell any item. Facebook encourages me to sell more" (Deb Roy 2020).

The easiness with which social media integrates individuals is the fundamental reason why this particular book exists. Social media fastens the process in which money – mainly in the form of cash in the Global South and virtual money in the Global North – is transferred into commodities, which in turn has an effect on the entire production and circulation of capital. The breaking up of Money (M) – Commodity (C), into two extrinsically distinct, yet intrinsically related processes of transformation, namely C-MP and C-L, has an interesting manifestation in the capitalist cycle. Social media commerce accelerates the process. It socializes the functions through which money gets converted into commodities, by increasing its frequency within society in general. Capital – the productive capital to be precise – then gets acquainted with a

---

2. See https://www.businessofapps.com/data/facebook-statistics/

The more the capitalist can buy L, the more the worker is impoverished, that was the basic theorem that Marx had put forward in the 1844 Manuscripts. Marx designates the process of transformation of M to C (or L to M),[3] as the precise moment in which the commodity gets transformed into money capital (Marx 1992, p. 113). This form of capital, according to Marx (1992, p. 140) is the most easily decipherable form in which capital, of the industrial kind, makes its appearance on the market. Capitalism works through providing an abundance and diversification of goods, [the market] allows for the ever-greater tailoring of consumption to the ever-more specific 'needs' [or wants] of the essentially private consumer- whose self-interested pursuit of goods disregards those of the community' (Soper 2020, Ch. 'Neither heroes nor dupes'). In this situation, if the people are to be made aware of the choices they make as consumers, they need to think of themselves as citizens. However, to effect real change, this has to be taken further than being mere citizens. Instead, the consumers have to reinvent themselves as being human beings and not *machines of consumption*. For that people have to realise that their needs are not constituted in isolation from the society, but rather, are articulated and brought into existence by a complex web of capitalist articulations, both physical and psychological.

Social media in today's day and age plays a crucial role in this techno-socio-cultural milieu. People have a diverse and complicated basis for articulating what they need. These are both subjective and objective in nature. A Marxist understanding of consumer society revolves around the manner in which the market dominates the individual subjectivity of the subjects within the society through mediations and control over the physical and ideological articulations about one's own selfhood available to any particular person. Marx in the Second Volume of *Capital* said:

> The workers are important for the market as buyers of commodities. But as sellers of their commodity – labour power – capitalist society has the tendency to restrict them to their minimum price. Further contradiction: the periods in which capitalist production exerts all its forces regularly show themselves in periods of overproduction; because the limit of the application of the productive powers is not simply the production of value, but also its realisation. However, the sale of commodities, the realisation of commodity capital, and thus of surplus value as well, is restricted not by the consumer needs of society in general, but by the consumer needs of a society in which the great majority are always poor and must always remain poor (Marx 1992, p. 391)

The signs which constitute the culture of consumption make objects appear as commodified needs on the market that 'superficially' satisfy the needs of sov-

---

3. M–C for the purchaser, i.e., the capitalist, is L–M for the seller i.e., the worker.

ereign consumers. These objects, or the ability to consume these objects, form the new basis of social status within the society, as Baudrillard (1972) has mentioned. This ability of the commodities to perform this function gets accentuated under capitalism. Commodities that appear as natural entities within naturalised exchange relations (Marx 1976, p. 165) constitute commodified and fetishised social relations by using sensual and psychological techniques apart from the routine economic techniques. As Soper notes: 'When products are advertised and sold on the basis of their authenticity and naturalness, the market promises to salve nostalgia for the very losses inflicted by its own advances into the everyday life' (Soper 2020, Ch. 'Consumption's Troubled Pleasures'). Advertisements under contemporary capitalism are produced keeping in mind an idealistically aesthetic sensual character of the object in question, based upon the promises that the object could potentially fulfil which are often unrealistic; 'What is being offered is not the socio-natural history of the commodity being sold, nor even the use-value of the product, but instead a *socio-fantasy* of identity and community that the consumer desires' (Duncombe 2012, p. 360). Marx's theory of commodity fetishism points towards concern about the consumer sense perception and the usage of goods within a capitalist mode of production (Skotnicki 2015, p. 3). Commodity fetishism renders invisible the social organisation of concrete labour relations in such a way that the commodity itself appears to be the central element of the society, both in the realms of production and consumption:

> ... as a use-value, the commodity appears as something independent. ... as value, it appears as something merely contingent, something merely determined by its relation to socially necessary, equal, simple labour-time. ... when the labour time required for its reproduction changes, its value changes, although the labour-time really contained in the commodity has remained the same (Marx 1976, p. 129)

The use-values of commodities used by workers tend to be appropriated by capitalism and its cycle of exchange value generation and circulation. Capitalist production and accumulation are designed so as to alienate the producers from the products and the means of production. Scholars following Marx (1844, 1976), such as Dunayevskaya (1958a, 1965), Fromm (1961), Harvey (1982), and Sanyal (2006) among many others have affirmed this idea. As Mulcahy (2017), in the process of being separated, the workers' replenishment and reproduction of their labour-power become merely another cost associated with production. The replenishment and reproduction mainly occur through consumption controlled by capitalists themselves without any autonomous production or use-value generation by the workers themselves (Gorz 1987; Mulcahy 2017). This is directly in synchronization with Marx's idea of consumption being merely a moment of production (Marx 1973).

There are quite a few allegations against Marx which find a place in the works of some scholars who theorize about consumption and its role in human societies. It is frequently theorised by many reputed scholars that Marx himself did not have much to say about consumption, or he did not give enough importance to consumption in society. Some, like Ritzer (2015, 2015a) and Toffler (1980), have attested to this idea by their expositions upon the idea of 'prosumption' involving 'both production and consumption rather than focusing on either one or the other' (Ritzer and Jurgenson 2010, p. 14). Mika (2019) talks about the *prosumerisation* of the population dividing the human evolution of the economy into three separate phases: the pre-industrial era when the producers were themselves the consumers, and as such there was no need to produce any surplus-value; the second wave of economic restructuration where there evolved a distinction between the producer and the consumer (Toffler 1980); and the modern era, where the differences between the producer and the consumer have been thinned down to almost nothing, thus creating 'prosumers' (Ritzer 2015). Mika (2019) expands the concept of prosumers into the domain of workers who work on the internet creating digital values which they themselves also consume with the same velocity as any other consumer thus creating a situation where the consumer produces the commodity that is to be consumed and becomes the abstract producer for some other consumer. The entire basis of the prosumption theory rests on the belief that under digital modes of commodity production, the activities of production and consumption have fused with each other.

Prosumer Capitalism has been the discussion of many theoretical studies over the past few years (Fuchs 2010, 2012a; Comor 2015). Fuchs (2010) argues that prosumer labour is one of the worst forms of exploitation of labour under contemporary capitalism because capitalism is exploiting them based on their everyday activities. In other words, the labour of the general users, like that of the creative workers or the intellectuals, has almost merged with that of the power of capital (Lund 2015). The internet has evolved as a site where constant prosumer labour is taking place, where users are engaging with the activities where they are constantly creating newer commodities – physical or mental – including communities themselves (Fuchs 2012a). In the domain of digital workers, to which Fuchs specifically catered, this theory might be applicable – the evaluation of which again is beyond the scope of this book. However, this theory definitely has certain issues when one starts analysing it with regard to social media commerce. Within social media commerce, the worker who sells the commodity is not a producer, the worker here is merely acting as a point of circulation. Even Comor's (2015) critique of Fuchs also does not sound convincing because he insists on relative freedom of the worker to sell the labour-power, which essentially does not take into account Marx's analysis of the worker as a consumer. Comor makes some further errors while critiquing Fuchs (2012b) who emphasises the idea that the production of the commodity itself is a form of exploitation, while Comor (2015) relegates value production only to the so-called productive labour. As Marx (1847, p. 118) says, the producer is always forced to sell the commodities produced under capitalism. Prosumption assumes certain independence of the functions of the producer and the consumer, but in reality, there is none. The consumer is as much constrained by capitalism, as is the producer (Marx 1847, p. 118). As stated in the last chapters, the needs and means of consumers determine the way in which the commodities produced by the producer will be consumed, which are themselves determined by social position and class. The scale at which the means of production in the society operate is not contingent upon the free will of the consumer or even the producer but upon the 'actual degree of development of the productive forces' (Marx 1847, p. 118).

It is true that Marx seldom spoke directly about consumption. It is also true that at times, Marxist theory often sounds like theories proposed through the vantage point of production. But to say that Marx did not have anything at all to say about consumption is outrightly a false notion that even Ritzer (2015) has agreed to. According to Skotnicki (2015), there are two reasons for Marxist theory not getting the sufficient importance it deserves within studies surrounding consumption: 'It entails a negative evaluation of consumers and consumption; It overlooks or ignores the varied meanings that consumers develop themselves' (p. 4). Sahlins (1976) argues that Marx was not much attracted to understanding the diverse natures of the various modes of consumption that produce the various use-values of the objects for different people. According to Sahlins (1976), this was because, for Marx, there was little sign of a distinct theory of meaning associated with the activity of consumption and its relationship with socially construed meanings of certain modes of consumption. Baudrillard (1981, pp. 130-34) again, argues that for Marx, the analysis of commodities was restricted to the analysis of exchange-values while the use-value of the commodity remains an abstract notion associated with it which remains outside the economic sphere of production.

Marx's analysis, in contrast to popular views such as Sutherland's (2008) and Skotnicki's (2015), does indeed lays emphasis on the ontological significance of the consumer. The only difference is that Marx does so from a perspective that is highly dialectical in nature. Marx does not analyse consumption as being a terrain that is completely divorced from production, rather he analyses consumption to be a part of the production process of capital (Marx 1973). As Dunn (2008, p. 24) notes, it was indeed Marx himself who laid the very basic foundation for the theorisation of consumption in capitalist societies in his *Grundrisse*: 'Production, then, is also immediately consumption, consumption is also immediately production. Each is immediately its opposite. But at the same time, a mediating movement takes place between the two. Production mediates consumption; it creates the latter's material; without it, consumption would lack an object. But consumption also mediates production, in that it alone creates for the products the subjects for whom they are products' (Marx 1973, p. 91). Marx's analysis of consumption comes alive in the Introduction to his *Grundrisse* where he articulated the threefold identities between production and consumption (Marx 1973, pp. 92-4).

Marx says, regarding the *Immediate Identity* between Production and Consumption: 'Production is consumption, consumption is production. Consumptive Production. Productive Consumption' (Marx 1973, p. 93). For Marx, the relation between production and consumption is mediated by commodities produced within a capitalist mode of production. This relationship is a relationship that is negotiated through the exchange between the positions of a subject and an object: 'each supplies the other with its object (production supplying the external object of consumption, consumption the conceived object of production' (Marx 1973, p. 93). Consumption in Marx's view is the final outcome of the process of commodity production:

> Consumption accomplishes the act of production only in completing the product as product by dissolving it, by consuming its independently material form, by raising the inclination developed in the first act of production, through the need for repetition, to its finished form; it is thus not only the concluding act in which the product becomes the product, but also that in which the producer becomes the producer (Marx 1973, p. 93)

It is production that creates consumption and not the other way round. Similar is the case with circulation and distribution of commodities. Though they are important parts of capitalism, perhaps of equal importance as well, it is at the point of production where the genesis of capitalism lies. Marx articulates them as all being the formational 'members of a totality, distinctions within a unity' (Marx 1973, p. 99). The distribution of commodities under capitalism becomes seemingly a social law, while in reality, the distribution of commodities takes place only after the distribution of the instruments of production and the distribution of 'the members of the society among the different kinds of production' has already taken place (Marx 1973, p. 96). Social media commerce focuses on consumption as an aesthetic activity in itself, through which it attempts to camouflage the already existing contradictions with regard to capitalist production. It does not let the working class articulate the prime functions of social media acting as an agent of circulation or distribution of commodities, which is the realisation of surplus-value in the society by redirecting working class possessed money towards becoming money capital and then on to commercial capital and at the final instance, new industrial capital. In this process, the commodities only get distributed through social media commerce because that is how the capitalist social division of labour has ordained the task of the workers within the realm of social media commerce. No exchange of commodities can take place without the division of labour being already established in the society be it 'spontaneous, natural, or already a product of historic development' (Marx 1973, p. 99).

Distribution and circulation of commodities are all 'presupposition(s) of production' as such that it is 'production [which has the] determinants and preconditions, which form its moments' such as distribution and circulation and finally, consumption (Marx 1973, p. 97). Marx (1865) also explicated this process through his analysis of supply and demand, where he explicitly demonstrated the causal reality of capitalist production, where both supply and demand are parts that were rendered in motion by capitalist production systems. Production of commodities is the domain, where the questions regarding distribution, circulation and consumption get articulated within capitalism (Marx 1973, Dunayevskaya 1965). The exchange of commodities which occurs regularly, and at an expedited pace within social media commerce is determined fundamentally by how the commodities are produced in the first instance. As Marx says, 'Exchange appears as independent of and indifferent to production only in the final phase where the product is exchanged directly for consumption' (Marx 1973, p. 99). Consumption satisfies the 'urgent' need of the individual, but in the process of this satisfaction, becomes in itself, a 'moment of production' because it reproduces the individual in the process becoming 'a moment of production' (Marx 1973, p. 94). Consumption in capitalism is a productive activity because it forms the basis for further exploitation and accumulation. Under capitalism, commodity production is not an 'objectified activity, but rather only as an object for the active subject' (Marx 1973, p. 91). Consumption provides an aim for production to happen by providing it with an objective in the first place, but 'it is clear that production offers consumption its external object' (Marx 1973, pp. 91-2). In other words, as Marx argued, without a need, production cannot take place *obviously*, but it is consumption that reproduces that need. And, this is where, the power of capital lies – the continuous reproduction of need through the fetishisation of commodities under capitalism.

Marx theorised consumption to be a part of the production process, something which was integral to the overall reproduction of capital (Marx 1992; Marx 1981). For Marx, factors such as circulation time and turnover time were all a part of the overall productive structure of capitalism, because he was not looking at production and consumption as two separate structural domains, but rather as being together within a single dialectical totality complementing and supplementing each other. Marx did not however fuse production with consumption. For Marx, it was the commodity that was at the genesis of capitalism. It was through the commodity that capitalism generates social patterns. Commodity production creates the avenues for the fulfilment of the two purposes of capital – '(1) as agent of production, (2) as source of income' (Marx 1973, p. 95). Ritzer's (2015, p. 416) argument that 'there can never be any production without consumption' is the main problematic element of the prosumption thesis. Marx, instead, shows that the private exchange of commodities only becomes possible because the private form of production exists in society. Marx treats distribution, circulation, exchange and consumption as moments of the overall circuit of capitalism where: 'A definite production ... determines a definite consumption, distribution and exchange as well as *definite relations between these different moments*' (Marx 1973, p. 99).

When the entire focus is on consumption, theories tend to forget the power which capitalism holds in terms of generating needs as Marx had shown. Such theories do not take into account that the intensity with which exchange takes place in society depends on the system and structure of production (Marx 1973, p. 99), which determine the supply and demand of commodities as well as the speed with which they get exchanged. The research conducted for this book reveals that people, either in the Global South or in the Global North, rarely question the commodities which end up on social media. Their entire focus remains on the act of consumption, while sometimes neglecting the indomitable power of capital to manipulate the commodities that the workers consume, including the way they consume it. A careful reading of Marx would reveal that Marx was never negligent of the use-value and its role within capitalism. Marx insisted upon the idea that it was only through the commodity being consumed in a particular way – the complete realisation of its use-value – that it became a 'real product' (Marx 1973, p. 91).

The very basis of Marx's theory was that with the ushering of advanced forms of capitalist domination over the society, use values get robbed of their importance within the society, a point which the book has already highlighted. Fetishism, plays a major role in this transformation, being a displacement of meaning through synecdoche, the displacement of the object of the desire onto something else through processes of disavowal (Gamman and Makinen 1994, p. 45). For Marx, as has been stated repeatedly, production and consumption were complementary parts of the total production process. The consumption of the commodity, the product, is taken to be the normal course of progress of the circuit of capital itself. Without consumption, there cannot be any production, while without any production there cannot be any consumption (Marx 1973). As Marx says: 'The individual consumption of the worker and the individual consumption of the non-accumulated part of the surplus product comprises, taken together, the total individual consumption' (Marx 1992, p. 173). The individual demands of a capitalist are usually the means pf production and the labour-power required for further production, of which the value of the former keeps on getting smaller in magnitude as the capitalist extends or expands the production process (Marx 1992, p. 197).

There are many different strands of social and political theories and movements which have taken up the struggle against this domination of consumer goods in society. Some groups, such as those formed by consumer activists and certain cooperative organisations that have been working against the mystification of the commodities by mainstream advertising firms, opine that the market as an institution has failed to connect the domains of production and consumption effectively as it has obscured the actual labour power and labour time embedded in those commodities. The networks of production and consumption through this obscuration create a mirage that all commodities are produced miraculously without the intervention of human effort and labour. As much as consumer activist groups sound radical and socially reformative in nature, they end up propagating the same production-consumption relation when they bring their own product into the market. Skotnicki (2015, pp. 7-8) reports a brief history of some of these cooperative organisations and brings forward their arguments supporting the existence of the 'ethical consumer' and the belief that the consumer is omnipresent within capitalist society: '[t]he unit of the co-operative movement is the *customer* – almost invariably a woman' (quoted from Skotnicki 2015, p. 8). Their fascination with the idea of the 'ethical consumer' was destined to fall into contentious disagreements with the working class who were averse to the idea of the consumer being a supreme figurative position within society. This was also characteristic of the methods in which these organisations worked, often with trade unions and socialist groups (Skotnicki 2015, p. 9), who were more interested in maintaining class harmony than advancing toward class struggle. As Skotnicki reports, these groups often took the side of the employers rather than the workers because of their adherence to the consumer being all-powerful and the workers as powerless elements within the capitalist network. The labels used by these companies run and managed by consumer activists, did not depict the working conditions literally but were rather used as triggering devices for instilling a sense of ethics among the consumers, but never really attempt to target the fetishism under capitalism. The arguments stemming from these consumer activists and cooperative groups can be mainly summarised through the two quotes from two different authors reproduced below:

> ... the consumer was universal as opposed to the partisan interests of businessmen and labourers. The consumer was also socially powerful. [Consumer activist Groups] identified the consumer as an "employer" of sweatshop and tenement labour. They proposed that consumers – not producers or owners – dictated the social relations of production. (Skotnicki 2015, p. 8)

> The force of one's actions as a consumer typically extends far beyond the local, making it necessary to relegate the senses to a lesser order power, in favour of an understanding of the causal impact of consumption along the axis of distant markets (Glickman 2009, p. 47)

Some of the arguments made by consumer activists, Skotnicki (2015, p. 23) agrees, can potentially reinforce the fetish of the commodity by connecting the commodity to the relations of production through a vantage point informed by that of the consumer. He rightly says that this process is at the heart of reinforcing the power of the commodity by continuing the sustenance of the social structure where the people only relate to the labour process and the workers who produce the objects through the commodities in the market. The general understanding of these groups rested upon the assumption that since the consumer was responsible for consuming the product and thereby was an "employer", he/she was also responsible for the working conditions within the production mechanisms in place (Skotnicki 2015, p. 8). However, the basic problem of this mode of theorisation is the assumption that they assume sovereignty of the consumer, i.e., they assume that within capitalist systems, the consumers have a kind of autonomy that can be used by them to effect changes. Freedom is a contested term within postmodern societies, like the one we inhabit currently. In the words of Zygmunt Bauman, postmodern freedom of expression 'in no way subjects the system, or its political organisation, to control by those whose lives it still determines, though at a distance. Consumer and expressive freedoms are not interfered with politically so long as they remain politically ineffective' (Bauman 1989, p. 88).

Individuals today, are more compliant than they have ever been. There have been many theories that have tried to divulge the cause of this compliance, such as Foucault's theory of the governance of individuality which argues that it is a diverse and expansive network of power that produces compliance (Soper 2020); or Boltanski and Chiapello's (2005) theory of the new spirit of capitalism. The 20th Century was a watershed moment for consumption globally. With the rise of Fordism, consumption had become an inevitable part of the working-class lives. Workers suddenly found themselves able to afford a lot of commodities that had historically been outside their grasp. Little did the working class realise then, that the affordability has come as a consequence of their own exploitation. Consumers grew exponentially with the growth of scientific management processes which not only boosted production but also had a dynamic impact on the existing 'needs' within the society. With more production and innovation within the already existing line of commodities, capitalism emerged as a global force because of its ability to generate new commodities which went on to create new kinds of needs in society as Marx had written in his *Grundrisse* (Marx 1973). Consumer activists have struggled against this within their own gambit of theoretical and practical domains. Some of these groups have turned out to be more inclusive than many established socialist and communist organisations, but they have all turned out to be rendered invisible the plight of the working class and other marginalised sections – the section which is the worst sufferer of any capitalist expansion. Consumer activists have been pushing for more regulatory practices in the production and sale of goods along with frameworks for creating more non-alienated production-distribution-consumption systems (Duncombe 2012, p. 361). Many consumer activists have taken upon de-fetishisation as a socio-political and cultural project. Sometimes, they have talked at length about the cruel labour conditions within which these commodities are produced in sweatshops (IGHLR 2011). But even consumer activists of the radical nature have taken onto understand and analyse the role of human beings within consumption to be essentially one which involves neglect on the part of the people along with their inability to notice and understand the true nature of the objects of their consumption (Duncombe 2012, p. 362). A discussion on the consumer activists in detail is not the purpose of the present work. However, the minor caveat has to, in the opinion of the current author, end with a quotation from Bill Talen, who is the creator of the character called 'Reverend Billy' and his 'Church of Stop Shopping': 'Corporate Commercialism has sped up to a roar, virtually unopposed. Consumerism is normalised in the mind of the average person, sometimes we even refer to ourselves as consumers forgetting that we are also citizens, humans, men, women, animals' (quoted from Duncombe 2012, p. 366).

For example, women, especially those coming from the upper and the middle classes, were particularly important in the formation of the early consumer activist groups in the West. These groups were highly active in demanding state regulation within the conditions of production, ethical purchasing practices, reforms of workplaces, etc. This was also coexistent with the gradual proliferation of cooperative societies, where the women were encouraged to take an active interest in the same. However, many societies were characterised by women becoming members of them only through the social identities of their spouses or guardians (Skotnicki 2015, p. 6-7). Such was the state of affairs in many early consumer activist groups. These groups maintained their differences from other radical groups because of their over-emphasising nature of giving importance to the ethical nature of the consumer rather than emphasising the civic or sacred duty of the people in maintaining ethical consumption practices. However, abolitionist groups were not advocating from the perspective of the people being consumers (Skotnicki 2015, p. 19). Other theories such as ethical consumption and contradictory consumption have evolved which have problematised the contemporary issues with regards to the distinction between consumption and consumer culture where consumption is posited as the general usage of commodities while consumerism is referred to as the logic of consumption located specifically within a definite social and political structure or system is known broadly as consumer capitalism (Lewis and Potter 2011; Littler 2011).

These theories mainly posited the replacement of old exploitation with a new form – one of the many characteristics of bourgeoisie rationality and philosophy (Adorno 1973) – and the implicit rationalisation of corporations supporting low priced commodities in the age of low wages (Weeks 2011), but never rupturing the system which produces these problems in its entirety. Kate Soper's (2020) critique, on the other hand, runs along the lines that in both Marxist and liberal ideas about the process of consumerization in contemporary society the consumer – the actual individual – is rendered powerless and is trapped within a particular mode of non-reflexivity. Marcuse (1941) analysed this condition as a foundational element of technological rationality under capitalism. Technology, as Marcuse (1941) rightly analysed, cannot be merely analysed as a disjointed artefact, but rather is a process that is directed by the individuals and groups associated with the technological form as creators, users, etc. In other words, the users themselves are part of the technological form in existence and cannot be detached from the same. However, users are not free individuals but are rather part of a process of social control, whereby capital attempts to control the minutest parts of their lives. Workers are victims of the existing system where their subjectivity is systematically dissolved or 'self-styling "constructs"' of the consumerist system where they freely choose to be consumers (Soper 2020, Ch. 'Neither heroes nor dupes'). She argues that one of the massive blind spots of socialist or Marxist thinking is that it lends itself to a contradictory position when it comes to thinking about the relationship between consumer reflexivity and the understanding of the self-constructed knowledge of the subjects. Soper argues that some Marxists and socialists turn to fetishise the notion of unfreedom prevailing in society to be the only cause of the problems arising under modern-day capitalism and in the process do not give adequate importance to the individualisation of consumption: 'it seems no more convincing to view shopping enthusiasts as merely unfortunate and unaccountable victims of the consumer society than to view them as fully autonomous and self-knowing beneficiaries of it' (Soper 2020, Ch. 'Neither Heroes nor dupes').

Conscious experience forms the basis of the acceptance of any political demand. The narrow materialism of consumer culture under contemporary capitalism can only be countered if the forces, advocating any form of social justice, can bring forward and start practising a form of materialism that is dialectical in nature including the value-form and its associated class character which restricts the worker for attaining the full realisation of individual potential (Dunayevskaya 1958a, p. 119, 1965). To understand the activities of human beings as consumers properly, what is required is a theory that focuses on consumers not as mere consumers, but towards a theoretical vantage point, which treats consumers first as human beings and then as consumers of the capitalist production-circulation-distribution cycle. In other words, the theory and social movements against consumption have to address the issues raised by consumption knowing that 'Man...is the objective foundation of the historical dialectic...and...is decisively involved in the dialectic process' (Lukacs 1971, p. 189), which leads the society into a stage of global capitalist control and domination. Lukács understood the point that it was actually existing human individual who is 'the subject and object of the social process coexisting in a state of dialectical interaction; but as they always appear to exist in a rigidly twofold form, each external to the other, the dialectics remain unconscious and the objects retain their twofold and hence rigid character [...] But because of the split between subjectivity and objectivity induced in man by the compulsion to objectify himself as a commodity, the situation becomes one that can be made conscious' (pp. 165-68). It is only the dialectics of history that can constitute the social basis for a radically different future based on theorising the dynamic and dialectical characteristics of the social existence of human beings (p. 188).

Consumer activists have attempted to counter these seemingly glaring contradictions and deficiencies in Marxist theory, which as we have seen in the preceding paragraphs were all addressed by Marx albeit in a different manner. Activities such as consumer activism rarely serve the purpose of a full-frontal attack on the power of capital. Much like how Hardt and Negri (2000) characterise postmodern movements and their relationship with structures of power, where they argue that these movements end up justifying the very power structure they set themselves to critique because they possess no self-ontological justification if those structures do not exist. Similarly, the radical activities of groups that engage in consumer activism only, as Duncombe (2012, p. 370) further notes, make sense within the paradigm of the consumerist world. They can never escape the overarching logic impended by capitalism, instead, in some way or the other, they reinforce the same by explaining the resistance in terms of the very object which creates the basis for their existence as a force of rebellion. What is needed is a radical understanding of consumption from a humanist perspective, a perspective that puts the focus on people, rather than the category of consumers. Of course, consumers are people, who have their own subjectivity and objectivity, but the onus must be placed on the actual person engaged in the process of consumption. In the past, the global anti-capitalist movement has witnessed the problems of conceptualising a homogenous working class as a category. Building such categories as homogenous entities – both in form and content hypothetically – renders invisible the fault lines which exist under capitalism.

10. THE CIRCULATION OF CAPITAL

Under capitalism, commodities that usually have a use-value, get quantified through their exchange-values and then by the price attached to them. For the circulation of commodities and the subsequent circulation of capital that the commodities represent, the invention of a universal standard was of utmost necessity (Marx 1859). Money has today become that global standard – 'money makes commodities commensurable' (Marx 1859, p. 306). It has become not only the universal standard as Marx (1976) had defined it to be, but rather has become the most important element in the overall machine of capitalism. Within social media, people have started creating new avenues of profit generation. The peculiarity of the space created by social media is that while the mainstream urban space, which is used by capitalism to exploit the working class (Lefebvre 1991; Harvey 2016), is actively managed by the capitalists, the digital space is transformed into an exploitative space by using the active will of the users, the majority of which come from the working classes. Unlike Adam Smith's (1776) notion that the market would act as an invisible force and settle all the problems and contradictions within society, it has taken an active role in promoting and amplifying those very social problems and contradictions that it was supposed to solve according to the proponents of free-market enthusiasts and capitalists. Within contemporary capitalism, the market does not only produce the needs but also creates hurdles in the route towards the fulfilment of those needs. 'Market' today means a social relationship that is mediated by the commodity, money, capital and human needs, both biological and social. But capitalism maneuvers the human actions performed for the fulfilment of those needs in such a manner that the attainment of the goals remains out of reach of the common populace. Under contemporary capitalism, actual human needs are seldom met. The market itself acts as a hurdle in the route towards complete satisfaction of the working class.

The regime of private property, which will be discussed in the next chapter, cannot come about without the development of a form of capitalism where the ontological essence of human beings is directly related to the possession of commodities. This entails within itself, the creation of an immense gambit of commodities capable of acting as points of exertion of human desires for enjoyment and activity as Marx (1844, p. 322) notes. Money essentially becomes the means through which human beings articulate their existence under capitalism as 'Money is the pimp between man's need and the object, between his life and his means of life' (Marx 1976, p. 165). Money becomes the bond, as Marx (1844, p. 324) says, between human beings and society and vice versa – 'the bond of all *bonds*'. The peculiar characteristic of money exists in it being the manifestation of human alienation as 'the alienated *ability of mankind*' (Marx 1844, p. 325). In other words, 'A particular individual may even today come into money by chance, and the possession of this money can undermine him just as it undermined the communities of antiquity. But the dissolution of this individual within modem society is in itself only the enrichment of the productive section of society' (Marx 1973, p. 223).

Capital is not an entity, but rather it is a process that represents the collective application of the various forms that capital assumes during its cycle of accumulation. Capital is a social relation that manifests itself throughout the capitalist society, be it within the realm of production or in the realm of distribution, or the realm of consumption. This social relationship exists because the point of production of the commodity form exists. Unless one addresses the point of production and its associated contradictions, one cannot get an idea of how capitalist logic circulates in society. Marx understood this basic contradiction very well. Production processes to Marx enabled the continuous reproduction of capitalism (Marx and Engels 1848). The total production process, under capitalism, splits up into two different departments: the means of production and the means of consumption. Marx defined the two departments as follows:

> (I). *Means of Production*: Commodities that possess a form in which they either have to enter productive consumption, or at least can enter this.
> (II). *Means of Consumption*: Commodities that possess a form in which they enter the individual consumption of the capitalist and working classes (Marx 1992, p. 471)

Marx then goes on to explain two vital components that the capital in each department possesses within itself:

> (1). *Variable Capital*: As far as its *value* goes, this is equal to the value of the social labour power applied in this branch of production, i.e. the sum of the wages paid for it. Considered in its material aspects, it consists of self-acting labour power itself, i.e. of living labour set in motion by this capital value.

> (2). *Constant Capital*: This is the value of all the means of production applied to production in this branch. It breaks down in turn into *fixed* capital: machines, instruments of labour, buildings, draught animals, etc.; and *circulating* constant capital: materials of production, such as raw and ancillary materials, semi-furnished goods, etc. (Marx 1992, pp. 471-72)

As Dunayevskaya (1965, p. 69) notes, the labour embedded within both constant and variable capital is forced labour, and 'this labour is so alien an activity that it has itself become a *form of capital*'. The mutual exchange of capital between the two departments leads to the grand circulation of capital in society in the form of money (Marx 1992, p. 474). Money circulation thus lies at the heart of the capitalist system, and it is exactly this aspect of capitalism that social media helps to sustain. Capital needs to ensure that the money which circulates in society has to flow back to the capitalists. This money is made to circulate in the economy for enabling the circulation of commodities under capitalism to ensure that the capitalist profit generation can continue. The circulation of capital usually takes place in the general form of commodity circulation in society as Marx says (1992, p. 139-140). Money or 'M' becomes the functional form of capital in the process of commodity circulation designed for the extraction of surplus value and profit generation (Marx 1992, p. 148), which then leads to the valorisation of value.

Surplus value is inherently present in both kinds of capital in both departments. Rejecting its centrality often can lead one into the trap of petty bourgeoise economism as Dunayevskaya (1958a, p. 127-130) notes. For the reproduction of capital, capital needs to flow between these departments creating more capital to bring into operation more means of production. That is the very basic element of social media commerce as well. When someone buys a saree in India from a seller or someone buys a book from one of those antique book dealers in the West, they are contributing to the capitalist surplus-value generation, though indirectly. Sellers of such commodities are rarely 'one timers' and are often either professionals or looking to be professionals. They use the narrative of the object's past for increasing the value of a particular object under capitalism (Susen 2018, p. 11). This stems from the deep capitalist desire to transform everything, including the immaterial forms of cultural expressions, into commodities meant for consumption. Social media here has been playing a major role. Previously the transmission of such cultural norms would take years, if not decades, and social media and technology speed up the process. So, it is entirely normal to have a thriving American comic book trade going on in India on social media. Sellers and buyers involved in which have revealed how technology and the proliferation of social media have made characters from those comics household names in India, creating an entirely different market itself that thrives through social media because new comics are too costly to buy for most potential readers. Under capitalism, there cannot be any mode of consumption that does not include payments of some form or the other. This complete monetisation of society 'ushers in frightening and disorienting confusions between persons and things, and as money becomes animated with powers of life and death and persons increasingly sell themselves, as if they were things' (McNally 2011, p. 150). Individuals begin to identify themselves in terms of money as money becomes the basis of their integration into society (McNally 2011, pp. 150-51).

Money becomes capital through the process of circulation when it ends up at the hands of the first capitalist, often the industrial capitalist, through a detour through the various circuits of capital by going through (multiple) cycles of realisation (Marx 1973, pp. 346, 402). Money capital is the most general expression of this process of valorisation (Marx 1992, p. 140), which has often been touted as the most important element of all the processes of capitalist exploitation of the working class (Marx 1976). Money capital does not exist, however, in a vacuum. It is always in a relationship with other forms of capital such as commodity capital. The relationship between money capital and commodity capital is an important one to understand if one is to get a complete grasp of the dynamics and potential outcomes of large-scale social media commerce. Commodities are the entities within capitalism that give rise to commodity capital. It is the actually existing form of capital that functions as a manifestation of the production process itself. It represents the 'already valorised capital value' which has been created by the capitalist production process (Marx 1992, p. 121). The commodity function of capital, according to Marx, contains in the ability of capital to create/produce the commodities, sell them on the market and then get converted into money thus realising the circuit of Commodity (C)-Money (M) (Marx 1992, p. 122). The money capital gets 'converted into a sum of commodities of equal value, *L* and *MP*, by way of M-C. These commodities no longer function as commodities, as articles for sale. Their value now exists in the hands of their buyer, the capitalist, as the value of his productive capital P' (Marx 1992:126). As Marx notes:

> In the circulation C-M-C, money is in the end converted into a commodity, that serves as a use-value; it is spent once for all. In the inverted form, M-C-M, on the contrary, the buyer lays out money in order that, as a seller, he may recover money. By the purchase of his commodity he throws money into circulation, in order to withdraw it again by the sale of the same commodity. He lets money go, but only with the sly intention of getting it back again. ... The exact form of this process is therefore M-C-M', where M' = M + DM = the original sum advanced plus an increment. This increment or excess over the original value I call "surplus-value". The value originally advanced, therefore, not only remains intact while in circulation, but adds to itself a surplus-value or expands itself. It is this movement that converts it into capital (Marx 1976, pp. 249, 251-52)

Money capital, as Marx says, that it serves two kinds of purposes for the capitalists. The first purpose is that it provides the capitalists with the means to invest in further means of production, while the second purpose is that it allows the capitalists to bring in more labour-power for the creation of commodities at an expanded scale. When capital is transformed into commodities, it performs the functions of a commodity. In everyday lives, commodities assume supreme importance under contemporary capitalism, as has been stated and analysed in Chapter 1. The initial step in this direction is taken by the productive industrial capital, which is in plain language, a means to transform the means of production and labour-power bought by the capitalist's money capital into a commodity that can be sold in the market for productive consumption (Marx 1992, p. 126). In the process, the means of production (which can be roughly taken to be the raw materials) are transformed into consumption-ready objects as commodities. This increases the value of the productive consumption by the industrial capitalist in the society, which contributes to the overall process of valorisation. Marx explains the implications of this process brilliantly:

> Through this real metamorphosis, the commodities withdrawn from the market in the first stage M-C are replaced by materially different com-

> modities of different value, which must now function as commodities, be transformed into money and sold. Hence the production process appears simply as an interruption in the circulation of capital value, which up till then had only passed through the first stage M-C. It passes through the final phase, C-M, with C altered both materially and in value. (Marx 1992, p. 126)

The circulation of capital in the socio-economic circuits dominating the everyday lives of the working class occurs through money capital and commodity capital. As Marx rightly attests, these are 'the two forms which value assumes within its circulation stages' after assuming and exhausting its productive capital form in the stage of production (1992, p. 133). Social media commerce ensures the mobility of capital in society in a manner that allows capitalism to counter this very problem. It uses the state of crisis to create a situation where the working-class property is sold on social media, which enables the working class to make a temporary gain out of the commodity as a response to the state of crisis or to fulfil their consumerist needs. During the course of the present study, not many respondents talked about being able to save their money or even wanting to do that. In other words, except for the exception of one respondent, who talked about saving money to repay a loan, which is also a form of capital accumulation, all the others affirmed investing the money back into the market directly or indirectly, sometimes through rent payments or by buying the same kind of consumer goods that they had sold. In the entire process of multiple transformations, however, the capital value does not change in form, but only changes in content:

> At the end of the process, the capital value is thus once again in the same form in which it entered it and can therefore open the process afresh and pass through it as money capital. And indeed because the initial and concluding form of the process is that money capital (M), we call this form of the circuit the circuit of money capital. It is not the form of the value advanced, but only its magnitude, that is changed at the end (Marx 1992, p. 127)

Commodity capital in its final form exists at the disposal of the capitalist in the form of money – 'the universal equivalent' (Marx 1992, p. 127). Like all other commodities, money is also produced by labour 'but unlike any other commodity, it is universally recognised to be just that and hence acts as a "natural" measure. But that measure is natural to it only because it is the recognised representative of labour in its abstract form' (Dunayevskaya 1958a, p. 86). The prevalence of money also produces the quintessential illusion about the non-existence of the valorised value of the capital originally advanced in the circuit, by emphasising the form of capital, i.e., money, in the process. The valorisation of capital, i.e., 'the fact that more value in the form of form is finally withdrawn from the circulation sphere than was originally advanced to it' is frequently hidden from the common view (Marx 1992, p. 141). These forms of capital are not completely distinct from each other but are rather related to each other. Marx argues that the entity which binds them is industrial capital (Marx 1992), which appropriates these various forms of capital and utilises them for producing surplus value and profit for the capitalists (Marx 1992, p. 133). It is the industrial capital, according to Marx (1992, p. 183) which acts as the complete and unified form of all the three circuits of capital – money, productive and commodity – and acts as various forms of capital at different points of the cycle of surplus-value generation so that the unified form manifested by industrial capital 'can only be such a unity in so far as each different part of the capital runs in succession through the successive phases of the circuit, can pass over from one phase and one functional form into the other' (Marx 1992, p. 183). Marx subsequently argues: 'Different fractions of the capital successively pass through the different stages and functional forms. Each functional form thus passes through its circuit simultaneously with the others, though it is always a different part of the capital that presents itself in it' (Marx 1992, p. 184).

A portion of the functional capital exists as commodity capital which with time, is transformed into money – the universal equivalent as Marx has famously remarked in the second volume of Capital. This money is entwined within a vicious circle of continuous reproduction. Another part of the functional capital existing as money-capital finds its way to being transformed into productive capital, while the productive capital finally gets transformed into commodity capital (Marx 1992, p. 184). The total circuit of capital in the society functions through the unity of all the existing circuits of capital in the society, by being a united process of production and circulation (Marx 1992, p. 183). The united action of this circuit uses machinery, people and the social structures built around them to subsequently increase the scale of production. The proportion and limits to which the production process can be improved are contingent upon numerous factors, some of which are technical while some of more ideological in nature. However, as Marx (1992, p. 158) rightly says, even if they are all meant for the generation of surplus-value or profit, they can only grow to the extent to which certain material forces permit them to grow and become part of the already existing circuits of capital or create newer circuits. In both cases, the moment the productive capital's role increases in conjunction with the circuits of capital, society begins witnessing the hoarding of surplus-value.

With time and the development of machinery as Marx (1976) points out, the capitalist invests a lesser amount in buying the means of production, with the value of the means of production being comfortably superseded by the value of the commodities the capitalist supplies to the market (Marx 1992, p. 197). The moment money gained from the sale and consumption of commodities has been used to buy the means of production, it ceases to exist as money or commodity but instead becomes a component of the mode through which industrial capital, the most important and overwhelming form of capital according to Marx, sustains itself (Marx 1992, p. 190). The gap which exists between the value of a commodity and the actual 'fictional' price attached to it operates as a site where capitalist exploitation works at its vicious best. This is an area where capital today has the power to regulate human behaviour and 'needs'. The satisfaction of needs, and their capitalist objectification functions in this gap to transform human beings into agents of need fulfilment only. However, when functioning as such agents, individuals tend to function in accordance with their alienated selves. Under contemporary capitalism, credits have functioned appreciatively to increase or sustain the accumulation of capital. It has also helped capitalism to move around the production-realisation contradiction without landing up in an abyss of debt. The contradiction between production and realisation, to Harvey (2014, pp. 82-3), forms an important part of capitalist exploitation in contemporary modernity. He says that demands can be increased if the total aggregate numbers in the labour force can be increased, or by significantly allowing the increase of conspicuous consumption or by simply increasing the number of people who are outside the production process but contribute a significant share of consumption i.e., the people who are rich mostly because they have inherited wealth. Credits are frequently used in contemporary society. Harvey (2014) argues that the domination of the credit system has somehow morphed the production-realisation contradiction into a contradiction between money and its innumerable forms today. The production-realisation contradiction remains intact, but it just gets relegated to the uncertainty of the future. Capitalism through the usage of credit within the society attempts to maintain the flow of capital in the system simultaneously while also creating the ground for what Harvey (2014, p. 83) calls speculative investment which in turn can potentially result in further accumulation.

The absence of any regulatory mechanism for private production and accumulation of capital is the fundamental contradiction of capitalism as Luxemburg (2003, p. 6) had noted, which leads to almost every major economic problem under capitalism including problems of overproduction and underconsumption. As long as capitalism evades the problem of realisation, the chances for it to avoid the crisis increase. Deregulated credit expansion however can lead to problems, an example of which the world had witnessed in the global financial recession of 2008. The fall in profits or the drop in the rate of accumulation is constituted by the lack of aggregate demand in the society creating contradictions to the expanding capitalist accumulation practices. It must be mentioned here that capitalist effective demand and the social demand for commodities' use values are two entirely different things. There might be a social demand for wood in cold places, but that does not mean that this demand will automatically affect the market. Capitalism and its desire to expand the networks of circulation and accumulation act as a two-edged sword. The more it oppresses the worker in a desire to maximise the productive capacities of the worker, the more it impoverishes the worker. The more it impoverishes the worker, the more their capacities to act as consumers drop. Thus, the drive to accumulate more surplus value effectively, and almost always, results in the constraining of the social agents of accumulation.

Consumer goods play a major role in the continuation of the circulatory system of capital in society. Social media commerce is centred upon consumer goods. In the Second Volume of *Capital*, Marx laid out the basis of this. In the previous chapter, the book described the importance of luxury goods in the consumptive cycle of capitalism. Critical Marxist theory has not often given hedonistic consumption the attention it deserves under contemporary capitalism (Turner and Rojek 2001, p. 80), which has often been used as a ploy against Marxist theory by labelling it as being insensitive to working-class desires of possessing and using consumer goods, by treating working-class consumption as a normal activity under capitalism (Shumway 2000; Mulcahy 2017). As Mulcahy (2017) argues, this distracts the theorising of workers as active consumers and reduces the importance of the commodities they use for the commodities' use-value, which again, they obtain through exchange under capitalism. In other words, Mulcahy (2017), and previously Fleetwood (2008), argue for an extension of Marxist theory which includes the workers not only as labourers but as active consumers under capitalism as well.

Marx (1859) mentioned the huge influx of consumer goods in the market in 1859, however, as Shumway (2000) notes this interpretation did not feature much when *Capital* was actually written in 1867 (Mulcahy 2017). A large portion of consumer goods is luxury goods, which are often outside the realm of necessity, regardless of how luxury is defined. Luxury goods generate more capital, but they also cost more to circulate. Manufacturers of luxury goods spend fortunes trying to make these products commonplace. Social media is one of the most important tools in that gambit of agents used to popularise these commodities. The exchange of such commodities on social media is more pronounced in the Global North than in the Global South. However, it must be said that, in the Global South, luxury has a certain aesthetic dimension, which is not commonly found in the Global North. So, while commodities such as laptops, tablets, etc are easily available through social media in the Global North, it is not only because these commodities are comparatively cheaper or commonplace in the West but also because, to a large extent, users in the Global North are a lot more engaged in the consumer economy than their counterparts in the Global South. In the Global South as well, these commodities find their way into the social media marketplace, but they are largely either extremely outdated or have been out of functional operation for a long time. Instead of used products, one finds a huge surplus of new commodities on the social media market in the Global South. This is primarily because of the way businesses are beginning to be structured in places like India. Luxury goods are not preferred to be consumed as used goods in the Global South. There are two reasons for the same: luxury goods even in their used forms are too expensive for a large section of the population, and the factor of trust. Considering that Indians still prefer to buy expensive commodities from brick-and-mortar stores, it is not unnatural that such commodities do not end up on the social media market. The kind of commodities which are found on the social media market and are most popularly bought and sold there thus, do not exist in a segregated society and are intimately related to the broader forces of distribution existing in the society.

Consumer goods or the commodities of Department II, in Marx's own words, can be subdivided into two kinds: *necessary means of consumption* referring to those goods that enter the consumptive cycle of the workers as means of subsistence and because being the means of subsistence also enter the consumptive cycle of the capitalists; and *luxury means of consumption* referring to those goods that enter the consumption of only the capitalists i.e., the luxury goods (Marx 1992, p. 479). Marx was well aware that in the case of the former kind of consumer goods, the quantity and quality of the value of the goods which enter into the consumption of the capitalists and the workers have differences. Marx here was also in affirmation to the idea that culture can play a vital part in determining the classification of commodities as necessary or luxury means of consumption such as tobacco. In the previous chapters, the book has engaged with the ideas of scholars such as Appadurai (1982), who had hinted that Marx lacked in providing a cultural idea of commodities. However, in reality, for Marx, a commodity was an all-encompassing identity, representative of a dialectical relationship between the use-value and the exchange-value that the commodity represents for the working class whose labour-power remains embedded within it.

The commodities that workers buy with the wages they gets are mostly consumer goods enabling the worker to survive and reproduce themselves (Perlman 1972). Perlman relates the extensive buying and selling of consumer goods by the workers to the general alienation in the society under capitalism where the workers become mere spectators in the process of capitalist exploitation of their own selves. Social media commerce functions in this space in contemporary society. It not only makes the workers engage in such practices but also accelerates the process, solving the issues of circulation for capitalists to a large extent. The Austro-Marxist Otto Bauer argued that capitalists who engage with the production of consumer goods constantly accumulate a portion of profits attributed to the production of producer goods, which then allow 'for a more rapid production growth of the means of production', and thus there exist no problem in the realisation of surplus value under capitalism (Kowalik 2014, p. 62). However, it is precisely the fear of a failure emerging in the process of this realisation that makes capitalism invent and invest in these newer and dynamic forms of capitalist accumulation and reproduction. Capitalism today has reacted to the realisation crisis by creating systems that do not allow capital to remain fallow. The necessity of capital being in circulation, being continuously invested and circulated, has been emphasised by Marx (1976, 1992), Engels (1843), and Mandel (1979) among others. However, Marx (1859, 1976) saw the basic contradiction of capitalism as being the commodity-form itself, a point which was emphasised later by Dunayevskaya (1952, 1958a, 1965). For the capitalist thus, any personal property of the working class is a hindrance because, in an overproduction crisis, it tends to block the worker to consume more commodities that have already been produced. The next chapter will go into detail about the importance of the idea of 'property' under capitalism and how social media commerce impacts the concept. These methods aimed at the complete realisation of value engage with the complete realisation of surplus-value already existing in the market. This realisation, however, does not and cannot happen through the conventional methods because, under the aegis of contemporary capitalism, the working class is always surviving under the conditions of economic and socio-psychological crises. The economic crisis inevitably results in lowering the capacities of the working class to consume commodities, which can call forth an overproduction crisis. The result of an overproduction crisis, again, is the failure of the capitalist infrastructure to realise the existing surplus-value in the market because with the dwindling wages and the rising prices, capitalism simply does not allow the working class to consume the commodities already available in the market (Deb Roy 2020).

Marx (1992, p. 419) argues that the total price of the entire corpus of commodities circulating in the society has not risen because of any general rise in prices, but because the number of commodities already in the market is much higher than those existing previously. Production, circulation and consumption are related to each other within a dialectical reality. With more production, there is the requirement of more circulation, which costs the capitalist. Marx brings forward that these costs have to be borne by the money already in circulation – 'either by a more economic use of the quantity of money in circulation ... or by means that accelerate the circulation of the same pieces of money – or alternatively by the transformation of money from the hoard to the circulating form' (Marx 1992, p. 419). The circulation of capital in society has to be manipulated in a way that it almost always lands up again at the hands of the capitalists, so as to ensure further productive consumption. Marx argues that a society can be fundamentally based on productive consumption only if production is carried out on a large scale (Marx 1981, p. 198).

One of the most important elements of this process of generating large-scale commerce in society is the influence of money – both as 'money' and as 'money capital'. The distinction between 'money as money' and 'money as capital' forms the foundation of the concept of commodity fetishism and that of the capitalist society itself in general. As Lotz (2017) argues, the latter provides a society, such as the one that is prevalent today in most of the world, with a specific direction in which the society is meant to progress in. The exchange of commodities does not merely mean the exchange of one object for another but rather, as a process, works towards the generation of further profits and surplus value (Lotz 2017, p. 367) – the most basic element of the sustenance of capitalism (Marx 1976). Under capitalism, every form of production of commodities is capitalist commodity production. The capitalist mode of production always takes large-scale production and sale as predispositions of the social mode of production (Marx 1992, p. 190). At this point, Marx distinguishes between the merchant and the individual consumer. It is the merchant who usually engages with capitalist industrial production directly. It is because the merchant is such an important component in completing the circuit of capitalist accumulation. At the same time, the merchant is also the most visible element of the entire circuit of capital, as is the capital that the merchant possesses: 'Thus we occasionally take its existence for granted in illustrating particular aspects of the capitalist circulation process; but in this general analysis we assume direct sale without the intervention of the merchant since this intervention conceals various moments of the movement' (Marx 1992, p. 191). Here, to make the point clearer to the reader, Marx quotes Sismondi, the summary of which points towards the idea that even though commercial activities (those of the merchants and the traders) engulf a good amount of the overall social capital, at the first glance, it does not seem to be a part of the social capital. Sismondi argues, something which Marx seconds (although he does mention that Sismondi's arguments are quite naive), that the activities of the seller, also constitute an important part of the total accumulative structure of capital in the capitalist society: 'Exchanged against the revenue of the consumer, [industrial and productive capital] divided into only two parts. One of these served as revenue for the manufacturer, in the form of profit, the other served as revenue for the workers in the form of wages, while they were manufacturing more [commodities]' (quoted from Marx 1992, p. 192). Money puts the commodity capital into circulation. It drives the industrial capital towards generating more circulation-ready industrial capital in the form of numerous individual commodity capitals. The speed with which money circulates in the economy, the greater the speed in which individual capitals of industrial nature can transform into commodities and then into, or even simultaneously, money. At this point, it is again worthwhile to quote Marx:

> Capital of the same value accordingly requires less money for its circulation, the more the money functions as means of payment and the shorter the periods of payment. On the other hand, assuming that the velocity of circulation and all other circumstances remain the same, the amount of money needed to circulate as money capital, is determined by the sum of the prices of the commodities, or alternatively, given the quantity and values of commodities, by the value of the money itself (Marx 1992, p. 192)

Two aspects of Marx's idea which have been emphasised in the quote above are (i) money functioning as the generalised means of payment; and (ii) the speed with which payments get made. In the first volume of Capital, Marx talks about the different kinds of functions that money performs within the capitalist scheme of things: as an entity to be hoarded, as a means of payment, and as a global force (Marx 1976, pp. 227-244). Hoarding, the first function mentioned by Marx, which is usually the utilisation of surplus-value that has not yet ended up in circulation, is conserved in the most convenient and universal form – money (Marx 1992, p. 163). Marx says that it is only in the underdeveloped and pre-capitalist economies, that hoarding usually becomes an end in itself while in other forms of economies, hoarding specifically entails within itself a desire to end up back in circulation (Marx 1992, pp. 164-65). In the advanced capitalist economies, however, the states have a much more sophisticated process through which they utilise banks and other such financial forms to ensure that they sustain themselves failing which the economies would be looking at stagnation in the circulation of commodities and capital (Marx 1976, p. 244). This could prove fatal to the capitalist economy itself, where labour and social relations formed on the basis of the exchange values of commodities are maintained by this very capital, which is in circulation in the public sphere (Lotz 2017, p. 378). Thus,

> ... the hoard [usually] appears as a form of money capital, and hoard formation as a process that temporarily accompanies the accumulation of capital, because and in so far as money figures here as *latent money cap-*

ital; because the formation of a hoard, the hoarded state of the surplus-value present in money form, is a functionality determined preparatory stage that proceeds outside the circuit of capital, and paves the way for the transformation of surplus-value into really functioning capital (Marx 1992, p. 164)

Money performs numerous functions in the overall circulation of commodities and the accumulation of surplus-value and profit. Sometimes, it does so by acting as 'latent money capital' which draws its name because of the characteristic ability of money to temporarily suspend (or camouflage) its functions as capital (Marx 1992, p. 158-165). Money capital functions as 'latent money capital' because it does not act directly on the circuit of capital (on any circuit of money, commodity or productive capital) in spite of it being able to act upon individual capitalists in ways peculiar to this particular form of capital. According to Marx, the purpose of this engagement lies in the expansion of the surplus-value produced contributing to the enrichment of the individual capitalist, sometimes in the form of credit securities, bonds, etc. which function as latent money capital (Marx 1992, p. 159). Marx says:

> If money functions as means of payment in our capitalist's transactions (so that the commodity only has to be paid for by the purchaser at a later date), then the surplus product destined for capitalisation is not transformed into money, but into claims for payment, titles to property equivalent to a sum that the purchaser either already has in his possession or expects to come into (Marx 1992, p. 159)

Marx argues that for capitalism to sustain itself, it is of utmost necessity that it does not only valorise the value within the circuits of capital, but also creates the conditions for the successful reproduction of capital, which also entails the valorisation of not only the original capital value, but also that of the surplus-value itself (Marx 1992, p. 173). The circuit of capital encompassing M-C and then further onto C-L and C-MP, a large part of the means of production, as Marx (1992, p. 189) rightly says, themselves become commodities functioning as commodity capital and then getting transformed into money capital. The distinction evoked between 'money as money' and 'money as capital' is a crucial element here because it functions as a basic cause of the distinction between the capitalist and the upper class/rich (Lotz 2017). Money can function simply as 'money' in certain circumstances. For example, in the cases where money is used as a gift and lands up directly within the sphere of consumption. But, within contemporary modes of capitalism, this scenario is, at best, an unrealistic utopia- and an impractical one – because with the complex network of circulation that capitalism has created, all money eventually finds its way into some form of 'capitalist circulation' where even stagnant money can 'work' (Lotz 2017), say for instance the case of fixed deposits in banks. In the opinion of Lotz (2017) arguments that dissolve the distinction between the two end up justifying the universality of capital as a thing, which in turn also dissolves the specific historicity associated with the usage of 'money as capital'. In more general terms, capital today has to be analysed as a subject rather than an object. With the overdetermining role which capital has taken within society in contemporary times, any analysis which does not take capital itself as a subject, at times, often falls into the trap of crude materialist analysis neglecting the subjectivity of capitalism itself. Capital has become overdetermining in nature because it has successfully created a situation where every social action or object finds its desired meaning within the capital-ist circulatory system:

> A subject is not only something that is related to itself, but also is something that is *related to itself in its other*, i.e., it is related to itself through something that is external to itself. Accordingly capital is a sub-ject because it is related to itself and because it is related to itself through abstract labour, i.e., labour that is exchangeable and monetised, as well as through the products of abstract labour, i.e., commodities as monetised products of monetised labour (Lotz 2017, p. 368)

Capital, as a self-valorising value, does not just comprise class relations, a defi-nite social character that depends on the existence of labour as wage labour. It is a movement, a circulatory process through different stages, which itself in turn includes three different forms of the circulatory process. Hence it can only be grasped as a movement, and not as a static thing (Marx 1992, p. 185)

Money capital's functionality is within the domain of general purchases and payments utilising its characteristics as money more than capital (Marx 1992, p. 112) – in everyday life. In other words, money capital can be said to be the most general form of capital that affects the everyday life of people, especially the working class. As Marx says, a part of the money-capital utilises itself in a way in which its characters as 'Capital' vanishes while only its 'Money' characters remain:

> M-L generally regarded as characteristic of the capitalist mode of produc-tion. But this is in no way for the reason just given, i.e. because the pur-chase of labour power is a contract of sale which determines that a greater quantity of labour is provided than is necessary to replace the price of labour power, the wage; i.e. because surplus labour is provided, which is the basic condition for the capitalisation of the value advanced, or, what comes to the same thing, for the production of surplus-value. It is rather on account of its form, because in the form of wages, labour is bought *with money*, and this is taken as the characteristic feature of 'money economy' (Marx 1992, p. 113)

Money eventually takes the form of a fictitious capital, which becomes highly concentrated in nature. Harvey (2014), in a way, defines fictitious capital to be the outcome of 'money capital loaned out to activities that create no value even as they are highly profitable in money terms and return interest' (Harvey 2014, p. 32). He bases his arguments on the idea that one of the major characteristics of money under contemporary capitalism is that money has the capacity to draw in profits from activities that bring forward no significant value. Investments that people make, be it on any platform in any form, are a form of this fictitious capital. This essentially, in plain terms means, the popularisation of the idea that money can lead to further generation of money capital – which has a positive impact on the circulation of capital in society, even within the working class.

Money, in the process, acts almost like a *spectre* – an invisible, all-powerful force. Jacques Derrida, arguing within the paradigm of what is now known as hauntology, argued, 'Marx always described money, and more precisely the monetary sign, in the figure of appearance or simulacrum, more exactly of the ghost' (Derrida 1994/2006, p. 55). Like a ghost, the influence of money is felt everywhere. Money, in the societies that we inhabit, not only dominates us through its actual physical presence but also through its spirit. The possession, or the desire of possession, of money, has wide implications for the social structure existing in any society. The aspect of social power and social status, which carries wide implications under capitalism, something which socialism tends to destroy, is dominated by a certain power associated with the possession of money under contemporary capitalism. In other words, money places itself at the heart of society and influences the most intimate aspects of human behaviour therein, including emotions such as 'greed' (Harvey 2014, p. 33), envy (Matt 2003), etc. There can be wide debates about whether human beings are inherently greedy or envious. But, as Harvey (2014) has highlighted, 'what is certain is that the rise of the money form and the capacity of for its private appropriation has created a space for the proliferation of human behaviour that is anything but noble and virtuous' (Harvey 2014, p. 33). Under conditions of extreme accumulation, a condition which is reminiscent of contemporary capitalism, money, irrespective of whether it acts as capital or not, gets concentrated at the hands of the few, it inevitably causes disruptions in the way society is organised. Capitalism takes these disruptions to new extremes.

11. COMMERCIAL CAPITAL AND SOCIAL MEDIA COMMERCE

Capital, in any capitalist society, is subject to fluctuations in value because of the general economic conditions which exist in the society. Marx uses the terms releasing and tying-up to make points surrounding the ways in which capital uses the revenues generated through the sale of commodities. Marx uses the phrase 'tying-up' to refer to the value of a commodity that is transferred back into its form of constant or variable capital so as to facilitate further production. By releasing up, Marx means the process in which a part of the value of the commodity is not transferred into any form of capital but rather becomes available for usage in other areas (Marx 1981, p. 206). In the second volume of Capital, Marx devotes a great deal of attention to the aspect of circulation time within the overall domain of reproduction of capital. Circulation time is an extremely important aspect of capitalist accumulation. The faster a commodity and money is circulated within society; the faster accumulation will be. There is a considerably large amount of interest-bearing capital or capital in the form of money existing at any given point of time in most major economies in the Global North and the Global South indiscriminately. They contribute to the growing drive for capital accumulation and profit generation through the exploitation of the social labour of the workers. David Harvey advocates that there is a symbiotic relationship between the appropriation of social labour and the appropriation of the commodities that social labour brings to life (Harvey 2014, p. 53). Bankers seldom care about the processes in which they generate profits or income, which can be at times, highly exploitative in nature (Harvey 2014, p. 54). Similarly, the creators or managers of social media platforms, rarely care about how anybody uses their platform. For them, the most important part of the entire process – from the creation of the platform to its massive popularisation – is that the process in which they engage should create profit.

Social labour produces the commonly held properties in society. These properties, as commodities, have distinct use-values, but when exchange value and prices become the dominating aspect of social life, like the bankers, even the human beings – the everyday human being – stop thinking about what the process in which these commodities were produced and witnesses them merely as agents to satisfy individual needs. All kinds of capitalist production harbour within themselves, a certain despotism, whereby it attempts to control the workers and their social labour (Dunayevskaya 1958a, p. 92). This is a point that Hardt and Negri (2000, 2004) also emphasise throughout their works. Social control in the modern world is mediated through numerous methods – debts, manufactured needs, crises, etc. The debts and other properties possessed by an individual have intimate connections with the financialised form of capital in the form of bank loans, credits, etc. The control over the circulation of capital allows the capitalists to control the productivity required by an individual. The revenue that a capitalist earns through the sale of commodities is usually divided into two parts: either it is, in the words of Marx, 'set free and can now serve either to expand his consumption or be transformed back into capital (accumulation)' (Marx 1981, p. 206). Marx quite correctly asserts that the tying up of variable capital is disadvantageous to the accumulation of profits, which can be countered by the releasing up of variable capital, to further the reproduction of capital (Marx 1981, pp. 211-12). This releasing and tying up of variable capital is intricately related to other vital aspects of the production process such as the utilisation of constant capital, wages, employability of workers both quantitatively and qualitatively, material conditions of production, and raw material procurement, etc. A detailed analysis of the process however is not the primary concern of the present work. Marx says that the release of variable capital for other purposes results in 'enabling it to function at an increased rate of surplus-value (Marx 1981, p. 210). At this point, it is entirely worthwhile to quote Marx in full:

> If wages fall, owing to a fall in the value of labour power, a portion of the capital previously laid out on wages is set free. There is a release of variable capital. For capital that is newly invested, this has simply the effect of enabling it to function at an increased rate of surplus-value. The same quantity of labour is set in motion with less money than before, and in this way the unpaid portion of labour is increased at the cost of the paid portion. But for capital that was already invested earlier, not only does the rate of surplus-value increase, but on top of this a portion of the capital previously laid out on wages is set free. This was formerly tied up and formed a portion constantly deducted from the proceeds of production, a portion which was laid out on wages and had to function as variable capital if the business was to proceed on the old scale. This portion now becomes available and can be used for new capital investment, whether to extend the same business or to function in another sphere of production (Marx 1981, p. 210)

Commercial capital, to Marx (1981), is a part of the overall merchant's capital, with another part of the same being money-dealing capital (which is similar but not identical to the second volume's money capital). While writing about the genesis of commercial capital, Marx said: 'Taking the social capital as a whole, one part of this is always on the market as a commodity, waiting to pass over into money, even though this part is always composed of different elements, as well as changing in magnitude; another part is on the market as money, waiting to pass over into commodities' (Marx 1981, p. 379). Capital, or rather the power of capital, is perennially existing in this cycle of shifting forms of capital in society. In simpler terms, Marx relates this process – the process of the formation of a very special kind of capital – to the overall process of capitalist reproduction and accumulation: 'In as much as this function [of metamorphosis] acquires independent life as a special function of a special capital and is fixed by the division of labour as a function that falls to a particular species of capitalists, *commodity capital becomes commodity-dealing capital or commercial capital*' (Marx 1981, p. 379). This is how Marx defines the origin of commercial capital. Commercial capital, in simpler terms, means the capital which is there in the market. The nomenclature of commercial 'capital' as a form of capital comes from the belief within Marx that every act which contributes to the reproduction and sustenance of capitalism – including transportation, storage systems, etc – should be designated and analysed as production process (Marx 1981, p. 380). Marx argues that certain activities like the ones listed above often get categorised as the only activities which are performed by commercial capital as its special function. However, 'as the social division of labour develops, so the function of commercial capital also evolves in a pure form, i.e., separately from these real functions and independent of them' (Marx 1981, pp. 379-380).

Commercial capital is an extremely important cog in the total machine which reproduces capitalism on an everyday basis in society. Marx understood the tremendous importance that commercial capital holds in the overall reproduction of capital, and thus gave considerable importance (and space) to the same:

> ... the existence of capital as commodity capital, and the metamorphosis that it undergoes as commodity capital within the sphere of circulation, on the market – a metamorphosis that breaks down into buying and selling, the transformation of commodity capital into money capital and of money capital into commodity capital – forms a phase in industrial capital's reproduction process and thus in its production process as a whole; but that at the same time, in this function as circulation capital, it is distinguished from its own existence as productive capital (Marx 1981, p. 380)

This process can manifest itself in many different ways depending upon the perspective from which one views the metamorphosis:

> ... the transformation of commodity capital into money capital, that presents itself for the merchant as M-C-M, in so far as he advances capital for purchasing the commodity from the producers; it continues to be the first metamorphosis of the commodity capital, even though the same act may present itself for a producer or for the industrial capital in the course of its reproduction process as M-C, the transformation of money back into commodity (the means of production), i.e. as the second phase in the metamorphosis (Marx 1981, p. 385)

Even though Marx asserted the importance of commercial capital within the overall process of capitalist accumulation, he was also equally assertive on the idea that commercial capital is nothing but a form of industrial capital. Marx never abandoned the belief that it is at the point of production (which often lies with industries) that capitalist social relations get formed. Social media commerce also is a part of the overall capitalist social relationship. The commercial relationships which get formed and then accentuated through social media, cannot exist if at the point of production the dehumanised notion associated with the commodity does not get abstracted.

The important part of commodity capital becoming commercial capital, in all forms of commerce including social media commerce, is the role of the merchant. Commercial capital is not an independent form of capital, as Marx (1981) repeatedly highlights. It is a part of the overall social capital that sustains capitalism. The role of the merchant becomes important because it is the merchant who advances valorised money capital within the system of circulation which enables the metamorphosis of commodity capital into full-fledged money capital, and then further onto more industrial capital. The merchant advances money, either the merchant's own or borrowed money (from the market itself), facilitating the circulation process of industrial capital that the commodity capital represents at the hands of the merchant. Through this activity, the merchant 'transforms money into money-capital, puts his M forward as M-C-M', and by this same process, he transforms commodity capital into commercial, commodity-dealing capital' (Marx 1981, p. 386). Marx argues that the primary reason behind the seemingly independent nature of commercial capital is because of the manner in which 'the merchant [advances] money capital that is valorised as capital and functions as capital' (Marx 1981, p. 386) but is only involved exclusively in the act of effecting the transformation of commodity capital into money and/ or money capital. Money capital performs this function through a continuous process of buying and selling, an activity that facilitates the circulation of industrial capital'. And, in the process, ensuring that the total social capital in the society is reproduced constantly. Social capital, as Marx explicitly states, 'is evidently nothing more than the part of industrial capital' which still is within the market waiting to undergo the process of metamorphosis into commodity capital and then towards valorised industrial capital itself. There is a very intricate process of transformation involved in this metamorphosis here. For the purposes of the present work, we divert ourselves a little bit from Marx's example of linen and instead focus our discussion on more tangible and relatable objects for the 21st Century – *smartphones*.

When smartphones are traded on social media, as is often the case within social media commerce, a form of merchant's capital, previously advanced only by the merchant, gets advanced by the working class. Social media commerce intensifies the process by creating numerous points from which such advances are made, creating a situation where a high percentage of commercial capital is enabled through the *working customers'* capital to go into the metamorphosis process, through which industrial capital gets reproduced. This reproduction is made possible through the accumulation that occurs at the physical merchant's store when the workers possess the money for getting into exchange relations with the original merchant's capital. Any merchant's capital is comprised of two parts – commodity and money capital. Social media commerce enables the constant circulation of both. The merchants, and the workers who act as merchants within social media commerce, are placed at the confluence of both these kinds of capital and can frictionlessly (in most cases) transform one capital into another by continuously engaging in activities of buying and selling. Social media commerce effectively transforms individuals into merchants. The more merchants exist in the society, the more commercial capital exists in the society. Stated simply, the more commercial capital exists in society, the more social capital is reproduced in society. Quoting Marx again, from one of the last paragraphs in the famous chapter on Commercial capital:

> Commercial capital is nothing more than capital functioning within the circulation sphere. The circulation sphere is one phase in the reproduction process as a whole. But in the process of circulation, no value is produced, and thus no surplus-value. The same value undergoes change in form. Nothing at all happens except the metamorphosis of commodities ... Commercial capital thus creates neither value nor surplus-value, at least not directly (Marx 1981, p. 392)

Commercial capital mostly exists in the form of money, which as Harvey (2014, p. 55) says, 'represents and symbolises social labour (value). The fact that money, as opposed to the social value it represented, is inherently appropriable by private persons means that money (provided it functions well as both a store and measure of value) can be accumulated without limit by private persons'. Enabled by the private appropriation of common wealth existing in society, this property of money contributes to its functionality as a marker of social status and power, which transcends both the individual desire for power and the social class power held by capitalists (Harvey 2014, p. 55). Within pre-capitalist societies, money did not assume the same power which it holds within the contemporary world. Commercial capital, emphasising again, is that portion of industrial capital, which exists physically in the market as a force that brings into effect the transformation of commodity capital into money (Marx 1981, p. 386). Marx says:

> ... it is only the *money* capital advanced by the merchant, the money capital exclusively designed for buying and selling, which never assumes any other form than that of commodity capital and money capital, never assumes that of productive capital, and remains forever penned into capital's circulation sphere – it is only this money capital that has now to be considered with regard to the overall reproduction process of capital (Marx 1981, p. 386)

Social media commerce begins from a seemingly Hobbesian point where it is already well-known and accepted that the amount of wealth that is present in the society in the form of commodities is not enough to satisfy everybody in the society such that they have to engage in competitive terms with each other to secure the plausible means of happiness (Fromm 1942). This was one of the ideas that Fromm draws from Hobbes but categorises it as an outmoded model because the model fails to take into account the dynamics associated with the ascent of the middle classes under capitalism towards economic rationality and a form of capitalist individuality, which again depends upon a form of working-class cooperation – albeit formulated and controlled by the capitalist schema. Social media commerce utilises this cooperative or participatory culture within social media, controlled by the monopolies (Fuchs 2014c), for profit-accumulation and valorisation of already existing capital within the society. Since social media is an important part of that communicative paradigm within digital capitalism, Fuchs (2014c) argument about the necessity of rethinking the simplistic models of participation which almost always place social media as a liberatory force within contemporary capitalism stand as an important and vital point. Fuchs (2014c) rightly states that true participation enables human beings "to be part of the decisions and to govern and control the structures that affect them" (Fuchs 2014c, p. 57). The differing elements or parts of the commodity capital which are almost always found in the market constantly evolve and reproduce themselves in various forms. Social media today has also become a part of this evolution. One of the main purposes of these forms of capital is to maintain the continuity of the productive capital and reproduction of the industrial capital. Capitalism cannot sustain without reproducing the profit and surplus-value which are essential to the regeneration of capital as a whole. Marx accorded tremendous importance to this function so much so that he explained through differing theoretical and practical examples, the process in which a portion of the social capital always exists as circulation capital. Circulation capital involves the continuous acts of buying and selling which take place between the industrial capitalists. A capitalist manufacturing bread buys tons of plastic wrappers from another capitalist. Similarly, a capitalist producing cigarettes buys from another capitalist manufacturing filter tips and paper. Circulation capital, effectively, forms the basis of the nervous system upon which the entire structure of reproduction is built upon. Circulation capital is also integral to the formation of commercial capital. Marx finally offers the readers the most exhaustive definition of commercial capital, when he discusses that in relation to circulation capital:

> Commercial capital, then, is nothing but the transformed form of a portion of [the] circulation capital, which is always to be found on the market, in the course of its metamorphosis, and perpetually confined to the circulation sphere ... Commercial capital, therefore, is absolutely nothing more e commodity capital of the producer which has to go through the process of transformation into money, to perform its function as commodity capital on the market; only instead of being an incidental operation carried out by the producer himself, this function now appears as the exclusive operation of a particular species of capitalist, the merchant, and acquires independence as the business of a particular capital investment (Marx 1981, pp. 380-82)

However, there is also a difference between commodity dealing capital, often labelled as commercial capital, and commodity capital. Some capitalists are also commodity dealers. Their capital appears on the market as money-capital since the capitalist does not produce anything but rather 'simply deals in them, facilitating their movement' which makes it mandatory for them to be the possessor of money capital. It is essential at this point to remember that Marx theorises the independent form of commercial capital because of two very specific reasons. The first reason is that commercial capital functions through the merchant or the agent, who is quite distinct from the producer. The whole seller of grocery goods in Hyderabad is not the same person who produces the rice or flour which the seller sells to the customers. Of course, even within the production process, there is a massive distinction between the industrial capitalist and the actual producer of the commodities, something which becomes the basis of Marx's theory of alienation (Marx 1844).

One of the easiest examples in this regard is to take the example of the capitalist firm which manufactures smartphones of a particular brand. The retailer does not produce the commodity, and nor does the retailer distribute the product. There are definite tasks assigned to each different capitalist along the cycle from production to consumption. Throughout this cycle, capital changes in its form continuously finally ending as surplus value for all the capitalists – of all kinds – engaged in the cycle. Commodity capital performs an important role in the cycle of distribution, a cycle very important if capitalism has to sustain itself. This is the function of commodity capital which makes it distinct from industrial capital, whose main purpose is to manufacture commodities. The main purpose which is fulfilled by commodity capital occurs outside the traditional domain of production and thus assumes an autonomy of its own. Marx (1981, pp. 384-85) explains this process in considerable detail citing numerous examples, mostly focusing on linen. The role and function of commercial capital also depend upon the possessor of the commercial capital. If a producer is by him/herself, the distributor or agent of the commodity within the market, their commercial capital simply becomes a part of the capital (industrial and/or productive).

Marx argues that this supposedly independent function of commodity and commercial capital is also related to the pre-existing dominance of industrial capital in society. On the supposed distinction or speciality of this kind of capital in comparison with industrial capital, Marx argues that, for the industrial capitalist, i.e., the capitalist who produces the commodity, this is only the commodity getting transformed into money (as the capitalist receives the money for the things the workers produce for the capitalist). But for the commercial capitalist, the money capital that the merchant or the trader parts within the beginning (of the circuit M-C-M') returns to the merchant at the end through the sale of the commodities. At times, the money capital increases in value (Marx 1981, pp. 384-85), which is then used for further profit generation. Money can only function as capital as long as it is in circulation, be it in any form. But, when it is taken out of the circulation process in the form of cash or other such forms, it does not function as capital, but only as money. However, if the cash is reinvested in property or other such investment domains, the money again becomes capital because then it sets in motion, or rather restarts in simple language, the network of capitalist accumulation. Capital, as Lotz (2017, p. 370) exists only within the domain of accumulation. Money, thus, is used by capital to make more money, which is one of the most important aspects of money (Harvey 2014, p. 32) under contemporary capitalism. This money then again goes on to form the commodity form – the soul of capitalism.

Selling is never the primary problem for capitalism, the problem for capitalism – or rather its overarching goal – is the realisation of the surplus-value which helps capitalism to reproduce itself (Dunayevskaya 1958a, p. 126). The commodity form and its associated value – the fundamental contradictions of capitalism – are not products of the market, but rather are creations of the capitalist production system, which manifests itself in every social relationship that exists under capitalism. The fetishism of the market, as has already been noted is the cause of numerous problems with Marxist analysis as Hudis (2012) notes, which fails to correctly understand the logic of capital itself. For example, such analysis usually takes private property and market-anarchy as being entities and processes intrinsic to capitalism, and as such direct, all their revolutionary energies towards them, while leaving out the basic fundamental contradictions of capitalism – value-form, commodity production and alienation (p. 14). Because of this issue within the articulation of the very logic of capital, they fail to analyse correctly the extent to which capital forms and structures the society.

The ubiquity of capital gets manifested in its act of splitting itself up into two different components, so as to maintain its overwhelming presence in society. Capital ensures that a part of it is always present in the market, to bring into effect the metamorphosis of productive and industrial capital to commodity capital and further into commercial capital. In doing so, capital ensures that it is reproduced at a social level. Social media commerce helps capital in doing just this. For the micro-scale entrepreneurs, who operate through social media platforms in the Global South, the process of the social reproduction of capital becomes very apparent. These sellers use other services such as courier services, packing professionals, etc., which are essential to the successful continuation of their businesses. In doing so, they aid in the reproduction of capital at a social level by making it circulate within the society. Most of the services that these sellers use are private services, often informal in nature, performed mostly in cash. The aspect of the usage of cash is an important one. Cash is what keeps small businesses running (Marx 1844). Some of the small-scale sellers on social media emphasise payments through cash. Some of them do that because it helps them meet their day-to-day costs. Some do that because it helps them feel secure. Conversations with people who drive for platforms such as Ola and Uber in India reveal this aspect of cash quite starkly.

In the Global North, depending on the location one is in, these services might be either private or public in nature. But regardless of their kind of functioning, these services are those everyday commodified services that keep money in circulation. Within social media commerce, there are multiple tendencies operating in terms of the mode of payment. Buyers, at times, prefer to pay through online means so as to save themselves the hassle, while some of them prefer to use cash merely because of the fact that paying through cash ensures that the buyer only has to pay once the commodity has transferred hands. But regardless of the mode of payment, this money formulates itself as commercial capital – a part of the overall social capital – which operates almost strictly in the circulation sphere. It is commercial capital that enables the creation of the 'money reserve' – a vital element of the sustenance of capitalism. The creation of commercial capital is a process that enables the original producer to reign supreme within the society because: '... one part of [the producer's] to be present in the market as a commodity, while another part carried on the production process so that when this latter part entered the market as a commodity, the other part would flow back in the money form' (Marx 1981, p. 387). Marx quite accurately notes the dialectical relationship between the merchant and the producer arguing about the complementary nature of their relationship such that without the one, the other would find it extremely difficult to sustain oneself. Taking a cue from these points, Marx advances three primordial assumptions regarding commercial capital. The first one is that commercial capital engaged exclusively with the activities of buying and selling within the market is almost always smaller in magnitude than what the magnitude would have been if the producer had himself/herself been engaged in the process of buying and selling: 'And besides the money that has to be laid out on the purchase of commodities, this capital also includes the money laid out for the labour needed to pursue the merchant's business, as well as for the merchant's constant capital, warehouses, transport, etc.' (Marx 1981, p. 388).

Since the merchant (the one possessing the maximum proportion of commercial capital) exclusively works within the domain of buying and selling commodities, it is very likely that the metamorphosis of commodities into money and then the money into productive capital will take place much sooner than what it would have been if the producer oneself would have been involved in the same. The third and last assumption put forward by Marx was based upon the relationship between commercial and industrial capital. Marx argued that commercial capital in a particular sphere (as usual, Marx explains this by taking the example of linen, and other such clothing materials), has the ability to facilitate the turnover of capital in other spheres, or in the same sphere (Spheres, in this case, refer to the production spheres of different commodities – linen, silk, etc.) (Marx 1981, p. 388). Commercial capital and circulation capital are indispensable to the furthering of the profits of industrial capital. The turnover of the industrial capital – the heartbeat of capitalism – faces numerous hurdles such as the problem of circulation time, the time taken by production, etc. Commercial capital helps in the mediation of these risks and problems. Commercial capital generated through exchange on social media commerce helps in the sustenance of other kinds of capital, just like Marx had predicted:

> The turnover of industrial capital is restricted not just by the circulation time, but also by the production time. The turnover of commercial capital, in so far as it deals with just one particular kind of commodity, is not restricted by the turnover of a single industrial capital but rather by the turnover of all industrial capitals in the same branch of production ... The turnover of the same commercial capital can just as easily mediate the turnovers of capitals in various branches of production (Marx 1981, pp. 388-89)

The declining usage of postal services in certain areas gets boosted by the sellers using them for sending their orders. The E-commerce revolution in India has already had a huge impact on the delivery services in India, including giving rise to numerous courier companies in the country. Social media commerce, however, because of the kind of people involved often with low amounts of commodity capital, relies heavily on the subsidised postal system. Social media commerce brings into effect a revolution in the overall system under which capitalist social relations exist. It necessitates a fast internet connection – a service which comes at a premium cost in most developing economies in the Global South – along with a constant emphasis on the logic of desiring faster modes of transport and delivery mechanisms. An increase in commercial capital and demand within the postal and other modes of delivery of products also creates a complementary increase in the commercial capital advanced in the sphere of transportation services.

Globally, individuals engaged in social media commerce use many associated services of the economy. Professional social media sellers have tie-ups with various delivery companies in India, which then, in turn, have professional relationships with other delivery companies and transportation agencies. The amount of revenue or profit that commercial capital can generate within a sphere of commodities, is contingent upon the quantity and quality of production in that sphere. However, the turnover of commercial capital does not depend upon individual capitals but rather depends upon the entire system of capitalist production, where numerous individual capitalists are engaged in the production of a similar kind of commodity (Marx 1981, p. 389). This turnover is only limited by the amount of time the merchant might need to reproduce the buying and selling cycle of the commodities. Commercial capital plays a pivotal role in the increase of the overall wealth in society. But the increase of wealth in society, almost inadvertently also results in an increase in poverty as well, for the marginalised sections (Marx 1844, p. 263).

Social media commerce fastens the turnover of commercial capital by making money change hands far more quickly than all previous forms of circulation techniques under capitalism. In a developing economy such as India where production is not sufficiently developed, commercial capital exists at a larger scale in comparison with the commodities in the society than the developed economies in the West, resulting in the constitution of monetary wealth for the merchants (Marx 1981, p. 389). The situation with commodities is in direct proportion to the mechanism of production in society. The speed with which production takes place and the speed of consumption determine the 'velocity' in which the circulation of money capital takes place within the economic structure (Marx 1981, p. 389). Merchants always play a crucial role in this regard, as has been noted by many scholars (Banaji 2020). Merchants within the capitalist economic system perform dual functions – first, they use the commercial capital to the full extent by buying newer commodities, and secondly, they again play a major role in selling those commodities in the market. This has not altered much from Marx's own day (Marx 1981, p. 390). For the merchant, it is extremely important that the commodities sold by the merchant yield a substantial profit, for which the merchant employs numerous and varied methods. Derek Sayer (1979, pp. 34-5) while talking about mercantile capitalism, says that for the merchant, it is always profitable to exchange the perishable materials at one's disposal for non-perishable or relatively fewer perishable goods. The relatively lesser perishable goods remain the most adequate replacement for value during longer durations of time. One shopkeeper of a grocery store, who exchanged his views on the kinds of items he stocks, in a conversation with the author, said:

> I, generally, focus on packed goods. Packed goods with MRP (Maximum Retail Price) help me in my own personal budgeting. The problem with selling loose products is that I have to alter the selling price with the fluctuations in the market. It is perfectly normal for me to incur a loss while selling those items because I cannot sell them at a price which is higher than what is accepted within the market. But with items which are packed by the manufacture, I have one significant advantage. They can always be sold at the same price, no matter what the state of the market. So even if I know that the products are virtually the same, my preference is always on stocking and trying to sell packed items, for instance wheat of a particular brand, rather than items which I buy in loose form from the wholesaler, even if that is wheat from the same field as the packed one.[1]

This can be just taken as an example of how prices and values influence everyday lives under capitalism. The same logic can be applied to the trading and commercial activities of used goods on social media. Commodities that end up on social media platforms as articles of sale are priced items, such that they have a marked price, are fairly tangible in terms of usage, and are capable of retaining some form of use-value for the subsequent user. There are instances in the Global North, where even perishable goods such as eggs, meat, etc. end up on the market digitally on social media, but the cases are few and far between. It is such that such goods do not hold much value over the course of time. In other words, their ability to yield profit for the seller is restricted by the time, which elapses between the moments in which they change hands. Harvey (2014, p. 17) argues that the exchange value associated with any product is determined by the cost of production and the profit along with the interest and the rent (which is often the ground and intellectual rent required for producing the item). The producers under capitalism tend to be heavily engaged and bent toward the production of exchange values rather than use-values. Exchange value under contemporary

---

1. The original statement from the shopkeeper was in Bengali and has been translated to English by the author. The statement has been condensed so as to convey the summary of the argument made by him which is relevant to the present discussion.

capitalism thus, 'moves into the driver's seat of' all forms of production (Harvey 2014, p. 17).

Circulation and Commercial capital are nothing alien to the capitalist circuit. All kinds of commodities under capitalism possess the capacity of generating surplus value and as such cannot be alien to the capitalist circuit. If a commodity does help in the production of surplus-value by being sold, the simple reason for the same is that the commodity already embodied the value. Social media commerce enables the functioning of commercial capital at a large scale by positively impacting (for the capitalists) the circulation time, both of commodities and capital, under capitalism. The desired end result, however, remains the valorisation of value. Though seemingly independent, as social media commerce and other forms of mass-scale commercial activities would like to paint it as it is at the end, 'nothing more than industrial capital itself in its form of money capital, in its own reflux in the money form' (Marx 1981, p. 390).

12. THE SOCIETY OF WORKING-CUSTOMERS

Social media commerce has created a society of Working-Customers – customers who are also workers, and workers who are also customers, all performing their share of alienated work within the same space to generate profits, often for the same capitalist. This society is fixated on the permanence of the consumer identity – the only fixed identity under contemporary capitalism. For individuals, the utility of a commodity ideally should be its use-value. But, in a society dominated by exchange value under capitalism, the utility of the commodity belongs to the person who can pay for the price of that utility (Dunayevskaya 1958a, p. 107) – the most effective consumer. Under contemporary capitalism, money is the dominant mode through which utilities can be bought and sold. The society of customers takes root from the point where money becomes ingrained within the nature of human sustenance (McNally 2011, p. 148). The society of customers takes root from the capitalist alienation at a social level which makes it normal for human beings to exploit other fellow human beings (Marx 1844, p. 307). Money exists under contemporary capitalism as an *'end in itself'* as a ' true *power* and the sole *end* – the extent to which in general' creates a human ontology under capitalism by making possible the possession of innumerable commodities (Marx 1844, p. 313). Marx (1844) also notes, as has also been stated in the previous chapters, that under capitalism, the human being also exists as a commodity in a state where human consciousness and self-action exist in a completely dehumanised form. Political economy analyses human beings as being a collection of various needs whereby each human being exists only for the satisfaction of the needs of other human beings – the mechanical nature of which makes it easier to classify the individual as being either a capitalist or a worker (Marx 1844, p. 317). But it is only when the concept of labour including the division of labour and its associated alienation under capitalism is conceptualised as the basic essence of private property, that the concrete development of the capitalist economy can be analysed. It is this analysis that lays bare the idea that every activity that human beings engage in under capitalism is a manifestation of their alienated mode of existence under capitalism and not their actual species-activity or real activity as a human being with an essence.

It is in the nature of capitalism to garner profit from every aspect of the production process, so it is not unnatural that 'The capitalist thus makes a profit, first, on the wages, and secondly on the raw materials advanced by him' (Marx 1844, p. 248). Under contemporary capitalism, human beings have become part of the raw materials, in fact, they have always been so. Social media commerce has only made it more explicit. Social practices associated with private property, form the core of the society that social media commerce envisages for the inhabitants therein. It is commonly accepted that society, in its essence, is a collection of social practices (Williams 1980) and their associated meanings (Bauman 2010). Technology and its associated innovation do not bring forward a new model of social behaviour, but it merely serves as a manifestation of already existing needs and processes (Bauman 2010). As Fuchs (2019b, p. 148) argues, by manipulating the digital means of communication, within which contemporary social relations are formed and mediated, capitalism creates digital spaces of alienation (Fuchs 2019b 148), where capital still dominates but only in a more indirect fashion by utilising the participatory culture of the individuals therein. This is the basic premise within which capitalism constitutes the basis of the creation of the society which is being termed as working-customers. This is a society where the workers are being actively encouraged to live the consumer life.

Engels's (1845) theory regarding the entrapment of the individuals within their narrow private interests through capitalist manoeuvrings also sheds light on the process in which an already existing communicative framework makes it not only easier but also attractive to the working classes to engage in social media commerce. The workers by engaging in social media commerce, not only act as active members of the community but also play their role as workers by allowing commercial capital and money to flow freely in society. That these people do not understand their predicament as workers and take themselves as sovereign beings is a part of the overall ideological domination of capitalism which carries forward the complete subversion and control of ideology as Dunayevskaya (1982, p. 144) predicted. However, while discussing ideology, it is worthwhile to take note of structural Marxists such as Althusser, whose theories on ideology, even with their problems, have proved to be helpful to the analysis of ideological domination. Althusser (2014) defined ideology to be an abstract 'imaginary' domain that only becomes concrete when it confronts social reality. Ideological emancipation within education does not merely mean maintaining the balance between erudition and scholarship, but rather it is about 'each [individual] becoming conscious of [one's] nature as an intellectual subject' (Ranciere 1991, p. 35). Under digital capitalism, social media is a conscious activity of schooling oneself on the rigours and nuances of everyday life. Just like how the reproduction of labour-power under industrial capitalism takes place through the capitalist schooling system, under digital modes of capitalist oppression social media becomes the place where individuals where along with learning the 'knowhow' to succeed and make themselves useful in a capitalist economist system and society:

> ... people also learn, [...] the 'rules' of good behaviour, that is, the proprieties to be observed by every agent in the division of labour, depending on the post he is 'destined' to hold in it. These are rules of professional ethics and professional conscience; that is, to put it plainly, rules of *respect* for the social and technical division of labour, and in the final analysis, the rules of *the order established by class domination* (Althusser 2014, p. 144)

The relationship between culture and any form of education and acclimatisation is an integral one. Culture, in the words of Williams (1960) does not refer to a natural process anymore but is rather 'a process of human training' (p. xiv). Of course, the connotations of training from Williams' times have altered significantly in the twenty-first century. However, Williams (1960) has very correctly described the shift in the way in which culture affects the everyday realities of the subjects under capitalism. Culture is, under capitalism, 'a thing in itself' whose connotations have been subjected to changes from being a state of mind or a habit to meaning the body of non-natural sciences to designate a way of life holistically (pp. xiv-xvii). For the purposes of the current paper, the emphasis is going to be on the usage of culture as 'a whole way of life, material, intellectual and spiritual' (p. xiv) as stated by Williams, to refer to how particular groups of individuals practice a certain set of cultural norms under very specific spatialities and temporalities within the society. Culture shapes individuals, as much as the individuals shape the cultures which are constituted around them (Williams 1960, 1961). This is a major underlying aspect of almost all the major works of Cultural Marxists such as Raymond Williams and Stuart Hall, who have attempted to theorise the relationship between culture, society and capitalism from a Marxist perspective. As Anthony Barnett (2011) rightly says in the Introduction to *The Long Revolution*: 'For Williams the most important part of the Long Revolution ... is the interrelationships of all [the] constituent parts to one another. Each needs to be understood for what they are, but it is the interaction, interpenetration and feedback – of industry, democracy and culture – that makes the transformation they entail' (Barnett 2011, p. NP).

This idea of analysing individual events and processes as being parts of a larger whole or totality is the very core of a dialectical understanding of society (Dunayevskaya 1961). Culture and Economics are parts of a complete social totality, whereby capitalism attempts to produce individuals who are comfortable or are made comfortable, within newer forms of social mechanisms brought into existence. Culture becomes the realm where antagonistic tendencies are diffused, and the potential of all revolutionary forces is stripped of their potentialities (Marcuse 1937). The power of culture in society, especially in the domain of disseminating standards of social practices, becomes an extremely powerful tool because it becomes synonymous with the expectations of the consumers and users often from the working class. Such cultural forms need not necessarily portray reality, but their effects on the general populace are such that they 'hear and read them and even let themselves be guided by them, so that accept the [so called] traditional values and make them part of their mental equipment' (Marcuse 2002, p. 60). Capitalism draws from the existing culture in society (Williams 1960, p. 300). Social media commerce did not emerge out of a vacuum but is rather the explicit manifestation of the way commodities and commercial relations have penetrated human society at a fundamental level. Contemporary capitalism, through its innovative insurgencies in the domain of both economy and culture, and by creating a successful economy around dominant cultural norms such as the usage of social media, has given rise to social media commerce. Social media commerce has enabled capitalism to generate a culture of 'selling' as an activity oriented towards exploiting and building commercial relationships based on the exchange value of a commodity with fellow human beings. The garb of anonymity that it provides has encouraged many from the traditionally stigmatised sections to engage in social media commerce. But as has been noted previously, anonymity also has a price – the price of self-stigmatisation, repression and the loss of selfhood.

Social media commerce encourages people to sell more by providing an easy, user-friendly interface. As a study conducted by the author in 2020 in New Zealand showed, Facebook Marketplace makes it highly attractive for people for engaging in commercial exchanges through social media. Some of the responses which were then recorded were explicitly in affirmation of the way in which social media explicitly made them sell more by providing them with easy access, making the process easier, and providing them with a ready customer base of individuals who would be willing to buy the commodities. Similar is the case with the Global South. Middle-class Indians use social media mainly to sell not because it provides them with profits – of course, the element of monetary revenue persists but it is not the main driving force – but because social media is an easy platform with which they have been engaged since years. One of the vital characteristics of capitalism, as Marx (1981, pp. 172-73) denotes is the concentration of not only the means of production in one place but also the workers in one place such as a colony or the space around a factory, in a cooperative manner which is able to transform their labour into combined social labour, which can be utilised for furthering the agenda of profit accumulation and surplus value generation by capital. This process entwines with itself some necessary aspects of cost reduction in the domain of constant capital which is extremely beneficial to the sustenance of the rule of capital. One commodity that forms the raw material for a particular production process is the final product of another production process (Marx 1981). This makes it necessary that once the production process in one branch of the industry is altered, often through the introduction of large-scale machinery, there must be changes in subsequent branches to complement the change (Marx 1976). Marx (1981, pp. 174-77) asserts here the centrality of the constant capital in sustaining capitalism, arguing that it is the constant capital that determines the rate at which profit will be potentially generated. It is the constant capital that allowed Marx to focus on the commodity, the cell form of capitalist society (Perelman 1981).

Under a highly developed capitalist system, most of the labour is cooperative in nature (Marx 1976). Coupled with cybernetic domination, it creates a scenario where every click and every message become a part and parcel of the profit-making mechanism of capitalism. The working class, to Negri, is never a finished construction, but rather, it was something that is imprisoned within a constant struggle with capital resulting in multiple working-class re-composition in a response to numerous capitalist restructuration (Witheford 1994). This cooperation between workers usually takes place within a social space, an all-encompassing element of the human society created by human beings themselves, as a means of production within capitalism (Lefebvre 1991a). Space is an important concept in the present discussion because this is where the exchange gets facilitated. Engels's (1845) emphasis on the living conditions of the working class and the dialectical relationship between those living conditions, their own properties such as housing and land, and the effect of those property holdings on their wages play a crucial part in explaining and analysing the social space which capitalism creates and utilises, as Lefebvre (1991a) says, as a means of production. The contemporary social space is being increasingly mediated by communicative technologies, where social relations themselves have become digitalised in nature. This digitalised social space constitutes the social relations without which it is possible for anything to find its way to the market (Marx 1976).

It is essential to realise that capitalism cannot generate profits on its own. It needs, as Dunayevskaya (1958a, p. 92) says, 'a whole army of foremen, managers, superintendents' working for capitalists to manage, regulate, exploit and control the workers. Within social media commerce, these are replaced by moderators, editors, and admins of the various groups who are at the central point of managing the entire structure of social media commerce. Global and networked structures of production mean that capitalism now needs more sophisticated control over the workers and even over those that it employs to control or manage the workers. In the kind of workplaces which are operating in contemporary society, cooperation is an important factor today for capitalism. Capitalism does indeed realise that bitter competition between workers can do more harm than good. It has to, under certain circumstances, work against its own fetish of achievement society where positivity runs amok creating existential crises, individually and collectively (Han 2018). Capitalism acts as the primary force in controlling the lives of the people it oppresses. Technology plays a crucial role in this process. Under the influence and patronage of capital, it not only furthers alienation but also uses the communitarian local market on social media – emphasised by Facebook as being the true reason for its invention of the Marketplace – to generate more avenues of profit accumulation for capitalism.

By bringing forward social media commerce, capitalism has evaded the problems that it faces with regards to the workers not being effective and aggressive consumers of the commodities that the capitalist production system creates at an increasing and inhumane pace. Under normal conditions, burdened by the systemic crisis whereby even the satisfaction of needs of sustenance becomes a struggle for most, the workers have little effect on the overall effective demand of commodities in the society (Harvey 2014, p. 80). Social media commerce enables the customers belonging to the working class to effectively 'contribute to the economy' by transforming them to being instruments of circulation which then go on to facilitate further accumulation. For capitalism to expand at a rate that it desires in a scenario where there are no limits to the growth of capital, it becomes imperative for it finds new avenues where it can constantly reinvest itself (Harvey 2010, p. 45). Considered as individual entities, the workers have little impact on the overall economy of consumerism that capitalism wants to promote within the society. Workers rarely have the means to satisfy their own needs, let alone contribute to the growing luxury goods economy, to which the working class contributes very little and only momentarily (Marx 1992).

Co-operation between the workers becomes an important element in this context as it helps capitalism to extend its influence on the collective whole of the working class. Dunayevskaya (1958a, p. 92) argues that the maintenance of cooperation between the workers under capitalism is of utmost necessity for a planned despotic rule of capital. One must not, however, confuse the cooperation that workers develop under capitalism with cooperative labour. Under advanced forms of capitalism, cooperation itself becomes a new skill for the worker (Dunayevskaya 1958a, p. 93). The definition of cooperation according to Marx was quite simple: 'When numerous workers work together side-by-side in accordance with a plan, whether in the same process, or in different but connected processes, this form of labour is called co-operation' (Marx 1976, p. 443). The cooperation between workers is a productive force (Marx 1976; Dunayevskaya 1958a) capable of producing surplus value for the capitalists. The biopolitical nature of control of modern-day capitalism has become an integral part of the workers of the effectual industries in both the Global North and the Global South. Tiqqun (2020), one of the most ardent advocates of the discipline of cybernetics being a new form of governance itself, argues that cybernetics is a system of domination and control which is autonomous in itself. Control over the means of communication is an essential aspect of capitalist hegemony today. This results in a collective consciousness that generates similar political inclinations and social behaviours (Battaggia and Campanile 1981). Capital, through its control of the means of communication, produces new forms of social relationships (Hardt and Negri 2000), which are then utilised to further the goal of accumulation.

The history of capitalist development revolves around three stages – cooperation, division of labour and manufacture, and 'machinofacture' (Dunayevskaya 1958a, p. 117). For the bourgeoisie to exist and continue to dominate, they have to continuously improve the standards and productivity of their means of production which would then go on to alter the relations of production thus changing the entirety of the social relationships in the society (Marx and Engels 1848). The affluent society or the consumer society can only come into being if there are a sufficient number of commodities operating within the society. To bring this into effect, capital must continuously evolve itself bringing in newer modes of production, and newer methods of profit extraction. The market of capital goods – the very basic means of production – is the only market that can 'expand beyond the limits of the workers paid at value ... Means of Production literally shoot up to the sky' (Dunayevskaya 1958a, p. 128). Constant capital thus will always receive a higher investment than variable capital because it is constant capital itself that possesses the highest profit-generating potential for capital. Thus, for the capitalist, it is never consumption that determines production, because that scenario would be a severe hurdle towards accumulation as it would create the foundation for the social proliferation of use-value, while for the capitalist, it is the exchange value that is the soul of capitalist production. At the same time, if consumption determines production, then capital would become the dependent variable in the equation between the people and itself, something which runs antithetical to the fiercely independent nature of socially controlling capital. The only way in which the capitalist can compete with other capitalists and sustain the reproductive powers of capital is by ensuring that the wages of the worker remain low, and productivity remains high (Dunayevskaya 1958a, p. 135), which potentially leads to an overproduction crisis.

From the internet to phones, the domination over the means of communication has resulted in a situation where science is being actively used by capital to reinforce hierarchy, surveillance, and measurements of all life activities (Dyer-Witheford 1999). The contemporary workers and the service class are not like the erstwhile industrial working class. They are not homogenous; they have different needs and different political views. They have their own subjectivities (Hardt and Negri 2012) as opposed to the definite objectivities of the industrial working class (Battaggia and Campanile 1981). It is, by all means, true that their oppression is similar, not identical, to the industrial working class, but as Marcuse (2002) says, capitalism has successfully made their oppression invisible resulting in a self-reflexive view where they are not 'workers' but professionals, who receive no wages but salary. For example, software workers do not work on direct physical matter. Their jobs revolve around creating mechanisms that somehow, directly, or indirectly, increase the rate of profit accumulation for their employers. The same is the case with other workers who work in industries and sectors whose work is directed upon non-materialist or post-materialist needs of the society such as hospitality, insurance, education, management, and the like. Co-operation within themselves assumes a significantly important place in their line of work. These workers work not through assembly lines but through lines of communication. Communication and coordination in their work are central to the creation of the final product. Negri (1989a) brings forward a paradigm that theorises the process in which capital completely owns the modes of cooperation among the workers. Software workers are living manifestations of workers working under regimes where information has been commodified and productive cooperation is a condition of labour and not the result of a process of labour (Hardt and Negri 1994).

The importance of cooperation was not left unnoticed by Marx, who designated it to be one of the bases upon which large-scale production under capitalism is based. Co-operation between workers allows capitalism to be flexible and as such more exploitative (Marx 1976, p. 446). Capital is the force that directs and controls the workers along with making them cooperate with each other all under the production plan of capital, either by being capital or being personified in the form of managers or supervisors. Co-operation allows capitalist production to obtain its goal of valorisation of value at a heightened speed resulting in the extraction of surplus value at the greatest possible value (Marx 1976, p. 449). Before most of the post-Marx Marxists, it was Raya Dunayevskaya (1958a) who theorised cooperation to be in itself, a productive force under capitalism as it represents the collective force of the social labour in its entirety. Co-operation under capitalism reproduces the inhuman foundations of capitalism as capitalism is formed on the basis of the existence of the 'unfree' individual never allows the complete development of the human potential. These new human energies cannot release themselves, as she notes, till the capitalist mode of production exists in society. Co-operative labour under capitalism forms the foundation of the contradiction between the machine's nature and the value-form under which it operates. Under capitalism, cooperative labour can never be the basis of a new society because:

> Its function is confined to the production of value. It cannot release its new, social, human energies so long as the old mode of production continues. Thus, the *nature* of the cooperative form of labour power is in opposition to the capitalist integument, the *value-form*. At the same time the monstrous creation of monotony, speed-up robs science also of its self-development, confining it to the single purpose of extracting ever greater amounts of surplus, unpaid labour from the workers (Dunayevskaya 1958a, p. 93)

Through cooperation, the individual labour-power of the workers could be transformed into the collective social power of the masses of people engaged in the production process (Marx 1976). To take an example, software workers, while working as a team, are encouraged by their bosses to get entangled with each other at a personal level through a variety of digital mechanisms, which allow for the employers' complete control and surveillance over the exchanges which take place between the workers. The traits are similar to Negri's (1992) classical social worker, who produces social cooperation prior to producing the commodities for capitalists. However, the emphasis on cooperation itself being a productive force is sometimes not focused enough within the autonomist current, something that Dunayevskaya (1958a 1973) regularly does following Marx (1976). Along with enforcing cooperation while retaining capitalist alienation, contemporary capitalism possesses an intrinsic desire to colonise time. Scholars like Postone (1993), Negri (2003), Weeks (2011), Shippen (2016) and many others have spoken at length about the process in which time becomes a weapon at the hands of capital to further its oppression. Time has socio-historically always been a method through which human beings orient themselves, sequence their lives and regulate their social lives (Elias 1992).

The element of time for capitalism becomes crucial because it is through the colonisation of time that it can deter the working class to gain a consciousness of the social and political demands and needs which Marxist theory attempts to represent at large which must be understood subjectively and propagated as such if they are to gain any foothold within the democratic paradigms of larger and advanced capitalist democracies (Negri 2003; Shippen 2013; Soper 2020). Capitalism understands, as Soper (2020) notes, that ideological needs and demands are different from other physical needs and can only be truly desired by people when they take these needs to be a part of their everyday selves. The complete domination of capitalism over the workers cannot take place unless capitalism becomes a force that can control the way the workers spent their time – both when within the productive process and when outside those productive relationships. The capitalist domination over time was explained by Postone (1993) through his differentiation of time into concrete and abstract time whereby the former was designated to be time understood through 'natural cycles and the periodicities of human life as well as particular tasks or processes' while the latter understood as '"empty" time ... independent of events' (Postone 1993, pp. 201-02). The domination of abstract time over concrete time produces the idea of time as an independent variable, which constitutes the way in which capitalism identifies the time for the working class. Martineau (2015, p. 113) further talks about the dual conception of time as equally important to capitalist exploitation as the dual character of labour itself.

Capitalism focuses on the abstract notions associated with both labour and time whereby time becomes something that people experience evenly within a continuum (Elias 1992). As Dunayevskaya (1952, p. 58) argues, 'The struggle to establish a normal working day was a veritable civil war between capital and labour'. She was following up on Marx himself, who all throughout his writings had established the importance of the working day and its relationship with revolutionary upheavals (Marx 1865, 1976). It is the capitalist desire to extract surplus value at all costs which leads it to devise unique ways which extend the working day of the workers under capitalism. The working day is bounded by the limits imposed upon it physically and socially, and as such is devoid of a certain rigidity (Marx 1976, p. 341). It is the desire of capitalism to extend the working day beyond limits, with the final target being the 24-Hour workday (Marx 1976, p. 367). Social media commerce makes this desire concrete. In Chapter 8, this book has talked about the serious leisure perspective, along with the causality behind why such leisure cannot be considered to be markers of freedom. Such leisure becomes a part of the capitalist working day when the activities that the workers engage in during those hours become a part of the valorisation process of capital.

Social media commerce and its relationship with the systemic crisis in society are also guided by this principle. When a social media user takes the commodity to the customer for transferring the ownership, the time spent is usually a part of the leisurely hours. The final value of the commodity now comprises the time which has been spent by the initial user or worker to transfer the commodity. The amount of labour that a worker or a user spends in using the commodity becomes the dead labour that the commodity represents when it is resold. This is the labour of consumption that the working customer performs day in and day out, all of which now is embedded within the commodity. The time which is required to produce a commodity is mediated socially and this is what, when taken on average, determines the value of any commodity (Postone 1993, p. 191). The exploitation of time as a unit of human activity has a long history that is beyond the scope of the present book. Postone (1993) shows the readers the process in which the varying conceptions of time, including the cultural and historical ones, are subsumed by capitalism to produce homogenous units of time whereby the labour time required to produce commodities could be accurately measured as 'The values of commodities are directly as the times of labour employed in their production, and are inversely as the productive powers of the labour employed' (Marx 1865, p. 125). The working day under any form of capitalism always varies taking into consideration multiple factors. In the struggle between capital and labour, the working day occupies a pivotal position (Dunayevskaya 1952). Marx realised that once the limits on the working day were set, capitalism would definitely be moving towards innovating its operations so as to produce newer avenues of surplus-value generation. Variable capital, as opposed to constant capital, which assumes the existence of a varying and constantly expanding pool of workers (Marx, 1981: 245), becomes an important aspect of modern-day capitalism, because it helps capitalism in successfully valorising the constant capital. Time or the socially necessary labour time plays a crucial role here. For the effective usage of time as an instrument of social domination, it is of utmost necessity to capitalism to create homogenous ways in which labour time is spent dissolving all quantitative and qualitative differences therein which would mean that every commodity contains the same amount of labour time (Marx 1847, 1859).

Marx (1847) talked about how under capitalism, time is an important factor that determines the value of the commodities, the monetary expression of which becomes price in the course of progress of the commodity (p. 120). Capitalism works through the complete objectification of this labour-time (Marx 1859, p. 288), where 'all commodities are merely definite quantities of *congealed labour time*' (Marx 1859, p. 272). Just like how cooperation becomes an instrument at the hands of capitalism to reproduce and further the influence of the value-form in society, time also is used by capitalism to manipulate the value attached to a particular commodity. Dunayevskaya (1952, p. 62) understood this basic contradiction within capitalism at a fundamental level which prompted her to posit value production as the final goal of all forms of cooperative labour under capitalism. Time occupies a pivotal position in this supreme goal of value production because 'Labour, being itself a commodity, is measured as such by the labour time needed to produce the labour-commodity' (Marx 1847, p. 125). That the exploitation of labour is the most important part of capitalist production and accumulation has not changed in all these decades of capitalist transformation, including the modern-day digital age. It is complemented by the idea that the internet today is both a factory site and a playground (Scholtz 2012). Factory, in the sense that it has been used by capital to generate revenue from unpaid work, and playground, in the sense of the ambience that the internet provides. ICTs have become an integral part of the economic structures across the world in asserting large-scale labour processes and labour market alterations (Huws 2016). The precarious nature of contemporary labour as has been highlighted by Standing (2011, 2014) and many others, is only set to increase in this day and age of digital labour relations working through the many modes of the gig economy, on-demand economy, etc (Huws 2016). The large-scale usage of ICTs has made possible an indiscriminate expansion of capital including the realisation of universally mobile recruitment and exploitation techniques, of which social media commerce is a small but hugely significant part. Within social media, even when a person works, the burden or sense of work is almost non-existent. To make the person realise that social media is a workplace is a very difficult job, even for the most competent labour organisers. Hjorth (2018) has analysed how this ambience within the internet is deliberately created in such a way, that the user, even if entrenched within the labouring process, never feels the burden or sense of work. People who trade aggressively on social media commerce, or the small-scale businesses which operate on and through social media, are at the risk of losing money the moment they log out of the system.

The amount of time an individual spends, while being 'logged on' is being actively used by capital to extract profit. Social media commerce is a part of this exploitative circuit, in fact, social media commerce has made it possible for capital to colonise and dominate the leisurely hours of the workers as has been stated in the previous chapter. By colonising the 'unproductive' time of the workers' lives, capitalism invents newer forms of power and control through which it can increase the productivity of its profit-generation mechanisms. The working day under capitalism tries to incorporate the after-work hours of the worker within itself as well. It uses the collaborative and participatory nature of social media to produce a collective mass of people who are engaged with each other on trans-actional terms. Brunhoff (1976) informs the readers about the relationship which money shares with social power – the mobility of power that is associated with money. Money as Marx (1859) argues, is the source of power in society mainly political in nature, the possession of which draws individuals to make efforts towards possessing it, social media commerce being a part of those efforts.

Money also plays a crucial role in the history of capitalism. As Marx (1993) argues, money has been a fundamental element of the generation of not only the capitalist production processes but also of the ideological structure of capitalism. Co-existing with elements of human nature such as greed and desires, money becomes the agency through which general social wealth 'become[s] individu-alised in a particular thing' (Marx 1993, p. 222). Money, as *material representative of general wealth, as individualised exchange value, ...* must be the direct object, aim and product of general labour, the labour of all individuals' (Marx 1993, p. 224). Harari (2018) argues that the development of complex economic systems makes it inevitable for societies to innovate toward generating entities that can be used to represent the values of goods and services independently of the restrictions imposed by the barter system. Both Marx (1993) and Harari (2018) agree that factors such as conquests and technological development play a role in the develop-ment of money. However, under capitalism, money emerges to be an operator of the 'social relationship of belonging' (Aglietta 2018, 'Monetary Crises'). In other words, it subsumes every aspect of human existence, which includes the processes of unalienated community formation:

> Money thereby directly and simultaneously becomes the *real community* ..., since it is the general substance of survival for all, and at the same time the social product of all. But as we have seen, in money the community ... is at the same time a mere abstraction, a mere external, accidental thing for his satisfaction as an isolated individual (Marx 1993, pp. 225-26)

Communities that human beings form under such circumstances are alienated communities. Groups, friendships and virtual communities formed on social media for trading and commercial purposes, such as the ones which have been referred to in this study, are typical examples of this process that Marx highlights. Individuals from these communities and social relationships therein under the illusion that they are doing so autonomously while in reality, these processes are markers of the extent to which the power of money has infiltrated into the human society such that 'the individual is not objectified in [one's] natural quality, but in a social quality (relation) which is ... external to' the individual (Marx 1993, p. 226).

The social system today is such that labour and leisure are being made to fuse with each other, but not in the way in which critical Marxists such as Lefebvre (1991b) or even Gorz (1987) would have wanted it to be. Capitalism uses leisure to further the fulfilment of its own needs of accumulation rather than those of the workers (Shippen 2013, p. 2). It is being done in a way where leisure itself becomes a part of the value-production mechanism of capitalism, being a part of an ideological construction that legitimises continuous and extended working hours. The social structure under contemporary capitalism is such that the worker can form meaningful relationships only once when they are outside the formal productive process (Lefebvre 1991a). The extended working hours represented by social media commerce are built upon this communitarian nature of social media itself, where the exploitation of workers' labour takes place through the relationships that the worker forms with others on social media (Fuchs 2012). Capitalism uses the cooperation and the feeling of a community that exists within social media. Co-operation not only allows the spatial expansion of the worksite but also allows the temporal elongation of productivity (Marx 1976, pp. 446-47) focusing on the collective potential and form of the working class. The despotic plan of capitalism (Dunayevskaya 1958a) comes true in its truest sense only in cases where a large number of workers are concentrated in a similar space and time (Marx 1976, p. 447). Horkheimer and Adorno (2002) theorised this concentration to be one of the most important characteristics of mass society, while Marx and Engels (1848) considered concentration to be the foundation of the capitalist process of urbanisation.

Social media affects this concentration into reality within a virtual paradigm, while making the workers remain in their alienated conditions of life as they would have been within the real social paradigm. Co-operation and communitarian among the working class can have revolutionary possibilities (Dunayevskaya 1958a, p. 94). The problem with capitalism is that under capitalism, the cooperative labour of human beings is not allowed to develop freely and is restricted to merely value-producing activities for the capitalists (Dunayevskaya 1958a, p. 93). Even under cooperative forms of labour, capitalism does not allow the workers to obtain the unalienated conditions of sustenance required to obtain the true freedom of the individual which Marx and Engels (1848) and later Dunayevskaya (1958a) and Marcuse (1966) talk about. Lefebvre (1991, p. 59) argues that since all forms of labour of the worker, under capitalism, is an entity that is always external to the worker and is rarely a part of the worker's intrinsic self, it is often during leisurely hours that the worker 'feels himself'. Leisure is also specifically a domain in which workers usually deviate away from the ways in which capitalism wants them to manage their lives. For capitalism, a worker is the most useful when the worker is engaged in productive activities i.e., when the worker is most likely to produce surplus value. Through digital capitalism, and especially through frameworks such as social media commerce, capitalism has extended the temporality of productive relationships. For capitalists and their ideological justifiers, it is the expansion of human productivity which matters the most – a desire which encourages them to introduce and proliferate technology within the production systems. The worker, for them, deserves no special attention but exists only as an object from which continuous surplus value and profit have to be extracted on an everyday basis. Capitalism through social media commerce has enabled the complete subsumption and colonisation of everyday life of the working class (Vaneigem 2012). Marx had classically designated the industrial factory to be the place where the process of surplus-value creation is primarily located, where the workers get into a formal contract with the capitalist to sell one's labour-power as a commodity (Marx 1865). Contemporary capitalism has transgressed the limits imposed upon it by Marx in terms of 'place' and has, through the utilisation of social space and communication, informalised the nature of contracts. The complete commercialisation and commodification of social relationships form the foundation of the kind of society, which is theorised in the present work, a society where everybody is a potential customer of everybody else in the society, provided the person is on social media. Autonomist Marxists such as Tronti (1962) and Negri (1989a) have argued for decades now that capitalism today has moved far beyond the mere walls of the factory. They have argued that contemporary capitalism functions through the creation of a 'social factory' (Tronti 1962), or as Negri (1989b) put it, the society itself exists being an extension of the factory by metamorphosising into a factory beyond the factory walls (Negri 1989b) resulting in the usage of the society as a means of production for capital, in turn, resulting in the formation of the social factory and the socialised worker (Negri 1989a). The basic definition of the 'social factory' can be put in these words:

> the relation between capitalist production and bourgeois society, between factory and society, between society and State achieves, to an ever-greater degree a more organic relation. At the highest level of capitalist development, the social relation is transformed into a moment of the relation of production, the whole of society is turned into an articulation of production, that is, the whole of society lives as a function of the factory and the factory extends its exclusive domination to the whole of society (Tronti 1964, p.NP)

Customers who work within the social media commerce paradigm are not the traditional industrial worker or the 'mass worker' – a term Antonio Negri (1988) used to define the semi-skilled workers who worked in factories (Witheford 1994) – who were objectively determined through a relationship which they shared with the production processes directly. They are similar to what Negri calls the 'socialised worker', a category of workers who come into being once society has transgressed from the industry being the major capitalist enterprise.

These workers are part of the newer avenues of capitalist exploitation, where they express themselves as active subjective beings, which is significantly different from the classical notions of people, masses or the 'working class' (Witheford 1994; Hardt and Negri 2004, 2012). This working class mainly works in the tertiary sector – outside the direct influence of the industrial capital – but becomes a part of the society by getting socialised through their massive involvement in the broader processes of value creation in the 'social factory'.

The control that capital exercises today is not limited by any boundaries but has transcended the walls of the factory (Tronti 1964; Negri 1989b). Hardt and Negri (1994) subsequently talk about how capitalism has moved away from considering labour within capital as the 'only productive labour' but instead has accepted various modes of labouring activities to be fully acceptable forms of productive and profit-making labour. As Witheford (1994) notes, the socialised worker of Negri (1988) was an attempt to alter the traditional theories on and about the nature of labour-power. The basis of the formulation is that previously marginalised aspects of the production process have been utilised within the circuit created by the capitalist social system. The software, care, hospitality, management industry workers and the like, represent the physical manifestation of Negri's "*Socialised Worker*" in the Indian context, whose job descriptions are significantly formed by the need for coordination and communication with others within and outside the workspace. Negri (1989a) emphasises the process through which capital steals information that the working class gets in possession of through continuous cycles of struggles. It is this information that capital then uses to create '*increasingly complex mechanisms of dominations*' (Negri 1989a). The associated social phenomena, which aid in transforming the mass worker into a socialised worker, convert in the process, almost all different forms of productive and unproductive labour to social labour.

Social media commerce uses the labour of the users to produce commercial capital and heighten the powers of industrial capital. The fieldwork from the research conducted for the book continuously shows that most of the individuals who sell commodities through social media do not simply sell but also reinvest the money they get by selling, into the process of obtaining newer commodities. A huge proportion of them carries forward the cycle that they are already a part of when they made the sale, by becoming new buyers, and then again, renewed sellers, and the cycle goes on. When asked whether they realised the existence of this continuous cycle, unsurprisingly, most of them replied in the negative. That their own spontaneous decision could be used by capitalism to further its own goals of accumulation was something that is beyond the general consensus in the society. Such unconscious nature of the way in which capitalism uses human labour leads to a normalisation of the competition that capitalism wants to create as a co-existing factor with cooperation. Competition, that capitalism launches in society, ensures that any process of the formation of any class solidarity faces an innumerable number of hurdles. Competition and technological rationality attempt to obstruct the formation of the class individual, while capitalist cooperation and bourgeoisie civility ensure that the workers remain loyal to the 'despotic' plan of capitalism.

Capitalism, as stated by Marcuse (1941), dissolves human life of all its spontaneity. It is this loss of spontaneity that social media commerce promotes. Even in the Global South, where the term 'affluent' might seem like a misnomer, individuals repeatedly invest in the same kind of commodity. Moving-out sales are common throughout the globe, the point of investigation however often remain restricted within patterning the kind of commodities that go out for sale but rarely divulges into how and why the act itself is mediated or brought into existence. When the author interviewed a certain individual who had just listed the entirety of the flat on social media for sale in the West, the person responded to have been completely driven by the virtual norms of which they had been a part for a very long time – 'list the objects as soon as you are done with them, sell and move forward'. One of the move-out sellers in the Global South said that it was the issues with transportation that had prompted the move, while another said that the person saw this as a service to the community because the person was selling the commodities extremely cheap. Regardless of the motive behind the activity, the significance of the activity remains in the fact that it has ensured certain mobility of capital in society. Customers or consumers are the most unstable part of the capitalist value production system because they do possess the will to reject commodities (Boltanski and Chiapello 2005, pp. 368-69), mostly within the realm of luxury commodities. By initiating social media commerce, capitalism has ensured that even if their spontaneous choices cannot be controlled to the extent that it wants to, it still 'enforces' upon them a necessity to put capital into motion, which can then initiate the valorisation of constant capital so as to positively affect the rate of profit accumulation.

Capitalism today, as Dunayevskaya (1973, p. 72) argues, had progressed from being a system that needs to extract surplus labour from the worker by extending the working hours. Through the introduction of machinery and automation, capitalism made it possible to extract surplus labour and surplus value from within the normal working day itself by increasing the productivity of the worker therein and making the worker akin to a machine. Digital media makes this condition more explicit in society. Under conditions of digital subsumption, human beings behave through pre-conceived patterns. Capital's control over society pre-conceives certain behavioural patterns that individuals are likely to follow within the digital space. For example, when somebody receives a message containing a picture or a website on WhatsApp or sees a message on Facebook, the first reaction usually is to click and check it. Once the person clicks the link or sees the picture of the product, the person is introduced into the digital space, whereby the forces of commodity fetishism and consumerism begin to act on the user creating value or creating the conditions for further production and valorisation of already existing value. This usually occurs in the form of views or 'clickbaits' leading to advertisements. Such means of valorisation are not created in a vacuum. It is the production relations existing in the society which give vent to these 'virtual' exchange relations. With constantly varying modes of production and newer forms of technology, there is a constant variation of the socially necessary labour time to produce the commodity (Dunayevskaya 1958a, p. 105). Such variations have diverse effects on the accumulation of capital in society.

The struggle for the reduction of the 'actual' working day remains a radical political demand in opposition to the exploitation of relative surplus value, which in reality has become the exploitation of absolute surplus-value itself as the workers today are always working.

For capitalism to accumulate on a large scale, along with the colonisation of time and the extension of the working day beyond its limits, it is necessary to diversify its points of accumulation. Marx talked about this tendency of capitalism through his opinions on the form of cooperative labour on a large scale under capitalism:

> ... cooperation on a large scale, can be realized only through the increase of individual capitals, only in proportion as the social means of production and subsistence are transformed into the private property of capitalists. Where the basis is the production of commodities, large-scale production can occur only in a capitalist form. A certain accumulation of capital in the hands of individual producers therefore forms the necessary pre-condition for a specifically capitalist mode of production (Marx 1976, p. 775)

Individuals form a class most favourably in situations where they are engaged in a struggle against another class (Marx and Engels 1845-46, p. 77). Individuals as Marx would say always articulate their selfhoods within the actually existing material conditions of the society they exist in. The articulation of the individual by the individual does not progress from a purely philosophical ideal conceptualisation but from the historical conditions which the division of labour and the social relations of production create in the society where these relations become autonomous in the society that capitalism creates and sustains (Marx and Engels 1845-46, p. 78). Social media commerce exploits the labour of the various users to generate commercial capital for the capitalists by transforming the labour-power of human beings into an appendage of the giant machine of accumulation just as how Dunayevskaya (1965, p. 69) talked about. Capitalism works through the idea that the more quickly capital is circulated in society, the more quickly it can manifest itself as commercial and circulation capital, as has been noted in the previous sections. In doing so, capital always has the tendency of increasing the working day of the workers, so as to enable the formation of surplus-value at an accelerated rate. Circulation depends to a large extent on the way in which human beings behave in society – in the contemporary form of which human spontaneity itself is a pattern curated for capitalist accumulation under conditions of alienated freedom.

Any opposition to such a state of existence has to oppose the capitalist homogenisation of the uniqueness of human existence. The importance and necessity of human spontaneity have to be re-established in opposition to capitalist repetitiveness and homogenisation. It has to be taken into cognisance that technology is a subjective force with diverse implications and the social practices resulting from technological advancements are not mere context-less 'practices' but are manifestations of social reality (Deb Roy 2020). The Communards during the Paris Commune showed how radical forms of social cooperation can produce revolutionary outcomes (Dunayevskaya 1958a, p. 98). The transactions between the buyers and sellers, or between the capitalists and the consumers, even if they are occurring under the garb of civility are not examples of cooperation, but rather they are manifestations of a bourgeoisie ethical and civil structure. In the society of working customers, such civilities are necessary so that every time one traverses through an exchange relationship, one not only feels satisfied but also empowered unconsciously by thinking of the civil behaviour which has been granted to the individual by another, something which capitalism continuously robs the individual off. The directives about being polite and civil in most social media websites reinforce the alienated conditions of labour that capitalism normalises. Natural civility and politeness can only result in a situation where the labour of being civil or polite is not labour at all. In other words, it can only occur in a situation where labour has been dis-alienated and disconnected from the processes of generation of value for the capitalists. The normalisation of the alienated conditions of existence outside the 'factory' also has a relationship with the labour process theory as the reduction in the cost of production can only be done through extreme control over labour (Braverman 1998). Subsequently, O'Connor (1998) writing about capitalism and its production process, spoke about how advanced capitalism always harbours an interest in commercialising not only the produced commodities but also the production process itself. In other words, in a drive to accumulate more profits, capitalism inevitably attempts to control the dynamics of the relationship existing between labour-power, labour control, the production process and the market. Taking a cue from Castells' (2010) argument about the increasing utilisation of ICTs by global monopolies in both production and circulation, it can be said that capitalism has performed both the above-mentioned processes identified by Braverman (1998) and O'Connor (1998) through the application of communication. The commercialisation of the means of communication has not only enabled capitalism to control the labour outside the formal production process but has also successfully allowed it to exploit people with a limited social life by getting them being involved with society through making it easy for them to engage in commercial practices on social media platforms. Social media enables the ready formation of social bonds, which can then be used for garnering commercial gains. A real-life situation within a commercial exchange relationship might seem daunting to many people, but social media effectively negates that. Within social media, one can 'freeze a sale' (using the term as used by an Asian worker in New Zealand) while still being completely anonymous.

This anonymity makes social media commerce highly attractive to people. Inferences drawn from real-world conversations urge one to believe that people when buying and selling commodities on and through social media temporarily become invisible. The happiness of alienated consumption (Wendling 2009, p. 110) makes the people focus on the commodities more than they notice the seller. This rendering invisible of the human being becomes the focal point around which negotiations take place, which becomes explicit in some of the responses which the sellers laid out which included, drawing from Deb Roy (2020): 'People usually just focus on the items and not the seller', 'the garb of invisibility helps me in getting around my ow confidence, and helps me in negotiating more aggressively', etc. Such responses, mostly associated with people who face some form of disadvantage in society, show few variations globally. There are countless platforms that are operating on the internet today, most of which have already been mentioned in this book by this time. Most of these platforms work within a global chain of information and communication structures through an on-demand economy setup. Numerous concepts can be used to theorise about the situation in which these workers find themselves socially, politically and culturally (Huws 2016). In the context of the current book, the approach that is found to be most relevant is that of crowd work, albeit with some modifications to the original concept. The idea of crowd work becomes an important one in the context because of its emphasis on the usage of the 'crowd' in getting things done, as the name itself implies. Crowd work constitutes a very important dimension of digital labour exploitation in contemporary society. The basic difference between crowd work and digital labour is the way the workers are renumerated for their labour. While mainstream digital labour is mostly conceptualised in the form of the labour that individuals perform in Information-technology companies or as consultants in paid jobs, crowd work is usually unpaid. Crowd work is mostly performed on online platforms and is crowdsourced to the extent that they virtually become free labour for capital (Ettlinger 2017). Crowd work under contemporary capitalism is a massive reorganisation of work where the work is usually facilitated by online work platforms and performed by crowds who 'are neither employed nor do they need to know the company they work for' (Gerber 2020, p. 2). Examples of crowd-sourced unpaid work can be cited to be the intense amount of data that Facebook puts up for translation in the public domain (Scholtz 2012). Other such forms can include Google Reviews and Maps, Facebook Check-ins, etc., all of which are performed online and without any wages but provide significant benefits to the enterprise in question. Within such kind of labouring process, the worker – the user – shares analytical and observatory skills with the digital system which then uses the data to gain financial profit from the same. Scholars such as Ettlinger (2017, pp. 31-2) have emphasised the similarity which exists between the routine and repetitive work in the online work platforms with the assembly line production of the yesteryears which includes the endless division of work, hurdles in building organisational structures among the workers, disconnect between the producers and the consumers of the product, etc.

The anonymity that social media commerce provides to the buyers, and sometimes the sellers, have been engaged with in detail by theorists working on crowd workers and the aspects of individuality and anonymity therein (Aytes 2012; Flecker and Schönauer 2016). Such processes and results are components of the overall techno-social system which is present in such labouring structures. Capitalism, by emphasising social media commerce, in certain ways, has used the power of socialisation to accumulate further profits. The final product of the time that human beings spend to build relationships and communities over digital medium – a human function (Shippen 2013) when a digital-social continuum is imagined – has become the basis upon which capitalism bases its exploitation within social media commerce. It not only aids in transforming people into customers, even from the perspective of other people who are customers themselves but also helps in sustaining the system by temporarily delaying the inevitable crisis of surplus-value realisation within capitalism, which as Ivanova (2019) rightly says is a manifestation of commodity capital not being able to transform itself into money-capital effectively at the pace which would sustain the capitalist circulation system. Social media commerce enables capitalism to temporarily evade the crisis. To a limited extent though, by creating a mechanism that ensures that capital does not remain fallow (Mandel 1978; Engels 1843) but keeps on getting invested and circulated – commodity capital getting constantly transformed into money capital. The power of the community is actively used by social media commerce to facilitate a kind of crowd work, where Haythornwhite's (2011) distinction between crowds and communities effectively disintegrates. Haythronwhite (2011) argues that the major distinction between crowds and communities, in addition to their size, is that while communities are composed of mostly mutually known members striving for a common goal with shared social practices, crowds are composed of anonymous members who act individually towards the same desired goal only to get dispersed at the end. One of the distinguishing characteristics of the community is that communities share a common characteristic of some kind (Hillery 1955) which helps them fraternalise with each other (Derrida 1997). Classical crowd workers' extreme heterogeneity makes it extremely difficult for them to be conceptualised as a community (Berg et al. 2018). However, a cooperatively planned work structure ensures more surplus value as Marx (1976) and then Dunayevskaya (1958a) had argued, quite correctly.

Even contemporary platforms are moving towards creating communities to introduce an indirect form of control within the platform-based work structures (Gerber 2020). While in classical crowd work, the worker needs to build a community, in social media commerce, capitalism exploits the community itself to produce workers who work *unconsciously but continuously* for capitalism. The first act as customers, and then act as workers employed by capital within the domain of commercial capital, and then again as customers for some other commodity. The process continues, producing within itself the working-customer, whose job is not only to buy but also to sell the commodity and contribute to the overall productivity of capitalist accumulation. Because of increased production due to advances made in the capitalist production systems, there is a transformation of the entire society into a customer pool, where each individual is a potential customer of not only the monopoly capitalist but also of every other individual, who is again a customer of the same monopoly capitalist. This digitally connected social pool of customers, aided by rising consumerism (Bauman 2005) transforms human beings into profit-bearing machines, which makes the exchange process smoother and faster. The digital hierarchy within the society is a product of capitalist exploitation (Witheford 2005), through which capitalism attempts to affect massive changes within the organic relationship between the worker and the environment within which the worker finds oneself. Online platforms, including those within the 'on demand' economy, work through the creation of dubious categories of workers (Huws, Spencer and Joyce 2016). The people who drive for Uber or those that work with are not the traditional blue or white-collar workers. These individuals seem to have certain control over the kind of work that they want to do, but in reality, it is the systemic crisis and needs under capitalism that controls the choices they make. The chronic rise of capitalist exploitation in society and the systemic crisis has put the entire society 'on display' for capital to exploit, not only as workers and as customers but as working-customers – unfree human beings working for their own exploitation.

13. THE REGIME OF PRIVATE PROPERTY

'... we have to grasp the intrinsic connection between private property, avarice, the separation of labour, capital and landed property; the connection of exchange and competition, or value and the devaluation of men, of monopoly and competition etc.- we have to grasp this whole estrangement connected with the money system'
– Karl Marx in the *Economic and Philosophical Manuscripts* (1844, p. 271)

Property is a widely contested term within the contemporary information and post-industrial society because of the inherent complexities which contemporary societies posit before social scientists and activists in the form of non-physical but material entities like information and knowledge increasingly entering the realm of transforming themselves into properties with significant exchange and rentier values (Fuchs 2019a). However, the significance of the term 'property', be it psychological or physiological, is immense within Marxist theory as, 'communists […] bring to the front, as the leading question ... the property question, no matter what its degree of development at the time' (Marx and Engels 1848, 519). The question of property assumes various forms in accordance with the state of progress in different societies (Marx 1847a, p. 322) contingent upon the state of society, the validity of free competition, personal holding of property, etc. What remains unchanged, however, is its vitality and centrality for any class to assert its domination within the society, be it the bourgeoisie in the feudal era, or the working class under capitalism (Marx 1847a, p. 323).

Capitalism in contemporary times cannot be analysed as an entity, but rather it has to be analysed as a process of domination because it is a process in itself (Marx 1992) – a social system encompassing facets of economics, culture, polity and history and not merely an economic system which creates newer processes which in turn, act upon or act through, existing processes. And, all institutions and platforms, digital or otherwise, publicly funded or privately owned, are a part of this overarching social reality, which dialectically determines the way in which individuals react to the varying situations they find themselves in within their everyday life (Lefebvre 2003). Human life under contemporary capitalism is a life lived within and through commodities that transform human life every day at every moment. Life today is a dominion of commodities produced by capitalism and for capitalism. Commodities that workers possess turn out to be the only property that they possess, which alienate them, dominate them and utilise them to further the cause of capitalist profit accumulation. They act in a way to ensure that 'the worker is the subjective manifestation of the fact that capital is man wholly lost to himself, just as capital is the objective manifestation of the fact that labour is man lost to himself' (Marx 1844, p. 283). The ownership of property often posited by Capital as being the antidote to all the problems under capitalism cannot be the solution, as long as the logic of capital prevails in the society.

Private property is the foundation of capitalism. It has developed through history transitioning through various forms and civilisational stages (Marx and Engels 1845-46, pp. 32-4). As Marx argued in his *The Poverty of Philosophy* 'to define bourgeois property is nothing else to give an exposition to the social relations of bourgeois production' (Marx 1847, p. 197). Without private property, there is no capital, and thus, subsequently no capitalism. Private property, understood in a radical Marxist sense, has to be analysed as something resulting from the appropriation of labour-power. The regime of private property represents the most blatant and most explicit form of capitalist domination over the working class. This regime cannot be destroyed through a mere communalisation or socialisation of private property. This point had been noted by Marx in his EPM. The primary definition of 'Communism' that Marx puts forward is the complete abolition of any form of bourgeois property. His definition of bourgeois property revolves around the conceptualisation of private property in the realm of it being a means of production (Marx and Engels 1848, p. 498).

The Marxist case against private property is different from others because Marx did not see crude forms of communism as being a substitute for capitalism. Marx did not argue that a mere re-distribution would cause any problems for private property under capitalism. Marx said that any analysis of private property without locating its centrality within the basic contradiction between labour and capital 'remains an indifferent antithesis, not grasped in its *active connection*, in its *internal* relation, not yet grasped as a *contradiction*' (Marx 1844, pp. 293-94). The mere abolition of private property cannot lead to communism or even socialism if it is abolished in the way crude communists want to abolish it. In crude communism, the state simply takes over private property and converts the same into communal property. The statist property becomes the manifestation of private property such that it categorises everything which cannot be possessed by everybody in the society as private property and 'wants to disregard talent, etc., in an arbitrary manner. For it, the sole purpose of life and existence is direct, physical *possession*. The category of worker is not done away with but extended to all men' (Marx 1844, p. 294). The previous relationship that private property shared with alienated labour under capitalism is then converted to a 'relationship of the community to the world of things', while in essence, the relationship between private property and labour remained intact (Marx 1844, p. 294). In other words, under such crude forms of communism, the logic of private property remains intact but in a very socialised form:

> The distinguishing feature of communism is not the abolition of property generally, but the abolition of bourgeois property. But modern bourgeois private property is the final and most complete expression of the system of producing and appropriating products that is based on class antago-

> nisms, on the exploitation of the many by the few. In this sense, the theory of the Communists may be summed up in the single sentence: Abolition of private property (Marx and Engels 1848, p. 498)

Crude forms of communism are only the first negation of capitalist accumulation processes which stops at the 'mere abolition of private property' which does not address the questions of expropriation positively (Hudis and Anderson 2021, p. 32). Under such forms of communism, basic human emotions still work in the same way. The essence of competition and private property persists in such a society in such a way that it is '*at least* turned against *wealthier* private property in the form of envy and the urge to reduce things to a common level, so that this envy and urge even constitute the essence of competition' (Marx 1844, p. 295). Thus, crude communism is only the levelling down of the capitalist society to the state where all the problems associated with capitalist private property are reduced to the lowest level or as Marx says to the '*preconceived* minimum' (Marx 1844, p. 295). The entire logic of private property remains intact and completely intact. Crude communism, a mere abstract negation of capitalist private property, is a stage where:

> The community is only a community of *labour*, and equality of *wages* paid out by communal capital – by the community as the universal capitalist. Both sides of the relationship are raised to an imagined universality – *labour* as the category in which every person is placed, and *capital* as the acknowledged universality and power of the community (Marx 1844, p. 295)

The proclamations of social media commerce being a democratic, fair and equal domain of exchange relations fall under this category of justification – the first negation of capitalist contradiction. It is true that within social media commerce there is an element of egalitarianism such that the prices are not directly determined by the capitalist process of valorisation. But such forms of non-capitalist structures are only the first negation of capitalist mechanisms. The method of Absolute Negativity as Dunayevskaya proposed proposes going beyond this bare negation and calls for an absolute negation which means doing away with 'not only ... the old, but also [establish] the basis for a forward movement' (Hudis and Anderson 2021, p. 27). Absolute negativity, as Hudis and Anderson state, not only means negating the external obstacles but also entangles negating the basis of all the internal obstacles of the path of human liberation – the very basis of value and commodity form – to move towards the negation of the negation 'for the positive is contained in the negative, which is the path to a new beginning' (p. 27). The narrow and limited logic of crude communism or other such forms of transcendence based on private property can only be overcome by a positive transcendence of private property:

> Communism as the *positive* transcendence of *private property human self-estrangement*, and therefore as the real *appropriation* of the *human* essence

by and for man; communism therefore as the complete return of man to himself as a *social* (i.e., human) being—a return accomplished consciously and embracing the entire wealth of previous development. This communism, as fully developed naturalism, equals humanism, and as fully developed humanism equals naturalism; it is the *genuine* resolution of the conflict between man and nature and between man and man — the true resolution of the strife between existence and essence, between objectification and self-confirmation, between freedom and necessity, between the individual and the species. Communism is the riddle of history solved, and it knows itself to be this solution (Marx 1844, pp. 296-97)

The positive transcendence of private property will reinstate the human essence, in its entirety, to the actually existing human being entrapped within an estranged human life under capitalism or crude communism. This transcendence to Marx would make it possible for human beings to return to being 'human beings' in their complete essence because the transcendence would bring an end to all forms of estrangement in society (Marx 1844, p. 297). Under capitalism, the proposed goal of human beings is not the immediate satisfaction of senses, needs or desires, but rather it is the complete annihilation of all forms of alienation and estrangement. This is what constitutes the positive transcendence of private property. Transcendence, as Dunayevskaya (1973, p. 82) argues, is a dialectical process, which takes into account multiple processes under its fold – fetishism, control, reification, etc. The abolition of private property does not merely mean doing away with private property as the crude and vulgar forms of communism posed to do. That is only the *first negation*, the most important part of abolition is to move towards the *second negation* – the *negation of the negation* – '"the permanent revolution" ... integral to the creation of "new Humanism" "beginning from itself"' (Dunayevskaya 1973, p. 186).

Private property regimes under capitalism create a situation where every human being 'must make everything that is [ones] *saleable*, i.e., useful' (Marx 1844, p. 310). The crude need of the worker is a greater source of profit than the needs of the rich which are far richer and refined in nature: 'Industry speculates on the refinement of needs, it speculates however just as much on their *crudeness*, but on their artificially produced crudeness, whose true enjoyment, therefore, is *self-stupefaction* – this *illusory* satisfaction of need — this civilisation contained *within* the crude barbarism of need' (Marx 1844, p. 311). Crude communism restricts the growth of human needs in society, and the complete development of human personality, which was an important element to the radical humanist in Marx. It completely overlooks the '*poor* and crude man who has few needs and who has not yet even reached it' (Marx 1844, p. 295). Such forms of communism are nothing more than a crude negation of capitalist private property and are manifestations of the continued logic of private property. Private property needs to be questioned through the paradigm of the harm it causes to the personality of human beings by instigating emotions such as envy, greed, etc in society (Marx 1844, p. 295). Envy and the urge to consume appropriate commodities are also foundational or important elements of other evils in society, which we have already talked about in the previous chapters such as consumerism, competition, etc. Marx credits the formation of crude communist or despotic communist regimes to their inability to grasp the positive essence of the transcendence of private property. These forms fail to analyse the *human* nature of need' (Marx 1844, p. 296). Crude forms of communism still retain the essence of private property as it is under capitalism, and as such is only an abstract negation of capitalist private property. As Sayers (2011, p. 103) notes, these forms simply work by bringing down the various aesthetic aspects of human existence. They do not grasp the positive nature of the generation of human needs and the relationship which needs share with human powers and human capacities, which in turn affect the positive growth and development of human nature (Sayers 2008; Sayers 2011). That individual's desire to possess commodities is nothing criminal or surprising. The problem remains that under capitalism, commodities become the basis of private property and capitalist accumulation.

The relationship between the capitalist state and private property within such situations is always a relationship manifesting harmony (Harvey 2014, p. 47). In some cases where the state, though capitalist in nature, gets to be governed by left-wing or progressively populist governments characterised by strong labour movements, it might attack the power which capital holds over private property in the society. Capital, at this point, does not get free reign over the private property existing in the society and instead is forced to search for alternative means. Before neoliberalisation, both in India and in New Zealand, Capital was forced to operate within a framework which is ridden with statist regulations due to the powers exerted by the state over taxation and business procedures in the country as is the norm in non-liberalised societies. These restrictions put a limit upon the movement of capital and create the grounds for the bourgeoning of the contradictions existing between the idea of the state and private property (Harvey 2014, p. 47). Capital has attempted to resolve this contradiction through multiple means, which is beyond the scope of the present work. The major idea is that bourgeois democracies, which are the prevalent form of state organisations in almost all the civilised nations in the world, have an inherently beneficial function for the sustenance of capitalism. Private corporations and statist bureaucracies have almost always tried to find solutions to their seemingly irresolvable conflicts by creating: 'broader political forces and to long-standing attempts to find collective forms of governance that effectively bridge the tension between the potential arbitrariness of state autocratic power and the popular desire for individual liberty and freedom' (Harvey 2014, p. 43).

Private Property and the analysis of its relationship with individuals within contemporary capitalism has to take into account the varying subjectivities therein. Not everybody analyses and interprets private property in the same way. Some see it as a kind of respite from the obnoxious effects of capitalism, which does not let the person accumulate like the way capitalists do. It is interesting in this case to note how the desire to accumulate has become a normalised human attribute under contemporary capitalism. Nobody raises an eyebrow over a person appropriating huge tracts of land and earning profits from rent and other forms of commercial activity. Accumulation today has become a naturalised dimension of human sustenance. However, that accumulation has become a natural dimension of human existence is not readily accepted by some intellectuals and activists, who associate private property to be a necessary marker of freedom. The first contradiction in this regard, as has been laid by Harvey (2014, p. 42) is that between the two ideological processes which advocate freedom of individual property rights and the collective powers which operate under capitalism such as the state to codify those rights into a formal system which protects, sustains and if necessary, exterminates them. This regulatory power that is held by the state is something that capitalism tries to overthrow, not always, successfully through. As Harvey (2005) argues, the state still retains a huge proportion of regulatory power within itself. The only difference between the present neoliberal system globally and the statist regimes is that it does not exercise it. The relationship between the state and the private property regime is such that the state uses its centralised power to regulate and manage the decentralised market, which often involves managing diverse sections of the population. Without the state, no regime of private property can sustain itself. Some form of overarching power, in the form of a state or something capable of reproducing power to that extent, is required to maintain the structures which sustain individual rights and liberty (Harvey 2014). The anti-thesis to this form of government cannot be a state-capitalist government as James, Dunayevskaya and Boggs (1986) have shown, as did Marx (1844).

In both these kinds of states, the worker exists only to work for capital, the moment the worker cannot work for capital, the entire existence of the worker is rendered useless. State capitalist regimes merely introduce a new central power but do little more than that. The fundamental ideas relevant to capitalist sustenance – commodity production, the law of value, the production of surplus-value, among others- still remain in force 'operative internally and externally' (Dunayevskaya 1973, p. 234). Similarly, social media commerce changes very little of capitalist exchange relations. Like all other exchange relations under capitalism, social media commerce also uses living human labour to valorise dead labour. It is nothing similar to the pre-capitalist non-commodified forms of exchange, where use-value was the value that mattered. One of the major differences between consumption in pre-capitalist societies and consumption in capitalist societies is that under capitalism, the act of consumption becomes one where in addition to the satisfaction of needs, it also needs to generate profit for the forces of capitalism (Lotz 2017, p. 367). Social media commerce, when placed within the overall logic of capitalism, is an intrinsic part of the total cycle of accumulation of capitalism. Social media commerce *marketizes* society in general. Social media commerce actualises the capitalist schema of diversifying the circulation of capital in domains hitherto unexplored by capital. It not only helps diversify capital but also helps in establishing the rule of accumulation. It enables the concrete multiplication of the points of accumulation, which further makes possible the intense accumulation of capital: 'The formation of many capital investments is only possible as a result of multilateral accumulation since capital comes into being only by accumulation; and multilateral accumulation necessarily turns into unilateral accumulation' (Marx 1844, p. 251).

The valorisation of capital within social media commerce, however, does not only occur through the exploitation of dead labour but also by exploiting the living labour performed by social media users in communicating and circulating the commodity within the society. This continuous valorisation under digital capitalism occurs through the exploitation of communicative technological systems and constitutes, in Negri's (2003) words, real subsumption of the entire society by capitalism. With the coming of this real subsumption, there has occurred, a possibility of complete blurring of the differences between personal and private properties, which has, in turn, resulted in the conversion of all use values to exchange values explicitly and universally. The individuals constituted by capitalism play a pivotal role in the creation of the consumption-oriented society that Bauman (1999) refers to as a liquid society. Through social media commerce, capitalism attempts to create a society where it can control not only the manner in which the workers produce and consumer but also how they engage with the refuse of production and consumption. One of the results of consumerism in society is the scattering of such refuses in society. Social media commerce enables the usage of such refuse for the benefit of capitalism. Rogers (2007) relates the utilisation of refuse to the broader processes of surplus-value creation by capitalism. The utilisation of the leftovers of the mass consumption society

The path of progress through the generation and sustenance of consumerist ideas leaves behind scores of 'collateral damage[s]'[1](Bauman 2007, p. 122), both in the form of commodities and actual human beings. Consumption on a massive scale results in a massive waste and then arises, the need to dispose of it (Bauman 2003a, p. 9). Social media commerce enables the proper utilisation of this refuse:

> As the capitalist mode of production extends, so also does the utilisation of the refuse left behind by production and consumption. Under the heading of production we have the waste products of industry and agriculture, under that of consumption we have both the excrement produced by man's natural metabolism and the form in which useful articles survive after use has been made of them (Marx 1981, p. 195)

The waste products of the everyday lives of human beings, from the rags from Marx's own example to headphones and smartphones which are sold at a massive scale through social media commerce, are definitely 'the refuse of consumption' (Marx 1981, p. 195). Marx theorised how such refuse is used by capital in other avenues to continue their domination and oppression of the working class:

---

1. Bauman descends into a larger debate about the underclass and the working class at this point, something which is, though very important, but beyond the scope of the present work.

The general conditions for this re-utilisation are: the massive presence of this refuse, a thing which results only when labour is carried on, on a large scale; the improvement of machines, so that materials which were previously unusable in their given form are converted into a form suitable for new production; and finally, scientific progress (Marx 1981, p. 196)

The kind of everyday commodities which find a place on social media commerce fulfils all these conditions. Examples in this regard can be cited of phones, laptops, headphones, etc. – all products of capitalist technological development, all coming with as Bauman (2005) says a fixed temporal nature of utility. Possessing an old smartphone, or using an old computer, under regimes of contemporary capitalism signifies that the person has missed 'the train of progress' (Bauman 2005, p. 5). Such ideological processes, which are materialistic in nature at the same time, create the ideal grounds for social media commerce to flourish. Progress cannot take place without the creation of commodities, but the creation of commodities also comes with its own share of refuse, the value of which capitalism desperately wants to valorise. The presence of such refuse at a massive scale result in the necessity of the creation of expanded markets- markets that can re-absorb these commodities. Books can be utilised as an example. The used books market (not the collectible books market) globally has been a testimony to the idea that used products can create a profitable market mechanism that can continue to produce surplus value by initiating further sales and more production by being entry-point products.

In previous chapters, I have gone into detail about how capitalism advances commercial capital in society through social media commerce, using human beings to make it rampant through society by the proliferation of exchange relations that germinate within social media. The human qualities which create the human essence, under capitalism exist only within the alienated paradigm that capitalism creates in the society, such that: 'The worker exists as a worker only when he exists *for himself* as capital, and he exists as capital only when some *capital* exists *for him*. The existence of capital is *his* existence, his *life*; as it determines the tenor of his life in a manner indifferent to him' (Marx 1844, pp. 283-84). Social practices of individuals are an intrinsic part of the human essence as the book has established in the previous chapters. Social media has to be analysed as part of these social practices which are dominant in society. The rise and proliferation of social media have been so huge that social media has become a part of the human social practice in contemporary society. The invention of social media commerce was thus a natural progression of social media considering the extremely capitalist nature of social media itself. Private property, again, becomes the basis of these social practices which are associated with social media commerce, because it is private property itself that under capitalism creates the foundations of the 'personal relations of dominion and servitude ... and the impersonal power that is given by money' (Marx 1976, p. 247). Private property and money are at the heart of the capitalist domination of society. The development of the production system under capitalism occurs through the development of property relations (Marx 1847, p. 119). At the same time, the 'property relations of any given era are the necessary result of the mode of production and exchange of that era' (Engels 1847a, p. 296). These are factors that create antagonistic tendencies in society, which not only keep the workers under control but also disregards their status as actively thinking human beings. It dominates the consciousness of human beings by impinging upon their actual life-process as 'Consciousness can never be anything else than conscious being, and the being of men is their actual life-process' (Marx and Engels 1845-46, p. 36).

Capitalism has used the human tendency to achieve a fulfilling condition of individualism to its own benefit by posing individual ownership as a means toward emancipation (O'Connor 1984; Bauman 2010). The creation of individual identity through the possession of commodities is the basis of capitalist sustenance as an ideological force in contemporary times. Social relations under digital forms of capitalism are not only structured by physical communities and organisations but also by organisational forms which are technologically mediated and created (Hall and Stahl 2012). Through such techniques, capitalism works to separate the individual from the broader human essence. The culture of exchange within a capitalist society results in a culture of individualism when it is coexistent with a capitalist state with extreme power and a powerfully deregulated monetary form of capital (Harvey 2014, p. 42). These are some of the fundamental characteristics of the construction of the capitalist individual. The capitalist individual is segregated and alienated from the class and community to which one belongs and uses those social relations to further capitalist accumulation. The continued creation of capitalist individuals is necessary to further strengthen the position of capital in society by reducing the situations in which capital itself might find itself to be weaker in comparison to the working class. This informalisation, driven by capitalism's desire to convert everything into profit-generating commodities, has enabled it to commercialise the social relations formed by human beings and makes them see other human beings within the society as the possessors of private property or customers, at times both. The basic character of private property under capitalism, as Marx exposes can be understood from these statements:

> The character of *private property* is expressed by labour, capital, and the relations between these two. The movement through which these constituents have to pass is: *First. Unmediated* or *mediated unity of the two.* Capital and labour are at first still united. Then, though separated and estranged, they reciprocally develop and promote each other as *positive* conditions. *[Second.] The two in opposition,* mutually excluding each other. The worker knows the capitalist as his own non-existence, and vice versa: each tries to rob the other of his existence. *[Third.] Opposition* of each *to* itself. Capital = stored-up labour = labour. As such it splits into *capital itself* and its *interest,* and this latter again into *interest and profit.* The capitalist is completely sacrificed. He falls into the working class, whilst the worker (but only exceptionally) becomes a capitalist. Labour as a moment of capital—its *costs.* Thus the wages of labour—a sacrifice of capital. Split-

ting of labour into *labour itself* and the *wages of labour*. The worker himself a capital, a commodity. *Clash of mutual contradictions* (Marx 1844, p. 289)

The construction of the capitalist individual depletes the potential of the assertive power of the working class by making capitalism stronger in areas where previously it would have been the object of serious criticism. Autonomist thinkers such as Tronti (2019) have always adhered to the belief that to attack capital, the working class must not choose the site where capital is the strongest but rather the site where the working class itself is strongest, in a manner that can make the most efficient use of the power that the working class possesses in terms of refusing to work for capitalism.

Private property and its relationship with capital is mediated through three relationships as Marx argues. The two relationships are the relationship between private property as labour and as capital, and the mutual relationship between these two (Marx 1844, p. 285). Capitalist competition and cooperation completely render the 'human' obsolete by transforming them into 'things' so that 'people regard each other only as useful objects; each exploits the other, and the end of it all is that the stronger treads the weaker underfoot; and that the powerful few, the capitalists, seize everything for themselves, while to the weak many, the poor, scarcely a bare existence remains' (Engels 1845, 329). It is a condition such as this that enables the continuous exploitation of workers within the realm of social media commerce. The working customers of social media commerce are entrapped within a never-ending cycle of capitalist accumulation, where their everyday activities are entrapped within a cycle of accumulation controlled by forces of capitalism. The working customers are the classical case of capitalist individualism where individuals see each other as sites of exploitation. The social media platform for them becomes their conception of a community, where everybody is competing with each other to meet their social needs, often at the expense of others. The huge concentration of individuals on the virtual platform is used by capitalism to permeate this tendency as something which is natural to human existence. As Engels said:

> The brutal indifference, the unfeeling isolation of each in his private interest, becomes the more repellent and offensive, the more these individuals are crowded together, within a limited space. And, however much one may be aware that this isolation of the individual, this narrow self-seeking, is the fundamental principle of our society everywhere, it is nowhere so shamelessly barefaced, so self-conscious as just here in the crowding of the great city. The dissolution of mankind into monads, of which each one has a separate principle, the world of atoms, is here carried out to its utmost extreme. Hence it comes, too, that the social war, the war of each against all, is here openly declared (Engels 1845, p. 329).

Individuals, under capitalism, are constituted by the social relations existing in the society including those determined by the networks of social production and consumption. Contemporary capital attempts to place absolute control over both production and consumption processes under which human existence becomes an act mediated by and influenced by the forces of capital. Social media commerce establishes human beings as commodities, one of the most important aspects of capitalist modernity as Bauman (1999) would have put it. It uses human beings as forces of circulation for capitalist accumulation. Technological advancements today, serve the purpose of further valorising the already existing value (Hall and Stahl 2012), and social media commerce plays an important part in this process because it allows capitalism to exploit the rising productive capacities of the working class, which had made it possible to produce enough for the society in the first place (Engels 1872). The primary aim of the capitalist system, however, is not mere production, but rather its final goal remains the generation of profits and surplus value through production. It aims to do that by altering the relation between living and dead labour in such a way that the latter dominates the former (Dunayevskaya 1973; Marx 1867). Social media commerce allows capitalism to create a system of successive consumption, which through the successive and continuous exploitation of dead labour, creates the basis for further accumulation within contemporary capitalism.

Technology has helped capital to manage not only the workers that it has already employed but also the potential worker who might find employment under the capital which runs the technology. The industry relations between producers and consumers have evolved over the years, but the ontological significance of the worker is something that has not changed. The utopian post-capitalist advocacy that digitalisation will lead to an end of capitalism (Mason 2016) does not hold good, when capitalism moves towards extracting surplus value and profits from each and every stage and level of the production process, including the digital components (Staab and Nachtwey 2016). Capitalism as a system recognises, if not explicitly then implicitly, that unless and until, there is a continuous circulation of valorised capital, it is impossible for capital to sustain itself. All societies are spaces that are constructed out of certain shared meanings (Bauman 2001). Because most individuals interpret society, both as a space and as an organisation, in a certain manner, there is a shared and dominant understanding of society. Capitalism, through its promotion of social media commerce, attempts to alter this very social understanding of the social space to satisfy its need for the circulation of capital which ultimately increases the value of capital. The only way to achieve this, while keeping the wages down and maintaining the class distinctions brought forward by distribution (Engels 1878), is by encouraging and/or coercing the working classes to start putting a value on their properties as Engels (1887) had described being the case of Germany in the preface to the second edition of his *The Housing Question*:

> ... bourgeois and petty-bourgeois socialism [...] strongly represented in Germany [...] wish[es] to turn the workers into owners of their dwellings [...] this is a point which has been shown in a very peculiar light by the industrial development of Germany during the past twenty years. In no other country do there exist so many wage workers who own not only their own dwellings but also a garden or field as well [...] With the intro-

duction of machinery all this was altered. Prices were now determined by the machine-made product, and the wage of the domestic industrial worker fell with this price. However, the worker had to accept it or look for other work, and he could not do that without becoming a proletarian, that is without giving up his little house garden and field, whether his own property or held by him as tenant. Only in the rarest cases was he ready to do this. (Engels 1887, pp. 427-30).

The dialectical relationship between use and exchange values constituted by the fact that a commodity always has a certain, as Marx says, non-use value for those who own the commodity and a use-value for those who do not own it, shapes the analysis of social media commerce and element of property within it. The sustenance of capitalism as an economic system depends on the sustenance of the capitalist society, a major aspect of which is to generate this exchange between the possessors and the non-possessors on financial terms. With the development of the modes of production under capitalism, which give rise to exploitative exchange relations based on and of property, there arise situations where capitalism itself fails to control the evils it creates (Marx and Engels 1848, p. 489). Consumption is one such aspect. No matter how much capitalism produces, it can never guarantee the productive consumption of everything that it produces. As Marx (1992) notes, capitalism produces numerous commodities, many of which almost never enter the consumption cycle of the working class – a point upon which Luxemburg (1913) had huge reservations. Consumption as has been noted earlier occupies an important position within social media commerce, but it is private property and the law of surplus value creation which creates the necessity of consumption – both physically and psychologically. To focus explicitly on consumption means to emphasise the law of demand and supply, which does not realise the problems associated with either overproduction or underconsumption (Ludenhoff 2021, p. 227).

Private property is the basis of production and consumption in a capitalist society (Marx 1844, p. 297). Under capitalism, it is through private property that individuals mediate the production of their demands and the consumption of commodities that are supposed to fulfil their needs. Private property comes to human beings as the only entity through which human beings can make sense of their social reality. The 'positive transcendence' of such property is the only way ahead for society if human society has to move ahead from the exploitative regimes which have been forced into existence by capitalism. It is especially crucial to talk about this, and theorise about this because it is only with a positive transcendence of private property regime that one can move towards talking about a human being as a human being – both in form and spirit. Crude communism, or other forms of society, do not fundamentally do away with the logic of capitalism. They might be successful in doing away with the capitalist semblance but can never do away with the capitalist fetish *per se*. The kind of communities that social media commerce helps to build is based on monetary transactions. Facebook groups mostly focused on trading are an example of this. These developments occur because of the fact that making payments has never been easier than today. Capital has invented a newer mechanism through which money can be made to circulate between buyers and sellers.

Technologies such as Apple Pay and Google Pay have made it easier for users to make payments to one another, which has contributed immensely to the accelerated growth of capitalism (Manzerolle and Kjosen 2015). Manzerolle and Kjosen (2015) present a circulation-based approach to the problems of capitalist accumulation and provide some important arguments. They argue that payment technologies have productively transformed the labour associated with checking out a product, thus having a positive effect on the speed at which commodities turn into money (p. 165). This is a conclusion that the present work agrees to. However, to posit the accumulation (and accelerated accumulation in certain cases) of capital exclusively to the sphere of circulation is to neglect the centrality of the commodity and private property within capitalist accumulation. It is true that the social being is only visibly manifested today in the realm of circulation and consumption, that is because capitalism makes it look like that by focusing on the socialisation of labour.

Capitalism, as Dunayevskaya (1958a, p. 121) notes proceeds through two basic laws, the first one being the centralisation of capital and the second one being the socialisation of labour. The establishment of private property regimes is the first manifestation of capitalist centralisation. The development of bourgeois modes of production depends upon the process in which the bourgeoisie concentrates the means of production in the hands of the few giving rise to 'concentrated property at the hands of the few' (Marx and Engels 1848, p. 488). The socialisation of labour is the basis upon which the subsequent capitalist structure is built. The history of the development of capitalist socialisation of labour is one based on the increasing cooperation between workers which not only the numbers but also at the same time disciplines and unites the total labour force (Dunayevskaya 1958a, p. 122) that continuously increases the tendency of labour productivity and thus capitalist accumulation. Such structures, in turn, promote the centralisation of capitalist accumulation whereby capital through mobile, always moves back to the hands of the few. One sells a smartphone to buy a new smartphone or pay a bill. One does away with the old car to get a new car or to pay off the mortgage. Such immediate acts of selling and the consequent buying, are the constitutive elements of a society of working customers. The immediate acts of buying and selling, transform these individuals into the eyes and consciousness of the participating individuals engaged therein, as sovereign beings free from the domination of the market relations. The relationships that individuals form within these situations, however, are just as much a product of capitalist domination as are the commodities in which they are dealing.

This feeling of sovereignty is something that social media commerce celebrates and banks upon to convert individuals into active workers working unconsciously to keep capital mobile within the society. Social media commerce is the capitalist solution to all forms of stagnant capital – either in the form of commodities or money. Capitalism realises, as Engels (1843) noted, that stagnant capital cannot generate any surplus-value. It is only the capital in circulation which allows capital to continuously valorise itself, in the process generating profits. Though the genesis of capitalist exploitation remains within the act and process of production, circulation enables capitalism to make the production relations dominate the society on a larger scale. With the changes in the way commodities are manufactured and distributed, property relations also change dramatically which has grave consequences on how social relationships are forged under capitalism, not only locally but also globally (Marx and Engels 1845-46, pp. 68-9): 'These different forms [of production] are just so many forms of the organisation of labour, and hence of property. In each period of unification of the existing productive forces takes place, insofar as this has been rendered necessary by needs' (Marx and Engels, 1845-46, p. 74).

Under conditions of technological rationality, Marcuse (1941, pp. 44-46) illustrates, there arise some forms of standardised norms and desired processes for individuals which establishes forms of standards and constitutes attitudes that make human beings subservient to alienating dictates. At the same time, technological rationality also makes human beings search for modes of aspirations that are measurable, physically or psychologically (Marcuse 1960). The decisions which individuals take under such forms of rationality are manifestations of the rationalised society that individuals constitute and through which they get constituted in their everyday lives. Every aspect of human life, previously spontaneous, becomes part of this patterning done by technological autocracy, where capitalism tries to create patterns of social behaviour, which fit its plans for accumulation. This kind of alienation creates the avenues for exploitation, whereby the truth behind these processes, which are themselves results of alienation, are hidden away from the general public and become part of the normalised notions established in society. Under the conditions created by contemporary capitalism, the entire society has become part of the cultural representative process or 'the culture industry', through innovations that make the spectator and the audience perceive the social reality as being an extended version of the screen (Horkheimer and Adorno 2002, p. 99). The audience starts seeing themselves in the characters on the screen enabling capitalism to create homogenous categories out of the different 'human' individuals who constitute the society (p. 116)

Capitalist alienation creates situations whereby the individuals voluntarily enter into a relationship of servitude to capital. The workerist philosopher, Mario Tronti (1973) was right in pointing out that the 'total process of reproduction of capital' is one that is based on circulation-controlled consumption to allow the reproduction of capital. The entire basis of a capitalist-controlled consumptive network is, as Bauman (2007) has rightly argued, to make individuals themselves wish to perform the requisite tasks for capitalist reproduction. Hebert Marcuse (2002) perhaps put it in a better way than Bauman, when he argued that it is the affluence of a society that renders the violence the society commits on its members completely invisible furthering the growth of capitalist administration (Forman 2017).

Marcuse (1967) opines that the 'transition from voluntary servitude ... to freedom presupposes the institutions and mechanism of repression. And the abolition of the institutions and mechanisms of repression already presupposes liberation from servitude, the prevalence of the need for liberation' (Marcuse 1967, p. 78). Such liberation can occur when the focus shifts back to the individual being conceptualised within a dialectical relationship with the society as a whole, as Marx himself put it: 'Modern universal intercourse cannot be controlled by individuals unless it is controlled by all' (Marx and Engels 1845-46, p. 88). Unless the stage is achieved, the conditions of servitude, propagated by multiple forces, including those of art and culture, which under capitalism act as components of the dominant capitalist alienating ideological discourse will continue to work towards resolving the antagonistic tendencies in the society (Marcuse 1972, p. 143) producing further alienation. This inevitably creates a condition where the organic and dynamic relationship between living labour and dead labour which Tronti (1962) claimed to be representative of the production system under capitalism, can be witnessed globally. The influence of capitalism has been widening in every domain of human sustenance including the very neighbourhoods and domestic spaces where one lives. Not only the workspaces which include the offices and factories but even households have also been internalised within the system of value production. Social media commerce is a living manifestation of the idea that advanced forms of capitalism can render everyday human activities as parts of a giant wheel of capitalist accumulation. From the domestic space to the public space, social media commerce has emerged as a framework that, because of its easy accessibility, pushes individuals towards working for capitalism, while seemingly retaining their individual spontaneity. One of the important directions of analysis of the social media commerce paradigm can be autonomist Marxism – it has been referred to in detail throughout the book. This has been partly because autonomist Marxism is a subjective mode of analysis (Hudis 2012), which often can be used to complement the overall subjective element within Marxist Humanist analysis, though there are certain contradictions in that regard as well. Under highly developed capitalism, however, both schools of Marxist analysis believe that it is at a social level that the contradictions of capitalism can be most easily witnessed and analysed, instead of narrowing down the effect of capitalism to factories or industrial sites *per se*.

Under a highly developed capitalism, the society itself emerges as a means of production for capitalism, where the entire society is put into use to achieve the quintessential capitalist objective of production merely for the sake of more production, thus resulting in the accumulation of profit. In other words, society becomes a mere extension of the factory. In the present case, the space of social media becomes an extension of the productive relations most easily and conveniently found within factories under capitalism (Tronti 1962). There are emergent forms of labour in this context, some of which have already been discussed in the preceding chapters, which are vastly different than the classical notions of the labouring process under capitalism. These processes are no longer conceptualised on the basis of 'work' or 'labour' being confined to the physical boundaries of the factory *per se* but instead encompass the immaterial and affective characteristics of human beings (Hardt and Negri 1994). Even though the autonomist tradition can be critiqued from numerous standpoints such as its adherence to a certain notion of the dissolution of the dialectics as Negri (2003) sometimes advocates, and its seemingly overt disregard for dialectics and the influence of Hegel on Marx (Anderson 2020, p. 159), it cannot be denied that the autonomist tradition has been instrumental in unearthing the role of communicative measures in the accumulation of profits (Negri 1989b). The specific form of the capitalist mode of production 'begins with the commodity phenomenon as "cell" and form which dazzles people into accepting as *a thing*, living labour which has been exploited and "reified," pounded into the saleable commodity, labour power' (Dunayevskaya 1973, p. 94).

Taking a cue from this Marxist Humanist position, Bauman's (2007) concept of a society of customers, though very important, is not an adequate tool to analyse the kind of society that social media commerce creates. It is true that consumerist societies treat consumers as commodities. The ability to consume becomes the basis of one's ontological justification in the world of customers where the inability to consume or being poor is itself posited as a crime (Bauman 2005a, 2007). However, Bauman's thesis does not focus much on the importance of private property and the commodity-form within capitalism. Though his departure rests on the assumption of capitalism being a force that needs to be countered, he does not say much about private property. Marx's words that 'Political economy starts with the fact of private property; it does not explain it to us. It expresses in general, abstract formulas the material process through which private property actually passes, and these formulas it then takes for *laws*. It does not *comprehend* these laws, i.e., it does not demonstrate how they arise from the very nature of private property (Marx 1844, pp. 270-71) seems to be the most logical explanation of Bauman's often very mainstream sociology. Even Bauman (2007), in spite of his rejection of the idea that contemporary social structures are still being built upon production relations, could not refuse the importance of commodity production in capitalist societies as he says 'Commoditization precedes consumption and controls the entry into the world of consumers' (Bauman 2007, p. 69). The dual character of the commodity creates the foundation of the society where money itself acts as a binding force of a community. Because of this immense power money possesses under regimes of private property accumulation brought forward by the dual character of labour and commodities, capitalism wants to accumulate money (Dunayevskaya 1958a, p. 86). The massive circulation of money within the society with a goal towards centralised accumulation by the redirection of the money towards proper capitalist commodities, which is evident from the way in which individuals spend the money in general, which is usually towards newer forms of commodity possession. These forms of commodity possession become the basis upon which renewed social media commerce takes place transforming these 'properties' into capitalist private property.

Communism means the concrete negation of capitalist private property. Wages and private property, even in their essence, draw their basics from the logic of capital. Actual communism needs to transcend this logic of capitalism itself. To understand the society of consumers, and to transcend that understanding to recognise the labour put forward by these consumers, a focus on the importance of private property is essential. To do so again, one needs to understand private property and capitalism from a perspective that sees it as a basic contradiction between labour and capital like Marx: 'The antithesis between lack of property and property, so long as it is not comprehended as the antithesis of labour and capital, still remains an indifferent antithesis, not grasped in its active connection, in its internal relation, not yet grasped as a contradiction' (Marx 1844, pp. 293-94). Social media commerce exposes the dialectical relationship between

Marx in his EPM argued that capitalism attempts to create a situation where the act of having become an essential part of the essence of 'being' (Marx 1844). In fact, under capitalism, Private property itself acts as an activity in itself, which makes the mainstream political-economic explanation of capitalism as being nothing other than depictions of the movement of private property under capitalism (Marx 1844, p. 290). Private property is the result of societal *alienated labour*, i.e., of *alienated man*, or estranged labour, of estranged life, of *estranged man*' (Marx 1844, p. 279). The relationship between capitalist private property and alienated labour is such that alienated labour causes private property to come into existence, but it is also the very reason why labour is alienated in the first place under capitalism (Marx 1844, p. 280).

The division of labour in society is one of the most important elements of the capitalist society as it determines the way in which individuals relate to each other while being in relation to the material realities of the society they are living in. The division of labour in society and its development depends upon the manner in which different forms of ownership (Marx and Engels 1845-46, p. 32). Marx understood the necessity of uncovering the causal relationship between the division of labour and capital and that between capital and property. This is one of the important aspects of Marx's critique of political economy (1844, p. 271). This is also a point where Marx's critique of classical political economy also becomes extremely aggressive in nature. For Marx and many Marxists who followed him, the division of labour in society was one of the most important elements of capitalism's continued sustenance because:

> Whilst the division of labour raises the productive power of labour and increases the wealth and refinement of society, it impoverishes the worker and reduces him to a machine. Whilst labour brings about the accumulation of capital and with this the increasing prosperity if society, it renders the worker ever more dependent on the capitalist, leads him into competition of a new intensity, and drives him into the headlong rush of overproduction, with its subsequent corresponding slump (Marx 1844, p. 240)

Competition between competing sellers is a natural manifestation of capitalism. For any commodity to become part of the private property regime, it is necessary to find its place within a competition orientated marketplace because 'Once thrown into competition, [properties and commodities such as] landed property [obey] the laws of competition, like every other commodity subjected to competition. It begins thus to fluctuate, to decrease and to increase, to fly from one hand to another; and no law can keep it any longer in a few predestined hands'

(Marx 1844, p. 269). Such competition creates collective amnesia in the society, where commodity fetishism becomes the basis upon which human relations are constituted obscuring the human labour embedded within the exchanged commodities. The cultural Marxist, Jameson (2015, p. 15) argued that to understand contemporary capitalism, it is necessary to understand this amnesic nature of contemporary capitalism which refers to the method in which capitalism reduces everything to its immediate existence. Under capitalism, the political economy fails to recognise the unemployed workers and the individuals who are outside the formal production relations (Marx 1844, p. 284). These individuals are utilised by social media commerce, in addition to those already existing within the production relations, to further the spread of capital in society. Social media commerce uses the human desire to possess and incorporate commodities, the basis of all consumption under capitalism (Marx 1844; Fromm 1976), to its advantage and to the service of capitalist accumulation.

Private property and its associated commodity fetishism do not only tend to physically possess, but also attempt to mentally possess everything that comes in its way of social domination. Private property, as Marx says, 'has made us so stupid and one-sided that an object is only ours when we have it – when it exists for us as capital, or when it is directly possessed, eaten, drunk, worn, inhabited, etc., – in short, when it is used by us' (Marx 1844, p. 300). Thus, it should not come as a surprise, given that we are all part of a capitalist social reality, which most of us actively reinforce through our everyday interactions with the reality, that social media commerce has assumed such huge popularity in such a short time. Private property, as Engels (1892) noted, is a methodological tool of social domination acting in the service of capitalism to keep the social status quo intact. Through social media commerce, capitalism uses the properties owned by the working class to suit its own needs (Engels 1872). Engels (1892) mentions that capitalism utilises the fact that the working class owns properties and is thus hypothetically placed in a position to extract monetary value out of the same, to reduce the general wage levels in the society. It does so, so as to provide the exploiter and purchaser of the labour-power of the working class, capitalism, the complete surplus value (Engels 1892). Engels (1878) also realised that this surplus-value cannot be appropriated unless there is a distributive mechanism that actively aids this purpose. This realisation made him progress from his ideas of property and talk about the method of distribution within capitalism and its impact on the creation of class differences (Engels 1892). He brings forward how new means and modes of production are initially resisted by the old mode of distribution (Engels 1892).

Social media commerce has emerged as a new mode of distribution in society – of both commodities and capital as has been stated in the previous chapters. These new modes of distribution rely on the continued increase in the culture of consumption in society. The logic of private property is directly related to this culture of consumption. The sense of 'having' has replaced all other senses in a way where 'being' has been directly equated with 'having': 'The human being had to be reduced to this absolute poverty in order that he might yield his inner wealth to the outer world' (Marx 1844, p. 300). The users engaging with the social space within and beyond social media commerce, are mostly workers. They are people whose living labour has become merely a means to satisfy external needs, which constitute the basis of alienation under contemporary capitalism. Labour has no intrinsic value, but merely is a part of the overall exploitative mediations that a working-class person has to engage in within capitalism. The result is that the worker feels that he is acting freely only in his animal functions – eating, drinking and procreating, or at most in his dwelling and adornment – while in his human functions he is nothing more than an animal (Marx 1844; Lefebvre 1991, p. 60) – a conceptual formation which has been challenged by thinkers such as Benton (1993). Capitalism transforms the entire ontological and epistemological basis of the lives of the workers into something which is dominated by self-estrangement and is ably enabled by the domination of private property: 'Private property [becomes] the only perceptible expression of the fact that man becomes objective for himself and at the same time becomes to himself a strange and inhuman object; just as it expresses the fact that the manifestation of his life is the alienation of his life, that his realization is his loss of reality, is an alien reality' (Marx 1844, p. 299).

Social media commerce is an instrument where the affluent classes protect the ways in which they perceive the world. It secures, for them, the consensus of the working class which is as Forman (2017, p. 30) says, both the victim and beneficiary of such processes. Social media commerce further delays any possible realisation of Marcuse's (2002) idea that true economic freedom can only mean freedom from the economy, by keeping the workers entangled within the productive relations. Capitalism through this, alienates the individual from the individual's senses, especially the working class. The affluent classes often, however, devise newer ways to protect their senses, but that act of saving itself locates itself within the capitalist alienation that private property and the alienated labour of workers create. To emancipate the human beings, it is thus of utmost necessity that the human senses, many of which have emerged through the long association between human beings and capitalism, are emancipated: 'The abolition of private property is, therefore, the complete emancipation of all human senses and qualities, but it is this emancipation precisely because these senses and attributes have become, subjectively and objectively, human' (Marx 1844, p. 300). Under capitalism, the very intrinsic relationship that a worker shares with one's own labour and the products of that labour is rendered distinct from the worker. Workers under the capitalist mode of production become poorer with the prosperity they bring to the capitalists for whom they work (Marx 1844) – that is a process that remains unaltered even after capitalism has made tremendous strides including the models of welfare capitalism. What one has to engage with in the contemporary decade of social media explosion is the processes in which these processes are still functioning, and perhaps even aggravating with regards to their effects on the working class. Capitalism is a world constructed through the alienation of the working class and the other marginalised sections of the populace – based on caste, gender, race, etc.

A regime of private property domination turns a human being away from society and forces the human beings to think of individual life as something which is radically distinct from their social life. All forms of societies that establish themselves based on the domination of private property are a part of this framework. Private property, as Marx (1844) notes, aids the conversion of every need into a physical and crude need, something which tends to find its solution or fulfilment within the logic of capital and private property. Freedom for Marx (1844, p. 304) refers to a society where the human being 'owes his *existence* to himself' and is not dependent on any other person, nor for survival nor for fulfilment. The roots of private property lie in the unfree society that the current book talks about in the second chapter. This unfree society under capitalism is characterised by the complete levelling down and fragmentation of labour which creates the foundation for the existence of private property as a direct extension of the alienation of the workers under capitalism (Marx 1844, p. 294). It is the relationship between the labour of one person with the labour-power of another that social relationships get constituted of under capitalism. Under situations, where the labour is still social or communal in nature, these social relationships between human beings do not get manifested as relationships between values or things (Sayer 1979, p. 40). Dunayevskaya (1958a) urges people to take this relationship between people as relationships between things because that is what they essentially are under capitalism.

The relationship between private property, the desire of human beings to accumulate private property, and money is a deep one. All of these aspects are related to each other. Under capitalism, private property becomes the primary basis upon which the entire structure of the society is built. It is something that can be named and identified (Harvey 2014); at the same time, it is also something that can produce surplus value and profit (Marx 1976). Classically, it is almost impossible to think of private property to be natural elements found freely in nature which is not quantifiable in easy human terms. However, under contemporary capitalism, this initial hurdle no longer exists as the world sees rapid privatization of necessary resources such as water and air under contemporary regimes using welfare and developmental policies. It is crucial thus, as Harvey himself opines, to think about the extent to which capital has extended itself to include within the gambit of private property almost everything that it can find: 'An individualized private property rights regime lies at the basis of what capital is about. It is necessary to condition and construct in the sense that neither exchange-value nor money could operate in the way it does without this legal infrastructure' (Harvey 2014, pp. 41-2). The abolition of private property, thus, is the absolute necessity of the liberation of the workers and any separation between the two ideas will result in a conceptual failure (Engels 1847a, p. 306):

> The slave frees himself by *becoming a proletarian*, abolishing from the totality of property relationships *only* the relationship of *slavery*. The proletarian can free himself only by abolishing *property* in general. ... The serf frees himself by driving out his feudal lord and becoming a property owner himself, thus entering into competition and joining for the time being the possessing class. The proletarian frees himself by doing away with property, competition, and all class differences (Engels 1847, pp. 100-01)

14. PERSONAL PROPERTY, SOCIAL MEDIA, COMMERCE AND ACCUMULATION

In *The Poverty of Philosophy*, Karl Marx notes:

> An oppressed class is the vital condition for every society founded on the antagonism of classes. The emancipation of the oppressed class thus implies necessarily the creation of a new society. For the oppressed class to be able to emancipate itself it is necessary that the productive powers already acquired and the existing social relations should no longer be capable of existing side by side. Of all the instruments of production, the greatest productive power is the revolutionary class itself. The organisation of revolutionary elements as a class supposes the existence of all the productive forces which could be engendered in the bosom of the old society (Marx 1847, p. 211)

Private property is one of the foundations upon which the capitalist society and its associated oppressed class of workers is constituted. Marx has repeatedly emphasised that private property under capitalism is one of the most important foundations upon which capitalism builds its empire. Capitalism draws its power from its dual ability to purchase both capital and labour-power, with the two abilities being dialectically related to one another. Capital is doubtless, 'stored-up labour' (Marx 1844, p. 247), but the act of storing up effortlessly under contemporary capitalism takes place not only through the traditional means of production and distribution but also through the intense amount of second-order circulation of commodities and circulation that it brings about through social media commerce. The latter being the complete exploitation of the living labour, not only of the worker who actually produced it, and the workers who then worked for distributing the commodity – which to Marx (1973) is also a part of the production process – but also of the living labour of the social media users who again put that 'used' commodity and its value, albeit of a different quantitative value now, back into the cycle of capitalist accumulation.

The transformation of the commodity into money and the money into capital is maintained as a sacrosanct law within capitalism. This transformation is necessary for the reproduction of the total social capital. Marx's (1976) analysis of the expanded reproduction of capitalism engaged with the distinction between constant and variable capital. In this regard, Marx (1992) proposes two departments – the departments producing the means of production and the means of consumption respectively – through which the capitalist production goes on merely for the sake of production and not for satisfying the demands of the consumer (Le Blanc 2012). Multiple debates have ensued between Marxists over the validity of the two departments within which Grossman's and Dunayevskaya's emphasis on the importance of constant capital and productive consumption of capital has been adopted as vantage points in this book (Grossman 2013; Dunayevskaya 1982; Luxemburg 1913). Rosa Luxemburg (1913) however argued that productive consumption i.e., production for the sake of production, the thesis of Marx was not a sufficient explanation of the process of capitalist reproduction but rather the emphasis should be on *who realises the surplus value* (Le Blanc 2012). Raya Dunayevskaya (1982) further critiqued Luxemburg as well stating that Luxemburg (1913) in her analysis of the process of accumulation and reproduction of capital, focused more on the aspect of consumption rather than production. Luxemburg's problem was that she was searching for answers to the fundamental contradictions of capitalism, as Ludenhoff (2021, p. 222) argues, in the forces of the market i.e., in the acts of buying and selling of commodities, and not in the sphere of production.

Marx (1847) had himself stated that it was within the sphere of production that the contradicting tendencies of capitalist life dominated the laws of supply and demand. Consumption does not determine production, but rather it was the method of capitalist production, and subsequently capitalist accumulation, which determined the methods of consumption. For understanding the effects and causality behind the capitalist accumulation process it is necessary to emphasise the sphere of production. For capitalism to develop it is of utmost necessity that human relations become relations between mere commodities, which have been not dehumanised, but also de-historicised and robbed of all their subjectivity. The personal relationships that a possessor used to share with the commodities have been disrupted, not completely, however, but surely to a large extent. The feelings of grief, mirth and solitude that people associated with certain commodities – largely cultural – have become in the age of social media commerce avenues to further profits and accumulation as has been noted in the little sections about institutional apparel and comics in India in the previous chapters. All such objects have become values of commercial interest today. With social media, the people who have probably possessed them for decades suddenly have found a market laid out with all kinds of possibilities to generate profits and further personal capital for the possessors. The cultural element of the objects, as was the case in the pre-capitalist formations, has been completely lost, with every object – from a needle to noodles – becoming commodities capable of bringing material wealth to the possessing hands. Of course, it is not to assume that pre-capitalist social formations were beyond criticism, but that the culture of exchange value was less dominant cannot be doubted.

With the development of capitalism, society progressed towards becoming a society of commodity producers, as Marx (1976, p. 133) states which subsequently gives rise to a social division of labour. In this kind of society, the use-values of material objects have no particular importance but rather what gains special importance is the exchange value that the object – now a commodity is laden with the power of 'value' – possesses and the kind of complicated social relations that it can develop by dissolving the aesthetic nature of all private and individual forms of labour. Marx has repeatedly argued that the domination of exchange value cannot be taken as natural law – it is not a divine revelation. It is something that a section of human beings creates and sustains through their roles within the flow of values in society. It is the flow of value in a society that presents before the workers a society, in which the workers themselves do not find any space, be it in the urban locales of New York City or the hinterlands of rural Bangladesh. As Marx noted while writing about the transition from feudalism to capitalism:

> Customs, character, etc., vary from one estate to another and seem to be one with the land to which they belong; whereas later [within capitalism], it is only his purse and not his character, his individuality, which connects a man with an estate. Finally, the feudal lord does not try to extract the utmost advantage from his land. Rather, he consumes what is there and calmly leaves the worry of producing to the serfs and the tenants. Such is *nobility's* relationship to the landed property, which casts a romantic glory on its lords (Marx 1844, p. 266)

Capitalism hates any kind of romantic association which falls outside its alienated and commodified sphere of influence. It tends to destroy all forms of romanticism existing in society because romantic notions attached to any commodity might harm its progress into the domain of circulation, essential to continued reproduction. As Marcuse (2002) rightly argued, in advanced industrial societies, 'The celebration of the autonomous personality, of humanism, of tragic and romantic love appears to be the ideal of a backward stage of development' (pp. 59-60). The aspect of aesthetic or romantic possessions is completely destroyed within capitalism. The realisation of any form of love or affection under capitalism is almost impossible because capitalism sustains itself by creating the conditions of *rabid* competition capitalism where every individual's individuality is a product that is to be sold and resold in the neoliberal market, often for its metaphorical or figurative values (Marcuse 1937). Relationships with human beings or one's affectionate possessions mean the 'complete surrender' of one's 'individuality in the unconditional solidarity', something which is a competitive achievement in society, under neoliberalism can only happen when one is dead (Marcuse 1937, p. 98) because the meaning of being alive within such a society comes to mean competing with others or struggling to possess more commodities laying the previously possessed commodities to waste. For the complete flowering of capitalism, 'it is necessary that this appearance [of any romantic or aesthetic association] be abolished – that landed property [or any other property held by individuals], the [potential] root of private property, be dragged completely into the movement of private property and that it becomes a commodity; that the rule of the proprietor appears as the undisguised rule of private property, of capital, freed of all political tincture' (Marx 1844, p. 267). Contemporary society is a society where the transformation of all social relationships into economic relationships which Marx was talking about has been established. Today, every person is personified by the commodities one possesses. The character of landed property has not changed though, it is still concentrated at the hands of a select few. However, our purpose here is to analyse Marx's statements with regard to landed property in a way that illuminates the ideas in relation to the personal properties of the workers, as Marx (1844, p. 264) analyses the relationship between large and small landed property with large and small (industrial) capital. All workers who possess substantial personal properties are small-scale non-industrial capitalists in a way under social media commerce. Some like the women entrepreneurs discussed in Chapter 2 are formal ones, while others are informal small-scale ones. The way in which these small capitalists and traders are related to the large capitalist accumulation process is a central part of the entire social media commercial system which capitalism has put into action in society.

Property ownership has always been an important issue because it tends to dictate the flow of solidarities in society (Engels 1847b). Property relations have historically been associated with legal structures and the state of needs in society (Engels 1847b). That the individual requires money to survive, is used by the large bourgeoisie to bring in processes that benefit the bourgeoisie as Engels analyses in the case of the landowner (Engels 1847b, p. 89). Similarly, the common individual – the property-less worker – needs money to survive is used by the capitalist system to induct the individual worker into the cycle of social media commerce. Both Marx and Engels had mostly equated the working class to be property-less (Marx and Engels 1848, Engels 1847c). However, the idea of property here actually refers to 'private property' – property ownership that can lead to the process of valorisation. Such property usually is only concerned with use-value as much as that use-value can lead to some sort of exchange value. The difference between pure personal property and private property can be stated to be that while the former is mostly engaged with use-value, the latter is engaged with the creation of not only use-value, but also exchange-value – and above all surplus value as Marx says regarding the capitalist production process. The commodities which are a result of capitalist production process are composed of use-values and exchange values and as such the production process itself is a composition of the dual processes of the labour process and value production – this is the basis of Marx's idea of the process of valorisation under capitalism (Marx 1976, p. 293).

Social media commerce and its proliferation under contemporary capitalism establish the rule of capital over the general unconscious of the working class. It predates the capitalist desire of establishing a general competitive emotion in society. The constant adaptation of the ways in which the products are listed on the platform, along with the continuous competition among the users to sell their products leads one back to the roots of the consumer society as the book has noted to be found in Marx (1849), where Marx talks about a society where the buyers and sellers constantly compete with each other to be the most efficient performer within social media commerce. Competitions destroy the individual subjectivities in the society and replace them with patterns of reactions that are deemed fit for a rationalised capitalist expectation from the workers within the society as subjects, normalising submissiveness and uncritical acceptance of social norms (Marcuse 1941, p. 48). Social media commerce, and in fact the entire idea of competitive selling and buying as Marx (1849) himself argued, hinges on the element of competition. Individuals compete with each other to buy commodities; they compete with each other to sell commodities – that is the fundamental reality of capitalist society. Competition under capitalism merely means the freedom to exchange, whereby the individual becomes able to 'use and abuse' the instruments of production (Marx 1844, p. 255). The socio-economic crisis does not allow the working class to utilise the full use-value of their properties and put it back into the market thus allowing the commodity to keep on generating exchange value. The temporary monetary gains, when invested again, in the purchase of commodities, lead to an accumulation of capital which becomes the living embodiment of the dead labour infused within not only the commodity itself but also of the many "hands" which circulated it. This scenario also bears testimony to Engels's (1872) point that the ownership of property by the working class, on its own, neither improves the conditions of the working class nor automatically results in class mobility. Engels (1872, 1845) directs one to think that it is the entire social whole that determines whether the ownership of any property can be indeed progressive in nature. In other words, as long as capital dominates the working class as an alien force (Marx 1867), the potential of the working-class ownership of properties as an emancipatory force remains abysmally low.

Social media commerce enables the extension of the competitive mindset that capitalism aims to extend within society. Classical political economy, or bourgeoisie political economy, does not grasp the relationship between competition and monopoly, between labour and capital, and between the exploiters and the exploited. Smaller capitalists and capital owners (who are not yet possessing enough capital to be classified as capitalists per se) suffer at the hands of the accumulating prowess of the larger capitalists when the latter starts concentrating on generating higher profits by eliminating the smaller players in the accumulation of capital. As Marx notes: 'The accumulation of capital increases and the competition between capitalists decreases, when capital and landed property are united at the same hand, also when capital is enabled by its size to combine different branches of production' (Marx 1844, p. 258). Social media commerce cannot exist without competition. The competition to sell, and the drive to buy, are the soul of social media commerce. Social media commerce makes human beings compete with each other for being the most efficient and cost-effective seller. The personal property of the worker becomes nothing more than a mere tool of labour that the worker uses for the benefit of Big Capital. Of course, from the standpoint of Marx, the worker becomes poorer with the increasing amount of wealth the worker produces for the capitalist – that forms the basis of Marx's theory regarding alienation (Marx 1844, p. 271). Marx equates bourgeoisie civility heavily tilted in favour of the benefits of the capitalist. Competition is an important element of that civility in the society that capitalism creates: 'competition comes in everywhere. It is explained from external accidental circumstances are but the expression of a necessary course of development, political economy teaches us nothing. We have seen how exchange itself appears to it as an accidental fact. The only wheels which political economy sets in motion are *greed* and the *war amongst the greedy – competition'* (Marx 1844, p. 271). Similar to the times in which Marx was writing, the worker even today is a cheap person. The worker does not have a voice. The working class today faces the same and often aggravated, risk of exploitation at the hands of capitalism in contemporary times. The separation from the products of one's labour combined with the other modes of alienation constitute a human being who is completely detached and separated from intrinsic human needs and is only devoured by the necessities that capitalism generates in the form of social needs (Marx and Engels 1845-46).

Capitalist accumulation takes place by converting human beings into puppets at the hands of the commodities that the human being possesses (Marx 1976, p. 772). For capitalist accumulation to take place, it is of utmost necessity that the workers do not think of themselves as workers, because the self-articulation of being a worker can have revolutionary outcomes as Marx (1847) had already shown. Social media commerce does not let the worker think of oneself as a worker but rather works towards destroying the individual subjectivity of the worker as a worker. It dampens the pace of the generation of the consciousness of the working class. And, to emancipate an ignorant person, one must be, and one needs to be, emancipated oneself, that is to say, one needs to become conscious of the true power of the human mind (Ranciere 1991, 15) in its unalienated form; social media commerce creates hurdles in this process of human development and as such forces more workers to become one with the capitalist logic of private property and accumulation. For a worker to emancipate oneself, both as an individual and as a class, it is necessary for workers to think of themselves as workers in the first place. It is necessary for the worker to realise the idea of the struggle and in the process initiate the transformation of the working class from being a class in itself to a class for itself:

> Economic conditions had first transformed the mass of the people of the country into workers. The domination of capital has created for this mass a common situation, common interests. This mass is thus already a class as against capital, but not yet for itself. In the struggle, of which we have pointed out only a few phases, this mass becomes united, and constitutes itself as a class for itself. The interests it defends become class interests. But the struggle of class against class is a political struggle (Marx, 1847, p. 211)

Social media commerce disrupts the process of the 'self-production of the human being' (Dunayevskaya 1958a, p. 308) which is a critical element of the construction of this class for itself, and the subjective human being itself. There is a dialectic relationship between the class and the individual. Without the class, there cannot be any individual in the Marxist sense, and without the individual, the class would only be a seemingly homogenous unit with no dynamicity of its own. Dunayevskaya's focus on the political relevance of the subjective selves of the workers remains one of the most unique aspects of her Marxist theory and Marxist Humanism in general (Spano 2021). The processes of capitalist accumulation, as Spano (2021) notes, can take place through both legislative means and disciplinary actions as has been the case under state-capitalist regimes. Capitalism through these processes aims to disrupt the ability of workers to make themselves conscious of the process of capitalist accumulation. Dunayevskaya's ideas about accumulation rest on the belief that capitalist accumulation runs parallel to the possibility of a workers' revolution with the two tendencies being at two poles of Hegel's Absolute Idea, which she draws directly from Marx (1976) (Hudis 2021). In her accounts of capitalist accumulation, Dunayevskaya understood the central focus of Marx's positive humanism which could theorise the revolutionary upheavals of the working class in the worst of situations, something that according to Dunayevskaya, Luxemburg did not give much credit to (Rich 2021, p. 96).

Exploitation within capitalist societies is directly related to the processes of capitalist accumulation. It is the desire to accumulate which leads capitalism to create the conditions where different forces can be ushered in within the society to achieve its final goal – total accumulation of everything that the working class produces, including the personal relationships of the workers. Being a successful small-scale seller on social media is contingent upon the kind of personal relationships which a seller possesses. Interviews with middle-class sellers in India and Bangladesh highlight this point. The more a person was entrenched within the community – or networked within the community – the more possibility there was of the sellers being successful. A lot of them confessed to having been positively impacted by the growth of social media because while in the earlier days, they would have to focus only on known relatives and friends, social media has put them into direct communicative contact with many second-order and tertiary acquaintances who have helped them in building their businesses within the community. Some of them, in the process, have competed with other sellers through their usage of nostalgic associations, kinship bonds, etc., all of which have been financialised in the process of them becoming full-fledged traders. Liberalism, especially of the neoliberal variety, has a tendency to disproportionately favour the ablest of its members (Horkheimer and Adorno 2002, p. 104). Liberalistic society was supposed to be a form of society whereby individualistic rationality was supposed to be rewarded, it has turned out to be a society where the achievements of the victorious individuals, which are the markers of the dominant individual's individuality, produce social needs hinging on the exclusion of the weaker populace or individuals (Marcuse 1941, pp. 43-4). The social needs in society are manifestations of the manner in which production processes of capitalist accumulation operate in society (Marx 1847, p. 119). Commercial practices on social media, such as the ones mentioned in this paragraph, would have been difficult to be exercised in a non-liberalised social setting where private production does not reach the great heights where it can effectively manipulate social needs and put sellers into direct competition with each other trying to dispose of the commodities resulting from the increased production.

Marx accredited tremendous importance to the element of competition for the sustenance of capitalism within society. It is the competition among the different capitalists that gives rise to the possibility of the generation of monopoly capitalism. It is true that accumulation of capital in the form of private property, as Marx (1844) had predicted, results in 'the *concentration* of capital in the hands of a few, it is, in general, an inevitable consequence if capital is left to follow its natural course, and it is precisely through competition that the way is cleared for this natural disposition of capital' (p. 251). The element of competition is very closely linked to the creation of an effective accumulation process of capital. At this point in the 1844 Manuscripts, Marx enters a terrain that will become extremely important in the context of the current work. This is the terrain of the 'small capitalist' and the relationship that the small capitalist shares with the large capitalist. When any form of crisis actually strikes, the first capitalist who faces the troubles of the time is the small capitalist. It is the small capitalist who bears the first 'burn' of the crisis, while the large capitalist has the time to plan and think of the various strategies which can be employed. The number of small businesses which went out of business during the Covid19 induced lockdowns exhibit the reality of capitalist societies where Big Capital could survive the shocks of Covid19, while the smaller capitalists faced their worst fears. The small capitalists are often left with no other choice but to become one with the large capitalist. It is worthwhile here to quote Marx in full:

> The small capitalist has the choice: (1) either to consume his capital, since he can no longer live on the interest – and thus cease to be a capitalist; or (2) to set up a business himself, sell his commodity cheaper, buy dearer than the wealthier capitalist, and pay higher wages – thus ruining himself, the market price being already very low as a result of the intense competition presupposed (Marx 1844, p. 252)

The small capitalists of Marx are similar, if not identical, to the professional social media sellers that the current book has encountered in the past chapters. They are instrumental to the continuing increase of wealth in society because of their role in the overall accumulation and reproduction of capital. The reproduction of capital as Marx (1992, p. 427) states occurs through a repeated circulation and turnover of the total social capital constituted by individual capitals each of which 'has acquired independence and been endowed with individual life'. The circuits of these individual capitals involve both the circulation of commodities and capital (Marx 1992, p. 428), processes which have been already referred to. The social media sellers live their lives in a state of constant chaos, something which Bauman (1999) takes to be one of the fundamental elements of contemporary modernity. Dunayevskaya (1949) however, was able to relate the chaos exhibited within the lives of the workers directly to the process of capitalist accumulation, something which Bauman did not emphasise much. In general, the debates about capitalism and socialism have always focused on the element of chaos versus planning, where the latter has generally been associated with socialist o state-capitalist tendencies while the former with capitalist systems *per se*. Dunayevskaya noted:

> Yes, planning is essential to capitalism and has always characterized the factory production and production relationship for it is the wherewithal of extraction of the greatest amount of surplus value. No, planning is not essential, chaos is, because while within production there resides the tendency to go outside the limits of production, class relations and existing values impose a limit on it, which expresses itself in the anarchy of the market. At the same time capitalism can never really plan because its law of motion is impelled by reproduction according to socially necessary labor time set by the world market, and thus even if all conditions are met as to planning in factory, external planning as to market, and labor paid at value, the incessant revolutions in production of necessity mean the "development of productive forces of labor at the expense of the already created productive forces." (Dunayevskaya 1949, p. 9217, quoted from Hudis 2021, p. 69)

For the reproduction of capitalism, it is necessary that capitalism continuously keeps on improving the social conditions of production. Capitalism affects many changes within the production mechanisms to improve the overall productivity of the workers. This includes the modification of natural conditions as well as the alteration of the conditions of the labouring process by the application of scientific knowledge (Marx 1976, pp. 773-75). In the last few decades, as scholars such as Zuboff (2019) and Greenfield (2017) have informed us, there has been a continuous rise in the popularity of digital transactions. However, even with this rise of digital transactions, the importance of *hard* cash has not been thwarted from gaining a seminal positional factor in the reproduction of capitalism, especially when considered from the point of view of the small capitalists because large scale capitalists continue to improve the socio-technical conditions of production but 'While every social improvement benefits the big estate, it harms small property, because it increases the need for ready cash' (Marx 1844, p. 264). Small-scale traders from the working class operating on social media thus have no other option than to engage in cash. This becomes extremely difficult for those people engaged in social media commerce who belong to historically stigmatised races in the west. In the course of the present research, the author conducted detailed interviews with five such sellers on social media, three from the west and two from the east. The common thread linking both these sets of accounts was their requirement for instant payments. The ones in the east preferred to be paid in cash, because of the overall importance of cash in the economy. Cash becomes extremely important for them not only because it is an easy mode of money transfer but also because of other social and technical factors involved in many countries of the Global South which include extremely poor transactional mechanisms, lack of trust, the desperation of sellers to obtain the payment, etc. With every transaction that social media facilitates, the capitalists potentially gain. If that transaction happens through digital means, they gain through the medium in which the transaction has been performed. If it happens through cash, the capitalist gains through bringing more cash into circulation, something which the book has examined in detail, in the previous chapters. In both cases, as the interviews have revealed, the capitalists gain because the domination of capitalism is experienced by the workers everywhere.

Marx makes a very important point with regards to the power of accumulation possessed by large capitalists in the EPM – the focal point of which remains on the aspect of cash and its importance. As Marx says, the large capitalist 'accumulates it itself the interest on the capital which the [small capitalist] has employed to improve [the commodity]. Small [capitalist] has to employ its own capital and therefore does not get this profit at all' (Marx 1844, p. 264). The relationship between the large and small capitalists is also affected by the relationship between fixed capital and circulating capital – something which Marx had also explored in the volumes of Capital – and which forms the basis of the competition between large and small capitalists. Marx began his discussion on the topic by drawing from the work of Garnier, who argued that circulating capital is the capital that is '"employed in raising" provisions, manufacturing, or purchasing goods and selling them again' (quoted from Marx 1844, p. 253). The relationship between 'fixed capital and circulating capital is much more favourable to the big capitalist than to the small capitalist. ... It is generally true that the accumulation of large capital is also accompanied by a proportional concentration and simplification of fixed capital, as compared to the smaller capitalists' (Marx 1844, pp. 253-54). At the same time, be it in the realm of fixed or circulating capital, the accumulation of capital – the desired result of capitalist production – always results in the pauperisation of the working class:

> Under the conditions of accumulation we have assumed so far, conditions which are the most favourable to the workers, their relation of dependence on capital takes on forms which are endurable or, as Eden says, ' easy and liberal '. Instead of becoming more intensive with the growth of capital, this relation of dependence only becomes more extensive, i.e. the sphere of capital's exploitation and domination merely extends with its own dimensions and the number of people subjected to it. A larger part of the worker's own surplus product, which is always increasing and is continually being transformed into additional capital, comes back to them in the shape of means of payment, so that they can extend the circle of their enjoyments, make additions to their consumption fund of clothes, furniture, etc., and lay by a small reserve fund of money. But these things no more abolish the exploitation of the wage-labourer, and his situation of dependence, than do better clothing, food and treatment, and a larger peculium, in the case of the slave. A rise in the price of labour, as a consequence of the accumulation of capital, only means in fact that the length and weight of the golden chain the wage-labourer has already forged for himself allow it to be loosened somewhat (Marx 1976, pp. 768-69)

Any practical business analyst – somebody who works on the shopfloor and knows the reality of business – will instruct one's followers that the real and most important ability to conduct business, especially in third world nations, is the availability of 'ready cash' at one's disposal. Businesses run with ready cash because it is cash with which you pay for your daily expenses. Platform workers such as Uber drivers in India repeatedly emphasise this during their demonstrations. Similar is the case for social media sellers in the Global South. Social media commerce provides the opportunity for small-scale traders to become capitalists on their own, albeit on a smaller scale. It allows them to profit from the products which other workers have created on a smaller scale. Social media commerce blatantly exhibits the petty-bourgeois utopian idea of turning every worker into a small capitalist by providing property rights, which Engels (1872) had critiqued. Engels' (1892, 1872, 1845) arguments that private property can never be the basis of liberation but only of domination find relevance when one analyses the reasons for which the working class gets engaged within social media commerce, which is almost always related to the existing social crisis, either materialistically or physiologically. These reasons as having already been stated are dependent upon the state of the society, which in turn depends upon the process in which social needs within the society are structured. Under social media commerce, everybody is a potential capitalist. The continuous flow of money within the society and the corresponding continuous change of hands creates an immense amount of potential money-capital being in circulation which gets accumulated by capitalism *at the last instance.*

Under contemporary capitalism, even though the workers have not become capitalists *as one knows it*, they are now a very vital part of its accumulation techniques through social media commerce. They are an entirely different breed of capitalist individuals, who are workers, customers and capitalists at the same time. They are workers in the sense that they play their part in the production of the commodities, and that they again play an important role in the circulation and re-circulation of commodities and the capital associated with that commodity in the society. They are capitalists as well because they are engaging with value production in a certain sense. The simple difference between private property – the bourgeois property – and personal property – the workers' tools and possessions – are that the former has the potential to produce profit for the possessors while the latter does not. The 'capitalist' produced by social media commerce does not want to, however, accumulate for furthering the rule of capital, but rather wants to accumulate for becoming more effective customers. Their social ontology is guided by a combination of their consumerist attitude that capitalism itself produces and allows to proliferate in society. In many ways, this new breed of capitalists is only 'temporal' capitalists. Their primary aim does not remain in accumulating capital for furthering their profits but rather in becoming more efficient consumers within the society because that becomes the basis through which they construct their being within the alienating conditions of capitalist existence, which makes their social existence similar – if not identical – to a small capitalist. Marx (1844) quite correctly says that the big capitalist has power over the small capitalist similar to the power that the big capitalist has over a worker. But the curious case of modern capitalism is that the distinction between the small capitalist and working class within social media commerce is increasingly porous in nature. In most of the processes of exchange within social media commerce, both the 'producer' and the 'consumer' within social media commerce almost always come from the same social class. The exchange of money and commodities within the working class comprises mostly the personal properties of the working class, which is itself entrenched within a crisis-ridden system, ensures that the class mobility of the working class remains stagnant because the moment the worker is in possession of the money, he/she cannot think of anything apart from possessing more commodities. The 'more commodities' firmly land the worker back into the cycle of accumulation that capitalism desires. The cycle then comfortably reproduces itself. In other words, as Marx says:

> ... the original transformation of money into capital takes place in the most exact accordance with the economic laws of commodity production and with the rights of property derived from them. Nevertheless, its result is : (1) that the product belongs to the capitalist and not to the worker; (2) that the value of this product includes, apart from the value of the capital advanced, a surplus-value which costs the worker labour but the capitalist nothing, and which none the less becomes the legitimate property of the capitalist ; (3) that the worker has retained his labour power and can sell it anew if he finds another buyer. Simple reproduction is only the periodic repetition of this first operation; each time, money is freshly transformed into capital. Thus the law is not broken; on the contrary, it gains the opportunity to operate continuously. ' Several successive acts of exchange have only made the last represent the first." (Marx 1976, pp. 731-32)

The increasing importance of private property within the process of capitalist accumulation cannot be offset by the emphasis on the working class amassing personal properties because the capitalists in these situations do not allow any other distributive mechanisms which would hamper their own accumulation and profits (Engels 1847a, p. 305). The entire cycle of social media commerce ensures that nobody has the potential for "rising above their class" (Engels 1845, p. 321) because the exchange value 'temporarily accumulated' by the working class again gets formally accumulated either as direct profit or as interest or as rent by the capitalists. Social media thus acts like how Marx analysed the role of machinery in society. Any technology or machinery causes a fundamental alteration within the agency which mediates the relationship that capital shares with labour (Marx 1976, p. 519). With the increased, and improved, means of production, which have a revolutionary effect on the existing class relations in society (Dunayevskaya 1958a), it becomes imperative for capitalism to also create new ways in which commodities can be distributed and exchanged in society. By the law of capitalist development, it is imperative that new modes of distribution produce conflicts and contradictions within the capitalist society. The initiation of commercial activities on social media platforms, allowed contemporary digital forms of capitalism to resist the opposition from the erstwhile controllers of distributive mechanisms in society. Social media commerce as has already been stated exploits the participatory culture existing on social media platforms to increase the tenacity of capitalist accumulation. It exploits the cooperative nature of social media groups, which become the primary sites of commercial trading on social media. Through social media commerce, Williams' (1980) idea that means of communication are in fact means of production becomes explicitly visible in society.

It is the imperative law of capitalist development that modes of production and exchange become more complicated as time progresses producing the material necessity of the complete change of the way in which property relations are structured in society (Engels 1847a, p. 304). The distributive mechanisms one witnesses in society are a direct manifestation of the way property relations are structured in society. Historically, merchants have occupied a pivotal position in the development of global capitalism (Banaji 2020). It is thus natural for them to oppose the new distributive mechanisms that capitalism brings forward continuously in the contemporary age and time. By initiating commerce through popular social media platforms, digital capitalism countered the resistance from the old modes of distribution through the immense participation of the people and by devising a process in which even the old modes keep on accumulating profits, partially at least, as well. In commercialising communication technologies and using them as a means of production (Fuchs 2020), capitalism has transformed communication into a medium to generate profits (Grohmann 2016). The reaction to a new state of things has not always been resigned abandonment of old values but rather a mad overdetermination, an exacerbation of these values of reference, function, finality and causality (Baudrillard 1990, p. 11). Social media commerce's emergence as a mode of distribution in society initially faced strong resistance from the established small capitalists in the society, and naturally so. The small capitalists globally often act as micro-scale distributing agents with their sphere of influence being restricted merely within the realm of commodity dealing capital.

The character of commodities, as Marx (1844, p. 254) reiterates, changes if the process of production of the commodities changes. With the change in the nature of commodities, there occurs a fundamental shift in the way in which human beings design and experience their everyday lives. The everyday lives of the workers today are constituted by an increasing number of commodities, which not only dominate the lives of the workers but also make sure that the workers live constantly under the influence of commodities, which generate the desire to possess more commodities. The changes in the way commodities are conceptualised have resulted in major changes in how they are utilised. The world today no longer possesses or desires to possess heavy computer systems, which have been replaced by light portable laptops. Landline telephone systems have been replaced by tiny mobile phones. In recent times, smartphones have taken the place of other trivial entities such as bus tokens, grocery lists, etc., whereby it has transformed these activities into a form of digital transaction (Greenfield 2017).

Such gadgets are commodities that are increasingly mobile in nature and are thus the perfect candidates for initiating systems like social media commerce which celebrates individual mobility and talks about a future where a cell phone will potentially replace many commonplace enterprises which are taken to be perennial in the present day. These movable personal properties of the workers are a characteristic feature of the modern age (Marx 1844, p. 287). The mystified nature of property under capitalist social systems is a result of the mystified nature of production and distribution relations in the society in the ways in which the instruments of production and the tools of distribution are scattered across the society (Marx 1847, p. 197). Social media commerce functions through converting the mostly movable working-class property into commodities – many of which are parts of the overall instruments of production – the commercial exchange of which leads to further profit-accumulation for the capitalist class because the monetary inflow of capital generated by the working-class seller through social media commerce gets diverted to either the consumption of further commodities or, as a response to the crisis, towards production and circulation. In this context, social media makes the capital accumulation process smoother by aiding the working class in generating monetary income so that capitalism can continue to realise the full surplus-value and exploit the complete labour-power available in society. The control that capitalism enjoys upon these workers cannot be miraculously erased, even by rapid direct-action movements. The working class will not wake up one day and discover their consciousness, rather when the day actually comes, it will have been a continuous process of de-alienation and destruction of capitalist logic itself.

Under capitalism, the relationship between production and exchange is such that without exchange, production can happen, but without production, there cannot be any exchange (Engels 1878). Capitalist production is aimed at the accumulation of profits. It is the desire to accumulate profits, which makes capitalism improve and alter the instruments of production (Marx and Engels 1848), which subsequently influence other spheres of production and circulation as well (Marx 1976, 1992). Capitalism always finds it profitable to invest in machinery rather than human labour because an investment in machinery results in a decrease in the dependence that the capitalist has on variable capital (Marx 1859, p. 198). The influence of machinery continues to grow at an exponential rate further worsening the condition of the workers under capitalism (Dunayevskaya 1958a), this is the general law of capitalist development. The continuous increase in the value of constant capital for the capitalist creates the ideal grounds for accelerated accumulation of capital: 'Out of the innermost needs of capitalist production, whose motive force is the production of surplus values, comes the drive to pay the labourer the *minimum* and to extract from him the *maximum*' (Dunayevskaya 1958a, p. 121). Every gain that the capitalist makes is complemented by a subsequent worsening of the lives of the workers. Capitalism's investment in technology reduces the amount of living labour and variable capital requisite for capitalist production (Dunayevskaya 1958a, p. 123). This enables the increasing reduction of externality effects and their influence on the rate of accumulation by capital. Externality effects, classically, are defined as effects that originate from costs associated with factors that are not registered in the market. Externality effects have the capacity to determine the price of a particular commodity without necessarily impinging upon its value.

The constant increase of constant capital in relation to variable capital is one of the primary requirements of capitalist accumulation (Marx 1976, p. 781). The capitalist reduction of externality effects frequently results in the creation of the reserve army of labour and the 'unemployed army' – what Dunayevskaya called the 'insoluble contradiction which is wrecking the entire system' (1958a, p. 123). Marx (1847b, p. 433) used the term 'reserve army of labour' to talk about the unemployed section of the working class which capitalism intentionally creates to keep the price of the labour-power as law as possible. This is only possible when the population concentration in any social space is higher than usual. Social media commerce has allowed capitalism to use the immense virtual concentration of workers on social media to its own benefit. Though capitalism keeps on creating more potential wage workers while constantly throwing a section of them into the abyss of unemployment, social media commerce has allowed it to use the 'reserve army' in complete synchronisation with the actual wage workers – both of whom engage with social media commerce and its associated accumulation.

The accumulation process within social media commerce is primarily mediated through individual users or small-scale collectives. It helps capitalism in creating smaller pockets of capitalist accumulation which enable the continuing mobility of capital in the society, increasing the overall value of capital. The diversification of capital also entails within itself the continuous increase in the wealth within the society, however, constricted in its distribution might that wealth be. Social media commerce helps capitalism to create and sustain a repetitive cycle of circulation and accumulation, essential to the reproduction of capitalism (Marx 1976, p. 711). Social media commerce has proliferated at a time when capitalist regimes have increasingly failed to provide complete employment or much prosperity to the people living under them, be it anywhere within the globe. The state of crisis in contemporary society has made the workers rethink their ontological sensibilities and their social belongingness. Personal property plays a large role in this regard. Historically, personal property has been mostly analysed as a foundation upon which social stability is built. Under contemporary capitalism, however, the personal property of the individuals of the working class is merely the commodities that the workers have the financial and social capacity to consume. The personal property of the workers is nothing but the limited means of consumption that the workers can possess (O'Connor 1984, pp. 17-9). The digital eco-system and its internal accumulation are integrally related to the accumulation which proceeds within the actual material world. The relationship between both these kinds of accumulation is mediated by the forces of economic crisis, consumerism, and the constant acceleration of capitalist production. Activities that go on within the virtual space are in no way completely alienated from the physical world and the real space that the individuals are located in (Jurgenson 2012; Nunes 2006). There are broader processes that operate within the society, which continuously work towards creating bridges between the virtual and real world so as to create a uniform cycle or pattern which keeps on reproducing and sustaining capitalist modes of accumulation. These processes gain immensely from the fact that digital monopolies such as

Google, Facebook and Instagram are essentially free to use (Fuchs 2019a). They sustain the idea that lower marginal costs and profits associated with digital production can be overcome by initiating large-scale accumulation through digital or physical means of accumulation or through a combination of both, by maintaining the circulation cycle of capital (Staab and Nachtwey 2016).

Innovations play a pivotal role in this regard. Innovations are also an important factor in the context of the current study. It is because of innovations, both scientific and managerial in nature, that we have an endless assembly line of commodities in contemporary society. In the third volume of Capital, Marx had a small segment dedicated entirely to the role of inventions in the economic structure of capital wherein he talks about the role of inventions and innovations within the capitalist economic structure (Marx 1981, pp. 198-99). Marx in this context takes note of none other than Charles Babbage and argues that it is the cooperative labour of the working class which builds upon the previously performed labour of the individuals to produce innovations – which are highly expensive when they are produced for the first time. The underlying idea here is that once an innovation is firmly entrenched within the capitalist accumulation process, it can be effortlessly utilised for capitalist accumulation (Marx 1981, p. 199). Such innovations, in the end, usually become important parts of the accumulation processes of 'the most worthless and wretched kind of money-capitalists that draw the greatest profit from all new developments of the universal labour of the human spirit and their social application by combined labour' (p. 199).

Under capitalism, the workers possess some commodities as personal properties as markers of potential individual freedom – which always exists as an abstraction never becoming concrete under capitalist domination. The personal property of the workers enables the existential justification of the worker under capitalism – a system that rests upon the belief in private property valorisation. The capitalist solution to the contradictions caused by its own processes of accumulation and valorisation is to give the opportunity to every worker to become capitalists of their own, who with time get inoculated with the germ of becoming complete capitalists themselves. Marx and Engels (1846) criticised these vulgar utopian models of social improvement, which at times flow from both ends of the spectrum – the capitalists as well as the communists – by labelling these ideas as: 'None other than that *everybody* should be turned into a *private-property owner*, a wish that is just as practicable and communist as that everybody should be turned into an emperor, king or pope' (Marx and Engels 1846, p. 44). The ownership of personal property by the working class as Engels (1872, 1845) had mentioned, does not hold any revolutionary potential as long as capitalism successfully initiates the commercial exchange of those properties by controlling the social processes. As long as the culture of value production remains the sole purpose of capitalist societies, the ownership of personal property and its communitarian usage can lead to nothing revolutionary, except meagre reforms. The mode of production in any society is not restricted only to the reproduction of the physicality of the individual as Marx says in *The German Ideology*. But rather, as Marx argues, reproduction encompasses everything that the individual stands for – the individual's mode of expressing the activities associated with living, the ways in which those activities are conducted, etc – which can be accurately summarised as '*mode of life*' itself: 'As Individuals express their life, so they are. What they are, therefore, coincides with their production, both with *what* they produce and with *how* they produce' (Marx and Engels 1845-46, p. 31).

For capitalism to survive, it is essential that it constantly increases the commodities available in the market. Capitalist systems, or any other social system, cannot go on producing unless it keeps on converting a part of its production into the means of production for further profit generation (Marx 1976, p. 711). Mere circulation cannot add value to the overall capitalist system. Claims that capital is self-moving, even if it adds value to itself in the process, expose only one side of the process. As Hudis (2012) argues, the self-movement of capital has certain internal limits, which must be highlighted. Value might appear to be self-expanding as long as one remains within the process of circulation only (Marx 1976, p. 255), but once the analysis moves into the phase of production, one realises that the dual character of labour produces internal limitations on the sphere of circulation is the only valorisation process:

> Circulation therefore does not carry within itself the principle of self-renewal. The moments of the latter are presupposed to it, not posited by it. Commodities constantly have to be thrown into it anew from the outside, like fuel into a fire. Otherwise it flickers out in indifference (Marx 1973, pp. 254-55)

Capitalism constantly gives back to the worker, as Marx (1976) says, a part of the product which the worker produces, while capitalism absorbs it in totality: 'The transaction is veiled by the commodity-form of the product and the money-form of the commodity' (p. 713). It is money that becomes a crucial aspect in these situations. It becomes the agency through which successful possession is accomplished which under capitalism and the regime of private property gets reduced to complete appropriation mainly through consumption. This transforms money from being a mere commodity to an '*object* of eminent possession' (Marx 1844, p. 323). This glorified status of money in society becomes the driving force behind the way exchange relations are maintained in society. The economic system in place generates the need for money (Marx 1844, p. 307), in such a way that money comes to represent the true quality of life under capitalism. Capitalism brings into life a general form of exploitation in the society where every need – social ones – becomes an avenue for exploiting one's neighbours and fellow human beings under the disguise of bourgeois civility and social norms which normalise exchange relations mediated through money to be the foundational basis of any society. This general form of exploitation constitutes the complete alienation of human beings from nature and the human society where everything, including the air that the workers breathe and the water that they drink, becomes an alien habitation to them as they tend to 'occupy [them] only *precariously*, it being for [them] an alien habitation which can be withdrawn from [them] any day – a place from which, if [the worker] does not pay, he can be thrown out any day. For any mortuary, he has to pay' (Marx 1844, p. 307). For the accumulation of capital, money plays a crucial part.

Social media commerce further creates hurdles in the creation of effective limits upon the valorisation of private property under capitalism. By introducing the possibility of comfortable exchange, capitalism through social media commerce tries to halt the progressive generation of the imposition of limits on the accumulation of private property and the proportional increase of social property which is integral to the generation of any kind of democratic socialist state of society as Engels (1847, p. 102) argues. The exploitative cycle of capitalism can only be resisted by rupturing the alienated digital spaces (Fuchs 2019b) through a socio-political struggle against the entire capitalist system itself, which, in turn, can re-establish a humane society, free from consumerism and commodification, which digital capitalism, or capitalism in general, establishes in the society. This humane society can finally be an antidote to the crisis that capitalism generates. In this process, there has to be a complete negation of the logic of property itself. Capitalist accumulation is based on private property and the class relations it creates in society. The ownership and circulation of the personal properties of the workers as commodities through social media commerce today constitutes an important part of this exploitative structure of capitalism. It constitutes an important part of the total machinery of capitalist accumulation. It not only enables capitalism to circulate both commodities and capital within the society but also creates the circumstances through which it begins to oppress the workers by using the personal properties of the workers as leverage against them: '... the ownership of the house, garden and field, and security of tenure in the dwelling-place is becoming today, [...] not only the worst hindrance to the worker but the greatest misfortune of the whole working class; the basis for an unexampled depression of wages below their normal level' (Engels 1887, 431). Under contemporary capitalism, the worker owns absolutely nothing. Commodities such as housing and cars, usually bought with money loaned out from the banks, or expensive electronic gadgets bought by workers by saving up the money the worker received for labour are not commodities wholly owned by the worker. These are commodities that the worker only *thinks* to belong to them, while in reality they are owned by the banks or the needs that the worker suppressed while saving for being able to possess the commodity. It is no surprise that these are the commodities that populate the highest space within the domain of social media commerce.

The working class, under advanced forms of capitalism, gets introduced to the idea of 'personal capital', which effectively in this context means the ability of any commodity or any form of capital to become a small personal 'capital' for the worker who possesses it. Herein enters the concepts of 'saving', 'hoarding' and 'buying for buying' in the context of social media commerce. Capital forces the worker to think that: 'The less you eat, drink and buy books; the less you go to the theatre, the dance hall, the public house; the less you think, love, theorise, sing, paint, fence, etc., the more you save – the *greater* becomes your treasure, which neither moths nor rust will devour – your *capital*' (Marx 1844, p. 309). This leads to an alienated state of human life wherein the more one amasses, the more alienated one becomes. In other words, life gets replaced by 'money and wealth' (Marx 1844, p. 309). The workers thus live only within an illusion thinking that they possess something, while in reality they absolutely do not. Thus, 'Many men, and even people in general, *do not know their own lives very well, or know them inadequately*' (Lefebvre 1991b, p. 94).

Capitalism has historically been at the forefront of the process in which the 'scanty property' of the workers has been continuously rendered 'quite worthless so that the capitalist was left with everything, the worker with nothing' (Engels 1847, p. 99). This usurpation of the rights of the workers has been the entire basis of capitalist production and accumulation. Capitalism has proven time and again that commodities, which the workers take for their own are in fact, nothing but temporary possessions which the capitalist can take back anytime by the exertion of power. Marx (1847a, p. 318) brings this forward eloquently when he says '"Power ... controls property!" Property, at all events, is also a kind of power'. The question of property is absolutely central to the working class because it is property that plays a crucial role in rendering obsolete the major contradictions which arise within capitalist societies. The personal property of the workers is produced by the industry with the help of industrial capital, and as such always remains a part of the capitalist cycle of accumulation. With time the kind of personal properties that the workers tend to possess have changed. While the struggle of the workers for possession in the times when Marx wrote was largely based on land, today's struggles are different. Land, of course, remains an important factor, but along with it, other everyday commodities also need to be problematised, as Henri Lefebvre had said:

> The most extraordinary things are also the most every day; the strangest things are often the most trivial, and the current notion of the 'mythical' is an illusory reflection of this fact. Once separated from its context i.e. from how it is interpreted and from the things which reinforce it while at the same time making it bearable – once presented in all its triviality, i.e. in all that makes it trivial, suffocating, oppressive – the trivial becomes extraordinary, and the habitual becomes "mythical"(Lefebvre 1991b, pp. 13-4)

Private property dominates personal property under capitalism. It treats all forms of personal property as being its adversaries and tries to completely destroy them of their essence and utility. This is the historical course of development through which capitalist private property destroys the 'unenlightened' feudal landowner (Marx 1844, p. 287-288). The kind of exchange of personal properties that one witnesses within social media commerce is not egalitarian in any way. It is not mutual aid, it is, rather a full-fledged explosion of commercial trading in the society aimed at capitalist accumulation just like all other social developments under capitalism as Marx (1976) shows.

Properties such as land and water become private property only once they become parts of the capitalist system. The landed property – the most primitive form of a kind of private property – confronted by industry turns into full-fledged private property because 'industry incorporates annulled landed property, the *subjective* essence of industry at the same time incorporates the subjective essence of *landed property*' (Marx 1844, p. 193). The final consequence of this process is the complete abolition of any explicit difference between the capitalist and other non-working classes, 'so that there remain altogether only two classes of the population – the working class and the class of capitalists' (Marx 1844, p. 266). The same kind of effect social media commerce has over the personal property of the workers. Of course, it must be mentioned in this regard that landed property is quite different from other commodities because of the socio-cultural connotations which are associated with the possession of land. The critical purpose here is to, for the time being, analyse land as just another commodity that the working class possesses so that it becomes possible to analyse every commodity as being a part of the capitalist system whose:

> ... final consequence is thus the abolition of the distinction between capitalist and landowner [or any other possessor of commodities], so that there remain altogether only two classes of the population – the working class and the class of capitalists. This huckstering with ... property, the transformation of ... property into a commodity, constitutes the final overthrow of the old and final establishment of the money aristocracy (Marx 1844, p. 266)

The law of capitalist production, as Marx argued, is nothing but 'relation between capital, accumulation and rate of wages' which again is 'nothing other than the relation between the unpaid labour which has been transformed into capital and the additional paid labour necessary to set in motion this additional capital' (Marx 1976, p. 771). Social media commerce allows capitalism to save the latter part of the payments to a certain extent by using the crisis-ridden conditions of existence that the workers find themselves to be in. These smaller and temporal capitalists that capitalism creates through social media are often ruthless in terms of pricing because they are already being exploited through a regime of systemic crisis. Mainstream capitalists – the capitalists possessing Big Capital – can afford to garner smaller profits from their sales because of the volume they produce under contemporary capitalism. The larger capitalist has the capacity to survive through cycles of losses, unlike the smaller ones for whom each loss-making cycle would potentially result in an economic disaster. The social media seller, usually even 'smaller', wants to make a profit with every sale (or resale) that is made. The desire to reap profits with every sale varies inversely with the size of the capitalist in question. There is thus nothing emancipatory about social media commerce. With large numbers of personal property holders entering the competition of selling within social media commerce, there develops a culture of exploitation and accumulation within the society.

Within contemporary capitalism, not only is there a valorisation of working-class property directly in terms of exchange value and accumulation of profits, but it is the mode of distribution and circulation itself, highly communicative in nature, which becomes an active facilitator of the new source of profit-accumulation. The dominant system of production, of both material and cultural values, makes its presence felt in the entirety of human existence. Thus, in a society where private property dominates, it is only natural that it will make its presence felt and exercise its domination, authority and control in every conceivable aspect of human life. Private property, as Marx notes, exercises its domination over human beings 'in its most general form, a world-historical power' (Marx 1844, p. 293). The development of the capitalist conception of property is intimately related to the development of the capitalist production process (Marx 1847, p. 197). Engels (1872, 1845) was able to bring forward the conditions within which the working class could be coerced by the system into doing away with their properties. His emphasis that mere owning of properties cannot alter the exploitative relationship between the capitalists and the wage earner (Engels 1872) can be witnessed even today. It is surplus-value, which provides the foundation for the continuous reproduction of private property and sustained domination of the capitalist division of labour. Heller (2018, p. 22) argues that division of labour within society also impacts the needs within society. It is the 'position of need within the division of labour (that) determines the structure of need, or at least its limits. This contradiction reaches its peak in capitalism and becomes [...] the greatest antimony in the antinomy-system of the society' (Heller 2018, p. 22). Capitalism stands on the basis of surplus value extraction from the workers, that is its fundamental principle.

The workers' consumption in the process of the reproduction of capitalism is, as Marx (1976, p. 717) rightly says, merely an 'incidental part of the production process'. The drive towards extending the duration of the working day, the capitalist emphasis on the element of cooperation – everything occurs because capitalism sees in these techniques a means to improve labour productivity and most importantly, increase the span of its cycle of accumulation. Capitalism does not care about workers, rather its focus remains on the ways in which they can be made more productive. Facebook or Instagram or Twitter, or more precisely, the ones who own these platforms, do not care about whether the users benefit from the platforms, but rather their idea about social development is restricted towards the increase of the power of capital in society. The entire gambit of commodities within which the workers entrench themselves is a part of the way in which the workers sustain themselves to work – for producing the labour which the capitalist appropriates, as Marx repeatedly states. The basic philosophy of capitalism which is to extract surplus value from the working classes, as Engels (1878) said, stands correct within the entire process of social media commerce. Facebook, it is widely known, generates a high amount of profits through the targeted advertisements listed on its user interface (Fuchs 2014c). It works by encouraging people into using Facebook for a variety of different purposes through which it can redirect those users to the advertisers, the main source of sustenance of Facebook itself. Through the proliferation of social media commerce, capitalism attempts to maintain the delicate balance between the need-satisfaction of the working classes and the profit-accumulation of the capitalists by rendering the oppression of the working classes invisible within digital capitalism so as to delay the socio-economic crisis or any form of social revolutionary movement.

That the personal property of the worker can be turned into private property by capitalists temporarily should not come as a surprise. Capitalist production process, of which social media commerce is definitely a part, constantly converts the labour of the workers into commodities by consuming it within the production process transforming *en route* the labour of the worker to capital and value. This capital, as Marx (1976, p. 716) argues, 'sucks up the worker's value-creating power, means of subsistence that actually purchase human beings, and means of production that employ people who are doing the producing'. Commodities, in the process in which they get produced and consumed, reinvent themselves every day and at every point in time. Social media is increasingly becoming the platform where used goods that have been exhausted of their use-values for a particular user find their places afresh in the market. This is a market where sellers repeatedly compete against one another in relation to their prices, trying to sell their commodities as soon as possible. The pace is dictated by the social reality within which the individuals find themselves. There are instances of sellers having to sell their commodities at a price that is far below the usual market price of the commodity because they wanted to 'get rid' of them as fast as they could. They treated these commodities as part of their personally held capital which they utilised to garner money, which can then enter the proper process of capitalist accumulation.

The freedom associated with being a consumer or a seller on social media is a sham, because, under capitalism, there are absolutely no free subjects, but rather everyone is entrenched within a system of economic rationalisation which is driven by a combination of crisis, power, empowerment and potential enrichment. Private property regimes provide modes of emotional satisfaction to the working class through the possession of commodities, only to coerce them into entering the cycle of capitalist accumulation. Through social media commerce, capitalism oppresses and exploits the workers both through the usage of space and time. Capitalism has colonised the entirety of the private and social existence of the working class, through which it commodifies the everyday life of the workers who are within the realm of social media. For capitalism to develop, it is of utmost necessity that property and possessions become commodified to the highest limits possible. It is necessary that the romantic notions of a commodity be abolished, and the commodity becomes a 'commodity' in the truest sense possible – an object which is merely available in the market without any 'essence' of its own. This commodification also paves the path for the complete dissolution of the distinctions between the commodity and the person possessing the commodity. This effectively means that the possessor becomes one with the commodity, ensuring that the possessor cannot be anything that the commodity is not. Immigrant social media sellers engaging more with exotic commodities rather than common everyday commodities such as clothing are a perfect manifestation of this. This is the force with which commodities affect the life of human beings under capitalism. Capital, as Dunayevskaya (1958a) rightly said, is a relation of production established by the 'instrumentality of things' (p. 121), where the relationships between people are actually relationships between commodities (Dunayevskaya 1973).

The greatness of Marx's theory was that it could point towards the final dismantling of the capitalist system as a whole (Dunayevskaya 1982) as such that 'The law of motion of capitalistic society is ... the law of its collapse' (Dunayevskaya 1958a, p. 124). The central point regarding understanding Marx's notion of accumulation is to emphasise the law of motion within capitalist societies. Marx considered that the contradiction between capital and labour was the central question in all capitalist societies. It is the power over the purchasing of capital that gives the power to the capitalists to control the society, but at the final stage (or rather the stage of the complete development of capitalism) when the power of capital grows extravagantly, it supersedes the power of the individual capitalist as Marx (1844, p. 247) predicts. The element of value has to be the central focus of any analysis of capitalism because it is value itself that subsumes within itself all the contradictions of capitalism. Luxemburg's (1918, p. 455) argument that it is within the anarchy of the market that the capitalist feels a certain dependency upon the society, creates some issues with regard to the importance of the growth of constant capital (the means of production and the raw materials) over variable capital (the living labour-power) being an important factor for capitalist accumulation (Ludenhoff 2021, p. 223). Luxemburg (1918) analyses free competition within the capitalists as a marker of the capitalist's dependency upon the non-capitalist classes such that she concludes the importance of the exchange relations by positing the mechanism of exchange as the root of the capitalist law of value and the generation of surplus-value, which as one can fathom from the quote above is, in reality, the domain of production. In her focus on the element of markets and individual consumption, Luxemburg (1913) 'transforms the inner core of capitalism into a mere outer covering' (Dunayevskaya 1982, p. 38, quoted from Ludenhoff, 2021, p. 223). In other words, commodity production, which is the central point of capitalism loses its sheen in the analysis of the overall structure of capitalism. In his *Grundrisse*, Marx tackled this issue quite eloquently and had said:

> It is commodities (whether in their particular form, or in the general form of money) which form the presupposition of circulation; they are the realization of a definite labour time and, as such, values ; their presupposition, therefore, is both the production of commodities by labour and their production as exchange values. This is their point of departure, and through its own motion it goes back into exchange value creating production as its result. We have therefore reached the point of departure again, production which posits, creates exchange values ; but this time, production which presupposes circulation as a developed moment and which appears as a constant process, which posits circulation and constantly returns from it into itself in order to posit it anew. (Marx 1973, p. 255)

It is the law of capitalist development that with the development of capitalism, the part of the capital invested in machinery and raw materials increases disproportionately in relation to the part which is kept aside for wages and other costs associated with the workers (Marx 1847b, p. 432). It does not matter if capitalism has allowed individual sections of the workers to gain some monetary benefits out of social media because, in the end, it is capitalism itself that reserves the power to direct those monetary gains *as it wishes, whensoever it wishes and howsoever it wishes*. Social media commerce can be described as a classic case of the futuristic truthfulness in which Marx's works are embedded. The rise of small-scale traders and the innumerable working customers, the constant circulation of money and the associated desired constant production of newer commodities produce the conditions of full-fledged capitalist accumulation. As Marx himself had said:

> When the prevailing system is the production of commodities, i.e. where the means of production are the property of private persons and the artisan therefore either produces commodities in isolation and independently of other people, or sells his labour power as a commodity because he lacks the means to produce independently, the above-mentioned presupposition, namely cooperation on a large scale, can be realized only through the increase of individual capitals, only in proportion as the social means of production and subsistence are transformed into the private property of capitalists. Where the basis is the production of commodities, large-scale production can occur only in a capitalist form. A certain accumulation of capital in the hands of individual producers therefore forms the necessary pre-condition for a specifically capitalist mode of production (Marx 1976, p. 775)

CONCLUSION: 'ACCUMULATE, ACCUMULATE! THAT IS MOSES AND THE PROPHETS!' SAID KARL MARX

'The challenge of our time is not to science or machines, but to men. The totality of the world crisis demands a new unity of theory and practice, a new relationship of workers and intellectuals'
—Raya Dunayevskaya in 'Marx's Humanism Today' (1965, p. 74)

The developments in the field of technology and communication have transformed a wide array of communicative mediums into means of production. They have enabled the further valorisation of value and have increased the efficiency of the total process of capitalist accumulation – from production to consumption. These developments have not only engulfed the production of knowledge and material commodities but also embed within themselves the means of communication such as the Internet and social media (Williams 1980; Hebblewhite 2016). The development of technology, and especially the innovations within the means of communication enable the usage of the human ontology as a means for reproducing capital and capitalist accumulation (Marx 1976; Habermas 1987; Hardt and Negri 2000; Tiqqun 2020). Social media in the contemporary age has given rise to culture, communities and relationships which are mediated through diverse platforms that raise important questions about authenticity and sociality (Miller et al. 2016).

Capitalism is different than all the previous historical epochs because capitalism is essentially based on the principle of value and surplus-value production and because of the fact capitalism stops at absolutely nothing to achieve its desired goal of surplus-value. It is this desire which leads capitalism to bring alterations within the production system bringing changes to the socially necessary labour time required to produce commodities which alters the value of the commodity and subsequently generates a ripple effect in the entire society and social relations therein (Dunayevskaya 1958a, p. 129). Marxism becomes important because Marx was able to negate the restrictions imposed upon a critical analysis of capitalism by classical political economy and simultaneously invent newer dimensions of analysis – rejecting the conceptualising of labour as a commodity and seeing it as an activity. In doing so, Marx posited labour-power as a commodity that the capitalist trades in and labour as the activity of human beings (Dunayevskaya 1958a, p. 103) – the force of any revolution against capitalism. Capitalism produces reified social relationships which dominate society – both materially and ideologically (Dunayevskaya 1973, p. 88).

The social state of fetishism is the naked reality of capitalism: 'Under capitalism, relations between men appear as relations between things because that is what "they really are." The machine is the master of man and consequently, man is less than a thing' (Dunayevskaya 1958a, p. 111). Commodities produce a false and mystified society that thrives on the total domination of abstract labour over concrete labour (Marcuse 1986). The fetishism created by the exchange of commodities and the relationship that capital shares with labour under capitalism completely renders invisible the class relations from which the commodities get constructed (Jhally 1987; Fuchs 2011). The commodity is the soul of the capitalist society which is 'deceptively simple, ... [and] makes its rounds as the most common of all things *yet it is an opiate which reduces all consciousness to* false consciousness' (Dunayevskaya 1973, p. 89).

Social media commerce is an important part of the capitalist exploitative structure today. Social media commerce has aided the complete colonization of everyday life similar to the way in which Vaneigem (2012) had described the process. Under contemporary capitalism, newer commodities come into existence every moment. These newer commodities as Chapter 1 notes, not only enable the increase of the number of commodities available in society but also give rise to an increase in the alien forces which oppress human beings. With every new commodity, as Marx (1844, p. 306) notes, there arises a new domain of 'mutual swindling and mutual plundering'. Money assumes a supreme role in society whereby the needs of human beings are directly related to the social needs that capitalism produces and allows to proliferate in society. Social media commerce forms communities based on transactions converting them into 'transactional communities' which are nothing but a constellation of social relations formed by 'transactional communication[s]' where money 'performs a relation between people in a moment of the transaction as well as relations between individuals and the larger imaginaries like "the economy" and "society"' becoming a shared belief penetrating into the psyche of the individuals as a recognisable force of society formation (Swartz 2020, pp. 16-8). Money thus, as Marx (1973) said becomes the basis of the community itself (Harvey 2014). It transforms fellow human beings – potentially everybody over time – as sellers and buyers who deserve nothing more than curt and often rude responses. Social media commerce establishes, in the words of Kosik (1968) a world where praxis is fetishised, and representations dominate consciousness leading to a complete alienation and invisiblisation of human activity.

In any capitalist society formed on the basis of commodity production, there needs to be a certain structure in place which makes the exchange of commodities occur in an automated fashion (Prodnik 2015). Capitalism does this through the commodification and usage of behavioural psychology and cognition for the development of capitalist accumulation processes. It creates a situation where the workers not only do what capitalism wants them to do automatically, but also provide active consent to their own exploitation. Scholars such as Marcuse

(1986, 2002) have hinted at this being the actual role of capitalism in affluent societies. Capitalism sustains the idea that the workers themselves affirm their own exploitation (Marcuse 1986; 2002). Marcuse, however, was often credited with harbouring a deep pessimism within his theories with regard to the potential of the working class (Cliff 1961, 1961a). But in spite of the language of deep pessimism – which the present author agrees with as well – about the role of human beings, Marcuse's revolutionary vision contained within itself the important need to totally overturn 'the capital relation, the class society upon which it was based, and its noxious by-products, from aggressive militarism to stultifying social conformity in the consumer society. In short, a total uprooting was needed [on Marcuse's view], however unlikely that might seem like a concrete historical possibility' (Anderson 2020, p. 184). Social media commerce is a part of the automated framework that capitalism wants to promote in society. The users of social media act as automatic machines, whereby their response toward certain issues becomes preconceived and within the paradigm that capitalism creates in society. Capitalism, in other words, through social media commerce, extends its domination right into the everyday consciousness of human beings, which is an immensely important site of any struggle:

> The production of ideas, of conceptions, of consciousness, is at first directly interwoven with the material activity and the material intercourse of men—the language of real life. Conceiving, thinking, the mental intercourse of men at this stage still appear as the direct efflux of their material behaviour. The same applies to mental production as expressed in the language of the politics, laws, morality, religion, metaphysics, etc., of a people. Men are the producers of their conceptions, ideas, etc., that is, real, active men, as they are conditioned by a definite development of their productive forces and of the intercourse corresponding to these, up to its furthest forms. Consciousness can never be anything else than conscious being, and the being of men is their actual life-process. (Marx and Engels 1845-46, p. 36)

The capitalism of today does not create humane relationships instead, it attempts to lure users within its fold of exchange relations, whereby the personal experiences of individuals are presented as products (Zuboff 2019). These social relationships are the foundations upon which capitalism builds its empire. Ideology and economy are inseparable elements of a dialectical analysis of capitalist society (Dunayevskaya 1958a). It is the individual subsumed under these social relationships who constitute the broader society. Capitalism through its improved production mechanisms and the cooperative labour of the workers create a society where all the needs of the individual become crystalised only in the form of money – 'Everything is within reach, can be bought, can be consumed' (Fromm 1956, p. 106). The proliferation of the commodity form played a key role in this transformation. Balibar (2007) argues that the development of money is necessary for capitalism to form a single holistic structure based on the production and exchange of commodities. This transformation is brought forward by the domination of the process of production where the production process gains superiority over the actual human being who affects the production process (Marx 1976, p. 175). Commodities are characteristic of the abstract labour contained in them which has a very specific social labour that mediates between the private labour of the individual worker and the labour market in conditions where the workers cannot access the means of production (Prodnik 2015). Smythe (1977) brings contemporary forms of communicative forms such as advertisements and mass media into the fold of capitalist production by using the concept of the 'audience commodity'. The mass media, which includes social media as well today, produces audiences as commodities who are then sold to corporations for profit. This occurs through capital using the audience themselves to market the commodities (Jhally and Livant 1986). For Smythe (1981, p. 233) the audience of the media becomes a commodity because it is the audience who is bought and sold at the market that technology creates. As Smythe (1977, p. 4) argues, the audience commodity provides the capitalists with the 'services of the audiences with predictable specifications who will pay attention in predictable numbers and at particular times to particular means of communication'. Most of the work that the audience does is mental, but even these mental forms of labour have a material basis (Smythe 1981). Smythe's (1977, p. 3) argumentative basis is the understanding that most of the non-sleeping time that the non-capitalist classes possesses is actual 'work time'.

Fisher (2015) explains this process through the struggle between the audience as workers and the media provides as capitalists based on the idea that capitalism mainly focuses on time as a factor of exploitation. Previous to Fisher (2015), scholars such as Postone (1993), Shippen (2013) and Martineau (2015) have also utilised this approach to the analysis of capitalism as has been noted in the present book as well. Contemporary capitalism exploits the worker both *intensively* and *extensively* to produce surplus value not only by extending their working hours but also by increasing their productivity (Jhally and Livant 1987) by fusing leisure with actual surplus value-producing labour converting workers in the process to automated machines whose every move and decision can be predicted. Capitalism achieves this by employing not only effective means of surveillance but also enforced modes of cognition. That capitalism can produce automated subjects depicts the perverse relationship between 'thinking' and 'practising' under capitalism which according to Smythe (1981) was the basis of the struggle between capital and labour – as far as the means of communication was concerned.

Information technology and automation have been massively reorganising society. They have changed the workspaces by bringing in more automation with an intention to reduce the variable capital associated with the production process (Dunayevskaya 1958a; Huws 2003). These changes, because of their effects on the entire production structure, cause further changes in the organisational structure as well causing more globalisation and exploitation of the labour market itself (Huws 2003). With time, the influence of automation has also reached the wider society. Any change in the production process does have a massive effect on the overall structure of the society just as Marx had stated numerous times (1847, 1973, 1976). This is the basis of the conceptualisation of the 'social factory' or the 'factory beyond walls' where the entire society emerges as a factory possessing the means of production ready to be utilised in the process of capitalist exploitation (Tronti 1962; Negri 1989b). Under these circumstances, new forms of labour emerge as do new forms of capitalist exploitation (Pleois 2016; Boutang, 2011). Social media commerce is a part of this process. In many ways, social media commerce uses the controlled and routinised biopower which technology helps capitalism reproduce on an everyday basis (Postone 1993; Hall and Stahl 2016). Like all other automated modes of production and circulation, social media commerce treats the entire society as a factory. It creates the basis upon which commodities enter the realm of exchange for a second time.

The value-form of the commodity under capitalism is supremely important in this context. As Dunayevskaya (1973, p. 88) says, it is the value-form that not only camouflages the relationship between human beings and their classes, but is also at the same time a perversion of the relationship between human beings and the machines – which dominate the realm of means of production – converting human beings as mere objects of the machinic subjects. There have been debates and discussions over whether it is the market or the value-form which dominates human beings (Harvey 2010a; Hudis 2012), some of which have been addressed in this book as well. But both sides of the debate conclude the importance of the process of accumulation within capitalism. As long as accumulation remains the causal force behind commodity production, capitalism will continue to attempt to extend the working hours of the working class (Dunayevskaya 1973, p. 227).

The centralisation and concentration of capital is the general law of capitalist development and accumulation (Dunayevskaya 1973, p. 83). The relationship between the crisis of overproduction and the statist advertisement of the consumerist life is well established (Cohen 2016). The sharing economy and its associated usage of communitarian ideals focused on Web 3.0 and Web 2.0 frameworks, is directly related to the historical development of capitalism as Cohen (2016) has established. There have been scholars who have focused on the aspects of fair trade and the ethicality of rampant consumption as political issues as well (O'Ruerke 2012). But these solutions do not attack the heart of capitalism – the point of production. They are mostly emphasising the law of demand and supply which does not desire to acknowledge that the number of people will always be more than the demand because that is the result of the capitalist production process (Marx 1844, p. 314). Social media commerce thus, cannot lead to an egalitarian society because it continues to use human activity as various forms of capital extinguishing all the natural elements of the object, further fetishising and de-socialising it (Marx 1844, p. 285) and reiterating, in the process, the capitalist basis of accumulation. The capitalist production process, it has to be realised is essentially a process of capitalist accumulation and exploitation (Marx 1981, p. 324).

Because of the inability of the working class to access the means of production, it is the class of the capitalists that produce the commodities, and the workers are enforced to buy the products of the production process either as means of subsistence (Prodnik 2015) or as means to satisfy their social needs (Marx and

Engels 1845-46). Mandel (1976) and Heller (2018) attempted to address the crisis of capitalism by using the idea of associated producers and their impact on the structure of human needs therein. This was a society where, as Heller (2018, p. 23) argues, the needs did not end up as commodities satisfying effective demand within the market. Rather, this society would be a society where the main focus of the social structures in place is to evaluate and assess the needs and then subsequently allocate the social labour-power and labour time to the satisfaction of those needs. Thus, they are not only mere objects appearing out of the thin air of effective consumer demands, but they become manifestations of human existence. This idea of the society of associated producers was criticised by Dunayevskaya (1976a) who emphasised that the society of associated producers did not contain an emphasis on the nature of the association. Her emphasis on the 'free association' of labour rested on the idea that 'Freely is the *specific* word, concept, living reality that was *the* determinate of Marx's "objective and strictly scientific way" not only of distinguishing his analyses from all others but characterising his *whole life*' (p. 73). It is only the freely associated labour that can destroy the fetishism associated with commodities (Dunayevskaya 1965, p. 67) 'because only they know it from the inside, from within the process of production, and thus only they have the power and the true knowledge of reality' (Dunayevskaya 1973, p. 88). The concept of freedom and the free individual cannot be a mere by-product of socialism, it has to be the very basis of the socialist society.

Within the liberal discourse, the usage of social media, like all other media, is usually associated with leisure (Fisher 2015). Leisure is usually the space and time associated with the life of a human being, where the human being is outside the production process and thus, possibly in the most humanised form possible (Lefebvre 1991a). Social media commerce penetrates this humane sphere of the workers' existence with the target of bringing it within the fold of capitalist exchange relations. In doing so, capitalism uses the pre-existing and normalised audience labour of the workers. Social media commerce is a method in which capitalism moves from the state of formal subsumption to a state of real subsumption of labour. Social media commerce uses the non-(productive)working time of human beings as an active facilitator of capitalist accumulation. Social media uses the social labour of workers to completely subsume the workers 'turning them into a means of piggybacking the circulatory requirements of capital onto the personal relationships (and unpaid cultural labour) of communicating subjects' (Manzerolle and Kjosen 2015, pp. 171-72). Marx (Marx 1861-63; Marx 1861-63a; Marx 1976, pp. 1019-38) used the two terms 'formal subsumption' and 'real subsumption' to indicate the transformation of capitalist emphasis on the extraction of absolute surplus value to relative surplus-value. The real subsumption of labour under capital takes into account the growing influence of science and technology within the production process. Formal subsumption entails within itself specific changes in the mode of production but induces no specific massive qualitative change. The stage of real subsumption under capitalism, however, embraces a fundamental qualitative change within the mode of production itself which it affects by bringing forward prolific technical changes within the system of production which completely transforms the entire production process (Marx 1861-63, pp. 92-3).

Formal subsumption does not change the socio-technical and natural conditions of production thus making it necessary to either increase the working day or make the working day more productive if more surplus value has to be extracted (Marx 1976). Formal subsumption is only the first stage of capitalism. With real subsumption, capitalism reduces the labour time but increases the constant capital abnormal limits, which further increases the labour productivity. Under conditions of real subsumption, the workers' relation to capital undergoes a complete change because the basis of exploitation itself undergoes a technological modification (Marx 1976, pp. 1034-36). The efficacy of real subsumption cannot reach great heights if the workers question the technology, and hence there arises the requirement of the total fetishisation of everything that results from technology – even exploitation and oppression.

Social media commerce attempts to move towards a society where for the working class, the aspect of the choice of the platform for consumption essential to the framing of the relationship between shopping and inequality (Williams 2006) is completely absent – '*I want something a bit expensive, I search on Facebook, the rest of the places? Oh, I can't even think of buying, too expensive*' as one respondent said. Social media commerce hampers the individual, as well as collective generation of class antagonisms, by creating a working class that remains acutely submissive, and completely entrenched within a community of buyers and sellers where the question of value though dominant but operates subtly through the usage of the community making the workers contribute to their own exploitation. Social media commerce enables quicker completion of the transformation of money to labour-power and means of production, by using actual networked human beings as agents of accumulation and circulators of commercial capital, after which the *Big* capitalist:

> ... has also a greater capacity to set labour power in motion, or a greater quantity of labour, than is needed to replace the value of the labour power, as well as the means of production that are required to realise or objectify this amount of labour. He thus controls the factors of production for articles of a greater value than their elements of production, for a mass of commodities containing surplus-value. The value that he has advanced in the form of money thus exists in a natural form in which it can be realised as value which breeds surplus-value (in the shape of commodities) (Marx 1992, p. 111)

Every historical epoch presents new challenges, and hence there arises a need to start from the actual material reality (Dunayevskaya 1973). The development of capitalism is in itself a contradiction and the law of motion of the development of capitalism is contradictory in its very nature (Dunayevskaya 1958a). For Dunayevskaya (1973) like Marx, capitalism begins with accumulation and inevitably moves towards a conflict between the expanded production processes and value creation. It is capitalism's desire to achieve limitless production which makes it move towards the crisis that it tries to evade by bringing in measures and tactics such as social media commerce. Social media commerce exploits the living labour of the users. The unpaid labour of the human users is used for the production of the surplus-value. The human beings themselves become the commercial capital that capitalism so desires to circulate in the market for creating avenues for further production. Social media commerce benefits from the usage of the communities (such as the Buy and Sell Groups) already formed in the virtual spaces mostly through some shared interests rather than through values or traditions (Fuchs 2008, p. 137). At the same time, social media commerce uses the power of cash to initiate further socialisation because as Friedman (2008, p. 83) says cash still remains a powerful mechanism of a transaction within the production relations in society. This socialisation creates the much-needed illusion of humanisation which is essential for social media to continuously reproduce the fetish of the technology to create more autonomous markets that, though located within society, are rather constructing a society of their own through exchange relations – all formed on the basis of value production and accumulation of capital.

The only way in which capitalism can be defeated is to defeat the law of value by conceptualising the entire 'needs of the productive system as a *human* system. A system where human needs are *not* governed by the necessity to pay the labourer at *a minimum* and to extract the *maximum* abstract labour for the purpose of keeping the productive system ... within the lawless laws of the world market, dominated by the law of value' (Dunayevskaya 1958a, p. 136). The construction of a new society cannot remain at the philosophical level but rather has to be a social practice in itself. The dialectical process not only has to get rid of the exploitative capital-labour relations pre-existing in the society but also build new human relationships (Dunayevskaya 1973, p.xxvii). This movement through the double negation towards the Absolute will articulate the transcendence of all the particularities as well as the whole 'overcoming ... [the] internal opposition' revealing the opposites and contradictions which lie within (Dunayevskaya 1973, p. 15). This movement will take into account the fact that the trading of commodities by the working class cannot be considered to be egalitarian in nature because it still rests on the concept of value and focuses on the exchange relation mediated by the commensuration-power of money. It does not reduce the extent to which the exploitative mechanism of capitalism acts upon the workers but instead further dehumanises the workers by providing them with the 'refuse' of consumption, often from their own but more able fellow workers.

The liberation from capitalism means to liberate each and every individual from the oppressive regimes of capitalist exploitation because it is only through this absolute rejection of the capitalist world order that a just society can be established: 'In place of the old bourgeois society, with its classes and class antagonism, we shall have an association, in which the free development of each is the condition for the free development of all' (Marx and Engels 1848, p. 506). This requires as Dunayevskaya (1958a, p. 53) says, a philosophy of human activity itself and not crude forms of negation or universality. The transcendence from the capitalist mode of production is a historical and dialectical process

(Dunayevskaya 1973, p. 82). This transcendence does not embrace idealism nor reject materialism nor vice versa, instead, it realises 'the truth of both, and therefore a new unity' (Dunayevskaya 1965, p. 72). In this process, property is an important idea because the amassing of property has been historically associated with the benefits of the process of labour associated with higher productivity and increased wealth (Sayers 2011; Gronow 2015). The contemporary form of property gained legitimacy in tandem historically with the '"free" worker who owns nothing but his own power to labour' (Sayers 2011, p. 111). The contemporary individual's social existence as a worker is the result of this development of history (Marx 1973, p. 472) which has legitimised private property and its associated exploitation of labour. In the legitimisation of private property, capitalism has sought to posit the common benefits of the workers and capital which as Marx (1849, p. 220) rightly said is a myth because the 'the interests of capital and the interests of wage labour are [always] diametrically opposed'. Social media commerce is not like the traditional business platforms which merely facilitate interaction between producers and consumers like how Parker, Alstyne and Choudhary (2016) describe normal platform models. The commodities within social media commerce update themselves automatically by using the unpaid human labour of the innumerable users, which potentially results in an ever-expanding arcade of commodities furthering the rise of surplus value in the society which often leads to imperfect valorisation and its associated overaccumulation (Grossman 1992).

In contemporary society, the machine has triumphed over the human will. Human lives today are increasingly being mediated by machines and automation. Paul Mason in his recent work has related the dominant anti-humanist perception of modern life to a capitalist mysticism surrounding machines and automation technologies (Mason 2019). Donna Haraway has argued that society is increasingly being characterised by entities that are 'hybrids of machine and organism – in short, cyborgs' (Haraway 2016, p. 7). Paul Mason, on the other hand, has argued that Haraway's notion of the domination of the cyborg is a pessimistic one arguing that Haraway's ideas usually tended to 'set aside all the dualisms on which revolts against oppression were based: mind versus body, nature versus machine, even man versus woman' (Mason 2019, 'The Anti-humanist Offensive'). However, even with their differences, both theorists agree on the disastrous effect that technological usage under capitalism has had on the imagination of human life under capitalism.

Such tendencies can only be negated through a positive and humanist transcendence of the capitalist system in its totality as Marx said: 'communism is humanism mediated with itself through the supersession of private property. Only through the supersession of this mediation—which is itself, however, a necessary premise—does positively self-deriving humanism, *positive* humanism, come into being' (Marx 1844, pp. 341-42). This *Positive Humanism* begins when the mental and manual aspects of the analysis of human labour are united within the paradigm of the '"all-rounded" individual' (Dunayevskaya 1965, p. 72). It is only this *positive humanism* that can lead human society towards true freedom. Freedom means to reinstate the self-activity and creativity of labour which has been rendered obsolete by capitalism (Marx and Engels 1845-46, p. 87). Theories focused on demand and supply are inadequate tools to realise this freedom because while they can point toward the necessity of reforms and restructurings, they can never point toward the absolute destruction of the value system itself. The inhumane nature of capitalist production cannot be altered, it has to be eradicated.

Social media is an important aspect of everyday life under contemporary capitalism. Social media commerce actively aids the sustenance of capitalist alienation in society by allowing commodity fetishism to run amok in society. For the attainment of freedom, it remains necessary to strategically dismantle the fetish of the commodity and the emerging praxis associated with the commodity which penetrates right into the consciousness of the individual workers. The struggle for freedom under contemporary capitalism is difficult because the contemporary surveillance form of capitalism today knows everything about individuals through which it draws them into a situation whereby even though knowing the harm individuals still go forward with certain activities. Complete freedom from capitalism means the obliteration of capitalist influence on both the spatial and temporal dynamics of human society. Such freedom is unimaginable without taking into account the technological domination that capitalism inflicts upon human beings in contemporary society.

Technological innovations under capitalism are a result of competition which are aimed at the increase of human labour productivity. Innovations such as social media commerce do not make life easier for human beings as this book has attempted to show, rather they are the only means which enable the complete subsumption of human life under capitalist social relations. Technological innovations do not allow human beings to imagine the end of capitalism, but rather they manifest the most profound images of capitalist realism where capitalism is imagined not only as an extremely stable system but also as a system that simply has no other alternative. Such technological advancements cannot produce a fulfilling life for human beings because they fail to reform the oppressive nature of the point of production under capitalism. A free society is a society where individuals do not toil but instead live a life of fulfilment where labour is synonymous with enjoyment and does not remain an alienated activity, something which can only be attained with a complete disruption of the point of production as it exists under capitalism.

Freedom means the complete rejection of capitalism itself!

BIBLIOGRAPHY

Adorno, T.W., & Horkheimer, M. (1972/2002). Dialectic of Enlightenment: Philosophical Fragments, Stanford, Stanford University Press.

Adorno, T. W. (1973/2004), Negative Dialectics, London, Routledge.

Adorno, T. W. (1991/2001), The Culture Industry: Selected Essays on Mass Culture, London, Routledge.

Aglietta, M. (2018). Money: 5,000 Years of Debt and Power, London, Verso.

Althusser, L. (1970). Lenin and Philosophy and Other Essays, New York, Monthly Review Press.

Althusser, L. (2005). For Marx, London, Verso.

Althusser, L.. Balibar, E., and Ranciere, J. (2009). Reading Capital, New Delhi, Aakar Books.

Althusser, L. (2014). On the Reproduction of Capitalism: Ideology and Ideological State Apparatuses, London, Verso.

Anderson, B. (1997). Imagined Communities, London, Verso.

Anderson, K. B. (2017). 'Marxist Humanism after Structuralism and Post-structuralism: The Case for Renewal', in Alderson, D., & Spencer, R. (eds.), For Humanism (pp. 68-119), London, Pluto.

Anderson, K. B. (2020). Dialectics of Revolution, Ottawa, Daraja Press.

Anderson, K. B. (2021). 'Two kinds of Subjectivity in Marxism and Freedom: Hegel, Marx, and the Maoist Detour', in Anderson, K.B., Durkin, K., & Brown, H.A. (eds.), Raya Dunayevskaya's Intersectional Marxism: Race, Class, Gender, and the Dialectics of Liberation (pp. 311-334) Cham, Palgrave.

Appadurai, A. (1986). 'Commodities and the Politics of Value', in Appadurai, A. (ed.), The Social Life of Things: Commodities in Cultural Perspective (pp. 3-63), Cambridge, Cambridge University Press.

Arendt, H. (1958). The Human Condition, New York, Harcourt Press.

Arendt, H. (1978). The Life of the Mind, Volume 1: Thinking, New York, Harcourt Press.

Aronoff, K., Battistoni, A., Cohen, D.A., & Riofrancos, T. (2019). A Planet to Win: Why we Need a Green New Deal, London, Verso.

Aytes, A. (2012). The "Other" in the Machine: Oriental Automata and the Mechanization of Mind. Doctoral Dissertation, UC San Diego.

Banaji, J. (2020). A Brief History of Commercial Capitalism, Chicago, Haymarket.

Baldi, G. (1972). 'Theses on the Mass Worker and Social Capital', Zero work, http://zerowork.org/GuidoBaldiTheses.htm

Balibar, E. (2007). The Philosophy of Marx, London, Verso.

Barbalet, J. (1983). Marx's Construction of Social Theory, London, Routledge, Kegan and Paul.

Bastani, A. (2019). Fully Automated Luxury Communism: A Manifesto, London, Verso.

Battaggia, A., & Campanile, F. (1981). 'Mass Worker and Social Worker: Reflections on the "New Class Composition"', No Politics Without Inquiry, no.1.

Baudrillard, J. (1965). 'The Masses: The Implosion of the Social in the Media', New Literary Theory, vol. 16, no. 3, pp. 577-589.

Baudrillard, J. (1968/2005). The System of Objects, London, Verso.

Baudrillard, J. (1970/1998). The Consumer Society: Myths and Structures, Thousand Oaks, Sage.

Baudrillard, J. (1972/1981). For a Critique of the Political Economy of the Sign, St. Louis, Telos Press.

Baudrillard, J. (1975). The Mirror of Production, St. Louis, Telos Press.

Baudrillard, J. (1988). 'For a Critique of the Political Economy of the Sign', In Poster, M (eds), Jean Baudrillard: Selected Writings (pp. 57-96). Stanford: Stanford University Press.

Baudrillard, J. (1990). Fatal Strategies, London, Pluto Press.

Bauman, Z. (1988). Freedom, Minneapolis, University of Minnesota Press.

Bauman, Z. (2000). Liquid Modernity, Cambridge, Polity.

Bauman, Z. (2001). The Individualized Society, Cambridge, Polity.

Bauman, Z. (2001a). Community: Seeking Safety in an Insecure World, Cambridge, Polity.

Bauman, Z. (2003). Liquid Love: On the Frailty of Human Bonds, Cambridge, Polity.

Bauman, Z. (2005). Liquid Life, Cambridge, Polity.

Bauman, Z. (2005a). Work, Consumerism and the New Poor, Berkshire, Open University Press.

Bauman, Z. (2007). Consuming Life, Cambridge, Polity.

Bauman, Z. (2010). 44 Letters from a Liquid Modern World, Cambridge, Polity.

Beiser, F. (2005). Hegel, London, Routledge.

Bell, D. (1973/1999). The Coming of Post-Industrial Society, New York, Basic Books.

Benjamin, W. (1936/1968). 'The Work of Art in the Age of Mechanical Reproduction', in Arendt, H. (eds.), Illuminations: Essays and Reflections, Selected Writings of Walter Benjamin (pp. 217-252), New York, Schocken Books.

Benjamin, W. (1968). 'The Task of the Translator', in Arendt, H. (ed.), Illuminations: Essays and Reflections, Selected Writings of Walter Benjamin (pp. 69-82). New York, Schocken Books.

Benson, J. (1994). The Rise of Consumer Society in Britain, 1880-1890, London, Longman.

Benton, T. (1993). Natural Justice: Ecology, Animal Rights and Social Justice, London, Verso.

Berg, J., Furrer, M., Harmin, E., Rani, U., Silberman, M.S. (2018). Digital Labour Platforms and the Future of Work: Towards Decent Work in the Online World, Geneva, International Labour Organisation.

Berger, P.L., & Luckmann, T. (1966). The Social Construction of Reality, New Jersey, Anchor Books.

Berger, A.A. (2015). Ads, Fads, and Consumer Culture: Advertising's Impact on American Character and Society, New York, Rowman and Littlefield.

Best, S. (2013). Zygmunt Bauman: Why Good People do Bad Things, Abingdon, Routledge.

Betancourt, M. (2016). The Critique of Digital Capitalism, Santa Barbara, Punctum Books.

Bhanver, J., & Bhanver, K. (2017). Click: The Amazing Story of India's E-commerce Boom and Where it's Headed, New Delhi, Hachette India.

Blackshaw, T. (2005). Zygmunt Bauman, London, Routledge.

Boltanski, L., & Chiapello, E. (2005a). 'The New Spirit of Capitalism' International Journal of Politics, Culture and Society, vol. 18 (Annual), pp. 161-188.

Boltanski, L., & Chiapello, E. (2005b). The New Spirit of Capitalism, London, Verso.

Boltanski, L., & Esquerre, A. (2020). Enrichment: A Critique of Commodities, Cambridge, Polity.

Boutang, Y. M. (2011). Cognitive Capitalism. Cambridge: Polity.

Bowlby, R. (2001). Carried Away: The Invention of Modern Shopping, Columbia, Columbia University Press.

Braverman, H. (1974/1998). Labor and Monopoly Capital: The Degradation of Work in the Twentieth Century, New York, Monthly Review Press.

Braudel, H. (1974). Capitalism and Material Life, 1400-1800, New York, Harper and Row.

Briziarelli, M. (2014). 'The Ideological Reproduction: (Free) Labouring and (Social) Working within Digital Landscapes', tripleC: Communication, Capitalism & Critique. Open Access Journal for a Global Sustainable Information Society, vol. 12, no. 2, pp. 620-631.

Brunhoff, S.D. (1976). Marx on Money, New York, Urizen Books.

Buck-Morss, S. (1977). The Origin of Negative Dialectics: Theodor W. Adorno, Walter Benjamin and the Frankfurt Institute, New York, Free Press.

Buhr, F. (2017). 'Using the City: Migrant Spatial Integration as Urban Practice', Journal of Ethnic and Migration Studies. DOI: 10.1080/1369183X.2017.1341715.

Burston, J., Dyer-Witheford, N., & Hearn, A. (2010). 'Digital Labour: Workers, Authors, Citizens', Ephemera: Special issue, vol. 10, nos. 3-4, pp. 214-539.

Callon, M. (1991). 'Techno-economic Networks and Irreversibility', in Law, J. (Eds.), A Sociology of Monsters: Essays on Power, Technology and Domination. London: Routledge.

Castells, M. (2009). Communication Power, New York, Oxford University Press.

Castells, M. (2010). The Information Age, Volume 1: The Rise of the Network Society, Oxford, Wiley-Blackwell.

Chaturvedi, S. (2016). I am a Troll: Inside the Secret World of BJP's Digital Army, Delhi, Juggernaut Books.

Chari, A. (2015). A Political Economy of the Senses: Neoliberalism, Reification, Critique, New York, Columbia University Press.

Chin, E. (2007). 'The Consumer Diaries, or Autoethnography in the Inverted World', Journal of Consumer Culture, vol. 7, no. 3, pp. 335-353.

Chin, E. (2016). My Life with Things: The Consumer Diaries, Durham, Duke University Press.

Clare, N. (2019). 'Composing the Social Factory: An Autonomist Urban Geography of Buenos Aires', Society and Space, vol. 37, no. 2, pp. 255-275

Cleaver, H. (1979/2018). Reading Capital Politically, New Delhi, Phoneme Books

Cliff. (1961). 'Belgium: Strike to Revolution',
https://www.marxists.org/archive/cliff/works/1961/xx/belgium.htm

Cliff, T. (1961a). 'The Belgian General Strike',
https://www.marxists.org/archive/cliff/works/1961/02/belgium.htm

Cohen, G.A. (1978/2000). Karl Marx's Theory of History: A Defence, Cambridge, Cambridge University Press.

Cohen, I.J (2016). Solitary Action: Acting on our own in Everyday Life, Oxford, Oxford University Press.

Cohen, M.J. (2017). The Future of Consumer Society: Prospects for Sustainability in the New Economy, Oxford, Oxford University Press.

Cohen, S. (1972/2013). Folk Devils and Moral Panics, London, Routledge.

Collins, J. (1989). Uncommon Cultures: Popular Culture and Post-Modernism, London, Routledge.

Crawford, K. (2012). 'Four Ways of Listening with an iPhone', in Hjorth, L., Burgess, J., & Richardson, I. (eds.), Studying Mobile Media: Cultural Technologies, Mobile Communication, and the iPhone (pp. 213–228), London, Routledge.

Dalla Costa, M., & James, S. (1975). The Power of Women and the Subversion of the Community, Berlin, Falling Wall Press.

Dant, T. (1996). 'Fetishism and the Social Value of Objects', The Sociological Review, vol. 44, no. 3, pp. 495-516.

Davies, W. (2015). The Happiness Industry, London, Verso.

De Certeau, M., Jameson, F., & Lovitt, C. (1980). 'On the Oppositional Practices of Everyday Life', Social Text, no. 3, pp. 3-43.

De Certeau, M., Giard, L., & Mayol, P. (1998). The Practice of Everyday Life: Volume 2, Minnesota, University of Minneapolis Press.

De Nora, T. (2000). Music in Everyday Life, Cambridge, Cambridge University Press.

Deb Roy, S. (2020). 'The Political Economy of Working-Class Social Media Commerce', tripleC: Communication, Capitalism and Critique, vol. 19, no. 1, pp. 171-194.

Deb Roy, S. (2020a). 'Early Marxist Explorations into the Woman Question', Peace, Land and Bread, vol. 1, no.2.

Deleuze, G., & Guattari, F. (1987). A Thousand Plateaus, Minneapolis, University of Minnesota Press

Derrida, J. (1994/2006). Specters of Marx: The State of Debt, the Work of Mourning and the New International, London, Routledge.

Derrida, J. (1997). The Politics of Friendship, London, Verso.

Dunayevskaya, R. (1949). 'Letter to Grace Lee, February 1', in The Raya Dunayevskaya Collection – Marxist-Humanism: A Half Century of its World Development, Detroit, Wayne State University Archives of Labor and Urban Affairs.

Dunayevskaya, R. (1952/2019). 'Capitalist Development and Marx's Capital, 1863-1883', in Dmitryev, F. (ed.), Marx's Philosophy of Revolution in Permanence for Our Day: Selected Writings by Raya Dunayevskaya (pp. 27-30), Leiden, Brill.

Dunayevskaya, R. (1958a). Marxism and Freedom...From 1776 until Today, New York, Bookman Associates.

Dunayevskaya, R. (1958b/2002). 'Letter to Herbert Marcuse July 15, 1958', in Hudis, P., & Anderson, K.B. (eds.), The Power of Negativity: Selected Writings on the Dialectic in Hegel and Marx by Raya Dunayevskaya, New York, Lexington Books.

Dunayevskaya, R. (1961). Rough Notes on Hegel's Science of Logic. In The Raya Dunayevskaya Collection – Marxist-Humanism: A Half Century of its World Development, Detroit, Wayne State University Archives of Labor and Urban Affairs, pp. 2815-33.

Dunayevskaya, R. (1965). 'Marx's Humanism Today', in Fromm, E. (ed.), Socialist Humanism, New York, Doubleday.

Dunayevskaya, R. (1965a). 'The Today Ness of Marx's Humanism', in Dmitryev, F. (ed.), Marx's Philosophy of Revolution in Permanence for Our Day: Selected Writings by Raya Dunayevskaya (pp. 27-30), Leiden, Brill.

Dunayevskaya, R. (1965b). 'The Theory of Alienation: Marx's Debt to Hegel', in Dmitryev, F. (ed.), Marx's Philosophy of Revolution in Permanence for Our Day: Selected Writings by Raya Dunayevskaya (pp. 27-30), Leiden, Brill.

Dunayevskaya, R. (1967). State-Capitalism and Marx's Humanism or Philosophy and Revolution, Detroit, News and Letters, https://bit.ly/3bNBdZ3

Dunayevskaya, R. (1968). 'Letter on Hegel's Theory of Tragedy November 17, 1968', in Hudis, P., & Anderson, K.B. (eds.), The Power of Negativity: Selected Writings on the Dialectic in Hegel and Marx by Raya Dunayevskaya, New York, Lexington Books.

Dunayevskaya, R. (1969/2002). 'Logic as Stages of Freedom, Stages of Freedom as Logic, or the Needed American Revolution', in Hudis, P., & Anderson, K.B. (eds.), The Power of Negativity: Selected Writings on the Dialectic in Hegel and Marx by Raya Dunayevskaya, New York, Lexington Books.

Dunayevskaya, R. (1969a). 'The Newness of our Philosophic-Historic Contribution', in The Raya Dunayevskaya Collection – Marxist-Humanism: A Half Century of its World Development, Detroit, Wayne State University Archives of Labor and Urban Affairs.

Dunayevskaya, R. (1972/2002). 'Letter on Lukacs'. In Hudis, P., & Anderson, K.B. (eds.), The Power of Negativity: Selected Writings on the Dialectic in Hegel and Marx by Raya Dunayevskaya, New York, Lexington Books.

Dunayevskaya, R. (1973/1982). Philosophy and Revolution: From Hegel to Sartre, and from Marx to Mao, New Jersey, Humanities Press.

Dunayevskaya, R. (1973a/2002). 'Lukacs' Philosophic Dimension', in Hudis, P., & Anderson, K.B. (eds.), The Power of Negativity: Selected Writings on the Dialectic in Hegel and Marx by Raya Dunayevskaya, New York, Lexington Books.

Dunayevskaya, R. (1976/2002). 'Hegel, Marx, Lenin, Fanon, and the Dialectics of Liberation Today', in Hudis, P., & Anderson, K.B. (eds.), The Power of Negativity: Selected Writings on the Dialectic in Hegel and Marx by Raya Dunayevskaya, New York, Lexington Books.

Dunayevskaya, R. (1976a). 'Today's Epigones who Try to Truncate Marx's Capital', in Dmitryev, F. (ed.), Marx's Philosophy of Revolution in Permanence for Our Day: Selected Writings by Raya Dunayevskaya (pp. 27-30), Leiden, Brill.

Dunayevskaya, R. (1979). 'Marx and Engels' Studies Contrasted: Relationship of Philosophy and Revolution to Women's Liberation', in The Raya Dunayevskaya Collection – Marxist-Humanism: A Half Century of its World Development, Detroit, Wayne State University Archives of Labor and Urban Affairs.

Dunayevskaya, R. (1980/2019). 'Preface to the Iranian Edition of Marx's Humanist Essays', in Dmitryev, F. (ed.), Marx's Philosophy of Revolution in Permanence for Our Day: Selected Writings by Raya Dunayevskaya (pp. 27-30), Leiden, Brill.

Dunayevskaya, R. (1981/1982). Rosa Luxemburg, Women's Liberation and Marx's Philosophy of Revolution, New Jersey, Humanities Press.

Dunayevskaya, R. (1983/2002). 'Marxist-Humanism: The Summation That is a New Beginning, Subjectively and Objectively', in Hudis, P., & Anderson, K.B. (eds.), The Power of Negativity: Selected Writings on the Dialectic in Hegel and Marx by Raya Dunayevskaya, New York, Lexington Books.

Dunayevskaya, R. (1987/2002). 'Presentation on the Dialectics of Organisation and Philosophy', in Hudis, P., & Anderson, K.B. (eds.), The Power of Negativity: Selected Writings on the Dialectic in Hegel and Marx by Raya Dunayevskaya, New York, Lexington Books.

Duncombe, S. (1997). Dreams: Re-imagining Progressive Politics in an Age of Fantasy, New York, The New Press.

Duncombe, S. (2012). 'It stands on its head: Commodity fetishism, consumer activism, and the strategic use of fantasy', Culture and Organisation, vol. 18, no. 5, pp. 359-375.

Dunn, R.G. (2008). Identifying Consumption: Subjects and Objects in Consumer Society, Philadelphia, Temple University Press.

Durkin, K. (2014). The Radical Humanism of Erich Fromm. London, Palgrave.

Dyer-Witheford, N. (1999). Cyber-Marx, Champaign, University of Illinois Press

Eagleton, T. (ed.). (1989). Raymond Williams: Critical Perspectives, Cambridge, Polity.

Elster, J. (1985). Making Sense of Marx, Cambridge, Cambridge University Press.

Engels, F. (1843/1975). 'Outlines of a Critique of Political Economy', in Marx Engels Collected Works: Volume 3, London, Lawrence & Wishart.

Engels, F. (1845/1975). 'The Condition of the Working-class in England', in Marx Engels Collected Works (MECW) Volume 4, London, Lawrence & Wishart.

Engels, F. (1847/1976). 'Draft of a Communist Confession of Faith', in Marx Engels Collected Works: Volume 6, London, Lawrence and Wishart.

Engels, F. (1847a/1976). 'The Communists and Karl Heinzen', in Marx Engels Collected Works: Volume 6, London, Lawrence and Wishart.

Engels, F. (1847b/1976). 'The Constitutional Question in Germany', in Marx Engels Collected Works: Volume 6, London, Lawrence and Wishart.

Engels, F. (1847c/1976). 'Protective Tariffs or Free Trade System', in Marx Engels Collected Works: Volume 6, London, Lawrence and Wishart.

Engels, F. (1872/1988). 'The Housing Question', in Marx Engels Collected Works: Volume 23, London, Lawrence & Wishart.

Engels, F. (1878/1987). 'Anti-Dühring: Herr Eugen Dühring's Revolution in Science', in Marx Engels Collected Works: Volume 25, London, Lawrence & Wishart.

Engels, F. (1887/1990). 'Preface to the Second Edition of The Housing Question', in Marx Engels Collected Works: Volume 26, London, Lawrence & Wishart.

Engels, F. (1892/1990). 'The Origin of the Family, Private Property and the State. In the Light of the Researches by Lewis H. Morgan', in Marx

Engels Collected Works: Volume 26, London, Lawrence & Wishart.

Elias, N. (1992). Time: An Essay, Oxford, Blackwell.

Elkington, S., & Stebbins, R.A. (2014). The Serious Leisure Perspective: An Introduction, London, Routledge.

Ettlinger, N. (2017). 'Paradoxes, potentialities and problems of online work platforms', Work Organisation, Labour and Globalisation', vol. 11, no. 2, pp. 21-38.

Farris, S. R. (2011). 'Workerism's Inimical Incursions: On Mario Tronti's Weberianism', Historical Materialism, vol. 19, no. 3, pp. 29-62.

Featherstone, M. (1991). Consumer Culture and Postmodernism, Thousand Oaks, Sage.

Fennema, M. (2004). 'The Concept and Measurement of Ethnic Community', Journal of Ethnic and Migration Studies, vol. 30, no. 3, pp. 429-447.

Fisher, E. (2015). 'How Less Alienation Creates More Exploitation? Audience Labour on Social Network Sites', in Fuchs, C, & Mosco, V. (eds), Marx in the Age of Digital Capitalism, Leiden, Brill.

Fisher, M. (2009). Capitalist Realism, Winchester, Zero Books.

Flecker, J. and Schönauer, A. (2016). 'The production of "placelessness": Digital service work in global value chains'. In Flecker, J. (eds.), Space, Place and Global Digital Work, London, Palgrave.

Fleetwood, S. (2008). 'Workers and their Alter Egos as Consumers', Capital and Class, vol. 32, no. 1, pp. 31-47.

Forman, M. (2017). 'Marcuse in the Crisis of Neoliberal Capitalism', in Lamas, A., Wolfson, T., & Funke, P. (eds.), The Great Refusal: Herbert Marcuse and Contemporary Social Movements, Philadelphia, Temple University Press.

Fraser, N. (2016). Contradictions of Capital and Care, New Left Review, vol. 1, no. 100.

Friedman, D. (2008). Future Imperfect: Technology and Freedom in an Uncertain World, Cambridge, Cambridge University Press.

Fromm, E. (1942/2001). The Fear of Freedom, London, Routledge.

Fromm, E. (1956/2002). The Sane Society, London, Routledge.

Fromm, E. (1961). Marx's Concept of Man, New York, Frederick Unger Publishing Co.

Fromm, E. (1976). To Have or to Be?, London, Continuum.

Fuchs, C. (2008). Internet and Society: Social Theory in the Information Age, New York, Routledge.

Fuchs, C. (2010). 'Labor in Informational Capitalism on the Internet', The Information Society, no. 26, pp. 179-196.

Fuchs, C. (2011). Foundations of Critical Media and Information Studies, London, Routledge.

Fuchs, C., & Mosco, V. (2012). 'Introduction: Marx is Back – The Importance of Marxist Theory and Research for Critical Communication Studies Today', tripleC: Communication, Capitalism & Critique, vol. 10, no. 2, pp. 127-140

Fuchs, C. (2012a). 'Google Capitalism', tripleC: Communication, Capitalism & Critique, vol. 10, no. 1, pp. 42-48.

Fuchs, C. (2012b). 'With our Without Marx', tripleC: Communication, Capitalism & Critique, vol. 10, no. 3, pp. 633-45.

Fuchs, C., & Sevignani, S. (2013). 'What Is Digital Labour? What Is Digital Work? What's Their Difference? And Why Do These Questions Matter for Understanding Social Media?', tripleC: Communication, Capitalism & Critique, vol. 11, no. 2, pp. 237-293.

Fuchs, C. (2014a). Digital Labour and Karl Marx, London, Routledge.

Fuchs, C. (2014b). Occupy Media! The Occupy Movement and social media in Crisis Capitalism, Winchester, Zero Books.

Fuchs, C. (2014c). Social Media: A Critical Introduction. London: Sage.

Fuchs, C. (2015). 'The Digital Labour Theory of Value and Karl Marx in the Age of Facebook, YouTube, Twitter and Weibo', in Fuchs, C., & Fisher, E. (eds.), Reconsidering Value and Labour in the Digital Age (pp. 26-41), Basingstoke, Palgrave Macmillan.

Fuchs, C. (2016). 'Towards Marxian Internet Studies', In Fuchs, C., & Mosco, V. (eds.), Marx in the Age of Digital Capitalism (pp. 22-67), Leiden, Brill

Fuchs, C. (2016a). 'Marx's Capital in the Information Age', Capital and Class, vol. 41, no. 1, pp-51-67.

Fuchs, C. (2017). Social Media: A Critical Introduction (2nd Edition), London, Sage.

Fuchs, C. (2018). 'Universal Alienation, Formal and Real Subsumption of Society under Capital, Ongoing Primitive Accumulation by Dispossession: Reflections on the Marx@200-Contributions by David Harvey and Michael Hardt/Toni Negri', tripleC: Communication, Capitalism & Critique. Open Access Journal for a Global Sustainable Information Society, vol. 16, no. 2, pp. 454-467.

Fuchs, C. (2019a). Re-Reading Marx in the Age of Digital Capitalism, London, Pluto Press.

Fuchs, C. (2019b). 'Henri Lefebvre's Theory of the Production of Space and the Critical Theory of Communication', Communication Theory, vol. 29, no. 2, pp. 129-150.

Fuchs, C. (2020). 'Towards a Critical Theory of Communication as Renewal and Update of Marxist Humanism in the Age of Digital Capitalism', Journal for the Theory of Social Behaviour, vol. 50, no. 3, pp. 335-356.

Gardiner, M. (2000). Critiques of Everyday Life, London, Routledge.

Gorter, H. (1921/1989). An Open Letter to Comrade Lenin: A Reply to "'Left-Wing' Communism, An Infantile Disorder", London, Wildcat Pamphlets.

Greenfield, A. (2017). Radical Technologies: The Design of Everyday Life, London, Verso.

Grohmann, R. (2016). 'Humanist and Materialist Perspectives on Communication: The Work of Alvaro Vieira Pinto', tripleC: Communication, Capitalism & Critique, vol. 14, no. 2, pp. 438-450.

Gamman, L., & Makinen, M. (1994). Female Fetishism: A New Look, London, Lawrence and Wishart.

Gerber, C. (2020). 'Community building on Crowd work platforms: Autonomy and Control of Online Workers?', Competition and Change. DOI:10.1177/1024529420914472

Geyer, R.F., & Schweitzer, D.R. (Eds.). (1976). Theories of Alienation: Critical Perspectives in Philosophy and the Social Sciences, Singapore, Springer.

Giddens, A. (1991). Modernity and Self-Identity, Cambridge, Polity.

Glickman, L.B. (2009). Buying Power: A History of Consumer Activism in the United States, Chicago, University of Chicago Press.

Goldman, R. (1983/1984). '"We Make Weekends": Leisure and Commodity Form', Social Text, no. 8 (Winter), pp. 84-103.

Gorz, A. (1987). Farewell to the Working Class, London, Pluto Press.

Gouldner, A.W. (1976). The Dialectic of Ideology and Technology, London, Macmillan.

Goonewardena, K. (2008). 'Marxism and Everyday Life: On Henri Lefebvre, Guy Debord, and some others', in Goonewardena, K., Kipfer, S.,

Milgrom, R., & Schmid, C. (eds.), Space, Difference and Everyday Life: Reading Henri Lefebvre (pp. 117-133), London, Routledge.

Gramsci, A. (1917/1977). 'The Revolution against "Capital"', in Hoare, Q. (eds.), Antonio Gramsci: Selections from Political Writings 1910-1920 (pp. 34-37). London: Lawrence and Wishart.

Gronow, J. (2015). On the Formation of Marxism, Leiden, Brill.

Gross, J. (2013). 'Conceptualizing Emotional Labor: An Emotion Regulation Perspective', in Grandey, A. A., Diefendorff, J. M., & Rupp, D. E. (eds), Emotional Labour in the 21st Century (pp. 288-293), London, Routledge.

Grossman, H. (1992). The Law of Accumulation and Breakdown of the Capitalist System, London, Pluto Press.

Grossman, H. (2013). 'The Change in the Original Plan for Marx's Capita; and its Causes', Historical Materialism, vol. 21, no. 3, pp. 138-164.

Gupta, D. (2008). India's Lagging Sector: Indian Agriculture in a Globalising Economy. Retrieved from https://acbee.crawford.anu.edu.au/acde/asarc/pdf/papers/2008/WP2008_05.pdf

Guillory, J. (1993). Cultural Capital: The Problem of Literary Canon Formation, Chicago, The University of Chicago Press.

Habermas, J. (1975). Legitimation Crisis, Boston, Beacon Press.

Habermas, J. (1987). Lifeworld and System: A Critique of Functionalist Reason, Boston, Beacon Press.

Hall, R., & Stahl, B. (2012). 'Against Commodification: The University, Cognitive Capitalism and Emergent Technologies', tripleC: Communication, Capitalism & Critique, vol. 10, no. 2, pp. 184-202.

Hall, R., & Stahl. (2016). 'Against Commodification: The University, Cognitive Capitalism and Emergent Technologies', in Fuchs, C., & Mosco, V. (eds), Marx and the Political Economy of the Media, Leiden, Brill.

Hall, J.R., & Neitz, M.J. (1993). Culture: Sociological Perspectives, New Jersey, Prentice-Hall.

Han, B. (2018). Topology of Violence, Massachusetts, The MIT Press.

Hands, J. (2019). Gadget Consciousness: Collective Thought, Wil and Action in the Age of social media, London, Pluto Press.

Harari, Y. N. (2018). Money, London, Vintage.

Haraway, D. (2016). A Cyborg Manifesto: Science, Technology and Socialist-Feminism in the Late Twentieth Century, Minneapolis, University of Minnesota Press.

Hardt, M., & Negri, A. (1994). Labor of Dionysus: A Critique of the State-Form, Minneapolis, University of Minnesota Press.

Hardt, M., & Negri, A. (2000). Empire, Cambridge, Harvard University Press.

Hardt, M., & Negri, A. (2004). Multitude, New York, Penguin.

Hardt, M., & Negri, A. (2008). Commonwealth, London, Penguin.

Hardt, M., & Negri, A. (2012). Declaration, Agro-Navis.

Hardt, M., & Negri, A. (2017). Assembly, Oxford, Oxford University Press.

Harvey, D. (2005/2019). Spaces of Global Capitalism, London, Verso.

Harvey, D. (2006). The Limits to Capital, London, Verso.

Harvey, D. (2009). Cosmopolitanism and the Geographies of Freedom, New York, Columbia University Press.

Harvey, D. (2010). 'Organising for the Anti-Capitalist Transition', Human Geography, vol. 3, no. 1, pp. 1-17.

Harvey, D. (2010a). A Companion to Marx's Capital, New York, Verso.

Harvey, D. (2010b). The Enigma of Capital, Oxford, Oxford University Press.

Harvey, D. (2014). Seventeen Contradictions and the End of Capitalism, Oxford, Oxford University Press.

Harvey, D. (2016). Rebel Cities, London, Verso.

Harvey, D. (2017). Marx's Capital and the Madness of Economic Reason, Oxford, Oxford University Press.

Haythronwhite, C. (2011). 'Democratic process in online crowds and communities', E-journal of the Conference for E-Democracy and Open Government, vol. 1, pp. 23-33.

Hebblewhite, W.H.J. (2016). '"Means of Communication as Means of Production" Revisited', in Fuchs, C., & Mosco, V. (eds), Marx and the Political Economy of the Media, Leiden, Brill.

Hegel, GWF. (1820/1991). Elements of the Philosophy of Right, Cambridge, Cambridge University Press.

Hegel, G.W.F. (1837/2004). Lectures on the Philosophy of History, New York, Dover Editions.

Heller, A. (1976/2018). The Theory of Need in Marx, London, Verso.

Hetherington, K. (2007). Capitalism's Eye: Cultural Spaces of the Commodity, New York, Routledge.

Higgins, J. (1999). Raymond Williams: Literature, Marxism and Cultural Marxism, London, Routledge.

Hillery, G.A. (1955). 'Definitions of Community: Areas of Agreement', Rural Sociology, vol. 20, pp. 111-123.

Hjorth, L. (2018). 'Ambient and Soft Play: Play, Labour and the Digital in Everyday Life', European Journal of Cultural Studies, vol. 21, no. 1, pp. 3-12.

Hochschild, A. R. (1983). The Managed Heart, London, University of California Press.

Holloway, J., & Piccioto, S. (1992). State and Capital, London, Edward Arnold.

Honneth, A. (2008). Reification: A New Look at an Old Idea, Oxford, Oxford University Press.

Hudis, P. (2012). Marx's Concept of the Alternative to Capitalism, Leiden, Brill.

Hudis, P., & Anderson, K. B. (2020). 'Dialectics in Brief', in Anderson, K.B., Dialectics of Revolution, Ottawa, Daraja Press.

Hudis, P. (2021). 'The Indispensability of Philosophy in the Struggle to Develop an Alternative to Capitalism', in Anderson, K.B., Durkin, K., &

Brown, H.A. (eds.), Raya Dunayevskaya's Intersectional Marxism: Race, Class, Gender, and the Dialectics of Liberation (pp. 65-89), Cham, Palgrave.

Hudis, P., & Anderson, K.B. (2021). 'Raya Dunayevskaya's Concept of Dialectic', in Anderson, K.B., Durkin, K., & Brown, H.A. (eds.), Raya Dunayevskaya's Intersectional Marxism: Race, Class, Gender, and the Dialectics of Liberation (pp. 23-44), Cham, Palgrave.

Huws, U. (2003). The Making of a Cybertariat: Virtual Work in Real World, New York, Monthly Review Press.

Huws. U. (2014). Labor in the Global Digital Economy: The Cybertariat Comes of Age, New York, Monthly Review Press.

Huws, U. (2016). 'Logged labour: a New Paradigm of Work Organisation?', Work Organisation, Labour and Globalisation, vol. 10, no. 1, pp.-7-26

Huws, U. (2016a). 'Logged In', Jacobin, https://www.jacobinmag.com/2016/01/huws-sharing-economy-crowdsource-precarity-uber-workers/

Huws, U., Spencer, N., and Joyce, S. (2016b). 'The Size and Characteristics of the on-demand economy in the UK and Europe', http://researchprofiles.herts.ac.uk/portal/files/10894858/Huws_Spencer_and_Joyce_2016_.pdf

Huws, U. (2017). 'A New Bill of Workers' Rights', https://www.compassonline.org.uk/publications/a-new-bill-of-workers-rights-for-the-21st-century/

Huws, U., Spencer, N., Syrdal, D. S. & Holts, K. (2018). 'Working in the Gig Economy: Insights from Europe', in Neufeind, M., O' Reilly, J., & Ranft, F. (eds), Work in The Digital Age, London, Rowman & Littlefield International.

IGLHR. (2011). Institute for Global Labour and Human Rights. Available at https://www.globallabourrights.org

Illouz, E. (2007). Cold Intimacies: The Making of Emotional Capitalism, Cambridge. Polity.

Ivanova, M.N. (2019). 'Marx's Theory of Money: A Reappraisal in the Light of Unconventional Monetary Policy', Review of Radical Political Economics. DOI: 10.1177/0486613419856727.

Jabareen, Y., Eizenberg, E., & Zilberman, O. (2017). 'Conceptualizing Urban Ontological Security: 'Being-in-the-city' and its social and spatial dimensions', Cities, no. 68, pp. 1-7.

James, CLR., Dunayevskaya, R., & Boggs, G.L. (1986/2013). State Capitalism and World Revolution, Oakland, PM Press.

Jameson, F. (2007). Conversations on Cultural Marxism, Durham, Duke University Press.

Jay, M. (2008). 'Introduction', in Honneth, A. (au.), Reification: A New Look at an Old Idea (pp. 3-16), Oxford, Oxford University Press.

Jenkins, H. (2008). Convergence Culture, New York, NYU Press.

Jurgenson, N. (2012). 'When Atoms Meets Bits: Social media, the Mobile Web and Augmented Revolution', Future Internet, vol. 4, no. 1, pp. 83-99.

Jhally, S., & Livant, B. (1986). 'Watching as Working: The Valorization of Audience Consciousness', Journal of Communication, vol. 36, no. 3, pp. 124-143.

Jhally, S. (1987). The Codes of Advertising, New York, St. Martin's Press.

Kellner, D. (1989). Jean Baudrillard: From Marxism to Postmodernism and Beyond, Stanford, Stanford University Press.

Kinnvall, C., & Mitzen, J. (2020). 'Anxiety, Fear, and Ontological Security in World Politics: Thinking with and Beyond Giddens', International Theory, vol. 12, pp. 240-256.

Kosik, K. (1968). 'Dialectics of the Concrete Totality', Telos, vol. 1, no. 2, pp. 21-37.

Kowalik, T. (2014). Rosa Luxemburg: Theory of Accumulation and Imperialism, London, Palgrave.

Lal, A. (2017). India Social: How social media is Leading the Charge and Changing the Country, New Delhi, Hachette India.

Latour, B. (1987). Science in Action: How to Follow Scientists and Engineers through Society, Cambridge Mass., Harvard University Press.

Latour, B. (2005). Reassembling the Social: An Introduction to Actor-Network Theory, Oxford: Oxford University Press

Lebowitz, M. (1992/2003). Beyond Capital, Basingstoke, Palgrave.

Lefebvre, H. (1968/1971). Everyday Life in the Modern World, New York, Harper Torch books.

Lefebvre, H. (1991a). The Production of Space, Oxford, Basil Blackwell.

Lefebvre, H. (1991b). Critique of Everyday Life: Volume 1, London, Verso.

Lefebvre, H. (2002). Critique of Everyday Life: Volume 2, London, Verso.

Lefebvre, H. (2016). Metaphilosophy, London, Verso.

Lenin, V.I. (1899/1977). 'The Development of Capitalism in Russia'. In Lenin Collected Works Volume 3 (pp. 21-607). Moscow: Progress Publishers.

Lenin, V.I. (1901/1961). 'What is to be Done?', in Lenin Collected Works Volume 5. Moscow: Progress Publishers.

Levin, C. (1984). 'Baudrillard, Critical Theory and Psychoanalysis', Canadian Journal of Political and Social Theory, vol. 8, nos. 1-2, pp. 35-52.

Lewis, T., & Potter, E. (2011). 'Introducing Ethical Consumption', in Lewis, T., & Potter, E.(eds.), Ethical Consumption: A Critical Introduction (pp. 27-40), London, Routledge.

Littler, J. (2009). Radical Consumption: Shopping for Change in Contemporary Culture, London, Palgrave.

Littler, J. (2011). 'What's Wrong with Ethical Consumption?', in Lewis, T., & Potter, E.(eds.), Ethical Consumption: A Critical Introduction (pp. 27-40), London, Routledge.

Lotz, C. (2016). The Capitalist Schema, New York, Rowman and Littlefield.

Lotz, C. (2017). 'Fiction without Fantasy: Capital Fetishism as Objective Forgetting', Continental Thought and Theory, vol. 1, no. 2, pp. 364-382.

Ludenhoff, K. (2021). 'On Capital Accumulation, the Tendential Fall in the Rate of Profit, and Crisis Theory', in Anderson, K.B., Durkin, K., & Brown, H.A. (eds.), Raya Dunayevskaya's Intersectional Marxism: Race, Class, Gender, and the Dialectics of Liberation (pp. 209-232), Cham, Palgrave.

Ludz, P.C. (1973). 'Alienation as a Concept in the Social Sciences', Current Sociology, vol. 21, no. 1.

Lukács, G. (1968/1971). History and Class Consciousness: Studies in Marxist Dialectics, Cambridge Mass., MIT Press.

Lukács, G. (1975). The Young Hegel. London: Merlin Press.

Lund, A. (2015). 'A Contribution to a critique of the concept of Playbour', In Fuchs, C., & Fisher, E. (eds.), Reconsidering Value and Labour in the Digital Age, London, Palgrave.

Luxemburg, R. (1913/2003). The Accumulation of Capital, London, Routledge.

Luxemburg (1918/2016). 'The Second and Third Volumes of Capital', in Hudis, P., & Le Blanc, P. (eds.), The Complete Works of Rosa Luxemburg: Volume 2, London, Verso.

Lysack, K. (2008). Come Buy, Come Buy: Shopping and the Culture of Consumption in Victorian Women's Writing, Athens, Ohio University Press.

Mackenzie, D., & Wajcman, J. (1999). The Social Shaping of Technology, Birmingham, Open University Press.

Malm, A. (2020). How to Blow Up a Pipeline, London, Verso.

Mandel, E. (1975). Late Capitalism, London, New Left Books.

Mandel, E. (1976). 'Introduction', in Marx, K., Capital: Volume 1, London, Penguin.

Mandel, E. (1978). The Second Slump, London, New Left Books.

Mann, G., & Wainwright, J. (2018). Climate Leviathan: A Political Theory of our Planetary Future, London, Verso.

Manzerolle, V., & Kjosen, A.M (2015). 'Digital Media and Capital's Logic of Acceleration', in Fuchs, C, & Mosco, V. (eds), Marx in the Age of Digital Capitalism, Leiden, Brill.

Martineau, J. (2015). Time, Capitalism and Alienation: A Socio-Historical Inquiry into the Making of Modern Time, Leiden, Brill.

Marcuse, H. (1937/2007). 'The Affirmative Character of Culture', in Kellner, D. (eds), Collected Papers of Herbert Marcuse Volume 4: Art and Liberation (pp. 82-112), London, Routledge.

Marcuse, M. (1941/1998). 'Some Social Implications of Modern Technology', in Kellner, D. (eds), Collected Papers of Herbert Marcuse Volume 1: Technology, War and Fascism (pp. 39-66), London, Routledge.

Marcuse, H. (1955/1986). Reason and Revolution, London, Routledge, Kegan and Paul.

Marcuse, H. (1960/2011). 'From Ontology to Technology', in Kellner, D., & Pierce, C (eds), Collected Papers of Herbert Marcuse Volume 6: Philosophy, Psychoanalysis and Emancipation (pp. 132-140), London, Routledge.

Marcuse, H. (1964/2002). One Dimensional Man, London, Routledge.

Marcuse, H. (1966/2001). 'The Individual in the Great Society', in Kellner, D. (eds), Collected Papers of Herbert Marcuse Volume 2: Towards a Critical Theory of Society (pp. 59-80), London, Routledge.

Marcuse, H. (1967/2005). 'Liberation from the Affluent Society', in Kellner, D. (eds), Collected Papers of Herbert Marcuse Volume 3: The New Left and the 1960s (pp. 76-86), London, Routledge.

Marcuse, H. (1972/2007). 'Art and Revolution', in Kellner, D. (eds), Collected Papers of Herbert Marcuse Volume 4: Art and Liberation (pp. 166-177), London, Routledge.

Marks, B. (2012). 'Autonomist Marxist Theory and Practice in the Current Crisis', ACME: An International Journal for Critical Geographies, vol. 11, no. 3, pp. 467-91.

Marshall, A. (1890/1964). Principles of Economics, London, Macmillan.

Marx, K. (1843/1975). 'Contribution to the Critique of Hegel's Philosophy of Law', in Marx Engels Collected Works: Volume 3, London, Lawrence and Wishart.

Marx, K. (1844/1975). 'Economic and Philosophical Manuscripts of 1844', in Marx Engels Collected Works: Volume 3, London, Lawrence and Wishart.

Marx, K. (1844a/1975). 'Economic and Philosophical Manuscripts', in Karl Marx: Early Writings, Harmondsworth, Penguin.

Marx, K., & Engels, F. (1845/1975). 'The Holy Family', in Marx-Engels Collected Works: Volume 4. London: Lawrence and Wishart.

Marx, K., & Engels, F. (1845-1846/1975). 'The German Ideology', in Marx Engels Collected Works: Volume 5, London, Lawrence and Wishart.

Marx, K., & Engels, F. (1846/1976). 'Circular Against Kriege', in Marx Engels Collected Works: Volume 6, London, Lawrence and Wishart.

Marx, K. (1847/1976). 'The Poverty of Philosophy', in Marx Engels Collected Works: Volume 6, London, Lawrence and Wishart.

Marx, K. (1847a/1976). 'Moralising Criticism or Critiquing Morality', in Marx Engels Collected Works: Volume 6, London, Lawrence and Wishart.

Marx, K. (1847b/1976). 'Wages', in Marx Engels Collected Works: Volume 6, London, Lawrence and Wishart.

Marx, K., & Engels, F. (1848/1976). 'Manifesto of the Communist Party'. In Marx Engels Collected Works: Volume 6, London, Lawrence and Wishart.

Marx, K. (1849/1977). 'Wage, Labour and Capital', in Marx Engels Collected Works Volume 9, London, Lawrence and Wishart.

Marx, K. (1859/1987). 'A Contribution to the Critique of Political Economy', in Marx Engels Collected Works: Volume 29, London, Lawrence and Wishart.

Marx, K. (1861-63/1988). 'Economic Manuscripts', in Marx Engels Collected Works: Volume 30, London, Lawrence & Wishart.

Marx, K. (1861-63a/1994). 'Economic Manuscripts', in Marx Engels Collected Works: Volume 34, London, Lawrence & Wishart.

Marx, K. (1863a/1963). Theories of Surplus Value, Volume 1 (Capital Volume 4), Moscow, Progress Publishers.

Marx, K. (1863b/1969). Theories of Surplus Value, Volume 2 (Capital Volume 4), Moscow, Progress Publishers.

Marx, K. (1863c/1971). Theories of Surplus Value, Volume 3 (Capital Volume 4), Moscow, Progress Publishers.

Marx, K. (1865/1985). 'Value, Price and Profit', in Marx Engels Collected Works: Volume 20, London, Lawrence and Wishart.

Marx, K. (1867/1976). Capital, Volume 1: A Critique of Political Economy, London, Penguin.

Marx, K. (1867c/1996). 'Preface to the First German Edition of Capital', in Marx Engels Collected Works: Volume 35, London, Lawrence and Wishart.

Marx, K. (1867d/1978). 'The Value-Form: An Appendix to the First German Edition of Capital', Capital & Class, vol. 2, no. 1, pp. 130–140.

Marx, K. (1868/1988). 'Letter to Ludwig Kugelman July 11, 1868', in Marx Engels Collected Works: Volume 43, London, Lawrence and Wishart.

Marx, K. (1885/1992). Capital: Volume 2, London, Penguin.

Marx, K. (1894/1981). Capital: Volume 3, London, Penguin.

Marx, K. (1973/1993). Grundrisse: Foundations of the Critique of Political Economy (Rough Draft), London, Penguin Books.

Mason, R.S. (1981). Conspicuous Consumption: A Study of Exceptional Consumer Behaviour, Hampshire, Gower.

Mason, P. (2016). Post Capitalism: A Guide to Our Future, London, Penguin Books.

Mason, P. (2019). Clear Bright Future: A Radical Defence of the Human Being. London: Allen Lane.

Matt, S.J. (2003). Keeping up with the Joneses: Envy in American Consumer Society, 1890-1930, Philadelphia, University of Pennsylvania Press.

Mavroudeas, S. (2020). 'Friedrich Engels and his Contribution to Marxism', Human Geography, vol. 13, no. 2, pp. 187-190.

McKendrick, N. (1982). The Birth of a Consumer Society: The Commercialization of Eighteenth Century England, Bloomington, Indiana University press.

McNally, D. (2011). Monsters of the Market: Zombies, Vampires and Global Capitalism, Leiden, Brill.

Michael, M. (2006). Technoscience and Everyday Life, New York, Open University Press.

Mies, M, & Shiva, V. (2014). Ecofeminism, London, Zed Books.

Mika, B. (2019). 'Transgressing between consumption and production: Materialistic outlook on the digital labour of prosumers', Capital and Class, vol. 43, no. 2, pp. 339-356.

Milanesio, N. (2013). Workers go Shopping in Argentina: The Rise of Popular Consumer Culture, University of New Mexico Press.

Miles, S. (1998). Consumerism: As a Way of Life, Thousand Oaks, Sage.

Miller, D. (1987). Material Culture and Mass Consumption, Malden, Blackwell.

Miller, D. (1998). A Theory of Shopping, Cambridge, Polity.

Miller, D. (2011). Tales from Facebook, Cambridge, Polity.

Miller, D. (2016). How the World Changed social media, London: University College of London Press.

Milner, A. (1994). Contemporary Cultural Theory: An Introduction, London, University College of London Press.

Mohandesi, S. (2013). 'Class Composition or Class Consciousness?', Science and Society, vol. 17, no. 1, pp. 72-97.

Mohun, S. (1996). 'Productive and unproductive labour in the labor theory of value', Review of Radical Political Economics, vol 28, pp. 30-54.

Morrison, K. (2008). Living in a Material World: The Commodity Connection, New Jersey, John Wiley and Sons.

Mosco, V. (1989). The Pay-Per Society: Computers and Communication in the Information Age, Toronto, Garamond Press.

Mulcahy, N. (2017). 'Workers-as-Consumers-Rethinking the Political Economy of Use-Value and the Reproduction of Capital', Capital and Class, vol. 41, no. 2, pp. 315-332.

Mylan, J., & Southerton, D. (2017), 'The Social Ordering of Everyday Practice: The Case of Laundry', Sociology, DOI: 10.1177/0038038517722932.

Negri, A. (1989a). 'Archaeology and the Project: The Mass Worker and the Social Worker' in Revolution Retrieved: Selected Writings on Marx, Keynes, Capitalist Crisis and New Social Subjects 1967-1983, London, Red Notes.

Negri, A. (1989b). The Politics of Subversion, Cambridge, Polity.

Negri, A. (1991). Marx Beyond Marx: Lessons from the Grundrisse, New York, Autonomedia.

Negri, A. (1992). 'Interpretation of the Class Situation Today: Methodological Aspects', in Bonefeld, W., Gunn, R., & Psychopedis, K. (eds), Open Marxism Volume 2: Theory and Practice, London, Pluto Press.

Negri, A. (2003). Time for Revolution, London, Bloomsbury Academic.

Neilson, T. (2018). 'Unions in Digital Labour Studies: A Review of Information Society and Marxist Autonomist Approaches', tripleC: Communication, Capitalism & Critique, vol. 16, no. 2, pp. 882-900.

Nunes, M. (2006). Cyberspaces of Everyday Life, Minneapolis, University of Minnesota Press.

O' Connor, J. (1984). Accumulation Crisis, London, Basil Blackwell.

O' Connor, J. (1998). Natural Causes, New York, Guilford Press.

O' Reilly, T. (2005). 'What is Web 2.0 Design Patterns and Business Models for the Next Generation of Software', www.oreilly.com/pub/a/web2/archive/what-is-web-20.html

O' Ruerke, D. (2012). Shopping for Good, Boston, The MIT press.

Ollman, B. (1976). Alienation: Marx's Conception of Man in Capitalist Society, New York, Cambridge University Press.

Ollman, B. (1990/2016). 'Putting Dialectics to Work: The Process of Abstraction in Marx's Method', in Ollman, B., & Anderson, K.B. (eds.), Karl Marx, London, Routledge.

Olsen, N. (2019). The Sovereign Consumer: A New Intellectual History of Neoliberalism, Cham, Palgrave

Parker, G.G., Alstyne, M.W.V., & Choudary, S.P. (2016). Platform Revolution: How Networked Markets are Transforming the Economy and How to make them work for you, New York, W.W. Norton and Company.

Perelman, M. (1981). 'Capital, Constant Capital and the Social Division of Labour', Review of Radical Political Economics, vol. 13, pp. 43-53.

Perelman, M. (1990). 'The Phenomenology of Constant Capital and Fictitious Capital', Review of Radical Political Economics, vol. 22, nos. 2-3, pp. 66-91.

Perlman, F. (1972/2016). 'The Reproduction of Daily Life', in Ollman, B., & Anderson, K.B. (eds.), Karl Marx, London, Routledge.

Pettifor, A. (2019). The Case for the New Green New Deal, London, Verso.

Pietz, W. (1993). 'Fetishism and Materialism: The Limits of Theory in Marx', in Apter, E., & Pietz, W. (eds.), Fetishism as Cultural Discourse (pp. 119-151), New York, Cornell University Press.

Plamenatz, J. (1975). Karl Marx's Philosophy of Man, Oxford, Oxford University Press.

Pleios, G. (2016). 'Communication and Symbolic Capitalism – Rethinking Marxist Communication Theory', in Fuchs, C., & Mosco, V. (eds), Marx and the Political Economy of the Media, Leiden, Brill.

Postone, M. (1993). Time, Labour, and Social Domination: A Reinterpretation of Marx's Social Theory, Cambridge, Cambridge University Press.

Prodnik, J.A. (2015). '3C: Commodifying Communication in Capitalism', in Fuchs, C, & Mosco, V. (eds), Marx in the Age of Digital Capitalism, Leiden, Brill.

Qiu, J.L., Greg, M., & Crawford, K. (2014). 'Circuits of Labour: A Labour Theory of the iPhone Era', tripleC: Communication, Capitalism & Critique, vol. 12, no. 2, pp. 564-581.

Ranciere, J. (1991). The Ignorant Schoolmaster: Five Lessons in Intellectual Emancipation, California, Stanford University Press.

Reckwitz, A. (2002). 'Towards a Theory of Social Practices: A Development in Culturalist Theorizing', European Journal of Social Theory, vol. 5, no. 2, pp. 243-263.

Rich, A. (2021). 'Raya Dunayevskaya's Marx', in Anderson, K.B., Durkin, K., & Brown, H.A. (eds.), Raya Dunayevskaya's Intersectional Marxism: Race, Class, Gender, and the Dialectics of Liberation (pp. 91-102),

Cham, Palgrave.

Rigi, J. (2014). 'Foundations of a Marxist Theory of the Political Economy of Information: Trade Secrets and Intellectual Property, and the Production of Relative Surplus Value and the Extraction of Rent-Tribute', tripleC: Communication, Capitalism & Critique, vol. 12, no. 2, pp. 909-936.

Ritzer, G., & Jurgenson, N. (2010). 'Production, Consumption, Prosumption', Journal of Consumer Culture, vol. 10, no. 1, pp. 13-36.

Ritzer, G. (2015). 'Prosumer Capitalism', The Sociological Quarterly, vol. 56, no. 1, pp. 413-445.

Ritzer, G. (2015a). 'Dealing with the Welcome Critiques of "Prosumer Capitalism"', The Sociological Quarterly, vol. 56, no. 3, pp. 499-505.

Ritzer, G., & Miles, S. (2019). 'The Changing Nature of Consumption and the Intensification of McDonaldization in the Digital Age', Journal of Consumer Culture, vol. 19, no. 1, pp. 3-20.

Rogers, H. (2007). 'Garbage Capitalism's Green Commerce', Socialist Register, vol. 43.

Rose, G. (1978). The Melancholy Science: An Introduction to the Thought of Theodor W. Adorno, New York, Columbia University Press.

Sahlins, M. (1976). Culture and Practical Reason, Chicago, The University of Chicago Press.

Said, E.W. (1979). Orientalism, London, Vintage.

Sanyal, K. (2006). Rethinking Capitalist Development: Primitive Accumulation: Governmentality and Post-Colonial Capitalism, London, Routledge.

Sassen, S. (1999). Globalisation and its Discontents: Essays on the New Mobility of People and Money, New York, The New Press.

Sayer, D. (1979). Marx's Method: Ideology, Science and Critique in Capital. New Jersey: Humanities Press.

Sayers, S. (1998). Marxism and Human Nature, London, Routledge.

Sayers, S. (2011). Marx and Alienation: Essays on Hegelian Themes, London, Palgrave Macmillan.

Scholtz, T. (ed.) (2012). Digital Labor: The Internet as Playground and Factory, London, Routledge.

Segal, L. (2017). Radical Happiness, London, Verso.

Seymour, R. (2019). The Twittering Machine, London, The Indigo Press.

Simmel, G. (1978/2012). The Philosophy of Money, London, Routledge.

Shipway, M. (2013). Anti-Parliamentary Communism, Basingstoke, Palgrave.

Shippen, N.M. (2016). Decolonising Time, Basingstoke, Palgrave.

Shrestha, N.R. (1997). In the Name of Development: A Reflection on Nepal, Lanham, University Press of America.

Shumway, D. (2000). 'Fetishising Fetishism: Commodities, goods, and the meaning of Consumer Culture', Rethinking Marxism, vol. 12, no. 1, pp. 1-15.

Simpson, D. (1982). Fetishism and Imagination: Dickens, Melville, Conrad, Baltimore, The John Hopkins University Press.

Sherlock, S. (1997). 'The Future of Commodity Fetishism', Sociological Focus, vol. 30, no. 1, pp. 61-78.

Skotnicki, T. (2015). 'Commodity Fetishism and Consumer Senses: Turn-of-the-Twentieth-Century Consumer Activism in the United States and England', Journal of Historical Sociology. DOI: 10.111/johs.12114.

Skotnicki, T. (2020). 'Commodity Fetishism as Semblance', Sociological Theory, vol. 38, no. 4, pp. 362-377.

Slater, D. (1997). Consumer, Culture and Modernity, Cambridge, Polity.

Smart, B. (2010). Consumer Society: Critical Issues and Environmental Consequences, Thousand Oaks, Sage.

Smith, A. (1776/1999). The Wealth of Nations, London, Penguin.

Smythe, D. (1977). 'Communications: Blindspot of Western Marxism', Canadian Journal of Political and Social Theory, vol. 1, no. 3, pp. 1-26.

Smythe, D. (1981). Dependency Road: Communication, Capitalism, Consciousness, and Canada, Norwood, Ablex Publishing Corporation.

Sohn-Rethel, A. (1972). 'Mental and Manual Labour in Marx', in Walton, P., & Hall, S. (eds.), Situating Marx (pp. 44-71), London, Human Context Books.

Sohn-Rethel, A. (1978). Intellectual and Manual Labour: A Critique of Epistemology, Basingstoke, MacMillan Press.

Spano, A. (2021). 'Unchaining the Dialectic on the Threshold of Revolution: Dunayevskaya's Discovery of Hegel in the Birth of Marxist-Humanism', in Anderson, K.B., Durkin, K., & Brown, H.A. (eds.), Raya Dunayevskaya's Intersectional Marxism: Race, Class, Gender, and the Dialectics of Liberation (pp. 45-64), Cham, Palgrave.

Srnicek, N. (2017). Platform Capitalism, Cambridge, Polity.

Standing, G. (2011). The precariat: The new dangerous class, London, Bloomsbury Academic

Standing, G. (2014). A Precariat Charter, London, Bloomsbury Academic.

Starbucks. (2011a). About Us. Available at https://www.starbucks.com/about-us/

Starbucks. (2011b). Store Design. Available at https://www.starbucks.in/coffeehouse/store-design

Stebbins, R. A. (2020). The Serious Leisure Perspective: A Synthesis, Basingstoke, Palgrave.

Strengers, Y. (2013). Smart Energy Technologies in Everyday Life: Smart Utopia?, New York, Palgrave.

Susen, S. (2018). 'The Economy of Enrichment: Towards a New Form of Capitalism?', Berlin Journal of Critical Theory, vol. 2, no. 2, pp. 5-97.

Sutherland, K. (2008). 'Marx in Jargon', World Picture, no. 1, pp. 1-25.

Suttles, G.D. (1973). The Social Construction of Communities, Chicago, The University of Chicago Press.

Swartz, L. (2020). New Money: How Payment became social media, London, Yale University Press.

Terranova, T. (2000). 'Free Labour: Producing Culture for the Digital Economy', Social Text, vol. 18, no. 2, pp. 33-58.

Terranova, T. (2004). Network Culture: Politics for the Information Age, London, Pluto Press.

Tiersten, L. (2001). Marianne in the Market: Envisioning Consumer Society in Fin-de-Siècle France, Berkeley, University of California Press.

Thompson, E.P. (1963/2013). The Making of the English Working Class, London, Vintage.

Thompson, E.P. (1978/2010). The Poverty of Theory and Other Essays, New Delhi, Aakar Books.

Thorburn, ED. (2017). 'Cyborg Witches: Class Composition and Social Reproduction in the GynePunk Collective', Feminist Media Studies, vol. 17, no. 2, pp. 153-167.

Thoburn, N. (2003). Deleuze, Marx and Politics, London, Routledge.

Tiqqun, R. (2020). The Cybernetic Hypothesis, Massachusetts, Semiotext(e).

Toffler, A. (1980). The Third Wave, New York, William Morrow.

Tonkiss, F. (2006). Contemporary Economic Sociology: Globalization, Production, Inequality, Abingdon, Routledge.

Tronti, M. (1962). Factory and Society. Retrieved from https://operaismoinenglish.wordpress.com/2013/06/13/factory-and-society/

Tronti, M. (1964). Lenin in England. Retrieved from https://www.marxists.org/reference/subject/philosophy/works/it/tronti.htm

Tronti, M. (1971). Workers and Capital. Retrieved from https://operaismoinenglish.files.wordpress.com/2010/09/workers-and-capital.pdf

Tronti, M. (1973). 'Social Capital', Telos, no. 17 (Fall 1973), pp. 98-121.

Tronti, M. (2012). Our Operaismo. New Left Review, vol. 1, no. 73.

Tronti, M. (2019). Workers and Capital, London, Verso.

Turner, B.S., & Rojek, C. (2001). Society and Culture: Principles of Scarcity and Solidarity, Thousand Oaks, Sage.

Vaneigem, R. (2012). The Revolution of Everyday Life, Oakland, PM Press.

Veblen, T. (1899/2007). The Theory of the Leisure Class, Oxford, Oxford University Press.

Vogel, L. (1996). 'Engels's Origin: Legacy, Burden and Vision'. In Arthur, C.J. (eds) Engels Today, London, Palgrave Macmillan

Vogel, L. (2013). Marxism and the Oppression of Women: Towards a Unitary Theory, London, Brill

Warde, A. (2017). Consumption: A Sociological Approach, London, Palgrave.

Weeks, K. (2011). The Problem with Work: Feminism, Marxism, Antiwork Politics, and Postwork Imaginaries, Durham, Duke University Press.

Wendling, A.E. (2009). Karl Marx on Technology and Alienation, London, Palgrave Macmillan.

Wengrow, D. (2010). Cultures of Commodity Branding, London, Routledge.

Wiener, N. (1948/1961). Cybernetics or Communication and Control in the Animal and the Machine, Cambridge, MIT Press.

Williams, C.L. (2006). Inside Toyland: Working, Shopping and Social Inequality, Berkeley, The University of California Press.

Williams, R. (1960). Culture and Society 1780-1950, New York, Anchor Books.

Williams, R. (1961/2011). The Long Revolution, Cardigan, Parthian.

Williams, R. (1977). Marxism and Literature, Oxford, Oxford University Press.

Williams, R. (1980). Culture and Materialism, London, Verso.

Witheford, N. (1994). 'Autonomist Marxism and the Information Society', Capital and Class, vol. 18, no. 1, pp. 85-125.

Witheford, N. (2005). 'Cyber-Negri: General Intellect and Immaterial Labor', in Murphy, T.S., & Mustapha, A.K. (eds.), The Philosophy of Antonio Negri, London, Pluto Press.

Wolin, R. (1994). Walter Benjamin, Berkeley, University of California Press.

Wright, S. (2002). Storming Heaven, London, Pluto Press.

Wrigley, E.A. (2010). Energy and the English Industrial Revolution, Cambridge, Cambridge University Press.

Zerubavel, E. (1981). Hidden Rhythms: Schedules and Calendars in Social Life, Chicago, University of Chicago Press.

Zerubavel, E. (1991). The Fine Line: Making Distinctions in Everyday Life, Chicago, The University of Chicago Press.

Žižek, S. (2002). For they Know not what they do: Enjoyment as a Political Factor, London, Verso.

Žižek, S. (2009). The Sublime Object of Ideology, London, Verso.

Žižek, S. (2017). Lenin 2017: Remembering, Repeating, and Working Through, London, Verso.

Zuboff, S. (2019). The Age of Surveillance Capitalism: The Fight for a Human Future at the New Frontier of Power, New York, Public Affairs.

Zukin, S. (2004). Point of Purchase: How Shopping Changed American Culture and Business, London, Routledge.